THE INVISIBLE WEAPON

THE INVISIBLE WEAPON

Telecommunications and International Politics 1851–1945

DANIEL R. HEADRICK

New York   Oxford / OXFORD UNIVERSITY PRESS / 1991

Oxford University Press

Oxford   New York   Toronto
Delhi   Bombay   Calcutta   Madras   Karachi
Petaling Jaya   Singapore   Hong Kong   Tokyo
Nairobi   Dar es
Salaam   Cape Town
Melbourne   Aukland

and associated companies in
Berlin   Ibadan

Published by Oxford University Press, Inc.,
200 Madison Avenue, New York, New York 10016

Oxford is a registered trademark of Oxford University Press

Library of Congress Cataloging-in-Publication Data
Headrick, Daniel R.
The invisible weapon : telecommunications and international politics,
1851–1945 / Daniel R. Headrick.
p. cm.   Includes bibliographical references and index.
ISBN 0-19-506273-6
1. Telecommunication—History.
2. Telecommunication—Political aspects—History.
3. Telecommunication—Military aspects—History.
4. World politics—1900–1945.
5. World politics—19th century.
I. Title.
HE7651.H43   1991   90–39697
384—dc20

987654321

Printed in the United States of America
on acid-free paper

Preface

Looking back on this twentieth century in its waning moments, I am struck by the ambiguous feelings humans have toward the world they have created. People the world over are fascinated by technology and look to it as a panacea to solve their problems. Yet modern technology comes with a host of surprising and unpleasant byproducts. Among the least understood is interdependence. For modern technology does not occur as isolated units, but as complex systems that require ever more widespread interactions and interdependence. Thus the more technologically advanced a country becomes, the more it depends on raw materials, manufactured goods, information, and services from around the world.

This interdependence is disturbing, even frightening to many people. It is no coincidence that the twentieth century has been the age of mass movements to withdraw from the very interdependence that modern technology requires, movements ranging from nationalist struggles of liberation to attempts to gain economic autarky or create racially homogeneous societies. Not only do humans fight one another, but they also rebel against the kind of world that unfettered technological and economic forces would impose on them, a world of interdependence, trade, and communications.

Telecommunications are among the technologies most involved in this process: they are very complex, they readily form systems and networks, and they both require and encourage global interdependence. Yet during much of our century, telecommunications have been controlled, twisted, and distorted by politics in order to separate and alienate peoples. This book is an attempt to understand this paradox.

A book like this is the result of the labors of many persons, and their mention on this page is but a small recognition of their important contributions. I would first like to thank the National Endowment for the Humanities for its support of this project through a Fellowship for College Teachers and two Travel to Collections grants.

I am also thankful to those who have helped me most in my research: Cable and Wireless plc and the keeper of their archives, Peter Travers-Laney; Jerry Hess and David Pfeiffer of the National Archives in Washington; R. M. Coppock of the Ministry of Defence in London; and the friendly, helpful staffs of the Public Record Office at Kew, the British Library in London, and the Joseph Regenstein and John Crerar Libraries in Chicago.

Numerous friends and fellow-scholars have encouraged my efforts, or given me their thoughtful criticism, or both. They are: Jorma Ahvenainen, Hugh Aitken, Jean-Claude Allain, Catherine Bertho-Lavenir, Andrew Butrica, Patrice Carré, Ivan Coggeshall, Donard de Cogan, Kate Ezra, Pascal Griset, Robert Kubicek, Bill and Jane McCullam, Joel Mokyr, David and Nancy Northrup, Jon Sumida, Yuzo Takahashi, Frank Thomas, Gary Wolfe, Mark W. Zacher, and Zhong Zhang.

My editor, Nancy Lane, deserves special thanks for her unfailing encouragement over many years.

This book is dedicated to the memory of my wife Rita, from whom I learned how to become a historian, and much else.

Chicago
Summer 1990   D.R.H.

Contents

THE INVISIBLE WEAPON

1

Telecommunications and International Relations

When the telegraph was introduced in Australia in 1853, the Melbourne *Argus* went into an ecstasy of rhetoric: "We call the electric telegraph the most perfect invention of modern times . . . as anything more perfect than this is scarcely conceivable, and we really begin to wonder what will be left for the next generation, upon which to expend the restless energies of the human mind."[1] Such raptures, not uncommon in the nineteenth century, expressed not only the admiration of progressives for the marvels of technology that gave humans such power over nature, but also the optimistic faith that this power was a blessing for mankind. Thirty years later Ferdinand de Lesseps, builder of the Suez Canal, put it in these words: "All these enterprises of universal interest—some already completed, others under construction or projected—have an identical goal: drawing peoples together, and thereby bringing about an era in which men, by knowing one another, will finally cease fighting."[2]

The enterprises to which de Lesseps was referring were the new means of transportation and communication—the railways, steamships, canals, and telegraphs—that thrilled so many in the nineteenth century. Had he lived to see the inventions of the next century, he might have been just as amazed, but he would surely not have thought that they could make people finally cease fighting. If we have learned anything in the past century, it is that technology confers power, but that the consequences of that power are anything but predictable.

Characteristics of Electrical Communications

The relations between communication and politics are complex, and to make sense of them we first need to identify some of the relevant characteristics of communica-

3

tions systems. Like the mails, point-to-point telecommunications systems convey information to specific recipients. In addition, they have five other important qualities. The first four of these—speed, coverage, reliability, and cost—are technical and economic, while the fifth, security, is political and organizational in nature.

Speed is the most striking characteristic of telecommunications. What triggered the explosion of demand for the new technology was the incredible speed of electricity and its inherent promise of "real-time" information. In 1901 Captain George Squier of the U.S. Army Signal Corps expressed the astonishment of his age when he wrote: "The fastest mail express, or the swiftest ocean ship, are as naught compared with the velocity of the electrical impulse which practically annihilates any terrestrial dimension."[3] Though much faster than the mail, the early telegraphs were by no means instantaneous in relaying information, but were slowed down by both technical and organizational delays. Because so much information quickly becomes stale, governments, businesses, and newspapers encouraged improvements in the efficiency of telecommunications.

Coverage refers to the number of participants in a network. The telegraph was not an isolated device, but appeared from the very beginning as a network, that is to say a complex sociotechnical system spread over a large geographic area. This was true of many other innovations of the recent past: railroads, aviation, and electric power, among others.[4] But whereas railroads and electric power reached their optimum efficiencies on a regional scale, telegraphs quickly became national and, in the case of submarine cables, intercontinental and even global.

Telecommunications networks tend to expand for two reasons. They meet a human need and therefore attract customers like any other desirable new product. Moreover, the number of possible connections in a network—a rough measure of its value to its customers—increases as the square of the number of customers. For these reasons, telecommunications networks spread farther than their creators expected. Within twenty years of its invention, the telegraph covered Europe and North America, reaching the smallest towns. Soon thereafter, regional networks joined to form continental ones, which submarine cables then linked into a global network. Recently, as the richer countries approach the goal of a telephone in every home and on every office desk, the public, far from satisfied, demands telephones in every room, car, and airplane, and will soon want one on every wrist, capable of reaching anyone in the world at any time.

The third characteristic of electrical communication—its cost—balanced the advantage of speed and restricted its spread. Like all economic phenomena, the communication revolution touched different social groups at different moments in history. At first, long-distance telegraph rates were staggering; on the Atlantic telegraph cable of 1866, a twenty-word telegram cost one hundred dollars, or two to four months' wages for an industrial worker. For many years, the public that applauded the technical miracle of telecommunication was restrained by its cost, and only sent telegrams on the most momentous occasions.

All new technologies start out expensive and gradually become cheaper. What is amazing is that the cost of communicating (unlike, say, transportation or housing) has continued to decrease for over a century, and the decline shows no sign of abating. The public's fascination with every advance in communications technology from the telegraph on is now being rewarded at last.

Businessmen were quicker to use the telegraph, for communication offered opportunities for profit and expansion. To the business world, the speed and reliability of telegraphy often justified its expense. Numerous businesses that arose in the nineteenth century, such as railroads, shipping lines, mail-order houses, and newspapers, were intimately connected with, even dependent on, the telegraph. Soon after its introduction, the telephone also became an essential tool of business. Similarly, the radio became indispensable to shipping and airlines and created the broadcast media. Thanks to telecommunications, local businesses became regional, then national, and finally multinational, developing the world economy.

What the public wanted but could barely afford, and what businesses could afford only within limits, governments craved at almost any price. When electrical communications began, governments did more than welcome them; they often supported them and subsidized their extension, regardless of the cost.

The fourth characteristic of telecommunications, their reliability, did not come easily. The early telegraphs suffered from numerous problems ranging from equipment breakdowns to human error. Messages often got lost, delayed, or garbled. To cure the telegraphs of their teething pains required many expensive investments such as duplicate lines, better equipment, and more experienced operators. The same was true for the radio in the early twentieth century. From a technical perspective, the history of telecommunications is one of constant gradual improvements periodically interspersed with astonishing advances.

Electrical communications has often been described as one of the great achievements of mankind. But when we look at it from a security point of view, we see an entirely different picture, for security is not a technical but a social and political characteristic. Since politics have not improved since the nineteenth century but have at times gotten noticeably worse, even the history of telecommunications has a dark side.

In offering to convey personal messages from one individual to another, telecommunications systems imply that no one else will see the message. For individuals this is a promise of privacy. Businesses value confidentiality, but they also value priority of access to information. The needs of governments are even more stringent: they want many of their communications to be secret.

At the same time, it is governments that threaten the security of communications. They alone have the means to impose surveillance on their citizens and to spy on other nations. While governments have engaged in prying since the dawn of history, the ubiquity of electrical communications and the tremendous increase in the flow of vital information have made communications more vulnerable than ever. Within a country, security is a matter of faith in the discretion of government rather than a characteristic of the telecommunications system itself. Internationally, and sometimes within a country as well, communications are vulnerable to the espionage of other governments.

Telecommunications and World History

Governments crave communication, for a timely flow of information is a vital instrument of power. Even the earliest rulers needed to know what was happening in their provinces and on their frontiers. In turn, they issued commands to their agents and subjects, hoping thereby to control events. In their foreign relations, governments were curious about other countries and eager to spread their influence, if not their raw power. And in wartime, information and control could determine victory or defeat.

Information has three levels of value: in itself, as knowledge; if it is timely, as news; and if it is exclusive, as secrets. Governments wanted all three. Large empires went to great lengths to speed the flow of information: the Romans built roads, the Persians and Mongols established relays of horses, the British subsidized mail steamers.[5] Before the electric telegraph, however, the slow and unreliable nature of communications acted as a restraint on governmental control. In large empires it could take months for a letter writer to receive a response. In spite of their poor communications, some empires—the Chinese, the Roman, and the Spanish, for example—survived for centuries, much longer than the creations of the "new imperialism" at the end of the nineteenth century.

By the eighteenth century, European governments were no longer content to establish their own communication networks; they also accelerated the advance of communications technologies. The development of semaphores, naval flags, and public postal systems was a sign that demand was pushing against the supply of communications media.

This book covers the period from 1851, the year the first telegraph cable linked France and Britain, until the end of World War II. From the perspective of international relations, this stretch of time divides into two distinct periods: forty years of relative peace among the great powers, followed by half a century of tensions and world wars.

In the 1840s, when the electric telegraph appeared, Europe and America were in the midst of an era of peace. Old enmities had been forgotten, and military requirements had given way to the demands of civilians. The rapid spread of the telegraph responded to the needs of businesses and railways as much as to those of governments. The public and the press hailed the magic of instantaneous electrical communication. What was so important to trade and so useful to diplomacy, many believed, could only lead to a greater harmony between the peoples and nations of the world.

Gradually, telecommunications turned from a miracle into another modern convenience, a proof of the progress of industrial civilization. As the new medium spread around the world, small networks merged into large ones, while technical improvements and economies of scale led to natural monopolies. Internal telegraph networks were built and operated by the government in every country but the United States, which tolerated giant corporations like AT&T and Western Union.

The late nineteenth century was an exceptional period in two respects. First, the great powers mostly avoided fighting one another, and turned their energies to trade and imperialism in Africa and Asia. Peace made them less sensitive to security concerns than ever before, and therefore less eager to spend vast amounts of money for better communications. Meanwhile, international trade expanded so much that economics, not politics, became the motor of expanded communications. After 1860 the cable business satisfied both its investors and its customers. Even governments that monopolized their domestic telecommunications left international telegraphy to private enterprise. As we shall see in Chapters 2 and 3, the history of telecommunications in the late nineteenth century is more a history of business than of politics.

As telegraph cables reached around the world, a small number of firms, most of them British, gained a stranglehold on international communications. This dominance aroused the admiration and envy of foreigners, but little hostility. In an age of free trade nations tolerated each other's comparative advantages. As long as the European powers were preoccupied with Continental problems and the United States with its own westward expansion, the seas were Britain's special sphere. Government involvement was mainly evident in the spread of telegraphy to the colonial empires and to non-Western countries like China, as we shall see in Chapter 4. The benefits of the telegraph for colonial administration, news, and world trade were so evident that the ownership of the cables was seen as a minor issue.

Throughout much of the nineteenth century, the rivalries of the European powers had been tempered by conservative restraint and respect for the balance of power, while the territorial ambitions of their more pugnacious elements were diverted to the vast unconquered lands of Africa and Asia. As the century neared its end, however, nationalism grew more virulent while unclaimed parts of Africa and Asia became scarce. What had been, for decades, a friendly rivalry between European powers engaged in the common enterprise of imperial expansion turned to jealousy, resentment, and suspicion. The events of the turn of the century—the Spanish-American War, the Franco-British confrontation at Fashoda, the Boer War, and the Anglo-German naval arms race—exacerbated tensions and transformed the long nineteenth-century peace into the first of the twentieth-century prewar eras.

As the reliance of nations on their communications increased, so did their fears of losing them. Cable cutting in the Spanish-American War and censorship in the Boer War showed the world how vulnerable were the lines of communication, and how much more vulnerable were the nations whose global communications depended on the goodwill of Great Britain. In reaction, France and Germany hastened to build their own networks, with heavy government subsidies, and the British government began rounding out its network with subsidized strategic lines. Only the United States remained satisfied with pure free enterprise. By 1914, instantaneous communications, far from smoothing out misunderstandings between the powers, only sharpened the jitters of nervous governments teetering on the brink of war. In the hopes of freeing themselves from their dependence on foreign cables, all the great powers helped push the infant technology of radio into an early adolescence. Telecommunications, once hailed as a miracle and later regarded as a public utility, had become a political tool in the rivalry between great powers. This will be the theme of Chapters 5 to 7.

The two world wars accelerated the politicizing of telecommunications that had begun at the end of the nineteenth century. In addition to the news and private messages, governments and the military used three special forms of information: propaganda, that which governments wanted the world to believe, whether it was true or not; secrets, or the information they tried to keep from unfriendly eyes; and intelligence, or secrets that unfriendly eyes had seen. During wars and cold wars, plain information tended to be overshadowed by these three hybrids. While every belligerent used secrecy and intelligence, control over information was especially critical for weaker nations on the defensive, for whom the smallest scrap of power could tip the balance between survival and disaster. It was in World War I that the military potential of electrical communication first became obvious, as we shall see in Chapters 8 and 9. Britain, the country with the best global communications, learned the lesson best of all.

The romance of espionage lingers on in literature long after it has been supplanted in the real world; after all, how can one compare the tedium of listening, hour after hour, to the faint crackling of a radio set with the excitement of Mata Hari's boudoir escapades? Unfortunately for literature, what the telegraph and radio did when they separated communication from transportation was to create a new form of espionage, one that was less thrilling but more powerful than any previous method of obtaining secret information. The telegraph and the radio enabled belligerents to control whole armies and fleets and to fight world wars instead of regional ones. In the process they also created communications intelligence to spy on each other. As information became easier and cheaper to transmit over long distances, governments found it more and more vital to control information by means of censorship and by secret interception, decryption, and analysis. Like so many other activities, espionage became first bureaucratic, then mechanized.

The interwar years, described in Chapters 10 and 11, did not witness a return to free trade but an exacerbation of rival nationalisms and state-controlled enterprises. Even in the United States, the last bastion of unfettered capitalism, the government became deeply involved in international telecommunications. The old British dominance was challenged on two levels: by the rise of American wealth and nationalism, and by the new kinds of cables and radio that threatened to make older technologies obsolete.

World War II was a replay of World War I with more advanced technologies. Once again Britain proved to be the master of communications. Not only were its own communications relatively secure, but it also succeeded in penetrating Germany's most secret codes and ciphers; the Americans did likewise with the Japanese. In this as in other fields, however, Britain paid for its security by relinquishing its place in the world to its ally and friendly rival, the United States, as we shall see in Chapters 12 to 14.

Though it has been over forty years since World War II, information and its hybrids—propaganda, intelligence, and espionage—are still part of the arsenal of international politics. de Lesseps to the contrary, it is questionable whether better communication will lead to peace and harmony among the peoples of the world.

International Telecommunications as a Field of Study

Information and the telecommunications systems that convey it are so essential to the modern world, it is not surprising that they have been studied from many points of view and by many different disciplines, from political science and economics to engineering and military science. A new discipline called *communication* has even arisen in the past few years specifically to study the interactions of the new media with society.

Of the two forms of communication, broadcast and point-to-point, the broadcast or mass media have captured most of the attention of communication scholars, for two reasons: first because, by their nature, they generate publicity and seek wide audiences; and second because they create their own information and preserve it for posterity.[6] The point-to-point media are by nature more discreet. They promise privacy, they only convey the information their customers bring to them, and they rarely retain copies of the messages. Yet they are more relevant to the conduct of government, to the outcome of wars, to the pursuit of business, even to the lives of ordinary people; who, indeed, does not value a personal letter or telephone call over a newspaper or television program? Because the messages of point-to-point media are so elusive, studies have concentrated on their structures, their origins and public history, the devices and techniques they use, and their business activities. With a few notable exceptions, the cultural aspects of point-to-point communications have yet to be studied.[7] The political impacts of telecommunications are so crucial that they have not escaped the notice of scholars, but, because the contents of the messages are preserved not by the media but by customers who keep them secret for many years, this awareness has mainly been felt among those scholars who can afford to wait, namely historians.

In the relations between nations, the advances in communications in the past century and a half have had a dual history. From a technical point of view, it has been an era of almost uninterrupted progress, resulting in falling costs and increasing coverage, speed, and reliability. In terms of security, on the other hand, as the world has become more dangerous, the political importance of international communications has turned it into a weapon in the rivalries of the great powers.

Like any work that deals with the social aspects of technology, this one also confronts the vexed issue of autonomy. For over a century, philosophers and writers have wondered whether technology has acquired a life of its own, independent of the will of its human creators, and whether this autonomous technology is the determining factor, the "independent variable" in modern history.[8] This question impinges strongly on our topic, since telecommunications technologies are complex and fast-changing and play an important part in the political life of nations. Yet they do not spring out of nowhere. While their origin is seldom predictable, their implementation and diffusion result neither from pure technical necessity nor from the rational choices of their inventors or their users. Rather, organizations mediate between the machines and society, influencing both. These organizations—the Eastern and Associated Telegraph Companies, the French Chamber of Deputies, the Western Union Company, the German Wehrmacht, to name a few—in effect control the flow of interactions between technology and society by purchasing, investing, subsidizing, patenting, sharing or withholding secrets, and many other means. While it often seems that technology influences the course of history—and this book is filled with examples thereof—it is in fact organizations that control the interactions between "technology" and "man" and, through their interactions with each other, make history. This book, then, is not a search for causes and consequences, but an inquiry into the interactions between telecommunications technologies, the organizations that use them, the information they convey, and the power of nations.

Notes

1. Quoted in Ann Moyal, "The History of Telecommunication in Australia: Aspects of the Technological Experience, 1854–1930," in *Scientific Colonialism: A Cross-Cultural Comparison*, ed. Nathan Reingold and Marc Rothenberg (Washington, 1987), 36.

2. Letter to Maxime Hélène, November 6, 1882, in Hélène, *Les travaux publics au XIXe siècle. Les nouvelles routes du globe* (Paris, 1882), 7.

3. Captain George O. Squier, "The Influence of Submarine Cables upon Military and Naval Supremacy," *National Geographic Magazine* 12, no. 1 (January 1901), 2.

4. On the idea of systems in the history of technology, see the pathbreaking book by Thomas P. Hughes, *Networks of Power: Electrification in Western Society, 1880–1930* (Baltimore, 1983).

5. Despite its importance, the subject of politics and communications before the nineteenth century still awaits its historian; the only work on the subject, Harold A. Innes, *Empire and Communications* (Oxford, 1950), is unfortunately inadequate.

6. See, for example, Everett M. Rogers, *Communication Technology: The New Media in Society* (New York, 1986).

7. Among the exceptions, we may cite: Ithiel de Sola Pool, *The Social Impact of the Telephone* (Cambridge, Mass., 1976) and *Technologies of Freedom* (Cambridge, Mass., 1983); Carolyn Marvin, *When Old Technologies Were New: Thinking About Communication in the Late Nineteenth Century* (New York, 1987); Stephen Kern, *The Culture of Time and Space* (Cambridge, Mass., 1983); and Patrice A. Carré, "Proust, le téléphone et la modernité," *France Télécom: Revue française des télécommunications* 64 (January 1988), 3–11.

8. This idea, most vigorously expressed in Jacques Ellul, *The Technological Society*, trans. John Wilkinson (New York, 1964), has been the subject of a searching inquiry by Langdon Winner in *Autonomous Technology: Technics-out-of-Control as a Theme in Political Thought* (Cambridge, Mass., 1977).

2

The New Technology

Origins of the Telegraph

During the French Revolution, the revolutionary government faced enemies on all sides, outside and within the country. While the size of armies and the speed of events had increased by quantum leaps, the means of communication—messengers on horseback—had not improved since Roman times. The revolutionaries, desperate for news from the battlefields and for means to control their armies, eagerly seized upon the aerial telegraph, a system of semaphores introduced by Claude Chappe in 1793. Chappe's system had many drawbacks. It was costly and complicated, for it required towers every few miles and hundreds of trained operators. It was also slow and unreliable, and only worked on clear days. Nonetheless it found favor with every French government for the next fifty years because it gave the nation's rulers a feeling of control, a priceless commodity in a country prone to dangerous dissent. By 1850 the whole country was covered with five thousand kilometers of lines and 556 stations.

Elsewhere, governments were either more frugal or more secure, and built few semaphores. Between 1797 and 1808, the English government built a semaphore network linking the Admiralty to its major harbors but abandoned it when peace returned. Commercial towns and private companies later built semaphore lines to announce the arrival of ships. Similarly in the United States a semaphore telegraph carried news of ships' arrivals from Sandy Hook, New Jersey, to New York City. In the 1830s, Prussia built a semaphore line on the French model, linking Berlin to the Rhineland.[1]

Despite its shortcomings, the semaphore whetted appetites. For the first time in history, information traveled more rapidly than the quickest means of transportation. By the 1820s, a new breed of information consumer had appeared: financiers and

11

speculators whose fortunes rode on the latest news of stock exchange fluctuations and ships' arrivals. To obtain this kind of information before others did was worth so much money to speculators that they were willing to bribe the semaphore operators to insert hidden code signals into official messages.

As long as governments monopolized the semaphore, the business community used another communication technology, the homing pigeon. Pigeons were the mainstay of the news agencies until the electric telegraph made them obsolete. In the 1830s, Correspondance Garnier and Agence Havas used them to carry messages between Paris, Brussels, and French provincial cities. With couriers and pigeons, Charles-Louis Havas got news from the Brussels morning papers to Paris by noon and to London by 3 P.M. *The Times* also had a pigeon post between Paris and Boulogne in 1837. By 1846 there were 25,000 homing pigeons in Antwerp alone.[2]

The electric telegraph was one of those inventions, like railways and airplanes, that arouse enthusiasm when they appear and retain their fascination for generations thereafter. While many people tried to convey messages by electricity, success in this venture is usually associated with the names of two Englishmen and an American. William Cooke and Charles Wheatstone built the first railway telegraph in Britain in 1837. Samuel Morse patented his code that same year and opened the first public telegraph line, from Baltimore to Washington, in 1844. Though Frenchmen were later to contribute significantly to the electric telegraph, in the 1840s, France had too much invested in the semaphore and too little in railways to feel the need as urgently as the English and Americans. Over the next century a significant gap opened, which France has been trying to close ever since.

By the late 1840s, webs of telegraph wires were beginning to cover Britain, France, Germany, and the eastern United States, and were appearing in Italy, Austria, and even further afield. As soon as electric telegraphs were opened to the public, telegraph agencies sprang up to transmit news to businesses and newspapers. In 1848–49 Bernhard Wolff and Julius Reuter positioned themselves in Berlin and Aachen, at both ends of the Prussian state telegraph line. From Aachen to Brussels, where the Franco-Belgian line began, Reuter sent messages by pigeon. Two years later, when a direct line linked Paris and Berlin, Reuter moved to England. Even foreign news was now only hours old.[3]

International Telegraphic Cooperation

When we turn to the international tensions and rivalries that arose later in the century, it will be important to remember the following: Before quarrels could arise over the control and security of international communications, there had to be telegraph lines connecting countries to one another, and these lines required international agreements. In other words, international cooperation preceded international disagreements.

The main motive for agreements was the desire to speed up international communications and overcome the obstacles that inevitably arose at every border crossing. An example will suffice. Before 1852 no telegram could cross the border between France and its neighbor across the Rhine, the Grand-Duchy of Baden. That year the two countries signed an agreement whereby an employee of the Baden telegraph administration was posted in the telegraph office at Strasbourg. When a telegram arrived from France destined for Baden, the French clerk handed it to the Baden clerk, who translated it into German, carried it across the river, and re-transmitted it on the Baden lines.[4] While this slow system was better than no communications at all, it cried out for improvements. Situations like this, arising all across Europe, forced governments to cooperate.

Nowhere was the need greater than in Germany. When the first telegraph lines were laid, Germany was still divided into myriad states, each with its own telegraph administration. Language, trade, and political pressures combined to erode the barriers. The first treaties linked Prussia and Saxony in 1849 and Bavaria and Austria in 1850. That year Prussia, Austria, and several smaller states formed the Austro-German Telegraph Union, to which most German states and the Netherlands later adhered.[5]

In the early 1850s France signed a series of treaties with its neighbors: Belgium in 1851, Switzerland in 1852, Sardinia in 1853, and Spain in 1854. The next year they formed the West European Telegraph Union, soon joined by the Netherlands, Portugal, the Vatican, and the Kingdom of the Two Sicilies. Belgium, France, and Prussia also signed the Berlin Convention of 1855, establishing through lines and pledging secrecy and efficiency.[6] By the early 1860s, dozens of treaties bound the states of Europe to one another and to the two telegraph unions. In 1864 Napoleon III invited all major European governments, except Britain, which had no state-run telegraphs, to create an efficient international telegraph system. The conference held in Paris in 1865 established the International Telegraph Union.[7]

There was more to cooperation than stringing wires across borders and allowing through telegrams. There were innumerable details to settle: through rates and their distribution among the various administrations involved, the order of priority among different classes of telegrams, the use of codes and ciphers, permissible words and languages, the routing of through messages, censorship and secrecy, and much else. Most of these questions were well beyond the competence or interests of the diplomats. At the next telegraph conference, held in Vienna in 1868, they therefore decided to establish the International Bureau of Telegraph Administrations in Berne to deal with such matters. It was the world's first permanent international organization.[8]

After that, periodic conferences made policy, while the Bureau administered day-to-day matters in the interim. The conference in Rome in 1871–72 admitted private companies to participate, though not to vote. As the great transoceanic cable companies coordinated their services with the state administrations, telegraphic unity spread to Asia and America.

The most important conference was the one held in St. Petersburg in 1875. Its convention codified the experience of the previous decade, including some important political decisions. While Article 2 assured the secrecy of correspondence, Article 7 violated that promise by giving the administrations the right to stop any telegram judged dangerous to state security, public order, or good morals: the influence of Russia and Germany was clearly evident here. Another suggestion—that telegrams be forwarded by the shortest possible route—was defeated on political grounds, for Russia and France did not want all of their mutual correspondence to pass through Germany.[9]

Countries outside Europe also joined the international telegraphic conventions: India in 1868, the Dutch East Indies in 1872, Egypt in 1875, and various European colonies in Africa and Asia as they became attached to the world network. There was a reason for this other than the practical need to coordinate technical matters. As the French director general of Posts and Telegraphs wrote in a letter to the minister of colonies:

> The adherance of our colonies is of great interest, because every administration that joins has the right to vote in international conferences, and every new adherance of one of our colonies has the effect of giving one more voice to France in the voting which follows the debates.[10]

The conferences were often dominated by the powers with the most colonies, Great Britain and France.

The United States was invited to the St. Petersburg conference but declined the invitation on the grounds that it had no state telegraph system. It also refused to sign the convention because of the censorship clause. Nonetheless the two major American companies, Western Union and Postal Telegraph, observed the regulations and made private arrangements concerning rates and other technical questions. Most countries in the Western Hemisphere followed the American example.[11]

St. Petersburg was the last diplomatic conference on telegraph matters until 1932. After it came a series of administrative conferences attended by representatives of the various telegraph administrations during the following years: 1879, 1885, 1890, 1896, 1903, 1908, 1925, and 1928.[12]

The First Submarine Telegraph Cables

To cross bodies of water, telegraph cables must be insulated. In the first half of the nineteenth century, many inventive minds considered this problem. Perhaps the most remarkable was William Brooke O'Shaughnessy, physician in the Bengal Army, professor of chemistry at the Calcutta Medical College, and an amateur scientist with an interest in electricity. Though he had never seen a telegraph, he was inspired by reports in British papers and discussions at meetings of the Asiatic Society of Bengal, and began experimenting with the new medium. In 1838 he put a twenty-two kilometer wire on bamboo poles and laid three kilometers of insulated wire underwater, using the Hooghly River as the return. It was the first underwater circuit.[13] In his own words:

> The progress of science is hourly adding to the catalogue of triumphs effected by the sagacity of man over the seeming impossibilities of nature. . . . A conquest still greater than all which I have quoted would be the annihilation of time and space in the accomplishment of correspondence. That a signal can be passed between places 1000 miles apart in less time than the motions of solar light through the firmament, is no less startling to assert than it is demonstrably and practically true.[14]

Although O'Shaughnessy's experiment succeeded, no one in Calcutta saw its utility, and it occurred too far from Europe to be noticed.

By the mid-1840s, however, two events combined to make underwater telegraphy possible. One was the spread of land telegraphs, which stimulated investigations into ways of carrying current underwater. The other was the discovery of an effective insulating material for wires. Gutta-percha, the latex of the *Palaquium* tree, which grows in the rain forests of Southeast Asia, was first brought to England from Singapore by two physicians, José d'Almeida and William Montgomerie. In Germany, Lieutenant Werner von Siemens of the Prussian artillery invented a machine to coat wires with this substance and laid cables across the Rhine and the harbor of Kiel. At the same time, in England Charles Hancock and Henry Bewley also solved the manufacturing problem, and experiments began in Folkestone harbor.[15]

Soon the process was sufficiently developed for a real trial. In August 1850 the brothers Jacob and John W. Brett laid the first submarine cable—a single strand of copper wire coated with gutta-percha—from Dover to Calais. Unfortunately it broke a few hours later when a fisherman hauled it up. In November of the following year, Thomas Crampton's Submarine Telegraph Company laid another cable made of four copper wires coated with gutta-percha and protected by an outer sheathing of iron rope. This one worked and lasted thirty-seven years.[16] It was also an international and economic success, for it linked the two wealthiest and most powerful nations in the world, France and Britain. Louis-Napoléon Bonaparte, president of France since 1848, was determined to establish closer ties with Britain. French financiers, eager to link the Paris Bourse with the London Stock Exchange, also supported the project.[17] Soon after it was laid, Julius Reuter opened offices at both ends to handle the flow of news. In the next few years, cables were laid between Ireland, England, and Scotland, between England and Belgium, England and Holland, and Denmark and Sweden. As Europe entered upon a decade of prosperity and free trade, the cable symbolized the hopes of an age.

The Mediterranean Cables

Until 1851, telegraphs were national enterprises, occasionally reaching across borders to speed up the everyday interactions between peoples. But the great powers extended their might as well as their trade. Britain and France, the greatest powers of the day, soon learned to value the telegraph as a means of projecting their will upon others. This first became clear in the Mediterranean, where both were deeply involved.

France had been trying to conquer Algeria since 1830, and by the 1850s it had 100,000 men engaged in the largest military operation since Napoleon. Several hundred thousand European civilians also lived in the colony. Two separate telegraph systems served the needs of the French administration and the settlers: a semaphore, which stretched 1,498 kilometers by 1854, and an electric network that began that year with 249 kilometers of lines and expanded to 3,179 kilometers by 1861.

After the success of the Channel cable, a telegraphic connection with Algeria was an irresistible temptation. When John Brett proposed in 1853 to lay a cable from France to Algeria via Corsica and Sardinia, he quickly obtained concessions from the French and Sardinian governments. He then floated the Compagnie du Télégraphe Electrique Sous-Marin de la Méditerranée, grandiosely promising to connect "Europe, Africa, India, and Australia, via France, Piedmont, Corsica, Sardinia, Algeria and Egypt." The portions between Genoa, Corsica, and Sardinia were successfully laid in 1854, but the final section of cable from Sardinia to Algeria was too heavy for the primitive laying apparatus and was lost.

The next cable, laid by R. S. Newall and Company in 1857, lasted only two years. The French government then turned to a third cable manufacturer, Glass Elliot and Company, which made two attempts. In the first attempt, from Toulon to Algiers, the cable broke in the laying; the second, laid in 1861 from Port-Vendres to Algiers via Menorca, only lasted a year. In desperation, France used a land line across Spain, with a short cable from Cartagena to Oran, laid in 1864 by Siemens, which also broke.

In 1870, the British-owned Marseilles, Algiers and Malta Telegraph Company laid the first direct and reliable cable between France and its North African colony. A year later that connection was duplicated when the India Rubber Gutta-Percha and Telegraph Works Ltd. (commonly known as the India Rubber or Silvertown Company) laid a second cable, this one for the French government.

In the 1870s, as more immigrants moved to Algeria and trade expanded, more cables were needed to keep up with the flood of telegrams. In 1879 and 1880 the India Rubber Company laid two more cables for the French government. In 1892 and 1893, when yet more lines were needed, the government signed a contract with two French firms, Société Générale des Téléphones and Société Grammont; their cables were the first manufactured in France.[18]

In the story of the first cables to Algeria, two points are worth noting. The first is that the French government's urge to communicate raced ahead of the capabilities of the new technology; in fact the technology advanced from one subsidized failure to another. The second is that France, which needed communications as badly as Britain, turned to foreign firms and thereby put off developing its own cable industry for two decades. It was a decision the French later regretted.

Great Britain was as deeply involved in the Mediterranean as France, less for territorial conquest than in order to maintain the balance of power between Russia, Turkey, France, and Egypt. Britain also imported Russian grain, Egyptian cotton, Italian wine, and other goods from the region. But most important of all was the route to India, Britain's greatest source of power and wealth. Since steamships began carrying mail and passengers in the 1830s, protecting that route had loomed ever larger in the minds of British statesmen, especially Foreign Secretary Lord Palmerston. British security depended on the Royal Navy and its bases at Gibraltar, Malta, and Corfu.

Communications, however, were much too slow for London to keep in touch with events in a region prone to sporadic upheavals. Even by steamship, a letter from England to Corfu would not receive a reply for six weeks.[19] As historian John Cell explains, "A telegraphic link with her Mediterranean possessions . . . would effectively double or treble Britain's naval strength in the area by enabling it to be brought to bear quickly where it was needed. No more need a Nelson search desperately for a Villeneuve."[20]

As often happened, war triggered the construction of telegraphs.[21] In March 1854, France and Britain declared war on Russia and proceeded to land troops in the Crimea. Messages went by telegraph to Marseille, then by ship to Constantinople, arriving there sixteen to twenty days later. In their eagerness to control their forces, the British and French governments could not wait for private enterprise to construct telegraphs. The governments erected a land line from Bucharest, the terminus of the Austrian telegraph network, to Varna on the Black Sea. From there they had Newall and Company lay a temporary unarmored cable to the Crimea.[22] In April 1855, for the first time, the French and British governments were in contact with their armies on a distant battlefield. While logistics and administration were improved, military operations suffered from long-distance interference. In his detailed history of the war, A. W. Kinglake had no kind words for the telegraph:

> But now, and even with suddenness, there began to interpose in the war that new and dangerous magic which has hugely augmented the already great powers of mischief conferred on an absolute ruler by carrying for him his orders with a speed so transcendent of space. . . .
>   Our Government did not abuse it; but—exposed to swift dictation from Paris—the French had to learn what it was to carry on war with a Louis Napoleon planted at one of the ends of the wire, and at the other, a commander like Canrobert, who did not dare to meet Palace strategy with respectful evasions, still less with plain, resolute words.[23]

Indeed, in one of his early telegrams to General Canrobert giving detailed instructions on troop movements, Napoleon III expressed his frustration: "I greatly deplore my not being able myself to go out to the Crimea."[24] It was probably just as well, since he had none of his uncle's talent for warfare and would have confused matters even worse in person. But his meddling was a portent of future campaigns directed from afar by self-appointed military strategists like Adolf Hitler and Lyndon Johnson.

The First Atlantic Cables, 1858–1866

While the British and French governments were eagerly seeking faster communications across the Mediterranean, private entrepreneurs were interested in the more profitable route to America. No telecommunications project in history aroused more excitement, nor has any been more written about, than the Atlantic cable.[25]

The idea of a cable across the Atlantic appeared very early. In 1845 the brothers Brett approached the British government for subsidies for such a venture but were rebuffed. The real moving force for the project was the American Cyrus Field. In 1854 he began promoting a cable from Newfoundland to Ireland, the two closest points across the ocean. In the United States he obtained the support of Samuel Morse and of Lieutenant Matthew Maury of the Naval Observatory, and aroused considerable popular enthusiasm. But he could not raise enough capital; so he went to England and joined John Brett, the telegraph engineer Charles Tilson Bright, and several capitalists in founding the Atlantic Telegraph Company in 1856.

The British and American governments offered various forms of assistance such as soundings of the ocean floor and the loan of warships, but no direct subsidies. After failing twice, in August 1857 and July 1858, the enterprise succeeded on the third attempt, to the great rejoicing of the press as well as the stockholders. On August 13, 1858, President Buchanan and Queen Victoria exchanged greetings, while speeches and celebrations marked the occasion on both sides of the ocean.

The signals were weak and slow, even with the ultrasensitive mirror galvanometer invented for the purpose by the physicist William Thomson. The cable proved its value when the British government cancelled an order for two Canadian regiments to sail to India, thereby saving £50,000. Beginning in September, however, the signals became weaker and less intelligible, and on October 25, they ceased entirely.

The disappointment was so great that the British government ordered an official investigation into the matter. Of the eight members of the Joint Committee, half were from the Board of Trade and half from the Atlantic Telegraph Company. The committee met 22 times between December 1859 and September 1860. Its report, issued in April 1861, went into every aspect of submarine telegraphy in great detail and became a classic in electrical engineering.[26] It blamed the final failure on Edward Whitehouse, a surgeon-turned-electrician and friend of Bright's, who pumped two thousand volts through the cable in the hope of reviving it. But as Donard de Cogan has recently shown, the real fault lay with the promoters, who were in too great a hurry, and with the manufacturers, Newall and Company and Glass Elliot and Company, who, in their haste, had made a cable that was too light, had too little insulation, and had been allowed to deteriorate.[27]

In the history of submarine telegraphy, the 1850s were a decade of enthusiasm, experimentation, and failures. Short cables, like those linking England to France or Canada to Newfoundland, worked reasonably well. For longer spans like the Atlantic, and in deeper waters like the Mediterranean and the Red Sea, the record was discouraging. Of 17,700 kilometers of cables laid by 1861, only 4,800 worked, and the rest were lost.[28] For a time, the cable situation looked so hopeless that there were proposals to connect the United States to Europe by way of Alaska and Siberia.

Eventually, however, technology caught up with its own problems. Manufacturers of cables and instrumentation and experts like William Thomson, Charles Bright, and Willoughby Smith learned from the experiences of the decade how to make cables, how to test, handle, and lay them, and how to send electrical impulses through them efficiently.

William Thomson, professor of natural philosophy at the University of Glasgow, played a crucial role in these events. He was associated with all the early Atlantic cable projects and served on the Joint Committee of 1859–60. Realizing that long cables act like condensers that smooth out electrical impulses and make signals hard to read, he devised a way to sharpen signals by sending a short reverse pulse immediately after the main pulse. He also invented better sending and receiving instruments and improved the efficiency of deep-sea soundings. For these and other contributions to physics, he was knighted in 1866 and raised to the peerage as Baron Kelvin in 1892.

From 1860 to 1864 the American Civil War and the fears of British investors hindered the expansion of telegraphy. When the war ended, the technology was ready, but investors were still somewhat apprehensive at the thought of sinking half a million pounds sterling into the ocean. At that point John Pender, a Manchester cotton manufacturer, engaged his whole personal fortune and business talent in the enterprise, thereby reassuring the timid. First he merged the Gutta Percha Company, makers of cable cores, with the sheathing manufacturer Glass Elliot to form a new company, Telegraph Construction and Maintenance, or TC&M. This firm traded its cable for shares in the Atlantic Telegraph Company. In July 1865 the new cable was loaded on board the *Great Eastern,* the world's largest ship and the only one able to hold an ocean's worth of cable. Some 2,200 kilometers east of Ireland, it broke. Unlike its predecessor of 1858, however, this cable was excellent in every other respect and needed only to be fished up and reconnected. The following year, Pender formed the Anglo-American Telegraph Company with a capital of £600,000 and sent the *Great Eastern* out again with a new cable.[29] This time everything worked, and the two sides of the ocean were connected on July 27, 1866. Six weeks later, when the 1865 cable was fished up and repaired, two cables spanned the Atlantic. The age of global communications had begun.

The Red Sea Cable, 1856–1860

British involvement in the Middle East did not cease when the Crimean War ended in 1856. Two of the new technologies of the mid-century, steamships and the telegraph, only increased the importance of that region as a corridor to India. The connection between the telegraph networks of Europe and of India was inevitable. Yet, like the Franco-Algerian links, there were innumerable political and technical obstacles it had to overcome. Attempts to connect Britain with India went through a time of failures from 1856 to 1860, a period of very inadequate communication from 1861 to 1866, and finally a series of successes from 1866 on.

In 1856 two teams of telegraph entrepreneurs, sensing an opportunity for profit, turned to the Middle East. The Brett brothers founded the European and Indian Junction Telegraph Company, proposing to connect the Mediterranean to the Persian Gulf by way of the Euphrates Valley. At the same time, Lionel and Francis Gisborne obtained exclusive concessions from the Ottoman and Egyptian governments to put a land line through Egypt and a cable down the Red Sea. Of the two schemes, the British government preferred the Bretts' and signed a preliminary agreement with them in February 1857.[30]

A few months later, on May 10, the Indian Rebellion broke out. From Lucknow, the center of the uprising, Sir Henry Lawrence telegraphed to the governor general in Calcutta on May 16: "All is quiet here but affairs are critical; get every European you can from China, Ceylon, and elsewhere; also all the Goorkas from the hills; time is everything." Two days later the dispatch left Calcutta, reached Bombay on the 27th, and was immediately sent by steamer to Suez. On June 21 the message was on board a ship at Alexandria, bound for Trieste. On June 26 it was telegraphed from Trieste and reached London in the middle of the night. It had taken forty days to make the trip.[31] The need for a telegraph required no further proof. The House of

Commons discussed the matter at length and with great urgency. Palmerston, who distrusted Egypt, supported the Euphrates Valley project. But the Ottoman government refused to grant the Bretts the necessary concession and decided instead to build its own telegraph line from Constantinople to the Persian Gulf. The European and Indian Junction Company was dissolved, and with it disappeared British hopes for quick action.

The capture of Lucknow in November and the end of the rebellion did not calm British anxieties, and so the government turned to the Red Sea route. In early 1858 Lionel Gisborne founded the Red Sea and India Telegraph Company. A tight money market prevented him from raising the capital he needed, so he asked the government for a dividend guarantee like the ones received by the Indian railway companies. *The Times,* London merchants, and the India Office supported the idea. In November 1858, despite the recent failure of the Atlantic cable, the government capitulated and signed a fifty-year contract guaranteeing the company a 4.5 percent dividend on its capital of £800,000. Between May 1859 and February 1860, R. S. Newall, the contractor, laid the cable. Though each section tested well for 30 days as stipulated in the contract, trouble soon arose, and, by March 1860, five of the six sections had failed. No telegram ever traveled the whole way between Bombay and Suez.

The cause of the disaster soon became apparent. The cable was thin, weighing only one ton per kilometer, one-fourth as much as later cables. Soundings taken in early 1858 showed a soft bottom, but no proper detailed sea-bed survey was ever made. The cable was laid in a straight line without slack; so it hung between underwater peaks and soon broke under the weight of the barnacles that fastened onto it. Elsewhere the thin armor wires rusted, allowing *teredo navalis* worms to eat their way through the insulation. Despite the disappointment, the governments of Great Britain and India felt duty-bound to respect the contract, and paid the stockholders of the Red Sea Company £36,000 a year for the next fifty years.

The disasters of the Atlantic and Red Sea cables chilled investors' faith and made the British government averse to subsidizing cable ventures for the next twenty years. Those events had one positive consequence, however: the formation of the Joint Committee, mentioned earlier, which turned submarine telegraphy from a speculative venture into an organized branch of engineering. Henceforth, all the technical variables would be studied beforehand, instead of in a post mortem.[32]

Telegraphs to India, 1861–1870

The British need to communicate with India was not diminished by the fiasco, but only deflected to an older technology, the land line. Land lines were slower and less secure than cables, but in the early 1860s they were considered more reliable. Whereas cables either worked well or failed completely, land lines suffered breakdowns that could be repaired. They were the fall-back technology after the failures of the Atlantic, Franco-Algerian, and Red Sea cables.

In 1858 the Turkish government decided to put up a land line from Constantinople to Bagdad and on to Fao on the Persian Gulf. It reached Bagdad in 1861 and Fao in 1865. Meanwhile, the British were approaching from the east. The Indian government's Indo-European Telegraph Department, formed in 1862 under Colonel Patrick Stewart, erected a land line from Karachi to Gwadur at the head of the Persian Gulf. To obtain the cooperation of the coastal tribes required a special mission by Major Frederick Goldsmid, bearing threats and promises. From Gwadur to Fao, a cable completed the line in 1864. Unlike its predecessor, this one was heavy and properly laid.[33]

In anticipation of the connection, Britain had signed a convention with the Ottoman Empire and another with Persia that allowed the Indo-European Telegraph Department to erect a land line between Teheran and Bushire on the Gulf, to connect with the cable to India. Meanwhile, the Russians were pushing a line from Moscow to Tiflis in Georgia and from there to Teheran. Finally in January 1865 the two lines met, and Great Britain could at last communicate by telegraph to India.

That is, in a manner of speaking it could communicate. Telegrams cost £5 for twenty words. They were extremely slow, for the text had to be received, written down, and retransmitted twelve to fourteen times. After the first few months, the average telegram took five to six days via the Turkish line. Once a message went from London to Bombay in just twenty-four hours, but at other times, especially in winter when the snow broke the wires in Turkey, telegrams could take up to a month. Worst of all, the messages arrived full of errors, sometimes in total gibberish. Though the Indo-Ottoman Telegraphic Convention of 1864 had stipulated that the Turkish administration would employ clerks "possessing a knowledge of the English language sufficient for the perfect performance of that service" and that the Constantinople office would have officials "thoroughly conversant with the English language," they hardly lived up to these high standards. The alternative, through Persia and Russia, was worse. In Russia, according to Goldsmid, "all was crude, very crude." Telegrams took a week or two to make the trip, when they were not simply lost.

Despite these drawbacks, the telegraph was popular. In the first nine months of operation, it conveyed 22,866 messages from Britain to India.[34] Julius Reuter, eager to obtain news from Asia, opened an office in Bombay in 1866 and had a cable laid from England to Germany, where it connected to the land line.

While the press and commerce adopted the land line, the governments of Britain and India had other concerns. They had to entrust their communications not only to Turks, Persians, and Russians, but also to Italians, Frenchmen, Prussians, Bavarians, Greeks, Dutchmen, and Belgians. Everywhere, the official messages of the local government had priority, and foreign telegrams were often put aside until the quieter night hours. There were also unconfirmed rumors of espionage and deliberate errors and delays. Russia, so recently an enemy, was a source of particular anxiety to Britain, which feared its designs on India.[35]

In 1866, in response to these complaints, the House of Commons appointed a Select Committee "to inquire into the practical working of the present system of telegraphic and postal communications between this country and the East Indies."[36] The committee sat from March to July and heard numerous witnesses from the telegraph industry and from government, commerce, and banking. All agreed on the poor service in Turkey and in India. The Russo-Persian line, some thought, was worse. Others voiced suspicions about the European administrations, such as this comment by the chairman of the Electric and International Telegraph Company, Robert Grimstone: "I believe that in Paris, but that is mere hearsay, that they make four copies of all that they think of importance, and send them round to the different bureaus."[37] In its report, the Select Committee concluded:

That, having regard to the magnitude of the interests, political, commercial, and social, involved in the connection between this country and India, it is not expedient that the means of intercommunication by telegraph should be dependent upon any single line, or any single system of wires, in the hands of several foreign governments, and under several distinct responsibilities, however well such services may be conducted as a whole, in time of peace.

And it recommended:

A line practically under one management and responsibility, between London and the Indian Presidencies, in the first instance, and afterwards with China and the Australian Colonies, is deserving of serious consideration, and such reasonable support as the influence of Her Majesty's Government may be able to bring to its aid.[38]

The Select Committee spoke of "reasonable support" rather than any more specific solution because the government was of several minds on the issue of subsidizing telegraphic communications with India. The Board of Trade and the Foreign, Colonial, and India Offices favored better communications, but the Treasury, still smarting from the fiasco of 1858, refused to bear any further risks.

The government's position was finally clarified on April 10, 1867, when the Chancellor of the Exchequer presented a minute to the House of Commons. This minute declared that there would be no subsidies. The government, however, could "cause surveys to be made of the proposed route and render assistance by Her Majesty's vessels in laying the cables, and also by using the good offices of the Government with foreign governments upon whose territories it may be necessary to land cables."[39] While this minute seemed a rejection of the telegraph promoters' incessant demands for subsidies, it was in fact a vote of confidence in the ability of private enterprise to achieve its goals without government money.

Evidence to back up this act of faith was soon forthcoming. In February 1867 Werner von Siemens, now head of the Prussian firm of Siemens und Halske, offered to erect a double land line from London to Teheran, where it would meet the lines of the Indo-European Telegraph Department. It was to be devoted exclusively to Anglo-Indian communications and operated by Siemens employees, not by local telegraph clerks. Siemens sent Major J. V. Bateman-Champaign of the Indo-European Telegraph Department to negotiate with the Russian and Prussian governments. Having obtained the necessary concessions, they founded the Indo-European Telegraph Company, based in London. The line was put up in 1869 and opened for business on January 31, 1870.[40]

The new line was immediately effective. The average time for a telegram between India and England via Russia fell from 9 days 10 hours 39 minutes to 1 day 13 hours 10 minutes in 1870, and to 3 hours 9 minutes by 1873. Not only were the telegrams fast, they were also, for the first time, accurate. Even the Turkish line, spurred on by the competition, cut its time from over 5 days in 1865–69 to 19 hours 12 minutes in 1873.[41]

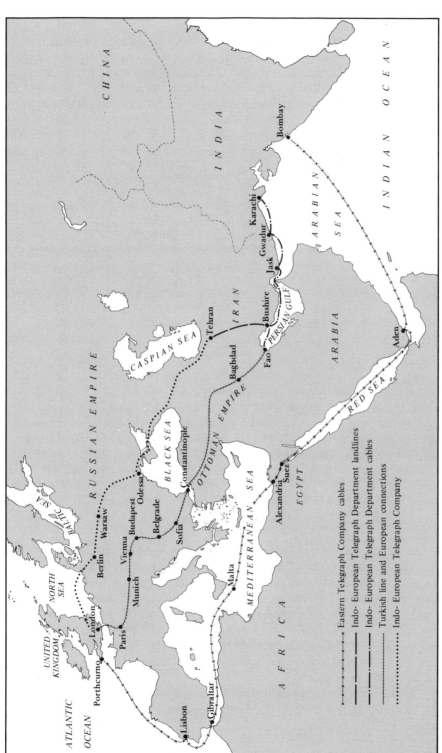

Figure 1. Telegraphs between Great Britain and India, c. 1875.

Meanwhile the success of the Atlantic cable of 1866 had suddenly put John Pender in a strong position. He turned his attention eastward. In May 1868 he founded the Anglo-Mediterranean Telegraph Company to lay a cable from Malta to Alexandria. The next year he created the Falmouth, Gibraltar, and Malta Telegraph Company to link England with its Mediterranean bases without passing through foreign countries. He also founded the British Indian Submarine Telegraph Company to connect Suez and Bombay. Though this company received no guarantee or subsidy, Pender was able to raise £1.2 million without difficulty. More important than any subsidy was the Telegraph Purchase Act of 1868. In nationalizing its domestic telegraph companies, the British government paid their shareholders £8 million, which now became available for new investments, especially for promising cable ventures.[42]

The new Suez-Bombay cable, manufactured by another Pender firm, TC&M, was laid by the *Great Eastern* in early 1870. This time, the work was done right. In May 1870 the three new cables were connected and messages began to flow.[43]

Conclusion

The history of telegraphy between 1850 and 1870 is significant in several respects. Those were the years in which submarine cable technology grew from infancy to maturity. Through a series of instructive disasters, cable manufacturers and engineers learned about insulation and armor, sounding and laying techniques, and the peculiarities of electricity and signaling over long distances. By 1870 British firms alone had developed the machinery to produce long cables and the ships and know-how to lay them. Only Britain had a capital market large and resilient enough to invest hundreds of thousands of pounds sterling in risky high-technology enterprises, lose them, and try again.

As a result, by 1870 Great Britain was in direct communication with North America, Europe, the Middle East, and India. At a time when France, Germany, Russia, and the United States were still filling in their domestic networks, Britain was ready to control the new medium of communication around the world. It would hold that position well into the next century.

In the process, the British learned some lessons about communication. One was that an integrated line was far more efficient than a series of short lines linked together. Another was that foreign telegraph administrations were technically incompetent, politically untrustworthy, or both. A third lesson, deduced from the first two, was that wherever there was a choice, a good cable at the bottom of the sea was much to be preferred to a land line through a foreign country. The fourth and most important lesson of all was the need to have alternative lines to fall back on, in case one was interrupted. Finally, the British government learned that on the trunk lines of the world, private enterprise could carry the burden of risk without state help.

In time, other powers would draw the same conclusions. By the time they did so, however, it was too late, for the British were there first and had obtained the best routes, built up an efficient service, and acquired the clientele that made the enterprise worthwhile.

Notes

1. On the Chappe telegraph, see Catherine Bertho, *Télégraphes et téléphones de Valmy au microprocesseur* (Paris, 1981), 9–58. On the English telegraphs, see Geoffrey Wilson, *The Old Telegraphs* (London and Chichester, 1976), Chapters 1–5.

2. Graham Storey, *Reuters: The Story of a Century of News-Gathering* (New York, 1951), 9–11; Jonathan Fenby, *The International News Services* (New York, 1986), 28.

3. Storey, 9–12; Fenby, 31–32; Vary T. Coates and Bernard Finn, *A Retrospective Technology Assessment: Submarine Telegraphy. The Transatlantic Cable of 1866* (San Francisco, 1979), 77.

4. George Arthur Codding, Jr., *The International Telecommunication Union: An Experiment in International Cooperation* (Leiden, 1952), 14.

5. Ibid., 13–14.

6. Ibid., 18.

7. Ibid., 21; George Sauer, *The Telegraph in Europe: A Complete Statement of the Rise and Progress of Telegraphy in Europe, Showing the Cost of Construction and Working Expenses of Telegraphic Communications in the Principal Countries etc. etc. Collected from Official Returns* (Paris, 1869), 12.

8. Codding, 23–24.

9. Keith Clark, *International Communications: The American Attitude* (New York, 1931), 97–98.

10. Letter of March 24, 1894, from the director general of Posts and Telegraphs to the minister of colonies in Archives Nationales Section Outre-Mer (Paris), Affaires Politiques 2554 dossier 4: Yanaon.

11. Clark, 103 and 116–19; Leslie Bennett Tribolet, *The International Aspects of Electrical Communications in the Pacific Area* (Baltimore, 1929), 10–12.

12. Codding, 27–30; "Telegraph Conferences" in General Post Office Archives (London) [henceforth POST] 83/30.

13. Sir William Brooke O'Shaughnessy, "Memoranda relative to experiments on the communication of Telegraphic Signals by induced electricity," *Journal of the Asiatic Society of Bengal* (September 1839): 714–31, and *The Electric Telegraph in British India: A Manual of Instructions for the Subordinate Officers, Artificers, and Signallers Employed in the Department* (London, 1853), iii–iv; Krishnalal J. Shridharani, *Story of the Indian Telegraphs: A Century of Progress* (New Delhi, 1956), 3–7; George W. Macgeorge, *Ways and Works in India: Being an Account of the Public Works in that Country from the Earliest Times up to the Present Day* (Westminster, 1894), 499–500; Mel Gorman, "Sir William O'Shaughnessy, Lord Dalhousie and the Establishment of the Telegraph System in India," *Technology and Culture* 12 (1971), 581–601.

14. O'Shaughnessy, "Memoranda," 20–21.

15. Donard de Cogan, "The Bewleys and their Contribution to Trans-Atlantic Telegraphy," *IEE Proceedings* (July 1987); Eugen F. A. Obach, *Cantor Lectures on Gutta-Percha* (London, 1898), 1–7; Alfred Gay, *Les câbles sous-marins*, Vol. 1: *Fabrication* (Paris, 1902), 45–46, and Vol. 2: *Travaux en mer* (Paris, 1903), 139–42; Th. Seeligmann, G. Lamy Torrilhon, and H. Falconnet, *Le caoutchouc et la gutta-percha* (Paris, 1896), 12–43; G. L. Lawford and L. R. Nicholson, *The Telcon Story, 1850, 1950* (London, 1950), 9–28. See also Daniel R. Headrick, "Gutta-Percha: A Case of Resource Depletion and International Rivalry," *IEEE Technology and Society Magazine* (December 1987), 12–18.

16. For a detailed and very technical chronology of these early cables by one of the pioneers in the field, see Willoughby Smith, *The Rise and Extension of Submarine Telegraphy* (London, 1891), 1–19. See also Lawford and Nicholson, 28–40.

26 *The Invisible Weapon*

17. Philippe Bata, "Le réseau de câbles télégraphiques sous-marins français des origines à 1914" (mémoire de maitrise, Université Paris-I Sorbonne, 1981), 3–5.

18. *Exposé du développement des services postaux, télégraphiques et téléphoniques en Algérie depuis la conquête* (Algiers, 1930), 49–50; Kenneth R. Haigh, *Cableships and Submarine Cables* (London and Washington, 1968), 302–304; Maxime de Margerie, *Le réseau anglais de câbles sous-marins* (Paris, 1909), 11–12, 18, and 27; Robert J. Cain, "Telegraph Cables in the British Empire 1850–1900" (Ph.D. dissertation, Duke University, 1971), 13 no. 1 and 75; Smith, 29–39.

19. Arthur R. Hezlet, *The Electron and Sea Power* (London, 1975), 2.

20. John Cell, *British Colonial Administration in the Mid-19th Century: The Policy-Making Process* (New Haven, Conn., 1970), 224.

21. On the early Mediterranean cables, see "Correspondence Repecting the Establishment of Telegraphic Communications in the Mediterranean and with India," *Parliamentary Papers* 1857–8 [2406] LX; Cain, 12–22; Cell, 224–26; and Hezlet, 4–7.

22. Smith, 40–42; Rupert Furneaux, *The First War Correspondent: William Howard Russell of the Times* (London, 1944), 39; Russell only sent one telegram during the Crimean War.

23. A. W. Kinglake, *The Invasion of the Crimea: Its Origin, and an Account of its Progress Down to the Death of Lord Raglan* (Edinburgh and London, 1892), 8: 263–64.

24. Ibid., 266.

25. Bern Dibner, *The Atlantic Cable* (Norwalk, Conn., 1959); Coates and Finn; Jeffrey Kieve, *The Electric Telegraph: A Social and Economic History* (Newton Abbot, England, 1973), 101–10; Smith, 44–51.

26. Great Britain, Submarine Telegraph Committee, *Report of the Joint Committee appointed by the Lords of the Committee of Privy Council for Trade and the Atlantic Telegraph Company to Inquire into the Construction of Submarine Telegraph Cables; together with the Minutes of Evidence and Appendix* (London, 1861), also in *Parliamentary Papers* 1860 [2744] LXII.

27. Donard de Cogan, "Dr. E. O. W. Whitehouse and the 1858 Trans-Atlantic Cable," *History of Technology* 10 (1985), 1–15.

28. Hezlet, 7.

29. On the *Great Eastern* see James Dugan, *The Great Iron Ship* (New York, 1953).

30. Manindra Nath Das, *Studies in the Economic and Social Development of Modern India: 1848–56* (Calcutta, 1959), 111–13; Shridharani, 7–8.

31. Coates and Finn, 101. Correspondent Russell's dispatches to *The Times* took an average of 43 days to reach London; see Furneaux, 100.

32. "History of Telegraph Communications with India (1858–1872) and an account of Joint Purse from 1874" (1897) in POST 83/56, pp. 3–23; "Correspondence Respecting the Establishment of Telegraphic Communications in the Mediterranean and with India," *Parliamentary Papers* 1857–8 [2406] LX; "Further Correspondence Respecting the Establishment of Telegraphic Communications in the Mediterranean and with India," *Parliamentary Papers* 1860 [2605] LXII; Halford L. Hoskins, *British Routes to India* (London, 1928), 374–78; Cain, 25–37 and 61–64; Cell, 226–33.

33. Christina P. Harris, "The Persian Gulf Submarine Telegraph of 1864," *Geographical Journal* 135 pt. 2 (June 1969), 169–90.

34. Cain, 116.

35. Frederick J. Goldsmid, *Telegraph and Travel: A Narrative of the Formation and Development of Telegraphic Communication between England and India* (London, 1874), 60–325; J. C. Parkinson, *The Ocean Telegraph to India: A Narrative and a Diary* (Edinburgh, 1870), 280–91; Hoskins, 379–89.

36. The report of the Select Committee is in POST 83/93 and in *Parliamentary Papers* 1866 (428) IX, 1.

37. Ibid., 27.

38. Ibid., xv–xvi.

39. "Special Report from the Select Committee on the Electric Telegraphs Bill," *Parliamentary Papers* 1867–8 (435) XI, pp. 29–30.

40. "Indo-European Telegraph Department 1865–1931," ed. Lesley A. Hall, in India Office Records (London), L/PWD/7; "History of Telegraph Communications with India (1858–1872) and an account of Joint Purse from 1874" in POST 83/56, 40–43; "Indo-European Telegraph, 1867–1871. Correspondence," in Public Record Office (Kew), FO 83/330; Colonel Henry Archibald Mallock, *Report on the Indo-European Telegraph Department, being a History of the Department from 1863 to 1888 and a Description of the Country through which the Line Passes,* 2nd ed. (Calcutta, 1890), 6–9; Hoskins, 389 and 396–97.

41. Goldsmid, 389.

42. Charles Bright, "The Extension of Submarine Telegraphy in a Quarter-Century," *Engineering Magazine* (December 1898), 417–20; Coates and Finn, 170; Kieve, 117–18.

43. On laying the British Indian cable, see Dugan, 218–39; Smith, 243–58; and Parkinson. On the telegraphs from 1866 to 1870, see Hugh Barty-King, *Girdle Round the Earth: The Story of Cable and Wireless and its Predecessors to Mark the Group's Jubilee, 1929–1979* (London, 1979), 26–35; Hoskins, 389–97; Mallock, 6–10; POST 83/56, 38–43; and Cain, 122–25.

3

The Expansion of the World Cable Network, 1866–1895

By 1866 telegraph engineers and entrepreneurs had learned much from two decades of experimentation and failure. They were ready to build a system that would dominate international communications for half a century. Until World War I the technology of telegraphs settled into a comfortable maturity, not yet challenged by long-distance telephony, radio, or airmail. Once cables could be made reliable and efficient, the network expanded until it reached almost every part of the world. Submarine cables, which totalled forty-six kilometers in 1852, stretched over 300,000 kilometers by 1895 (see Table 3.1 and Figure 2). Meanwhile, the world's land lines had grown to over a million kilometers. Between them, cables and wires carried some 15,000 messages a day.[1]

Yet telegraphic equipment was costly to manufacture and difficult to operate and maintain. Telegraphs could not be manufactured everywhere they were needed; instead, many countries had to import the equipment, and the less developed countries and colonies had to import the technicians as well. Despite its wide diffusion, this technology encouraged the concentration of manufacture and control; until the 1890s only the industrial nations manufactured their own telegraphic equipment.

The tendency towards concentration was even more powerful in the case of submarine cables. Until the 1890s, only Great Britain had a commercial and financial organization and a level of demand sufficient to warrant a cable industry. Moreover, only Britain had colonies and islands in every ocean suitable for cable relay stations. In 1887 Britain owned 70 percent of the world's cables; from 1894 to 1901, it still retained a 63 percent share.[2] More important, Britain's share of the world's cables included the trunk lines to India, East Asia, Australasia, Africa, and the Americas. Though other countries had feeder cables, most of the world's important business traffic traveled over British lines. The period from 1866 to 1895 was one of British hegemony in international communications.

28

Table 3.1.   Length of Cable in Existence at the Beginning of Each Year, 1852–1908[a]

Year	Companies (km)	(%)	Governments (km)	(%)	Total (km)	Year	Companies (km)	(%)	Governments (km)	(%)	Total (km)
1852	46	100			46	1879	110,873	93	8,740	7	119,613
1853	91	98	2	2	93	1880	128,567	92	10,440	8	139,007
1854	178	95	9	5	187	1881	135,388	92	12,125	8	147,513
1855	178	94	11	6	189	1882	140,286	92	12,577	8	152,863
1856	178	94	11	6	189	1883	156,204	92	13,892	8	170,096
1857	357	97	11	3	368	1884	160,828	92	14,624	8	175,452
1858	357	75	122	25	479	1885	182,103	92	16,333	8	198,436
1859	574	82	122	18	696	1886	187,038	91	19,365	9	206,403
1860	724	86	122	14	846	1887	196,826	91	19,613	9	216,439
1861	880	79	240	21	1,120	1888	202,482	91	20,576	9	223,058
1862	1,028	81	242	19	1,270	1889	204,653	90	22,264	10	226,917
1863	1,231	78	357	22	1,588	1890	215,548	91	22,378	9	237,926
1864	1,231	68	576	32	1,807	1891	225,841	91	22,561	9	248,402
1865	1,231	32	2,613	68	3,844	1892	241,258	91	24,205	9	265,463
1866	4,744	62	2,891	38	7,635	1893	247,558	90	28,370	10	275,928
1867	8,419	73	3,110	27	11,529	1894	260,545	90	29,732	10	290,277
1868	11,693	79	3,110	21	14,803	1895	271,787	90	30,064	10	301,851
1869	12,601	80	3,228	20	15,829	1896	272,919	90	31,250	10	304,169
1870	20,357	82	4,436	18	24,793	1897	279,068	89	32,880	11	311,948
1871	41,290	90	4,775	10	46,065	1898	282,880	89	34,435	11	317,315
1872	53,674	89	6,480	11	60,154	1899	293,053	89	35,346	11	328,399
1873	55,107	89	6,602	11	61,709	1900	303,644	89	35,634	11	339,279
1874	69,098	91	6,768	9	75,866	1901	328,065	90	37,885	10	365,950
1875	85,483	92	6,934	8	92,417	1902	349,520	89	41,860	11	391,380
1876	96,223	93	7,626	7	103,849	1903	357,229	86	60,450	14	417,679
1877	102,134	93	7,854	7	109,988	1904	371,145	86	61,742	14	432,887
1878	108,842	93	8,426	7	117,268	1908	389,818	82	83,290	18	473,108

[a] Maxime de Margerie, *Le réseau anglais de câbles sous-marins* (Paris, 1909), 21.

The Technology of Cables

Submarine telegraphy was the high technology of the late nineteenth century, involving phenomena that challenged the minds of the best physicists. The subject can be divided into the cables themselves, their laying and repair, and the transmission of signals.

Telegraph cables consisted of two parts: a core made of copper insulated with gutta-percha, and an armor to protect it. Engineers had learned that different conditions demanded different types of cable. The longer the cable, the more the signals became blurred and hard to read, and therefore the slower the transmission. This effect, called *attenuation,* could be reduced by using a thicker conductor with a heavier insulation. While thin cables were adequate on shorter routes—to cross the English Channel seventeen kilograms of copper per kilometer were quite sufficient—to cross the Atlantic companies learned that an initial investment in a heavy core paid off in faster service. The cable laid in 1894 by the Anglo-American Telegraph Company contained 159 kilograms of copper, compared with 98 kilo-

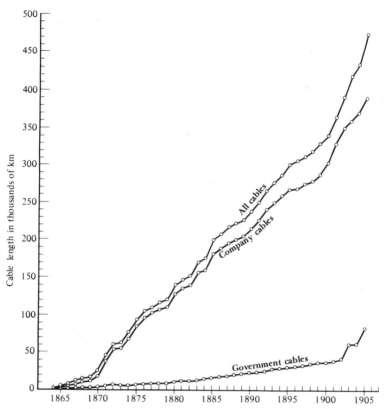

Figure 2. Length of cables in existence, 1864–1908.

grams for the 1873 cable. The direct New York–Brest cable of 1898 was, at six thousand kilometers, the longest in the world and therefore had to be the heaviest, with 162 kilograms of copper per kilometer.

The second aspect of cable design was its armor. This consisted of multiple windings of soft iron wire covered with layers of tarred hemp or jute to protect it from the salt water. On the soft bed of the Atlantic, the armor served mainly to prevent the cable from breaking while it was being laid or lifted for repairs. On the continental shelf the cable had to be stronger for protection against trawlers, and as it neared the coast it had to be even stronger to withstand the force of currents and the impact of rocks and ships' anchors. In tropical waters a thin brass tape was wound around the core to protect the gutta-percha from teredo worms, and on some Atlantic cables the iron wire served as a return for the electric current. Because of the differing types of cores and armor, cables could weigh anywhere from one to thirteen tons per kilometer.

Not only did cables have to be designed for specific tasks, but they had to be almost perfect. Impurities in the copper reduced conductivity, and, under the extreme pressures of the ocean floor, the least air bubble or flaw in the gutta-percha would inevitably cause an electrical failure. The armor also had to be perfect, for a broken wire could penetrate the core or cause the cable to break during laying operations. So exacting were the requirements of cable manufacture that the industry was dominated by a very few firms. One of them, the Telegraph Construction and Maintenance Company, made two-thirds of the world's cables in the nineteenth century. The other third was made by three other English companies: Siemens Brothers; India Rubber, Gutta Percha and Telegraph Works, and W. T. Henley Telegraph Works.

France also made cables, but in smaller quantities. In 1881 the French government opened a factory at La-Seyne-sur-Mer that made cable armor; the cores came from the Société Industrielle des Téléphones in Saint-Tropez and the Etablissements Grammont in Calais. Together they made shorter cables, such as those between Marseille and Oran (1892) and between Australia and New Caledonia (1893). Germany did not manufacture cables until the 1890s. The United States bought its cables from Britain until the 1920s.[3]

Another reason for the concentration of the industry was the complexity of cable laying and repair. The first cable ships were converted steamers, and laying operations were rather haphazard. By the mid-1860s it was clear that cable laying required careful preparations. Laying ships had to be large enough to hold thousands of kilometers of cable coiled in a tank and submerged in water to prevent the gutta-percha from drying out. At first only the *Great Eastern,* the largest ship built before the twentieth century, could hold an ocean's worth of cable. Then in 1873 the *Hooper* was launched: It was the second-largest ship in the world, and the first one specially built for cables. Cable ships were also designed to navigate along a precise path even in rough weather, and carried special equipment to unwind the cable at the right speed and with the right amount of slack. Electricians on board continuously tested the cable and communicated through it with the starting point.

In spite of every precaution, cables frequently needed repairs, especially near shores and along jagged sea beds like the Caribbean and Red seas. Cable-repair ships, smaller than cable-laying ships, were stationed along the major cable routes. With electrical and navigation equipment, accurate maps, and grappling gear, cable ships could locate a break in a cable within 0.05 percent of its length (i.e., within 1.5 kilometers on an Atlantic cable), haul it up from the ocean floor, and repair it, sometimes in a few days, sometimes after weeks of searching. Because of the complex techniques and equipment involved, cables were laid and mostly repaired by their manufacturers, and only a few repair ships belonged to telegraph companies or governments. The concentration of the industry meant that, of thirty cable ships in the world in 1896, twenty-four were British and only three were French, all of them small cable-repair ships purchased in Britain. Britain not only owned the ships but also the knowledge required to cut as well as repair cables. In the wars of the next century, it would give the British a powerful advantage over their enemies.[4]

In the early days of submarine telegraphy, capitalists hesitated to invest in cables that might wear out in a short time. Not until the end of the century did it appear that cables sunk in the oceans might last indefinitely, as water pressure actually improved the insulating properties of the gutta-percha. While some sections needed frequent replacement, others lasted as long as a century, with an average life span estimated at seventy-five years. As a consequence, at any given time, most of the world's submarine cables were technically obsolete. Rather than replacing them, telegraph companies put their effort into seeking advances in transmission techniques that would prolong the economic life of existing cables. More commonly still, they sought exclusive concessions and cartel arrangements that would protect their investments from competition. By the late nineteenth century, the international telegraphs had become the most conservative of all industries.

While cables changed very little from the 1860s to the 1920s, there was considerable progress in transmission techniques. The first inventions were the work of William Thomson. As the instruments used on land lines were not sensitive enough to detect the feeble currents coming from long cables, he devised the mirror galvanometer in 1858, a device that permitted a "mirror clerk" to read up to twenty-five words per minute, while another clerk wrote down the message. The mirror galvanometer, however, was subject to human error, left no record, and required two employees. In the early 1870s, Thomson introduced the siphon recorder, in which a pen drew an undulating line on a moving paper tape, which then served as an accurate and permanent record of incoming signals, transcribed by a clerk at up to sixty words per minute.

Early in the history of cables, a number of other improvements appeared, all driven by the need to bring the cables' efficiency up to that of land lines. James Graves, telegrapher for the Anglo-American Telegraph Company, devised the "sea earth" in which the electric current returned through the iron wires of the cable armor, rather than through the water; though introduced on the Atlantic cable in the late 1860s, this technique was only perfected twenty years later. Several other improvements clustered in the 1870s. In order to speed transmission, cable code, which used positive and negative impulses of equal length, replaced the Morse code with its dots and dashes. Duplexing, introduced between 1875 and 1879, allowed signals to be transmitted in both directions at once; by making each instrument insensitive to its own outgoing signals, it effectively doubled the capacity of cables. The automatic transmitter, invented by the French engineers Belz and Brahic, transmitted continuously at maximum speed the message prerecorded on punched paper tape by several telegraph clerks.[5]

All of these innovations had one purpose: to increase transmission speed. Engineers measured the electrical efficiency of cables and apparatus in words per minute. The increases in speed in the last third of the century were truly remarkable. The first long cables were excruciatingly slow. While the Atlantic cables of 1858 to 1873 could reach twenty-five words per minute in an occasional burst of speed, their average was between seven and thirteen. By the 1880s, Atlantic cables carried twenty-five to thirty words per minute, and the heavy cable of 1894 carried around fifty, with bursts of up to ninety.[6]

Customers had another measure of speed: the time it took a message to reach its destination. Here what counted was not only electrical but also human efficiency, especially on long routes along which telegrams had to be relayed several times. The fastest route was the North Atlantic, with several competing cables and only two retransmissions. By the 1890s the London and New York stock exchanges were two or three minutes apart from handing-in to delivery. So fast were the Atlantic cables that it was quicker to send a telegram from Paris to London via New York than directly.

Other routes were much slower because of retransmissions and a lack of competitive incentives. Between London and Bombay, for example, messages were received and retransmitted at Porthcurno in Cornwall, Carcavelos in Portugal, Gibraltar, Malta, Alexandria, and Aden; at the turn of the century, a telegram took an average of thirty-five minutes. A cable from England to Argentina took sixty minutes, to China, eighty, and to Australia, one hundred—slow by today's standards, but quite an improvement over the weeks and months by boat mail.

Cables were capable of amazing speeds on special occasions. In June 1870, at a party he threw to celebrate the inauguration of a cable to India, John Pender sent a telegram to Bombay and received an answer in four minutes and twenty-two seconds. News of the death of Queen Victoria on January 22, 1901 was relayed to Georgetown, British Guiana in twenty-two minutes. And at the British Empire Exhibition of 1924, King George sent himself a telegram that went around the world in eighty seconds.[7]

The Atlantic Cables

From Great Britain, cables fanned out in four directions: toward Europe, toward North America, toward the Mediterranean and Asia, and toward South America. Lines to the West Indies and Africa were essentially branches on one of the trunk lines.

In two of these directions, toward Europe and North America, the cables led to nations that had their own telegraph networks. Though numerous and heavily used, cables in European waters were but short links that connected national networks and required small investments. Most often, they were the joint property of the governments whose networks they linked.

More interesting was the North Atlantic route. Here cables demanded heavy investments available only to well-capitalized private enterprises. Britain and the United States both practiced free trade in cables, allowing foreign companies easy access to their coasts and cities. French companies operated in the shadow of the British. The story of the Atlantic cables in the last third of the century is one of considerable commercial but little political interest.

Cables across the North Atlantic were laid in three periods of intense activity separated by lulls: from 1866 to 1884, from 1894 to 1910, and finally from 1923 to 1928. The Anglo-American Telegraph Company, having pioneered the field, laid two more cables from Heart's Content (Newfoundland) to Valentia (Ireland) in 1873, 1874, and 1880. Though it dominated the field, it was burdened with debts inherited from the defunct Atlantic Telegraph Company and the high costs of the 1866 cable, a total of £7 million; it was therefore never very profitable. When the British government bought out its domestic telegraph companies for £8 million in 1869, former shareholders were eager to invest their newly liquid capital in other telegraph enterprises.

The first was the Société du Câble Transatlantique Français, organized by the news agency entrepreneur Julius Reuter and the French financier Baron Erlanger. In 1869 it laid a cable from Brest to Duxbury, Massachusetts, via the island of St. Pierre. In 1871 it joined the Anglo-American in a "joint purse" or cartel by which

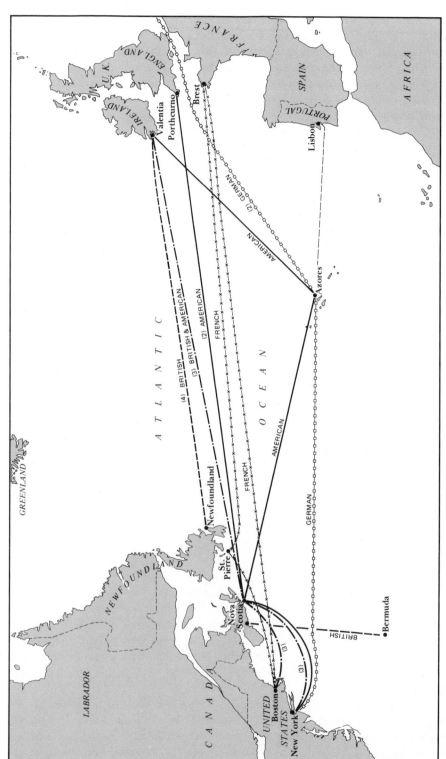

Figure 3. Atlantic Cables, c. 1904.

they agreed to charge the same rates and divide the income in proportion to their traffic. In financial difficulties two years later, it was sold to the Anglo-American. In 1874 another competitor, the Direct United States Telegraph Company, had a cable to Halifax laid by Siemens Brothers for only £1.3 million. Unable to compete with the Direct Company on the basis of rates, the Anglo-American bought half the shares of its competitor and forced it into the joint purse. In 1879 there appeared another French enterprise, the Compagnie Française du Télégraphe de Paris à New York—familiarly known as the PQ after its founder, Senator Pouyer-Quertier—which laid a new cable from Brest to Cape Cod. The PQ joined the purse, then attempted to leave it, and ended up in financial trouble.

More menacing competition appeared in the 1880s from two American enterprises. In 1881 Jay Gould's Western Union Telegraph Company had two cables laid from Nova Scotia to Cornwall. Though it joined the purse in 1883, it did so on its own terms. That same year the mining tycoon John W. Mackay and the publisher of the *New York Herald,* Gordon Bennett, founded the Commercial Cable Company, which had cables laid from Nova Scotia to England. With a more direct route, they offered both faster service and competitive rates.[8]

After a ten-year lull, more cables were laid in 1894 and in 1898. By the end of the century, of the sixteen cables lying on the bottom of the Atlantic, twelve were working, and eleven would still be working fifty years later: seven British, three American, and one French. In the first decade of the twentieth century, they were joined by two German cables, two American, and one British.

The North Atlantic route, which began as a monopoly and turned into a cartel, gained a measure of competition when well-funded Americans arrived on the scene. Thereafter, British capitalists gradually lost interest in this market; finally in 1911 the Anglo-American and Direct United States companies leased their cables to Western Union. The British, however, still firmly retained their dominance of cable manufacture, laying, and maintenance.[9]

The Cable Companies

As they gave way to Americans in the North Atlantic, British enterprises found more lucrative opportunities in connecting Europe with Asia, Australia, Africa, and South America, where they faced no rivals in the cable business. Instead they encountered countries that were technologically backward, many of which were in the British Empire or soon to be. The disparity in wealth and power between Britain and the lands at the other ends of the cables and the symbiosis between cable communication and maritime power made these enterprises exceptionally political. Just as Great Britain towered above the countries of the non-Western world, so did one firm tower above its rivals. The history of the Eastern and Associated Telegraph Companies coincides with the growth and decline of the British Empire after 1870.[10]

In 1868–70 John Pender founded several cable companies in quick succession: the Falmouth, Gibraltar and Malta; the Anglo-Mediterranean; the Marseilles, Algiers and Malta; the Mediterranean Extension; and the British Indian Submarine Telegraph companies. They were created separately so that a disaster in one would not pull the others down. In 1872, when they had proved themselves technically and financially viable, he merged them to form the Eastern Telegraph Company, with a capital of £3.8 million.

As soon as the cable to India showed promise, Pender repeated the pattern beyond India. In 1869 and 1870 he founded the British Indian Extension, the China Submarine, and the British Australian telegraph companies. In 1873, once their cables were laid and working, he merged them into the Eastern Extension Australasia and China Telegraph Company, with a capital of £3 million.

The Eastern and Eastern Extension companies were the heart of Pender's cable empire and, as orators phrased it, "the nerves of the British Empire."[11] In later years he founded several other enterprises: the Brazilian Submarine Telegraph Company (1873) between Europe and Brazil; the Western and Brazilian Telegraph Company (1873) along the Brazilian coast to Buenos Aires; the West Coast of America Telegraph Company (1877); the Eastern and South African Telegraph Company (1879) between Aden and Durban, South Africa; the African Direct Telegraph Company (1885) along the west coast of Africa; and other smaller ones. These companies were nominally separate, but they had interlocking directorships, and almost all had John Pender, his son Denison-Pender, or the Marquis of Tweeddale as chairman. To reinforce the links, they also shared directors with the Anglo-American and Direct United States Telegraph companies, and with the Telegraph Maintenance and Construction Company, which owned shares in the cable companies and which manufactured, laid, and repaired most of their cables. Lest anyone still think they were independent, the companies also shared the same building, Winchester House on Old Broad Street, London, and in 1902 they all moved to Electra House in Moorgate. Here telegrams marked "Via Eastern" could flow from one end of the earth to the other in a matter of minutes. Almost half the world's cables came through this building and, with them, more than half of the world's international news, commercial information, and diplomatic dispatches.[12]

These were all private firms with no more connection to the government than any button manufacturer. The Treasury minute of 1867 had promised that the government would help the companies "by using the good offices of the Government with foreign governments upon whose territories it may be necessary to land cables."[13] The cable companies took every precaution to obtain the maximum benefit from these words. Although most of the capital invested in cables came from trade, in Pender's case the textile industry, the boards had a disproportionate number of aristocrats with connections in the Foreign Office and the Colonial Office.[14] For example, at a dinner at John and Emma Pender's house in February 1876,

> "Herbert of the Colonial Office" came up to him and congratulated him. In the course of the conversation that followed, according to Emma Pender, Herbert assured the chairman of the Eastern Telegraph and Eastern Extension [i.e., John Pender] that if he should ever want any business transacted "in his office" connected with telegraphs, he would take charge of it himself.[15]

In July 1882, during the British invasion of Egypt, John Pender offered to lay a cable from Alexandria to Suez via the Suez Canal to replace the vulnerable land line, but he asked for an assurance of no competition. The Treasury replied:

While Her Majesty's Government . . . do not deem it expedient that anything in the nature of a guarantee of monopoly should be given to the Companies whom you represent, they are able to assure you that, in their opinion, it would be highly inexpedient to encourage, upon light grounds, competition against a Company in the position of the Eastern Telegraph Company which has embarked large capital upon existing lines; and these considerations would apply with especial force to competition which might be threatened from foreign sources.[16]

During the Colonial Conference of 1887, Pender wrote to Sir Henry Holland at the Colonial Office:

Our telegraph system is now very much in touch with Her Majesty's Government, and we have letters from the Foreign Office to the effect that whatever discussions take place in regard to submarine telegraphs we shall have full information on the subject, and representation during such discussions. I, therefore, hope that the Colonial Office, looking to the vast interests involved in the submarine telegraphic system, will grant to my companies similar recognition on the present occasion.[17]

The Eastern and Associated Companies did not always get the full support of the British government, nor did the government always obtain full satisfaction from the companies; but until 1902 at least, their ties were closer than those of any other industry.

In comparison to the Eastern group, the history of the other British cable companies is singularly uninspiring. Three small firms served the Caribbean: the West India and Panama Telegraph Company, the Cuba Submarine Telegraph Company, and the Halifax and Bermudas Cable Company. They made few profits because traffic was poor, while their cables, resting on coral beds, needed constant repairs. By the turn of the century, Eastern had bought enough of their shares to operate them as subsidiaries. The India Rubber Company, a rival of TC&M, tried to enter the cable business by serving countries that Eastern avoided. Its Direct Spanish Telegraph Company linked Marseille to Barcelona; its Spanish National Company laid a cable from Cadiz to Tenerife in the Canary Islands, where it met the West African Telegraph Company's cable that served the non-British colonies, and the South American Telegraph Company's cable to Brazil. None of these enterprises flourished. Eastern bought out the Direct Spanish, Spanish National, and West African cables in 1884, while the South American, almost bankrupt, was sold to France in 1902. The lesson was clear: Companies that served the British Empire and cooperated closely with the British government flourished, while British companies that served foreign countries shriveled and were swallowed up, either by their competitors or by their clients.

There were also some non-British cable companies outside the North Atlantic. A Danish firm, the Great Northern Telegraph Company, connected Britain with Scandinavia and Russia, and Siberia with Japan and China. It bought its cables from TC&M and cooperated closely with the Eastern Extension company. A small French company founded in 1888, the Société Française des Télégraphes Sous-Marins, operated cables in the Caribbean and between Australia and New Caledonia. Like all French companies, it relied on government subsidies. In 1895 it merged with the Compagnie Française du Télégraphe de Paris à New York to form the Compagnie

The Invisible Weapon

Table 3.2. Distribution of Private Cables in the World in 1892[a]

	Number of cables	Length (km)	Percent of world total
Eastern and Associated Companies			
Eastern Telegraph Co.	117	50,843	20.6
Eastern Extension . . . Telegraph Co.	27	13,597	5.5
Eastern and South African Tel. Co.	12	12,586	5.1
Brazilian Submarine Telegraph Co.	6	13,647	5.5
West African Telegraph Co.	12	5,594	2.3
African Direct Telegraph Co.	7	5,086	2.1
Western and Brazilian Telegraph Co.	10	7,341	3.0
West Coast of America Telegraph Co.	7	3,147	1.3
Black Sea Telegraph Co.	1	624	0.3
River Plate Telegraph Co.	3	256	0.1
Subtotal	202	112,711	45.5
Other British Companies	4	1,311	0.5
Direct Spanish Telegraph Co.	1	1,574	0.6
Halifax and Bermudas Cable Co.	7	3,998	1.6
Spanish National Submarine Tel. Co.	14	19,261	7.8
Anglo-American Telegraph Co.	2	5,741	2.3
Direct United States Cable Co.	5	2,778	1.1
Cuba Submarine Telegraph Co.	22	8,440	3.4
West India and Panama Telegraph Co.	55	43,103	17.5
Subtotal			
Total of British Companies	257	155,814	63.1
Non-British Companies			
Great Northern Telegraph Co. (Denmark)	27	12,838	5.2
Cie Fr. du Télégraphe Paris à New York	4	6,475	2.6
Soc. Fr. des Télégraphes Sous-Marins	14	6,952	2.8
Western Union Telegraph Company (U.S.)	8	14,340	5.8
Commercial Cable Company (U.S.)	6	12,849	5.2
Mexican Telegraph Company (U.S.)	3	2,821	1.1
Central and South American Tel. Co. (U.S.)	10	8,977	3.6
Canadian Pacific Railroad Co. (Canada)	5	78	
Total of Non-British Companies	77	65,330	26.5
Total of all Companies	334	221,144	89.6

[a]U.S. Department of the Navy, Bureau of Navigation, Hydrographic Office, *Submarine Cables* (Washington, 1892), 41–59.

Française des Câbles Télégraphiques. Not until the turn of the century did French and German companies begin to offer the British any significant competition, and when they did it was from political motives.

Tables 3.2 through 3.4 show the distribution of the world's cables in 1892. They reveal two important aspects of submarine telegraphy: private ownership and British dominance. While governments owned the largest number of cables, they were mostly very short, connecting islands and crossing bays and fjords. In length, 89.6 percent of the world's cables belonged to private companies; they were to the short

Table 3.3.   Distribution of Government Cables in the World in 1892[a]

	Number of cables	Length (km)	Percent of world total
British Empire			
Britain	111	2,963	1.2
India	93	3,671	1.5
Canada	22	396	0.2
Other	25	774	0.3
Total	251	7,804	3.2
French Empire			
France	53	6,954	2.8
Indochina	4	1,472	0.6
Total	56	8,432	3.4
Other Nations			
Italy	34	1,976	0.8
Germany	45	1,541	0.6
Netherlands and Dutch East Indies	24	1,007	0.4
Spain	9	961	0.4
Greece	48	926	0.4
Turkey	10	628	0.3
Norway	255	526	0.2
Russia	8	524	0.2
Denmark	55	363	0.1
Belgium	2	202	0.1
Austria	31	194	0.1
Others	96	644	0.3
Total Government Cables	892	25,728	10.4

[a]Same as for Table 3.2.

government cables like ocean liners to river ferries. The other obvious statistic is the British predominance: two-thirds of the world's cables were British, and 45.7 percent belonged to one group: the Eastern and Associated Companies, the greatest multinational corporation of the nineteenth century.

Table 3.4.   Company and Government Cables Combined in 1892[a]

	Number of cables	Length (km)	Percent of world total
British cables	508	163,619	66.3
American cables	27	38,986	15.8
French cables	74	21,859	8.9
Danish cables	82	13,201	5.3
Others	535	9,206	3.7
Total World Cables	1,226	246,871	100.0

[a]Same as for Table 3.2.

Cables to India and Australia

After the North Atlantic and Mediterranean routes, the route to India was the busiest in the world, handling not only Indian traffic, but also that of Australia, Southeast Asia, and parts of the Far East. As soon as the Eastern cable to Bombay opened for business, it captured half the traffic between India and England, a share that gradually rose to two-thirds. Traffic on the Turkish line fell to 1.49 percent of the total. The Indo-European Telegraph Company held its own but ceased making profits. When it was interrupted for three months by the Russo-Turkish War of 1877, Eastern took the opportunity to lay a second Suez–Bombay cable. It could have annihilated the competition, but instead was persuaded to join the Indo-European Telegraph Company and the Indo-European Telegraph Department in a joint purse. This satisfied the governments of Britain and India, which wanted to maintain alternative routes in case the cables were interrupted.[18]

In 1870, as the first Suez–Bombay cable was being laid, the British Indian Extension Telegraph Company leased a land line between Bombay and Madras from the Indian Telegraph Department and laid a cable from Madras to Penang and Singapore. Beyond Singapore, the cables branched out in two directions: toward Australia, and toward Indochina and China.

At the time Australia was not one country but several colonies that squabbled more often than they cooperated. Vast internal distances and isolation from Britain, to which most settlers were still very attached, made Australians greet the telegraph with enthusiasm. Yet, unlike Americans, they were too few and poor to construct it all themselves.[19] Australians had been putting up telegraph wires since 1853. Before the first cable reached the continent, there were already networks in New South Wales, Victoria, and South Australia, and lines to Queensland and Western Australia. But none yet reached Darwin on the north coast, where the British Australian Telegraph Company landed its cable from Singapore in October 1871. The line across the Australian Desert from Darwin to Adelaide was completed, after the most harrowing difficulties, on June 23, 1872. It carried amazing news, as K. S. Inglis wrote: "Among the first messages from London to Adelaide in 1872 was an announcement that England and the United States were about to go to war. Then the wire went dead for several weeks, while English newspapers refuting the report were traveling out in the mail steamer."[20]

The line was finally repaired in August 1872, eighteen months behind schedule. Its effect was most remarkable. News that had taken fifty-four days to travel from England by the fastest ship now took only fifteen to twenty-four hours. Australians threw banquets to celebrate the event with as much fervor as Americans had shown in 1858, but they soon learned the drawbacks of telegraphy. The land lines were easily damaged and were down half the time. Messages were garbled crossing Java. Worst of all were the high rates: at first £9 9s. for twenty words, then, from 1872 to 1891, 10s. a word. Australians, the most prolific telegraph users on earth, could seldom afford to send a message "home" to England. The telegraph served mainly to send price quotations and orders for wool, wheat, and other goods in the tersest codes available.[21]

Cable Rivalries in the West Indies and Latin America

As soon as the Atlantic cable of 1866 showed what could be done, entrepreneurs turned their attention to the West Indies and Latin America, regions that seemed as promising as India and the Far East. Here, however, Britain competed both commercially and politically with the United States and France. The rivalry between British and American cable interests was purely commercial and did not involve the governments. As we shall see in the next chapter, French interests in the region were cultural and political as well as commercial.

The first cable entrepreneur to see lucrative opportunities in the Caribbean was the American James Scrymser. At the end of the Civil War, he obtained concessions from Spain and the United States to lay cables between Key West and Havana. By 1868 his firm, the International Ocean Telegraph Company, was operating a cable at a profit. Due to disagreements among the partners, however, it did not seek landing rights in the British West Indian colonies, and in 1868 it was refused a landing right in Brazil.[22]

What Scrymser could not do, the British did. The West India and Panama Telegraph Company, founded in 1869, obtained landing rights in all the British colonies in the Caribbean as well as in Cuba, Guadeloupe, and Martinique. Another firm, the Cuba Submarine Telegraph Company, got the concession for a cable along the coast of Cuba. By 1872, all these lands were connected to one another and, via the Havana–Key West cable, to the United States and Europe.[23]

At that point John Pender turned his attention to South America. In 1873 his Western Telegraph Company got what Scrymser had been refused: a thirty-year concession to connect Brazil to Europe. Two other subsidiaries, the Western and Brazilian Submarine Telegraph and the London Platino-Brazilian Cable companies, got landing rights along the Brazilian coast and to Argentina, respectively. Finally, in 1875–76 the West Coast of America Telegraph Company, whose network was connected to the Western cables by a land line across the Andes, extended the network up to Peru. By 1877 Pender was in control of most South American communications.[24]

Scrymser, however, had not retired from the cable business. Although he lost his International Ocean Company to Jay Gould's Western Union Company in 1878, he obtained the concession for telegraph links between the United States and Mexico, which he joined by a Galveston–Vera Cruz cable two years later. His Mexican Telegraph Company did well enough to attract a group of New York bankers led by J. Pierpont Morgan, rivals of Jay Gould. With their money, Scrymser founded the Central and South American Telegraph Company in 1882 and laid cables down the west coast to Peru. In 1891 his company laid a cable to Chile and bought the Transandine Telegraph Company's land line to Buenos Aires. It now competed with Pender's companies for the traffic between South and North America, and even some of the traffic to Europe. As they had in the North Atlantic a decade earlier, the British were encountering some unpleasant competition. Not until the 1920s, however, was it seen as a rivalry between the two nations.[25]

The French entered the cable business in the Americas belatedly. In comparison to Britain and the United States, France did relatively little business in the Caribbean. It owned two sugar islands, Guadeloupe and Martinique, and the undeveloped territory of Guyana. While the British were eagerly acquiring the best cable routes around the world, France was occupied by the war with Prussia in 1870 and its aftermath. Furthermore, there was no French cable industry, and what capital the nation had went to maintain a large standing army or was invested in Algeria and Europe. Only in the 1880s, after many years of frustration with the British cable companies, did France extend its cable network to the Caribbean.

In July 1886 the government introduced a bill to the Chamber of Deputies, granting a concession for a French cable to link Brazil, French Guyana, Martinique, the Dominican Republic, and the United States. The project also involved the creation of cable factories and required a subsidy of a million francs (£40,000) per year.[26] Supporters of the bill invoked the national glory and predicted vast profits; opponents were sure the cable would lose money and end up a burden on the taxpayers. The Chamber of Deputies, skeptical of every scheme that did not contribute to the defense of France against Germany, put off the bill until the following year.

Meanwhile in Britain the journal *The Electrician,* voice of the cable industry, derided "the sentimental idea that France must have French cables to French colonies, and should have cables built in France."[27] The British were not content to make fun, however; as *The Financial News* stated: "We congratulate Mr Thomas Fuller, the managing director of the Brazilian Submarine Company, on the great victory he has just scored in Paris for the English telegraph industries."[28] When the bill came to the floor of the Chamber, it was debated at length, then sent back to committee.[29] Between February and July 1887 it was the subject of articles and editorials in the Parisian press, almost all of which opposed it on the grounds that it was unrealistic and represented "lucre" and "speculation" at the taxpayers' expense. Finally in July the Chamber of Deputies rejected the bill for the last time.[30]

Defeat in the parliament did not deter the cable promoters for long. In 1888 they founded the Société Française des Télégraphes Sous-Marins. Two years later it began laying cables, without subsidies, between the Dominican Republic, Guadeloupe, Martinique, French Guyana, Surinam, and Brazil. As its detractors had predicted, it lost money and by 1895 was in such financial difficulty that it had to be rescued by the government and merged with the equally unprofitable Compagnie Française du Télégraphe de Paris à New-York.[31]

In 1892–93 France again narrowly missed having a cable to the Caribbean. In February 1892, when the Portuguese government granted exclusive landing rights in the Azores to TC&M, French Foreign Minister Ribot persuaded the Portuguese parliament not to ratify the agreement. Instead, the concession was given to the Société Française des Télégraphes Sous-Marins, which signed an agreement with the French Ministry of Posts and Telegraphs to lay a cable from France to Haiti via Lisbon and the Azores, a project very similar to the one defeated in 1887. However, Minister of Commerce and Industry Jules Siegfried found the proposed dividend guarantee of 2.3 million francs a year too high, and persuaded the budget committee of the Chamber of Deputies to reject it. The Portuguese government then granted the concession to the European and Azores Telegraph Company, an Eastern subsidiary, which later sold it to the German Post Office.[32] France finally acquired a connection to the Caribbean in 1896, when the United States and Hayti Telegraph Company, a nominally American firm but owned by the French, linked France's New York–Brest cable to its West Indian cables.[33]

Time and again, the French attempts to create a cable network were stymied by the poor fit between the economy of France and its role in the world. In the late nineteenth century, France was wealthy but largely self-sufficient, with a lagging industrial sector. Yet culturally, politically, and militarily, France was a great nation in the process of conquering a global empire. To some Frenchmen, worldwide communications seemed essential; to others, wasteful.

Only in the Americas, a battleground of rival empires since the sixteenth century, did the British face serious competition. It was a portent of more widespread challenges in the years to come.

Across Russia to Japan

The telegraph approached the Far East from two directions at once: from Southeast Asia and across Russia. As we saw, the Eastern group reached Singapore in 1870. Let us now turn back a few years and watch the telegraph approaching from the north.

The first proposal to bring telegraphy to the Far East came from the United States. In 1858 Perry Collins presented a proposal to the Russian court at Saint Petersburg to link Europe with North America via Siberia and Alaska. The failure of the Atlantic cable of 1858 and the growing Russian interest in the Far East made his proposal seem eminently sensible. Collins also offered to run his wires to Japan and across China to Australia. He was able to obtain the backing of Samuel Morse, the Western Union Telegraph Company, and the Russian government, which wanted to communicate with the Maritime Provinces it had acquired in 1860; he was also encouraged by the American and British governments. In 1864–65 Western Union began erecting a line in British Columbia, while the Russian Telegraph Administration extended its wires eastward from Irkutsk, and surveyors charted the gap in-between. In 1866, however, the Atlantic cable put an end to this project.[34]

The next project came from an even less likely source: Denmark, a country with no diplomatic representation and almost no commercial interests in the Far East. Two enterprising Danes, the banker C. F. Tietgen and Lieutenant Edouard Suenson of the Danish Navy, were able to use these weaknesses to their advantage. In 1868 Tietgen and others founded three small cable companies, the Danish-Norwegian-English, the Danish-Russian, and the Norwegian-British Submarine, to connect the countries so named. A year later they merged to become Det Store Nordiske Telegraphenkompagnie, the Great Northern Telegraph Company. This firm enjoyed the favor of the Russian government for two reasons: Russia, until then connected to Britain by the land lines of the Indo-European Company, wanted an alternative route that did not cross Prussia; furthermore, the Crown Prince, soon to be Czar Alexander III, was married to Dagmar, the daughter of King Christian IX of Denmark.

But Tietgen was not content to operate in European waters. He therefore offered the Russians a telegraph line to China and Japan, and possibly another to America, free from both Prussian and British control. In exchange, the Russian government would let the Great Northern use its land line across Russia and Siberia. He won the concession in October 1869, and three months later founded the Great Northern China and Japan Extension Telegraph Company.[35]

If the Danes were able to use their political connections with Russia to good effect, they were equally able to use their good relations in Britain. Their efforts, far from being seen as anti-British, received the backing of British business circles; the Great Northern Extension was underwritten by a London bank and obtained three-quarters of its capital from British investors.[36] The British Foreign Office added its support to that of Russia, Denmark, France, and the Netherlands to help the company obtain landing rights in China and Japan. Even John Pender readily agreed to let this rival land a cable in Hong Kong. In their efforts to open the Far East to Western trade and influence, Europeans were more often allies than rivals.

It was a fortunate coincidence that cable enterprises approached Japan just after the Meiji Restoration of 1868, when the country came under the sway of a modernizing elite eager for Western technology. In 1869 the Japanese government hired the English telegraph engineer George Gilbert and erected a land line between Tokyo and Yokohama. When Lieutenant Suenson arrived in early 1870 to seek landing rights for his company, the Japanese government quickly approved. As the Great Northern had already sent a cable ship out east, work proceeded quickly. In 1871 the company laid cables from Vladivostok to Nagasaki and Nagasaki to Shanghai, and opened offices in those cities and in Hong Kong. It also laid a cable from Nagasaki to Yokohama for the Japanese Telegraph Administration. The telegraph from Japan to Europe opened for business on January 1, 1872. The Company celebrated its success by merging the Great Northern Extension into its parent company, the Great Northern Telegraph Company.[37]

The Japanese rapidly built up their telegraph network. In 1872 the first group of students was sent to Europe to study telegraphy, and the government began manufacturing telegraph equipment. After the Satsuma Rebellion of 1877 demonstrated the value of rapid communication, the network was expanded and opened to the public. In 1891 the country had 435 telegraph offices linked by 11,610 kilometers of land lines and 387 kilometers of cables.

For its international communications, Japan found it more expedient to rely on foreigners. It signed the International Telegraph Convention in 1879 and agreed to use Japanese words transcribed into Roman characters for international telegrams. In 1882 it granted the Great Northern a twenty-year exclusive concession on its communications with Asia (and thereby with the rest of the world) in exchange for new cables to Russia, China, and Korea. In communications, Japan did not become assertive until the turn of the century. By being so accommodating with the Great Northern, it gained a measure of independence internally.[38]

Commercial Codes and the International Telegraph Union

There are two kinds of secret writing. A code is the substitution of words and phrases with code words, and requires a codebook to encrypt and decrypt. A cipher is the substitution of numbers for letters, and requires a fixed system (such as a table of encipherment) and a readily changed key. Both methods offer conciseness and promise confidentiality, and sometimes secrecy.

The first codes were developed to ensure a measure of privacy to private correspondence. As early as 1845, Samuel Morse's agent Francis Smith published *The Secret Corresponding Vocabulary*.[39] In the introduction to the 1869 edition of his *Telegraphic Code*, Robert Slater wrote:

> On the 1st February, 1870, the telegraph system throughout the United Kingdom passes into the hands of the Government, who will work the lines by Post Office officials. In other words, those who have hitherto so judiciously and satisfactorily managed the delivery of our sealed letters will in future be entrusted also with the transmission and delivery of our . . . telegraphic communications, which will thus be exposed not only to the gaze of public officials, but from the necessity of the case must be read by them. Now in large or small communities (particularly perhaps in the latter) there are always to be found prying spirits, curious as to the affairs of their neighbors . . . and proverbially inclined to gossip. . . . The community will frequently have occasion to employ the telegraph in the transmission of messages which they will be most anxious to forward in such terms as shall be unintelligible to the operators through whose hands they pass.[40]

Very quickly, customers discovered the other advantage of codes: their economy. Long-distance cables, with their astronomical rates, encouraged the publication of standard business codes like William Clausen's *ABC Code* and the best-selling *Bentley's Complete Phrase Code,* and even special codebooks for particular industries or individual companies.[41] In 1902 Eastern published the *Via Eastern Telegraphic Social Code* for the benefit of travelers.[42] Though the cost of writing a codebook was very high, the economies it provided were phenomenal. In social codes, a code word replaced an average of 5.95 plain words, and in one commercial code, each code word did the work of 27.93 plain words.[43] On the longer cables, where nine-tenths of the telegrams were commercial, 95 percent were in code. Thus between 1885 and 1898, while the trade between Britain and India increased several times over, the number of words transmitted remained static as the increased use of codes gave the traffic an ever greater density of meaning.[44]

The private telegraph companies encouraged the use of codes as an alternative to lowering their rates, and generally accepted a code word of up to seven syllables as the equivalent of a plain word. European governments and the International Telegraph Union tried to regulate the practice, partly out of bureaucratic zeal, and partly out of concern for national security.[45] Codes and ciphers had been permitted within Europe since 1865, but it was the St. Petersburg Convention of 1875 that officially admitted codes with a maximum of ten letters per word. The London conference of 1879 restricted telegrams in extra-European traffic to English, French, German, Italian, Dutch, Spanish, Portuguese, and Latin; in the spirit of imperialism then in fashion, the languages of non-European peoples were simply forbidden. In 1890 the Paris ITU conference decreed that an official ITU codebook would be written to replace all private codes. Its publication in 1894 aroused such protests that the ITU had to back down and authorize existing codebooks. Finally in 1903 the ITU surrendered to the private code makers and allowed artificial words of up to ten letters. The result was a surge in code making, with books like *Whitelaw's Tele-*

graphic Cypher consisting of 20,000 five-letter words that could be joined to form 400 million different ten-letter combinations admissible in international telegraphy.

Conclusion

In the last third of the nineteenth century, the telegraph was so new that people still viewed it as a technological miracle, and politicians, businessmen, and the public gave this magnificent invention their enthusiastic support. Governments of every sort—autocracies like Russia, democracies like the United States, colonial regimes like India, even non-Western states like Turkey and Japan—all seized upon it as a means of enhancing their power and improving their efficiency. Only China stood back, seeing in the telegraph an alien intruder.

As the telegraph was springing up everywhere, the cables were reaching out, sometimes preceding local networks, sometimes following. It all happened quite suddenly: it reached North America in 1866; India in 1870; Japan, China, and Australia in 1871; the Caribbean in 1872; South America in 1874; East and South Africa in 1879; and West Africa in 1886. In twenty years the world was wired up. Unlike the land telegraphs, this was not a case of technological diffusion; the cables spread to every continent, but the equipment and knowledge stayed firmly in the possession of a small elite, almost all British and, among the British, almost all of them members òf the Eastern group and TC&M.[46]

Commercially, it was a well-deserved hegemony. British engineers had developed the technology, their entrepreneurs had promoted them, their investors had risked their capital, and, in most places, they provided value for money. The companies were greedy and unscrupulous, and, in the face of serious competition, as on the North Atlantic or in China, they joined their rivals to exploit their customers. Throughout the era of expansion, the British government stood aside, helping only indirectly. Since cables were commercial enterprises created in a seemingly apolitical atmosphere, few suspected just how much political power they gave their owners. In the long run, the might of Britain did not just rest on her trade or on the Royal Navy, but on access to the information the cables provided.

Notes

1. Maxime de Margerie, *Le réseau anglais de câbles sous-marins* (Paris, 1909), 21; Charles Bright, *Submarine Telegraphs, Their History, Construction and Working* (London, 1898), 167.

2. Margerie, 36.

3. On cable manufacturing, see Bright, *Submarine Telegraphs* and "The Extension of Submarine Telegraphy in a Quarter-Century," *Engineering Magazine* (December 1898), 417–28; G. L. Lawford and L. R. Nicholson, *The Telcon Story, 1850, 1950* (London, 1950), 72–80; Frank J. Brown, *The Cable and Wireless Communications of the World: A Survey of Present-Day Means of Communication by Cable and Wireless, Containing Chapters on Cable and Wireless Finance* (London, 1927), 25–30; and Alfred Gay, *Les câbles sous-marins*, Vol. 1: *Fabrication* (Paris, 1902).

4. "Navires câbliers" in Ministry of Posts and Telecommunications (Paris), archives, 2997; Gay, Vol. 2: *Travaux en mer* (Paris, 1903), 167–70; Gerald R. M. Garratt, *One Hundred Years of Submarine Cables* (London, 1950), 36–38; Kenneth R. Haigh, *Cableships and Submarine Cables* (London and Washington, 1968), 17–25; James Dugan, *The Great Iron Ship* (New York, 1953).

5. On the sea earth, see Donard de Cogan, "Development of the Distributed Sea Earth in Transatlantic Telegraphy," Institute of Electrical Engineers, *Proceedings* 134 (July 1987), 619–32. Other inventions are described in Vary T. Coates and Bernard Finn, *A Retrospective Technology Assessment: Submarine Telegraphy. The Transatlantic Cable of 1866* (San Francisco, 1979), 159; and Garratt, 35–38.

6. John D. Scott, *Siemens Brothers 1858–1958: An Essay in the History of Industry* (London, 1958), 124; Brown, 51–55; Garratt, 31–36 and 53; Coates and Finn, 157–59.

7. Halford H. Hoskins, *British Routes to India* (London, 1928), 395–96; Thomas Lenschau, *Das Weltkabelnetz*, 2nd ed. (Frankfurt, 1908), 60–62; Garratt, 29–36; Coates and Finn, 74.

8. Alvin F. Harlow, *Old Wires and New Waves: The History of the Telegraph, Telephone and Wireless* (New York and London, 1936), 425–28.

9. A good business history of the North Atlantic cables after 1866 is still to be written. But see Bright, "Extension," 420–25; Coates and Finn, Chapter 5; de Cogan, "Sea Earth," 630–32; Garratt, 30; and Haigh, 316–21.

10. There are two official biographies of the Eastern group (now called Cable and Wireless): K. C. Baglehole, *A Century of Service: A Brief History of Cable and Wireless Ltd. 1868–1968* (London, 1969); and Hugh Barty-King, *Girdle Round the Earth: The Story of Cable and Wireless and its Predecessors to Mark the Group's Jubilee, 1929–1979* (London, 1979). But see also Robert J. Cain, "Telegraph Cables in the British Empire 1850–1950" (unpublished Ph.D. dissertation, Duke University, 1971); and Margerie, 44–47.

11. For example, George Peel, "The Nerves of Empire," *The Empire and the Century: A Series of Essays on Imperial Problems and Possibilities* (London, 1905).

12. Margerie, 42–58.

13. Barty-King, 25.

14. Jorma Ahvenainen, *The Far Eastern Telegraphs: The History of Telegraphic Communications between the Far East, Europe and America before the First World War* (Helsinki, 1981), 18.

15. Barty-King, 53–54.

16. Letter from Treasury to John Pender, 27 July 1882, in "Eastern Telegraph Company Limited 1868–1919, Agreements British Government," no. 1018 in archives of the Cable and Wireless Ltd. (London).

17. Barty-King, 80.

18. "Telegraph Communications with India," 1–10, in British Post Office Archives (London) [henceforth POST] 83/56; "Indo-European Telegraph Department," i-iii, in India Office Records L/PWD/7; Henry A. Mallock, *Report on the Indo-European Telegraph Department, being a History of the Department from 1863 to 1888 and a Description of the Country through which the Line Passes*, 2nd ed. (Calcutta, 1890), 3–11; Peel, 256–57.

19. Ann Moyal, "The History of Telecommunication in Australia: Aspects of the Technological Experience, 1854–1930," in *Scientific Colonialism: A Cross-Cultural Comparison*, ed. Nathan Reingold and Marc Rothenberg (Washington and London, 1987), 35–54.

20. K. S. Inglis, "The Imperial Connection: Telegraphic Communication between England and Australia, 1872–1902" in *Australia and Britain: Studies in a Changing Relationship*, eds. A. F. Madden and W. H. Morris-Jones (London, 1980), 30.

21. Inglis, 21–30; Moyal, 36–43; Barty-King, 38–42.

22. James A. Scrymser, *Personal Reminiscences of James A. Scrymser, in Times of Peace and War* (Easton, Penn., 1915), 67–70; Leslie B. Tribolet, *The International Aspects of Electrical Communications in the Pacific Area* (Baltimore, 1929), 42; Barty-King, 23 and 29.

23. Baglehole, 6; Barty-King, 30–31; Cain, 113–14.

24. Ludwell Denny, *America Conquers Britain: A Record of Economic War* (London and New York, 1930), 369–70; Bright, "Extension," 420–21; Tribolet, 42–43.

25. Scrymser, 67–78; Bright, "Extension," 422–23; Tribolet, 45–46; Denny, 370; Margerie, 23–24; Keith Clark, *International Communications: The American Attitude* (New York, 1931), 151; Harlow, 300–301.

26. "Projet de loi portant approbation d'une convention relative à l'établissement de câbles télégraphiques sous-marins destinés à desservir les colonies françaises des Antilles et de la Guyane française," *Journal officiel de la République française* 18, no. 118 (13 July 1886), 1444–46.

27. *The Electrician* (July 23, 1886), 1.

28. *The Financial News* (July 20, 1886).

29. "1re délibération sur le projet de loi portant approbation d'une convention relative à l'établissement de câbles télégraphiques sous-marins," *Journal officiel de la République française* (February 13, 1887), 420–38.

30. Charles Cazalet, "Les câbles sous-marins nationaux," *Revue économique de Bordeaux* 12, no. 71 (March 1900), 41–51; *Journal officiel* (July 19, 1887).

31. Memorandum, Ministre du Commerce, de l'Industrie et des Colonies to Sous-secrétaire d'Etat aux Colonies, January 12, 1892, in Archives Nationales Section Outre-Mer [hereafter ANSOM], Affaires Politiques 2554/5; Harry Alis, "Les câbles sous-marins," in *Nos africains* (Paris, 1894), 547; Léon Jacob, "Les intérêts français et les relations télégraphiques internationales," *Bureau des questions diplomatiques et coloniales* 230 (1912), 10–11; Cazalet, 47; Margerie, 180–81.

32. Charles Lesage, *La rivalité anglo-germanique. Les câbles sous-marins allemands* (Paris, 1915), 94–97; Haussmann, 261–69; Bright, "Extension," 427; J. Depelley, *Les câbles sous-marins et la défense de nos colonies. Conférence faite sous le patronage de l'Union Coloniale Française* (Paris, 1896), 30–31.

33. Kenneth R. Haigh, *Cableships and Submarine Cables* (London and Washington, 1968), 321.

34. Robert L. Thompson, *Wiring a Continent: A History of the Telegraph Industry in the United States 1832–1866* (Princeton, N.J., 1947), 371–80; Ahvenainen, 25–30; Cain, 90–91; Clark, 112–15.

35. Store Nordiske Telegraf-Selskab, *The Great Northern Telegraph Company: An Outline of the Company's History, 1869–1969* (Copenhagen, 1969), 9–11; Ahvenainen, 21–25 and 35–36.

36. Ahvenainen, 36–37.

37. Store Nordiske, 11–14; Ahvenainen, 39–46.

38. Japan, Teishinsho (Department of Communications), *Outline of the History of Telegraphs in Japan* (Tokyo, 1892); *Résumé historique et statistique de la télégraphie et de la téléphonie au Japon* (Tokyo, 1899); Japan, Teishinsho (Department of Communications), *A Short History of the Post and Telegraph Services in Japan* (Tokyo, 1902); Yuzo Takahashi, "Institutional Formation of Electrical Engineering in Japan" in *Histoire de l'électricité, 1880–1980: Un siècle d'électricité dans le monde. Actes du Premier colloque international d'histoire de l'électricité, organisé par l'Association pour l'histoire de l'électricité en France (Paris, 15–17 avril 1986),* ed. Fabienne Cardot (Paris, 1988); Yuzo Takahashi, "The Beginnings of Telegraph System in Japan" (Paper read at the colloquium on "Télécommunications,

espaces et innovations aux XIXe et XXe siècles," Paris, January 5–7, 1989). I am grateful to Professor Takahashi of the Tokyo University of Agriculture and Technology for these papers. See also Ahvenainen, 65–67, 186, and 210.

39. David Kahn, *The Codebreakers: The Story of Secret Writing* (New York, 1967), 189–90.

40. Robert Slater, *Telegraphic Code, to Ensure Secresy in the Transmission of Telegrams,* 7th edition (London, 1923), iii.

41. Kahn, 836–46.

42. Hugh Barty-King, *Girdle Round the Earth: The Story of Cable and Wireless and its Predecessors to Mark the Group's Jubilee, 1929–1979* (London, 1979), 147.

43. George Peel, "The Nerves of Empire," in *The Empire and the Century: A Series of Essays on Imperial Problems and Possibilities* (London, 1905), 281.

44. Maxime de Margerie, *Le réseau anglais de câbles sous-marins* (Paris, 1909), 77–79.

45. On codes and the ITU, see "Plain language, code and cypher in international telegrams: historical summary and conference decisions from 1858 to 1896," in Post Office Archives (London), POST 83/30; George A. Codding, Jr., *The International Telecommunication Union: An Experiment in International Cooperation* (Leiden, 1952), 65–75; and Kahn, 842–43.

46. For a discussion of the contrast between the cultural diffusion of technology and its geographic relocation, see Daniel R. Headrick, *The Tentacles of Progress: Technology Transfer in the Age of Imperialism, 1850–1940* (New York, 1988).

4

Telegraphy and Imperialism in the Late Nineteenth Century

In the late nineteenth century the world witnessed a sudden surge of European expansion and conquest known as the *new imperialism*. This surge made a dramatic impression on the public at the time, as it has on historians ever since, both because Europeans took most of Africa and much of the Pacific, and because the traditional imperialist powers—Britain, France, Russia, the Netherlands—were joined by eager newcomers: Germany, Belgium, Italy, the United States, and Japan.

If we think in terms of population and trade instead of territory, however, we get a different impression. The majority of the world's colonial subjects in 1900 were Indians, and their country had been under British rule in 1850 as well. India was the economic center of the colonial world, and its trade was a major factor in Britain's prosperity and maritime supremacy and the primary motivation for extending British rule over South and East Africa, Egypt, Aden, Burma, and Malaya.

Yet if the "new imperialism" was not as new as some historians have claimed, it was different from all previous imperialisms in one important respect: In the late nineteenth century, Europeans came to Africa and Asia equipped with new techniques and devices that could overcome both the obstacles of nature and the resistance of the indigenous peoples. Among them were two new communications media: the mail carried by steamships and railroads, and the telegraph.[1]

Empires had always needed secure and rapid means of communicating with their provinces and their agents abroad, and they went to great lengths to obtain them. The advent of the telegraph seemed to herald an era in which central governments could communicate with their remotest outposts and control their most distant agents as easily as they could those near home.

Imperialism was neither a clearcut phenomenon nor a momentary event. Since it was so ubiquitous in the nineteenth century, it is hard to find a case of the use of telegraphy outside of the North Atlantic nations that was not, to one degree or another, part of the imperialist movement. In this chapter we will see how the telegraph was introduced by Europeans into non-Western societies by various forms of duress.

While the telegraph had a remarkable impact everywhere, its introduction and consequences differed markedly from one part of the non-Western world to another. India, Algeria, and the West Indies were densely populated and under effective European control when the telegraph arrived. China, Persia, and the Ottoman Empire had indigenous governments that came under heavy European pressure to open up to trade and concede valuable privileges. The interiors of Australia, North America, Arabia, and Africa were thinly populated and had only local governments or none at all. Geographical differences influenced the choice between landlines and submarine cables. In each situation, the establishment of the telegraph faced very different challenges, depending on the societies it encountered, the natural environment, and the degree of European control. Let us consider a few cases where the telegraph interacted with the new imperialism in especially interesting ways: India, Indochina, China, the French West Indies, and Africa.

The Telegraph in India

India was one of the birthplaces of the electric telegraph, thanks to William O'Shaughnessy's experiments in the Hooghly River in the late 1830s. In the 1840s, when telegraphy was all the rage in Britain, Europe, and America, various people drew the attention of the Court of Directors of the East India Company in London to the advantages of electric telegraphy in India. In September 1849 the Court directed Governor General Dalhousie to look into the matter. Remembering O'Shaughnessy's experiments, Dalhousie asked him and Lieutenant Colonel Forbes of the Royal Engineers to investigate. In 1850–51 O'Shaughnessy and Forbes built the first telegraph line in India between Calcutta and Diamond Harbour at the mouth of the Hooghly River. The line consisted of iron rods hung on granite poles or buried underground in rows of roofing tiles. Despite storms, animals, and vandals, it worked and gave advance notice of the arrival of ships from England, a matter of consummate interest to the Europeans of Calcutta.[2]

Lord Dalhousie, by temperament an impatient man, once complained:

Everything, all the world over, moves faster now-a-days than it used to do, except the transaction of Indian business. What with the number of functionaries, bards, references, correspondences, and several Governments in India, what with the distance, the reference for further information made from England, the fresh correspondences arising from that reference, and the consultation of the several authorities in England, the progress of any great public measure, even when all are equally disposed to promote it, is often discouragingly slow.[3]

In his eagerness to force the pace of progress in the lethargic East, Dalhousie seized upon the telegraph. He appointed O'Shaughnessy Superintendent of Electric Telegraphs in India and sent him to London in April 1852 to persuade the Court of Directors to authorize a 5,000-kilometer network linking Calcutta, Agra, Bombay,

Peshawar, and Madras. Much to O'Shaughnessy's amazement, the East India Company approved his request immediately: "Such rapidity in the dispatch of an important measure is, perhaps, without parallel in any department of Government."[4]

Armed with this authorization, O'Shaughnessy purchased 9,000 kilometers of iron rod and 1,100 of copper wire and hired sixty "artificers" to train as telegraphers. He also inspected the telegraph systems of Britain and the Continent.[5] What he brought back to India was not the British Cooke-Wheatstone system, then the epitome of high technology, but the simpler Morse system, which was better suited to Indian conditions because its crude instruments could be repaired by Indian craftsmen and soldiers.[6]

Construction began in November 1853. To avoid the destruction of wooden poles by termites, the lines were carried on masonry posts or 5-meter-high slabs of granite.[7] Iron rods were used for fear that copper wires would be stolen or broken by monkeys. The line from Calcutta to Agra was completed by March 1854, and the whole network was opened to the public in February 1855. Dalhousie even had a line built to the hill station of Ootacamund, where he spent the hot season of 1855. In 1856, India had some 7,200 kilometers of lines and 46 telegraph offices.[8]

By the time of the Telegraph Act of December 27, 1854, Dalhousie had made the telegraph a government monopoly in India, in contrast to Britain where telegraphs were private. He viewed telegraphy not as a business enterprise but as an instrument of British power. As he wrote his friend George Couper in December 1854: "The post takes ten days between [Calcutta and Bombay]. Thus in less than one day the Government made communications which, before the telegraph was, would have occupied a whole *month*—what a political reinforcement this is!"[9] Elsewhere, he praised the telegraph for contributing to "the early realisation of a vast magnitude of increased political influence in the East."[10]

Little did Dalhousie realize at the time how soon and how sorely that political influence would be tried, and how valuable the telegraph would prove to be. In 1857, after he had left India, sepoys or soldiers of the Indian army mutinied and killed their officers. Soon much of northern India was engulfed in rebellion in the greatest challenge to the British Empire since 1776. While the rebels were numerous and well armed, their communications were poor. The British used the telegraph to good effect. Military telegraphers under Colonel Patrick Stewart accompanied General Colin Campbell, commander-in-chief of the British forces,

> to put the end of the telegraph wire in Sir Colin's hand wherever he went. No sooner were headquarters established at any spot, than the post and the wire were established also. It was the first time that the telegraph had been made to keep pace with the advance of an army in the field.[11]

John Lawrence, commissioner of the Punjab, is said to have exclaimed: "The telegraph saved India."[12] He meant for Britain.

After the end of the Indian Rebellion, the telegraph spread rapidly under a double impulsion: the military and political needs of the British rulers, and the personal and business needs of the Indian people. From 1856 to the end of the century the internal network of India grew at an annual rate of 5.9 percent (see Table 4.1). In length, the Indian network could be compared with that of most European

Table 4.1. The Indian Telegraphs, 1856–1900[a]

Year	Length of lines (km)	Number of offices
1856	6,800	46
1868	22,200	
1891–92	61,800	3,246
1900	84,700	4,949

[a]George W. Macgeorge, *Ways and Works in India: Being an Account of the Public Works in that Country form the Earliest Times up to the Present Day* (Westminster, 1894), 502; Krishnalal J. Shridharani, *Story of the Indian Telegraphs: A Century of Progress* (New Delhi, 1956), 21 and 58.

countries. By 1883, when the Telegraph Department was merged with the Post Office Department, it reached every major town; runners forwarded the telegrams to village post offices.[13]

The quality of the service was poor. At first it was slow and erratic, as lines broke and poorly trained telegraphers struggled with unfamiliar equipment. Later there were complaints about the lack of security; according to historian Halford Hoskins, "it was an open scandal that commercial intelligence was peddled in Indian markets by Government telegraph clerks."[14]

Because India had poorly paid telegraph clerks, it had the cheapest service in the world. In 1855 a sixteen-word telegram cost one rupee per 640 kilometers, roughly half the European rate. In 1868 the one-rupee rate was applied to any ten-word message between any two points in India.[15] Telegrams became popular among Indians and, along with the railways, helped create a subcontinent-wide market. At the time, the unification of the subcontinent benefited the British rulers and merchants. Only much later did Indian unity turn against the British.

The Telegraph in Indochina

Indochina was conquered piecemeal, beginning in the 1850s. As the French moved north from Cochinchina to Annam and Tonkin, they built telegraph lines. In 1866 the Ministry of Colonies considered a project for a cable between Indochina and Europe, but rejected it as too expensive.[16] Five years later, when Pender's China Submarine Telegraph Company proposed to lay a cable from Singapore to Hong Kong, a delegation from Indochina called upon the company's representatives in Singapore to request that the cable stop in Indochina on the way. The company agreed, and in July 1871 Indochina was connected to the cable at Cap St. Jacques, with a span to Saigon.[17]

In the 1880s, as the French moved north into Tonkin, they felt the need for a cable, for the country was not fully pacified and land lines were vulnerable to rebels. In November 1883 the Ministry of the Navy and Colonies signed a contract with the Eastern Extension, Australasia and China Telegraph Company (successor to the China Submarine) to lay a cable from Cap St. Jacques to Hué, Haiphong, and Hong Kong, for an annual subsidy of 265,000 francs (£10,600); it opened in

Table 4.2. Telegraphs in Indochina, 1864–1921[a]

Year	Length of lines (km)	Number of offices
1864	400	15
1871	1,200	22
1902	11,951	224
1921	31,155	425

[a]A. Berbain, *Note sur le service postal, télégraphique et téléphonique de l'Indochine* (Hanoi–Haiphong, 1923), 6; Camille Guy, *Les colonies françaises*, Vol. 3: *La mise en valeur de notre domaine colonial* (Paris, 1900), 567–68; France, Conseil Supérieur de l'Indochine *Note sur la situation et le fonctionnement du Service des Postes et Telégraphes en 1902* (n.p., n.d.), 8–9; Lucien Cazaux, "Le service des Postes et Télégraphes en Cochinchine depuis 1871 à 1880," *Bulletin de la Société des études indochinoises de Saïgon* (1926), 185–207.

February 1884.[18] Six years later Hanoi was connected to China by a land line.[19]

After the first telegraphers arrived in Indochina in 1861, the telegraph network spread quickly, even more rapidly than that of India (see Table 4.2). Like the Indian network, the Indochinese telegraphs were built for the Europeans, as Inspector Berbain explained: "The postal and telegraph services had to be created from scratch; their development followed the occupation of this immense territory, not to help a possible economic growth, but for purely strategic or political purposes."[20]

Cables and News in the French West Indies

The French may not have had Britain's commercial interests, but they were eager to spread their cultural influence around the world, especially to the Latin nations. And they knew that culture flowed over the cables. Jacques Haussmann, a cable lobbyist at the end of the century, explained the motives of France: "It is not only her commerce and industry that are involved; it is also her influence, the diffusion of her ideas, her good name in the entire universe." He quoted a French agent in Central America, who lamented:

> General news bulletins arrive every day from the United States and are immediately published by the local newspapers. They contain only news of the great republic of the North and of England. Only exceptionally do they carry some information concerning France. . . . By a natural process, you become interested in those about whom you hear every day, you live their lives, and quite naturally you enter into ongoing relationships. As for those whom you never hear of, they are quite soon forgotten.[21]

In the 1870s and 1880s Frenchmen in the Caribbean were most sensitive to the cultural power of cables. In 1871, Martinique and Guadeloupe, like other Caribbean islands, had contracted with the West India and Panama Telegraph Company to provide cable service. Article 8 of the contract with Martinique, similar to those signed with the other islands, reads:

> In consideration of an annual subsidy of 50,000 francs, the French telegraph office will receive, for publication and at no additional expense, a dispatch giving the general,

political and commercial news of Europe and the United States, as well as the current prices in the markets, especially the four great commercial ports of France and, if appropriate, the important events which might take place in the West Indies, at the discretion of the company, which will be the sole judge of the contents of said publication.[22]

The French islands needed this information, especially wholesale prices, in order to compete in the cut-throat sugar business. Yet complaints arose almost immediately. The General Council of Martinique first asked the company to send the bulletin in French instead of English, then objected to the choice of news:

The National Assembly [of France] met in November; it adjourned on January 11; the colony did not hear of this until many days later and without knowing why. They tell us that such-and-such a prince of England is ill, that Princess So-and-so is getting married, that a horse won a race, but interesting news? None, or not much. We would have some serious suggestion to make on this subject to the agent of the company.[23]

When the contract came up for renewal in 1881, the governor of Martinique complained that "dispatches containing news of France only give short and indirect items and also include information that is inexact and sometimes hostile to our country."[24] In reply, the president of the West India Company, C. D. Earle, requested an increase in the subsidy.[25]

In early November 1882, when news arrived of disturbances in Lyon and fears of a royalist conspiracy, the conflict grew sharper. The governor of Martinique protested against

alarming lies written in New York and transmitted by cable to the West Indies and Central America. They caused emotions and worries to the population of Martinique. This dispatch . . . troubled the friends of the Republic and gave joy to the adversaries of our institutions, as well as to foreigners. . . . I realized then the deplorable effects produced by misleading dispatches; what would it have been if they had told the truth?[26]

Earle answered:

It is one of the regrettable characteristics of the Company's service that it has been burdened with the obligation to furnish a general news bulletin. You will agree that the role of a submarine telegraph company is not to provide such information, but only to transmit it.[27]

In spite of these disagreements, the General Council of Martinique decided it could not forego the bulletin while neighboring islands get exact news of sugar prices.[28]

Both parties would have been satisfied with a news bulletin written by the French government and cabled to the French islands; in fact, the governor of Martinique suggested just that. But who would write the official news bulletin? The Ministry of the Navy and Colonies refused, as did the ministries of Posts and Telegraphs and of Foreign Affairs. Finally the Ministry of the Interior and of Religions got the job.[29] The Compagnie Française du Télégraphe de Paris à New York at first balked at sending the bulletin free of charge, but eventually agreed to transmit up to one hundred words a week to New York.

The bulletins began in May 1883. The French consul in New York wrote the minister of foreign affairs in Paris that he could not afford to send them by Western Union to Key West (where the West India cables began), and was keeping them in a box.[30] He eventually sent them on by boat mail, and they reached the governor of Martinique two months later.

Earle agreed to incorporate the official French bulletin in the general news dispatch, but pleaded:

> I would further earnestly request M. le Directeur [des Colonies] to move their Excellencies the Governors of La Guadeloupe and La Martinique to exercise the power of censorship held by them over the News Bulletin. . . . All the inconveniences that have arisen would have been avoided had the authorities in the French Colonies supervised the telegrams previous to their publication, and it would obviate all possibility of offence, which the Company is most desirous not to give, if measures were taken for exercising the power of the Government in this direction.[31]

Thus the islands got an official news bulletin from France censored by the colonial governors.

Meanwhile colonial interests in France were beginning to lobby for French-owned cables. Unfortunately, in competition with well-entrenched British firms, their projects required heavy subsidies, which the government would not grant. Once again the French were caught between their ambition to spread French culture and their reluctance to pay for it.

The Telegraph in China

Almost everywhere, telegraphy was greeted with enthusiasm or at least acquiescence. From Britain to Persia and from Canada to Chile, governments, businesses, and the public immediately recognized its utility. Only the odd ethnic group not under full government control—nomadic Arabs of Mesopotamia or Indians of the American West—attacked the new device.

China was the exception to this generalization. The Chinese reaction to the telegraph, especially in comparison to the Japanese, reveals cultural and social implications of telegraphy elsewhere hidden behind its technological glamor. Unlike Westerners, who saw the telegraph as a device that enabled humans to conquer nature, the Chinese saw it as a tool of the Western barbarians, a wedge to penetrate China.

Throughout the 1860s, even before the cables reached the East, the Chinese were under pressure to accept the telegraph. Westerners, feeling expansionistic after the British and French victory over China in 1860, wanted to open it up to trade and investments in railways, coal mines, and other boons of European civilization. In 1862, as the Russians were erecting a line eastward into Siberia, their ambassador in China, de Balluseck, tried to obtain a concession to prolong the line to Peking. Although he failed, he did get the Chinese government to agree that "whenever foreigners are allowed to construct telegraphs, the Russians will be the ones to start."[32] In 1864–65 the representatives of Britain, France, and the United States asked permission to install land lines or cables linking Hong Kong, Shanghai, Amoy, Foochow, and the other treaty ports opened after the Anglo-Chinese War of 1857–58. In 1865, as the Russian telegraphs were nearing the Chinese border, the Russian government again asked to prolong its wire to Peking.[33]

The Tsungli Yamen, China's foreign ministry, rejected all these requests, as did local officials. Faced with what they considered obstructions to progress, the Westerners sometimes took matters into their own hands, causing conflicts with local officials. In 1864–65 the British customs commissioner of Fukien Province, Milliken, had a land line erected from Foochow to Lo-hsing-t'a. After some incidents, Governor General Hsü Ch'ung-kan ordered the work to stop and bought the equipment from Milliken. Similarly, when a British merchant put up poles and strung wires between Shanghai and the harbor of Woosung, local officials pulled them down, whereupon the British consul demanded an indemnity on the grounds that the treaty of 1860 did not prohibit the erection of telegraph lines![34]

There has been some debate about the causes of the Chinese resistance, based on contradictory Chinese explanations and Western misunderstandings. At the time, Westerners thought the Chinese opposed the telegraph out of "superstition," that is, traditional Confucian values and respect for the spirits of the dead. Recent scholars, however, have argued that the Chinese compared the costs and benefits of the telegraph and found the balance negative. Tseng Kuo-fan, the man who introduced modern shipbuilding to China, declared: "[I]f [we] allow telegraphs and railways to be introduced, the livelihood of cartmen, muleteers, innkeepers and porters will be taken away."[35] In 1866 the governor of Guangdong and Guangxi wrote to the Tsungli Yamen: "The request to construct a telegraph line from Canton to Shanghai is meant to establish a precedent. Once started, [foreigners] will have excuse to demand lines from Canton to adjacent provinces, and from the adjacent provinces to the capital city, without limits."[36] In 1868, the representatives of eleven foreign countries petitioned for a sixty-kilometer-long telegraph line from Shanghai to Chuan Sa to speed up rescue efforts in case of shipwrecks, promising "in the future, we will absolutely not take this as a precedent to infer others." To this, the Tsungli Yamen responded:

> All countries have cast their greedy eyes on the construction of telegraphs in China. . . . [The request] sounds quite proper. Yet, the evil intentions they harbor are not voiced. It should be clear that this is to pander to all foreign ambassadors' desire to take an opportunity to get in, and one successful case will lead to demands for more. What they say about not taking this as a precedent to infer others is apparently a bait. How can we count on it?[37]

To Chinese officials, the telegraphs were less a means of communicating than a wedge to pry China open to foreign influences, a threat to their sovereignty, and a source of potential conflicts with the Europeans. In the 1860s they resented the fact that telegraph offices were manned by European clerks who only accepted messages in a European language that could be transmitted in Morse. This meant that foreigners would learn all official communications before their recipients did.[38] In addition, there were the concerns of special groups, as Jorma Ahvenainen explains:

> Representatives of the foreign companies gained the impression that in many cases the provincial authorities opposed the telegraph because it made their activities more effectively subject to control from Peking than before. . . . The landed gentry feared that rapid means of communication would give the Central government a firmer hold.[39]

All these resentments were mixed with a general dislike of the pushy Western barbarians and their devices. Only merchants "saw the economic and commercial advantages of a speedy means of communication."[40] Not until the 1880s did Chinese officials begin to look upon the telegraph and other Western technologies as means of "self-strengthening" and resistance to foreign encroachment.[41]

The arrival of the cables simultaneously from the south and the north intensified the pressure on China. John Pender had founded the China Submarine Telegraph Company in 1869 for the purpose of operating cables from Singapore to China and Japan. Since Hong Kong was a British colony, he had no difficulty obtaining a landing license there. Prolonging the cable to Shanghai, however, required a Chinese landing license; so Pender sent John George Dunn, a merchant with experience in China, to negotiate with the Chinese government. In Peking, Dunn obtained the backing of British Ambassador Thomas Wade, but the Tsungli Yamen refused him the license he sought. Finally, in May 1870 Dunn and the Chinese reached a compromise. The cable was not to touch land, but would end at a hulk moored outside the Woosung anchorage, where messages were to be carried to Shanghai in rowboats.[42]

Meanwhile the Great Northern had also requested a landing license, but was refused on the grounds that it would only stir up the Russians to demand the right to build a land line to Peking. The Chinese government, fearful of the encroaching foreigners, hoped to keep them at bay by playing one off against the other.

The divide-and-rule tactic failed, for the companies were not really competing. Given the strong and inelastic demand for communication, they had more to gain from squeezing their customers than from fighting over them. Toward the Chinese they presented a united front. In May 1870, before the first cable entered Chinese waters, the two cable companies signed an agreement. While the Great Northern would lay the Hong Kong–Shanghai cable, both would maintain offices in the two cities and would share the receipts equally. The China Submarine Company promised not to extend its lines north of Shanghai, and the Great Northern would not operate south of Hong Kong.[43]

To counter the obstinate but weak Chinese officialdom, Westerners developed an effective tactic: the *fait accompli*. At the end of 1870, the Great Northern's cable ship landed its cable on Gutzlaff Island, a barren rock near Shanghai. Then one night it laid another one from Gutzlaff to the foreign settlement at Shanghai, but did not notify the Chinese of this blatant violation of their sovereignty. In early 1871, the ship laid yet another cable from Shanghai to Hong Kong, which opened for business on April 18. The China Submarine Company's cable ship arrived soon after, and in June 1871 Shanghai and Hong Kong were connected to Europe by the southern route as well.[44]

This connection with the world cable network exacerbated the tensions between Chinese and Westerners. The conflict came to a head in Fukien Province, the most important tea-exporting region of China. It began in 1873 when the Great Northern, without Chinese permission, spliced a piece of cable between its Hong Kong–Shanghai cable and the town of Amoy. That same year, when the company erected a land line from Shanghai to a new cable landing at Woosung, the government ordered it torn down but, in the face of protests by the Western consuls at Shanghai, did not enforce its order. While the Chinese saved face, the Europeans were only encouraged to push harder.[45]

The following year the Western merchants and consuls in Foochow, a major tea emporium, requested permission to put up a land line to Pagoda Anchorage, sixteen kilometers away. Twelve days after they received permission from the local officials, the line was up. The Europeans then sought to extend their line to Amoy, to link up with the cable. To them, this was an obvious and logical connection, but to some Chinese, it was exactly the foot-in-the-door tactic they had long warned against. When local officials let the Great Northern put up a line between Foochow and Amoy in early 1874, Russian Ambassador Butzow reminded the Tsungli Yamen of their promise of 1862 and demanded the right to put up a land line between the Russian border and Tientsin.[46]

Meanwhile the Japanese, in their first foray into empire building, invaded Taiwan in April 1874. The Chinese high commissioner for Taiwan, Shen Pao-chen, suddenly needed better communication and proposed a government-controlled cable between the island and Amoy. At the same time he wrote to Li Ho-nien, governor of Fukien Province, to protest the Great Northern's land line from Amoy to Foochow. Caught in the middle, the imperial government demanded that the new line be removed. When that order was ignored, "popular uprisings" began to attack the line. This brought protests from the European ambassadors. Finally, in May 1875 the Chinese government agreed to purchase the line from the Great Northern Company and hereafter place all telegraphs under its protection.[47]

Thus in April 1876 the Chinese government found itself in possession of a telegraph line. It thereupon took steps that surprised the Europeans. First it dismantled the line to appease the popular opposition. Then it hired two foreign consultants and rebuilt the line in Taiwan where Shen Pao-chen needed it. As there were only five Chinese who could operate a telegraph, it contracted with the Great Northern Company to open a telegraph school. To bridge the cultural gap, the Chinese telegraphs adopted a code published in Shanghai in 1875, which translated Chinese characters into numbers, that could be transmitted more cheaply than words in a European language. The Chinese government became reconciled to a telegraph network operating under its own auspices and serving its own needs.[48]

It had taken eleven years, from 1864 to 1875, for China to accept the telegraph as a neutral device. It took six more before the government viewed it as beneficial. In 1876 Li Hung-chang, viceroy of Chihli Province and commissioner of the northern ports, contracted with Danish engineers to put up a land line from Tientsin to the Taku Forts that defended the approaches to Peking. Two years later he sent the businessman Sheng Hsuan-huai to arrange with the Great Northern Company for the construction of more lines. With the acquiescence of the Chinese court, Sheng and Li founded a company, the Imperial Telegraph Administration, to operate telegraphs throughout China. They began in 1881 with a line along the Grand Canal from Tientsin to Shanghai, followed by lines to Nanking in 1882 and to Canton, Peking, and Port Arthur in 1884. Thus, after years of resisting, procrastinating, and playing off one Western country against another, the Chinese officials accepted a nationally owned telegraph network as a useful tool of government.[49]

The nature of the Telegraph Administration was purposely left ambiguous under the motto "government control and merchants' profit." But, as historian Albert Feuerwerker pointed out, it showed "a sharp contrast between the profitable returns realized by its managers and shareholders on the one hand and the relative lack of success in providing China with a modern communications network on the other."[50]

The Administration was also important internationally, for it gave China, for the first time, a knowledgeable representative when dealing with the Westerners. No longer could foreign merchants and diplomats impose their will on China while claiming that they were only providing it with the benefits of modern technology. They now had to negotiate with Sheng Hsuan-huai.

In 1881 Sheng formed an alliance with the Great Northern, promising to hand over to it all telegrams for foreign destinations and not allow other countries (i.e., Russia) to put up land lines that would compete with the company's cables. In exchange, the company lent its engineers to the Administration, opened a school, and offered to transmit Chinese government telegrams free of charge.[51]

This agreement aroused the protests of John Pender and of the British, German, French, and Russian ambassadors. For two years the Eastern Extension and the Great Northern companies argued and negotiated. In 1883 the Eastern Extension was brought into the cartel with a new Hong Kong–Shanghai cable and a joint purse to share all receipts from telegrams between China and Europe. Finally, in 1887 the Administration, the Great Northern, and the Eastern Extension agreed to avoid all further competition. The Imperial Telegraph Administration had all the benefits of a monopoly within China without the responsibilities of a government agency, while the two cable companies cooperated so smoothly they became known as "the amalgamated companies."[52]

Once again the telegraph companies found it in their best interest to patch up their differences and present a united front to their customers. The customers, mainly Western businessmen in the treaty ports, were the victims of this collusion. Whereas telegraph rates all over the world had fallen since the 1870s, between China and Europe a telegram now cost 8.50 francs per word, more than in 1871 (100 francs for twenty words), and not much less than in 1875 (10 francs per word).[53] The cartel was strong enough to ignore their protests.

Lines of communication are more sensitive to politics than to geography, as the Sino-Russian land line demonstrates. The Russian line had reached Irkutsk in 1863 and could have been extended to Peking a year later, if the Chinese had allowed it. They refused again in 1875 when the Russian line reached the border town of Kiachta. Periodically thereafter, the Russian government demanded that the Chinese allow a land line, but this pressure was evidently a bargaining chip for other more important demands; after all, the Russians could telegraph to China via the Great Northern cable, which they wanted to preserve for other reasons. The cable companies were naturally worried that a direct land line could offer far lower rates between China and Europe, and ruin them. Faced with a potentially dangerous new competitor, they did what came naturally: they invited the new rival to join their conspiracy against the customers. In 1892, after years of negotiations, Russia and China agreed to link their networks. Connections were made at Helampo in Manchuria in 1893 and at Kiachta in 1900. Traffic between Russia and China was much improved, but through telegrams to Europe had to pay the same exorbitant rate as on the cables.

The Boxer Rebellion of 1900 gave the Westerners a chance to force their wedge

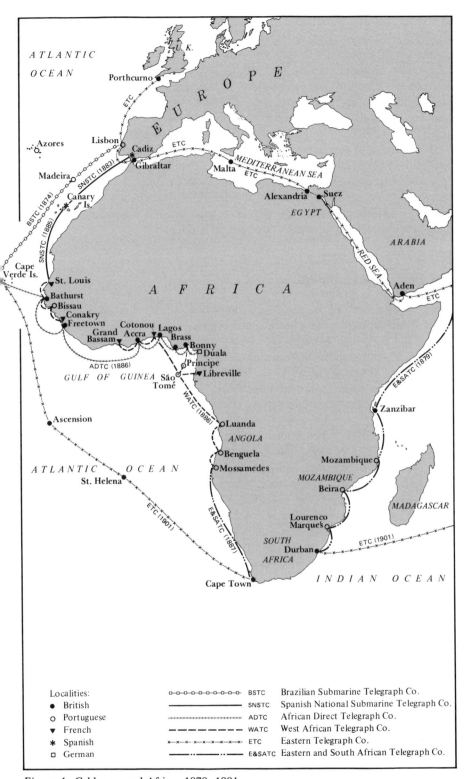

Figure 4. Cables around Africa, 1879–1901.

deeper into China. Without Chinese permission, the British and Germans laid cables from Shanghai to Taku near Peking and from Chefoo to the foreign naval bases of Kiaochow, Weihaiwei, and Port Arthur, and seized the Peking–Taku land line "until peace and the normal state of affairs in the North of China shall have been reestablished." The cable companies seized the opportunity to extend their monopoly on China's foreign communications for another thirty years.[54]

For thirty years the Chinese had resisted the telegraph, seeing in it only a means of European penetration. The long delay, far from protecting China from foreign encroachment, only made it more vulnerable to harassment. In the end, it had to accept the new technology, but in the form of an inefficient and costly private monopoly operating in collusion with unscrupulous foreign companies. As in all things Far Eastern, the contrast with Japan is striking.

The East African Cables

The great trunk lines of the world cable network—on the one hand from Europe to North America, on the other to India and beyond—were laid in response to commercial demand, with governments playing a supportive rather than an indispensable role. Magnifying their commercial viability was the fortunate circumstance that the domestic telegraph networks of North America, India, and Australia were already in place before the arrival of the cables; thus, all telegrams to and from those regions could be funnelled through one telegraph office at New York, Bombay, or Port Darwin.

Not so in Africa. When cables reached maturity after 1866, Africa—with the exception of Egypt, Algeria, and South Africa—was still telegraphically virgin. Furthermore, there was little business or private demand to justify the costs of telegraphy. And finally Africa was just beginning to be nibbled at, piecemeal, by various European powers from beachheads strung out along its coasts. Cables were therefore more political than commercial, and had to serve simultaneously as trunk lines and as linear networks connecting the coastal towns. In West Africa, competition for colonies led to the laying of two parallel cables that leapfrogged one another. All of this made communications far costlier and less efficient than in the more developed and homogeneous parts of the world.

East Africa was connected before the west coast, not because it had more trade, but because it lay closer to the British imperial trunk line. The pressure for this connection came from white South Africans. In 1867 the parliament of the Cape Colony proposed a "concerted action" with the British Colonial Office to lay a cable from England to Australia via South Africa, but the Treasury rejected the idea.[55] In 1871–73, Hooper's Telegraph Company offered to lay a cable down the east coast from Aden to Mauritius and Natal, but failed to raise sufficient private capital or obtain subsidies from the British or French governments. Nor could Colonial Secretary Lord Carnarvon persuade the Treasury to pay for a government-owned cable.[56]

Poor business prospects and Britain's refusal to pay did nothing to dampen the South Africans' eagerness for a telegraphic link to Europe. In July 1877 Thomas

Watson, president of the Cape Town Chamber of Commerce, wrote to Sir Bartle Frere, governor of the Cape, advocating a land line across Africa:

> The construction of a line of telegraph through the centre of this great country would not only put us in immediate communication with the mother country, but at the same time open up a vast field for commercial enterprise. The maintenance of a series of stations along the route would do more to abolish the slave trade than . . . a fleet of cruisers on the African coast. Mission stations would be protected, savage tribes civilized, and in a few years a complete revolution would be effected.[57]

This view was echoed by the general manager of telegraphs for the Cape Colony, J. Sivewright, in a paper on "Overland Telegraphs" read to the South African Philosophical Society, which was relayed by Frere to Colonial Secretary Sir Michael Hicks Beach.[58] The parliament of the Cape Colony passed the Anglo-African Telegraph Act of 1878, which offered a subsidy of £15,000 a year for fifteen years, to which Natal added another £5,000, for any telegraph line between England the Cape.[59] Advocates of the land line proposed to build it from Pretoria—then the northernmost point on the South African telegraphs—to Khartoum, which was connected to Egypt by a land line and by a Nile cable.[60] They estimated the cost at one-half to one-third that of a cable and claimed it would be no more difficult to build than the lines across America, Siberia, Australia, or the Ottoman Empire.[61]

Various explorers gave their views on the scheme. Verney Lovett Cameron was enthusiastic, and Henry Morton Stanley supported the plan, while Charles "Chinese" Gordon and John Kirk, British consul at Zanzibar, suggested bypassing the more dangerous stretches with short coastal cables. There were also skeptics. Sir Samuel Baker said: "I do not think any police supervision would protect a wire of gold from London to Inverness, and I think it would be equally impossible to protect a wire of iron through the tribes I have named."[62] Others mentioned the diseases of the interior and the African custom of using copper wire as ornaments. In fact, no one knew, since the regions where the line was supposed to be built had not yet been well explored, let alone colonized. The issue was not so much technical as political, as Hicks Beach told Frere in November 1878 when he pointed out that the line, to be secure, would have to be erected in British territory.

Meanwhile John Pender was actively lobbying against the land line and sent his son James to negotiate for concessions for a cable from Aden to Durban via Zanzibar and Mozambique; however, he wanted a subsidy of £35,000 a year.

The interested parties could have gone on discussing the Cape-to-Cairo telegraph project for quite a while longer, but for a sudden and shocking turn of events. During 1878 Sir Bartle Frere prepared to go to war against King Cetywayo of the Zulu. Hicks Beach told Prime Minister Disraeli: "I cannot really control him without a telegraph. . . . I don't know that I could do with one."[63] Then on January 22, 1879, the Zulu defeated the British at Isandhlwana. This convinced Hicks Beach, who now recognized the "excessive and urgent importance upon political and military, as well as commercial grounds," to accept Pender's offer.[64]

Thus a precedent was set; or rather, the precedent of the 1858 Red Sea cable was revived. As a matter of principle, the British government refused to subsidize cables except in times of crisis. However, given the global reach of the British Empire, crises tended to arise more frequently and politicians felt less secure with each passing year. Eventually the exceptions became more common than the rule.

The West African Cables

On the west coast of Africa, telegraphic connections were first delayed, then hastened, by political events. In 1873–74, during the war between Great Britain and the Kingdom of Ashanti, communications with the British forces depended on steamship service between the head of the cables in the Canary or Madeira Islands and Cape Coast Castle; it often took two months to get a reply. Yet the Colonial Office refused to consider cable projects because they all included a subsidy, and besides, the outcome of the war was a foregone conclusion.[65]

In 1881 a war scare on the Gold Coast revived the issue. The War Office and the Colonial Office agreed that a cable would let them reduce troop strength in West Africa for a savings of £2,500 a year, and might even prevent another expensive campaign like the Ashanti War, which had cost £900,000. But the required subsidies—£10,000 a year to the Cape Verde Islands and another £15,000 to the Gold Coast—were still too high to ask of the tight-fisted Treasury.[66]

If the Ashanti could not loosen the Treasury's purse-strings, other European nations could. In the 1860s the French had installed some short land lines in Senegal, from which telegrams were forwarded by boat to Europe.[67] In 1883 the Spanish National Submarine Telegraph Company, a subsidiary of the India Rubber Company, linked Cadiz with the Canary Islands. Two years later the French government contracted to have that cable extended to Saint-Louis in Senegal, at a subsidy of 1.7 million francs (£68,000) a year.[68]

All of this was part of a plan by Matthew Gray, director of the India Rubber Company and rival of John Pender, to lay cables to South America via Senegal. The competition for business, however, coincided with another more political rivalry, for in the year 1884 the "scramble for Africa" had begun in earnest. French military units began moving from Senegal into the hinterlands of Sierra Leone and the Gold Coast and along the upper Niger. Germany was in the process of annexing Togoland. Agents of the European powers were so far beyond the reach of their governments—it took over a month to send a dispatch from Europe to the West African coast, and weeks more to penetrate inland—that they acted on their own initiative. This made the British Colonial Office, hitherto used to a lethargic pace of events in that uncontested backwater, suddenly quite nervous. Misunderstandings between the agents of European powers could easily turn into embarrassing diplomatic incidents. When the Colonial Office pointed this out to the Treasury in April 1884, it had the support of the War Office, the Admiralty, and the Foreign Office as well. The Treasury, once again softened up by arguments of national security, agreed to subsidize a cable from the Cape Verde Islands to Accra. It got bids from Pender's Brazilian Submarine Telegraph Company and from the India Rubber Company. The Treasury opted against India Rubber because it was "rather too closely allied to a Spanish-owned cable company to suit the Colonial Office's sense of the requirements of national security," and the Colonial Office "would not hear of official messages passing through French or Spanish territory." Thus the Eastern group, now tightly associated with British imperial interests, was brought into West African waters.[69]

1885 was the decisive year for the West African telegraphs. While the British government pondered its next move, it was caught off guard by a private entrepreneur. Count Tadeusz d'Oksza-Orzechowski, a Polish physician, diplomat, and speculator, obtained from the Portuguese government a concession to lay a cable from Senegal to Portuguese Guinea, Sao Tomé, Angola, and Cape Town.[70] Oksza had no intention of laying cables himself, of course, but only of selling his concession to someone else. That someone was the India Rubber Company, which had just obtained a concession from the French government for a cable linking Senegal, the Ivory Coast, Dahomey, and Gabon. For this purpose, it founded the West African Telegraph Company, which combined the two concessions into a project linking all the French and Portuguese colonies along the coast.[71]

Stung into action, Pender founded the African Direct Telegraph Company. In January 1886 he obtained a concession from the British government to lay a cable linking the British possessions on the West African coast, with a subsidy of £19,000 per year. From the India Rubber Company he purchased a cable between the Gambia and the Cape Verde Islands, where it joined the Brazilian Company's line to Europe.[72]

Throughout 1886 cable ships were busy laying cables up and down the coast. By the end of the year the African Direct Company had a cable linking the Cape Verdes with the Gambia, Sierra Leone, the Gold Coast, and Nigeria—in other words, the British possessions. The West African Company, meanwhile, connected the French and Portuguese possessions, but also stopped off at the Gambia and the Gold Coast to allow communication with the British towns.

Small networks tend to link up into larger ones, for doubling the number of subscribers in a system quadruples the possible interconnections and the potential traffic. But this technical tendency was reinforced by the notorious business urge to conglomerate. In West Africa, it only took three years. Already in November 1889 the Eastern and the India Rubber companies had worked out traffic agreements, or, in other words, a cartel for West Africa.[73] When the Eastern and South African Telegraph Company laid a cable from Cape Town to Loanda linking up with the West African cable, the African continent was surrounded. To complete the merger, Matthew Gray was replaced by John Denison-Pender (John Pender's son-in-law) on the board of the West African Company.[74] Though the West African Company still served the French and Portuguese possessions, it had in fact become part of the Eastern group, that pillar of the British Empire.

In the colonial era, Europeans learned that it was far more difficult to erect land lines in Africa than in other parts of the world. In 1892, Cecil Rhodes formed the African Transcontinental Telegraph Company to construct a land line from Rhodesia to Egypt, another variant of his Cape-to-Cairo dream. His aim was partly to compete with the cables, but, more important, he hoped it would open the interior to European colonization. However, the line had barely reached Ujiji on Lake Tanganyika when commercial failure put an end to the scheme.[75]

Similarly, the French made several attempts between 1897 and 1912 to build a telegraph line from Gabon to Lake Chad in the interior of equatorial Africa. Part of the way they used a Belgian line along the Congo River, and in other places, to save the expense of transporting poles and wires into the savannas of Ubangi-Shari, they erected an optical line. This line was also never completed and worked poorly until it was supplanted by the wireless.[76]

These and other lines in the interior of Africa suffered from two problems. One was the horrendous difficulty of transporting heavy materiel across deserts and swamps and through regions where beasts of burden died of sleeping sickness. The other was the low density and poverty of the population, which meant that the telegraph companies could not expect to get enough local business to defray their expenses. In Africa, unlike India or Latin America, the telegraph remained a device used by Europeans to communicate with Europe—in other words, a part of the colonial but not of the indigenous economy.

Cables and Colonial Control

Earlier we saw how rapidly the world cable network was extended to the major French and British colonies, often at the behest of the cable companies, without waiting for official subsidies or encouragement. To lay cables to the minor colonies, especially those that were not located on a trunk line, the companies had to be bribed with subsidies. Colonial administrators were always eager to improve their communications, but small colonies could not afford to subsidize a cable, and needed the help of the home government. Colonial officials, both at home and in the colonies, argued that cab'~s would save money by allowing a smaller number of troops and warships to be deployed more efficiently, thus preventing small incidents from swelling into major confrontations. To overcome the Treasury's skepticism, the most persuasive argument was a military crisis or, better yet, a war.

This is what General Wolseley, commander of the British forces in the Ashanti War of 1873–74 in the Gold Coast, tried to do. He won over the Colonial Office and the War Office, but the Treasury, secure in the knowledge that the British were sure to win with or without a cable, was not moved. When the British suffered a defeat in the Zulu War of 1879, however, the Treasury relented, and agreed to subsidize a cable to South Africa. When West Africa got a cable seven years later, it was not because of the resistance of Africans to British encroachment but because of the far more dangerous activities (in British eyes) of French and German agents along the coast.

As in foreign affairs, the use of the telegraph spread slowly to the colonial ministries. In 1866–67 the British Colonial Office budgeted only £100 for telegrams. The telegraph began to have an impact on colonial administration between 1874 and 1878, during Lord Carnarvon's second term as colonial secretary. The Colonial Office, like the Foreign Office, hired clerks to pick up telegrams at night and decode them for consideration by the staff in the morning. Crises in South Africa, the Straits Settlements (Malaya), and Barbados forced the Colonial Office to spend £2,951 on telegrams in 1875–76. By 1881–82 the cost had soared to £9,660. In subsequent years, the number of telegrams between the Colonial Office and the governors of the various colonies increased steadily, except in wartime, when it shot upward: 1,997 in 1892, 4,747 in 1899, 9,058 in 1902 (the height of the Boer War), and back to 6,067 in 1903. Though official telegrams cost half the normal rate (e.g., 4s 6d instead of 8s 11d to Cape Town in 1890), they were still expensive because they were usually longer than business messages. No wonder the Treasury was not thrilled at the thought of instantaneous global communication.[77]

The flood of information that came in over the cables far outstripped the Office's ability to handle it effectively. In West Africa, writes Robert Kubicek,

> local imperial agents (governors &c) sent more telegrams to the Colonial Office than they received. Between 1887 and 1896 the Gold Coast on an annual average sent 75 to the CO while the latter sent only 43 to the former. The figures for Lagos–CO telegrams were 48 and 35 . . . most telegrams had to do with staffing, replacing the sick and dying administrator more quickly.[78]

The last decades of the century, the age of the new imperialism and the scramble for Africa, saw small crises popping up all over the world. Lord Kimberley, colonial secretary in the early 1870s, wanted "all telegrams of any importance" sent to him immediately.[79] The result, in one historian's words, was that "the calming effect upon the most excited despatch of lying unread for a month in the darkness of a mailbag was lost."[80] Harried clerks and assistant undersecretaries were rushed to draft quick responses without taking the time to look up previous correspondence or even read the dispatches in sequence. The Colonial Office was overwhelmed by the information explosion. As its historian, John Cell, explains: "The great dividing point was the telegraph. By this medium information was transmitted piecemeal; abstractions from reality arrived and departed quickly, irregularly, and unpredictably. . . . Not regularity but jerkiness came to characterize the process of imperial decision making."[81]

Despite the administrative problems it caused, telegraphy promised to increase the control of great empires by their central government, something rulers of empires had always yearned for. Yet historians who have considered this question have argued that it did not. The Colonial Office continued to give its governors the benefit of the doubt in the crisis situations that regularly broke out on the periphery of the Empire. And the men on the spot eagerly took the initiative, knowing London had no other reliable source of information about events on the imperial frontiers and would in any case back them up after the fact. Thus in 1873 Sir Andrew Clarke, governor of the Straits Settlements, imposed a British resident upon the Malayan state of Perak without bothering to consult London, in spite of the newly laid telegraph cable. Colonial Secretary Kimberley later wrote him: "I am not in a position to form an opinion on the details of your arrangements, but as far as I was able to judge from your telegraphic despatches which I received before I left office, I anticipated that I should have approved the course you had taken."[82] Similarly, in 1883 Queensland annexed New Guinea first, and informed London afterward.[83]

In South Africa, in the weeks that preceded the Boer War, Colonial Secretary Chamberlain's attempts to control events were in vain because British High Commissioner Sir Alfred Milner was eager for war; as Robert Kubicek noted: "Clearly, the telegraph did not extend the office's opportunities for learning of or controlling

events in South Africa. In fact, its operation reinforced the office's passive characteristics and the activist propensities of the man on the spot."[84] While the telegraph
did not allow the Colonial Office to prevent or control the war, it was nonetheless
used successfully to persuade the Australian colonies to furnish troops, because
Chamberlain's telegrams to the colonial governors and jingoist press dispatches
provoked a patriotic fervor among Australians. The governor of Victoria, Lord
Brassey, called the telegraph "a great Imperial binding force." Not until the *Manchester Guardian* arrived, five to seven weeks later, could Australians read an
opposing view on the South African war.[85]

Even the French government, despite its centralizing traditions, did not feel
sufficiently in control of its colonies; thus we find the director general of posts and
telegraphs pleading with the minister of colonies in 1894: "It is absolutely indispensable that, on questions of general interest, the directors of colonial telegraph
administrations make no decision unless it has been determined that it is not contrary to the decision of the metropole."[86]

The impact of the telegraph on colonial power relations is ambiguous, however.
As the expansion of telegraphy coincided with the new imperialism, uncertainty on
the frontiers of empire, ambitious imperial agents, a lack of information, and an
overwhelmed central administration combined to enhance the power of the men on
the spot at the expense of their home governments. But this was a temporary
phenomenon associated with the phase of warfare and expansion. As soon as areas
were pacified, bureaucratic controls replaced the free-wheeling agents of the frontier period. And inevitably the controls operated through the telegraph wires and
cables. After the turn of the century, one no longer hears much about independent
proconsuls. Instead, colonial officials began to worry about the rivalries between
the colonial powers and, increasingly, the stirrings of nationalism in the colonies.

Conclusion

Imperialism introduced a new set of relationships into the already complex world of
great-power relations. By imposing European rule on non-Western peoples, it created, in theory, two new political relationships: that of European colonists over their
native subjects, and that of the home country over its agents in the colonies. These
relationships did not arise without struggles: not only the often violent resistance of
Africans and Asians to European rule, but also the power struggles between Europeans in the colonies and their metropoles. South Africa is the most dramatic but
hardly the only example.

To complicate matters further, the nations of the West were often rivals both at
home and overseas. On the ill-defined frontiers between expanding colonial empires, the agents and colonists of one nation encountered those of another, and their
relations did not always coincide with the official relations between the governments they technically represented. In some cases the men on the spot dragged their
governments into embarrassing and potentially hostile confrontations. As the imperialist powers took over the last remaining "unclaimed" parts of the earth at the turn
of the century, their colonial rivalries exacerbated existing tensions and contributed

to the prewar atmosphere. Rapid communications only made these tensions more instantaneous and more difficult to defuse.

Notes

1. On the connections between technology and European imperialism, see Daniel R. Headrick, *The Tools of Empire: Technology and European Imperialism in the Nineteenth Century* (New York, 1981); and *The Tentacles of Progress; Technology Transfer in the Age of Imperialism* (New York, 1988).

2. Manindra Nath Das, *Studies in the Economic and Social Development of Modern India: 1848–56* (Calcutta, 1959), 115–18; Krishnalal J. Shridharani, *Story of the Indian Telegraphs: A Century of Progress* (New Delhi, 1956), 4–8 and 25–26; Mel Gorman, "Sir William O'Shaughnessy, Lord Dalhousie and the Establishment of the Telegraph System in India," *Technology and Culture* 12 (1971), 584–85; Sir William Brooke O'Shaughnessy, *The Electric Telegraph in British India: A Manual of Instructions for the Subordinate Officers, Artificers, and Signallers Employed in the Department* (London, 1853), iv.

3. Minute of April 14, 1852, quoted in O'Shaughnessy, *The Electric Telegraph*, xi–xii.

4. O'Shaughnessy, *The Electric Telegraph*, v.

5. Ibid., v–vi.

6. Deepak Kumar, "Patterns of Colonial Science in India," *Indian Journal of History of Science* 15, no. 1 (May 1980), 109; Gorman, 591–93.

7. Dalhousie letter of February 1856, cited in Das, 156.

8. Das, 137–50; Shridharani, 21.

9. Quoted in Gorman, 597.

10. Quoted in Shridharani, 21.

11. "Stewart, Patrick (1832–1865)," in *Dictionary of National Biography*, Supplement, 22: 1230–31.

12. Gorman, 598–99.

13. Shridharani, 55–56.

14. Hoskins, 386–87.

15. India, Telegraph Department, *Summary of the Principal Measures Carried out in the Government Telegraph Department during the Administration of Sir John Lawrence, Bart., G.C.B., G.M.S.I., and D.C.L., Viceroy and Governor General of India, 1864–68* (Calcutta, 1869); Das, 148; Shridharani, 27.

16. "Câble du Tonkin" in Archives Nationales Section Outre-Mer (Paris) [henceforth ANSOM], Colonies Séries Modernes 313 Indochine W30 (1).

17. Letter of agreement of July 9, 1871 between the French Ministry of the Navy and Colonies and the China Submarine Telegraph Company Ltd. in ANSOM, Colonies Séries Modernes 313 Indochine W31 (1); Lucien Cazaux, "Le service des Postes et Télégraphes en Cochinchine depuis 1871 à 1880," *Bulletin de la Société des études indochinoises de Saigon* (1926), 206.

18. Agreement of 29 November 1883 between the French Ministry of Navy and Colonies and the Eastern Extension, Australasia and China Telegraph Company, in the archives of the Cable and Wireless Company [henceforth Cable and Wireless] D/370; "Câble du Tonkin" in ANSOM Colonies Séries Modernes 313 Indochine W31 (1) and (4).

19. Jorma Ahvenainen, *The Far Eastern Telegraphs: The History of Telegraphic Communications between the Far East, Europe and America before the First World War* (Helsinki, 1981), 64.

20. A. Berbain, *Note sur le service postal, télégraphique et téléphonique de l'Indochine* (Hanoi–Haiphong, 1923), 2.

21. Jacques Haussmann, "La question des câbles," *Revue de Paris* 7, no. 6 (March 15, 1900), 274–76.

22. Contract between Martinique and the West India and Panama Telegraph Company Ltd., June 23, 1871, in Cable and Wireless B2/675: "Martinique and Guadeloupe, 1868–1871."

23. *Gazette officielle de la Guadeloupe* (December 1874), in Cable and Wireless B2/675.

24. Letter from the Minister of the Navy and Colonies to C. D. Earle, President of the West India and Panama Telegraph Company, October 21, 1881, in "Communications périodiques télégraphiques avec les Antilles, 1882–84," ANSOM, Affaires politiques 2554/3.

25. Memorandum from C. D. Earle to the Minister of the Navy and Colonies, November 2, 1881, in Cable and Wireless B2/675. Because cables broke frequently on the coral-encrusted bed of the Caribbean Sea, while a depression in the sugar islands kept demand low, the West India and Panama Telegraph Company was the least profitable of the British cable companies, paying dividends of less than 1 percent until 1899, and none thereafter; see Maxime de Margerie, *Le réseau anglais de câbles sous-marins* (Paris, 1909), 60–61.

26. Letter from the Governor of Martinique to the Minister of the Navy and Colonies, November 9, 1882, in Cable and Wireless, B2/675.

27. Letter from Earle to the Director of Colonies, February 26, 1883, ibid.

28. Minutes of the meeting of the General Council of Martinique, December 17, 1882, ibid.

29. Letter from the Ministry of the Interior to the Ministry of the Navy and Colonies, April 28, 1883, in ANSOM, Affaires politiques 2554/3.

30. Letter from the Consul General of France in New York to Minister of Foreign Affairs Challemel Lacour, May 18, 1883, ibid.

31. Letter from Earle to the Director of Colonies, July 25, 1884, ibid.

32. Zhong Zhang, "The Transfer of Networks Technology to China, 1860–1898" (Ph.D. dissertation, University of Pennsylvania, 1989), Chap. 1: "The Destruction of the Woosung Railroad and the Foochow Telegraph." I am grateful to Mr. Zhong Zhang for permission to cite his paper.

33. Saundra P. Sturdevant, "A Question of Sovereignty: Railways and Telegraphs in China 1861–1878" (Ph.D. dissertation, University of Chicago, 1975), 18–21 and 150–51; Ahvenainen, 31–32; Zhong Zhang, Chap. 1.

34. Sturdevant, 20 and 25–26.

35. Zhong Zhang, Chap. 1.

36. Ibid., 4.

37. Ibid., 10.

38. Zhong Zhang, private communication, January 1990.

39. Ahvenainen, 59.

40. Ibid., 60.

41. Sturdevant, 22–24, 152–154, 102–203, and 215–18; Zhong Zhang, Chap. 1.

42. Zhong Zhang, Chaps. 1 and 3: "Harnessing the Telegraph Network: The Chinese Management of its Introduction."

43. "Agreement between the China Submarine Telegraph Company Ltd and the Great Northern Telegraph of China and Japan Extension Company of Copenhagen" (May 13, 1870) in Cable & Wireless, D/248.

44. Albert Feuerwerker, *China's Early Industrialization: Sheng Hsuan-huai (1844–1916) and Mandarin Enterprise* (Cambridge, Mass., 1958), 192; Hugh Barty-King, *Girdle*

Round the Earth: The Story of Cable and Wireless and its Predecessors to Mark the Group's Jubilee, 1929–1979 (London, 1979), 28 and 39; Robert J. Cain, "Telegraph Cables in the British Empire 1850–1900" (unpublished Ph.D. dissertation, Duke University, 1971), 138; Ahvenainen, 17–19 and 32–52; Sturdevant, 157–62.

45. Sturdevant, 163–68; Store Nordiske, 14; Ahvenainen, 48–54.

46. Ahvenainen, 48; Sturdevant, 178–86 and 208.

47. Ahvenainen, 55–57; Feuerwerker, 192; Sturdevant, 186–94; Zhong Zhang, Chap. 1.

48. S. A. Viguier, *Mémoire sur l'établissement de lignes télégraphiques en Chine* (Shanghai, 1875); Ahvenainen, 60; Sturdevant, 199–206; Zhong Zhang, Chap. 1 and private communication, January 1990.

49. Zhong Zhang, Chap. 3.

50. Feuerwerker, 206. On the Telegraph Administration, see Ahvenainen, 60–62, and Feuerwerker, 190–207.

51. Ahvenainen, 68–69; Store Nordiske, 17.

52. Ahvenainen, 70–99, 106–107, 113, and 209.

53. Ibid., 41–42, 51–52, and 113.

54. Ibid., 143–45; Leslie B. Tribolet, *The International Aspects of Electrical Communications in the Pacific Area* (Baltimore, 1929), 77–81.

55. Cain, 151.

56. Ibid., 152–58.

57. Colonial Office, "Correspondence Respecting the Projected Telegraphs to South Africa" (1879) in Public Record Office (Kew) [henceforth PRO], C.O. 879/15/194.

58. Lois Alward Raphael, *The Cape-to-Cairo Dream: A Study in British Imperialism* (New York, 1936), 49–62.

59. Leo Weinthal, "The Trans-African Telegraph Line," in *The Story of the Cape to Cairo Railway and River Route from 1887 to 1922,* ed. Leo Weinthal, 5 vols. (London, 1923–1926), 1:211–12.

60. Richard Hill, *Egypt in the Sudan 1820–1881* (London, 1959), 131.

61. Cain, 163; Weinthal, 1:212.

62. Weinthal, 1:214–15.

63. Cain, 165–66.

64. George Peel, "The Nerves of Empire," in *The Empire and the Century: A Series of Essays on Imperial Problems and Possibilities* (London, 1905), 264; Cain, 166–69.

65. Brian L. Blakely, *The Colonial Office, 1868–1898* (Durham, N.C., 1972), 65.

66. Cain, 150 and 171–74.

67. Decree organizing the telegraph service in Senegal, February 28, 1868; dispatch from the governor of Senegal to the minister of the navy and colonies, March 2, 1868, in ANSOM, Affaires Politiques, 2554/1.

68. Law of July 9, 1883, in West African Telegraph Co. Ltd. Guard Book, in Cable & Wireless 924/139; Charles Bright, "The Extension Of Submarine Telegraphy in a Quarter-Century," *Engineering Magazine* (December 1898), 423.

69. Cain, 176–81.

70. Boleslaw Orlowski, "The Person who Stood Firm against the Might of England," in Cable and Wireless archives. I am grateful to Mr. Orlowski for permission to cite this paper.

71. "Copy of the Report of the Budget committee to the French Chamber of Deputies on the Convention between the French government and Matthew Gray of the West African Telegraph Company Limited, 10 July 1885" in Cable and Wireless 924/139; "Agreement of 22 April 1886 between Eastern TCL, Brazilian Submarine TCL, African Direct TCL and India Rubber, Gutta Percha, and Telegraph Works CL and West African TCL" in Cable and Wireless 728/10.

72. African Direct Telegraph Co. Ltd., West African Cables, 1886, in Cable and Wireless, 1980; Eastern and South African TCL, "Correspondence relating to West Coast of Africa cables no. 4, 1886 & 1889," ibid., 2195.

73. "Africa Agreements," Cable and Wireless, 728.

74. "Correspondence relating to West coast of Africa cables no. 4 (ex. 334), 1886 and 1889," Cable and Wireless, 2195.

75. "Prospectus of the African Transcontinental Telegraph Company Limited," Cable and Wireless, 1741; Barty-King, 86–90; Weinthal, 1:215–17.

76. "Télégraphes 1888–98," ANSOM, Série géographique, Gabon-Congo, XII, dossier 22; "Câble de Loango à Libreville," ibid., dossiers 23a and 24b; and "Ligne télégraphique de Loango à Brazzaville" (1899), ibid., dossier 24b; Captain P. Lancrenon "Les travaux de la mission télégraphique du Tchad (1910–1913)," *L'Afrique française: Bulletin du Comité de l'Afrique française* (January 1914), 34–40, and (February 1914), 55–69; Martial Merlin, "L'oeuvre des récentes missions en Afrique équatoriale française," *Bulletin de la Société de géographie commerciale de Paris* 36 (1914), 249–67; Daniel R. Headrick, "Les télécommunications en Afrique Equatoriale Française, 1886–1913," *Recherches sur l'histoire des télécommunications* 2 (December 1988), 73–86.

77. Robert V. Kubicek, *The Administration of Imperialism: Joseph Chamberlain at the Colonial Office* (Durham, N.C., 1969), 30–32; Cain, 188–192; Blakeley, 65–66.

78. Robert Kubicek, private communication, December 1989. I am very grateful to Professor Kubicek for this information.

79. Blakeley, 66.

80. Cornelius W. de Kiewiet, *The Imperial Factor in South Africa: A Study in Politics and Economics* (Cambridge, 1937), 293.

81. John W. Cell, *British Colonial Administration in the Mid-19th Century: The Policy-Making Process* (New Haven, Conn., 1970), 43.

82. C. D. Cowan, *Nineteenth-Century Malaya: The Origins of British Control* (London, 1961), 266; Sir Andrew Clarke, *Life of Lieut.-General the Hon. Sir Andrew Clarke, G.C.M.G., C.B., C.I.E.,* ed. R. H. Vetch (New York, 1905), 155–56; Cain, 193–94.

83. Blakeley, 67.

84. Kubicek, 109; for a similar opinion, see P. M. Kennedy, "Imperial Cable Communications and Strategy, 1870–1914," *English Historical Review* 86 (1971), 751.

85. K. S. Inglis, "The Imperial Connection: Telegraphic Communication between England and Australia, 1872–1902," in *Australia and Britain: Studies in a Changing Relationship,* ed. A. F. Madden and W. H. Morris-Jones (London, 1980), 21–38.

86. Letter of March 24, 1894, in ANSOM, Affaires Politiques, 2554/4.

5

Crisis at the Turn of the Century, 1895–1901

In the early days of cables it seemed miraculous to send a message over thousands of kilometers in a matter of hours. Pulpits, podiums, and editorial pages resounded with paeans of praise for the "annihilation of time and space." By the 1880s, when cables had reached every continent, telegraphy was no longer celebrated as a miracle but had become a daily necessity of business and governments in an age of expanding global trade.

In Europe and America, the years from 1871 to 1898 were a time of peace. In the tropics, to be sure, Europeans quickly and almost effortlessly conquered whole empires. But the world was huge, there was so much land still to be taken, and diplomats were able to resolve the differences that arose between the great powers. In the last years of the century, the peoples of the Western world could admire the new technologies they had brought forth and see in them a great increase in their power over nature, ignoring, for the last time, the power these technologies gave some men over others.

This naive euphoria did not last. In the 1890s, when the advancing Western empires swallowed the last unconquered lands in the tropics, the collisions of their far-flung agents in the heart of Africa and in the expanses of the Pacific reverberated back to Europe and America, inflaming the press and agitating the chanceries. From a miracle for all mankind, the telegraph became a means of political power, a dangerous weapon in the hands of potential enemies.

Telegraphy and Diplomacy

The relationship between the diplomatic establishments and the telegraphs was two-sided, for diplomacy was also affected by the telegraphs, often in unexpected ways. The ministries of foreign affairs, with their ancient and sacred rituals, entered the age of speedy communications with reluctance. Until 1859 the British Foreign Office received and sent telegrams at the telegraph office during normal business hours. That year, it hired two clerks to accept telegrams after hours. The State Department in Washington was much slower to enter the modern age: Not until 1868 did it have a clerk send and pick up telegrams at the Western Union office thirteen blocks away.[1]

Gradually, the telegraph forced itself upon the attention of the diplomats. By the 1870s, the Foreign and Colonial Offices in London had direct telegraph lines, and some high officials, like Foreign Secretary Lord Granville and Colonial Secretary Lord Derby, had lines installed to their homes or their country estates.

As the world grew more complex, the foreign offices increased their use of the telegraph proportionately. Vary Coates and Bernard Finn have collected some statistics on the State Department's use of the telegraph. By 1910 it was handling a thousand messages a month, and by the 1930s, 200 a day. Just between the State Department and the U.S. embassy in London, the number of telegrams varied from an average of 200 a year between 1866 and 1910, to 552 a year from 1910 to 1914, 15,000 a year from 1914 to 1919, 500 to 900 a year in the 1920s, and 700 to 1300 a year in the early 1930s.[2]

In the nineteenth century, most telegrams were purely internal and bureaucratic: travel plans, personnel and ceremonial matters, requests for information, and the like. The telegraph was also much used for lesser foreign relations issues, such as consular matters, apprehending and extraditing criminals, and reacting to epidemics and other natural disasters.[3] While this was clearly beneficial to the public, it led some diplomats to deplore, in the words of British ambassador to Vienna Sir Horace Rumbold, "the telegraphic demoralization of those who formerly had to act for themselves and are now content to be at the end of the wire."[4]

The impact of the telegraph on important events was a matter of some debate. Edmond Hammond, permanent undersecretary of the Foreign Office from 1854 to 1873, complained that the telegraph tended to "make every person in a hurry, and I do not know that with our business it is very desirable that it should be so," for it tempted officials to "answer off-hand points which had much better be considered."[5] The French historian Charles Mazade, writing in 1875, believed that the Franco-Prussian War could have been avoided if diplomats had deliberated slowly instead of reacting to the telegraph.[6] Not only were telegrams hasty, they were also too succinct, leaving out important details, and they often arrived out of order. At the time of the *Alabama* dispute between Britain and the United States, Foreign Secretary Granville wrote to Prime Minister Gladstone: "This telegraphing work is despairing. It will be a mercy if we do not get into some confusion."[7]

Others were more sanguine. Sir John Pender, speaking before a banquet at the Imperial Institute of London on July 20, 1894, praised telegraphy for having "prevented diplomatic ruptures and consequent war, and been instrumental in promoting peace and happiness. . . . No time was allowed for the growth of bad feeling or the nursing of a grievance. The cable nipped the evil of misunderstanding leading to war in the bud."[8]

Whether they liked it or not, diplomats could not simply ignore the telegraph and carry on in their traditional custom of long delays, for the press also got its information by telegraph, the public demanded an immediate reaction, and that reaction was then relayed by the press to the foreign governments concerned. It was still better to have diplomacy by telegraph than by public opinion.

Charles Bright, a leading expert on submarine telegraphy, summed up its impact on international relations:

> If the peoples have been brought more in touch with each other, so also have their rulers and statesmen. An entirely new and muchly-improved method of conducting the diplomatic relations between one country and another has come into use with the telegraph wire and cable. The facility and rapidity with which one government is now enabled to know the "mind"—or, at any rate, the *professed* mind—of another, has often been the means of averting diplomatic ruptures and consequent wars during the last few decades. At first sight, the contrary result might have been anticipated;* but, on the whole, experience distinctly pronounces in favour of the pacific effects of telegraphy.
>
> *Indeed, it cannot be denied that there *are* occasions when rapidity in the interchange of diplomatic communications may have had—aye, and may still have—the effect of producing ruptures which "a little more time to think" would have avoided.[9]

Bright published these words in 1898, at the end of a long era of peace. What he sensed darkly, but could not openly believe, is that telegraphy could just as easily contribute to the tensions leading to war as to the rational pursuit of peace, if the men in power were so inclined.

British Cable Strategy to 1898

Great Britain's cable policy in the nineteenth century aimed at encouraging and protecting its growing cable network. The first requirement was to induce cable companies to land their cables on British soil, a goal facilitated by the location of the British Isles in the Atlantic.

Great Britain, like every country, reserved the right to grant licenses to land cables on its shores. Most countries used this right to demand concessions in return, such as lower rates for official telegrams, but Britain granted landing rights to all without restrictions. This liberal policy had encouraged cable companies to land their cables in Britain, even the French and American transatlantic cables that could technically have gone directly to the Continent. This in turn contributed to Britain's primacy as the information center of the world. As Maxime de Margerie explained:

> If, despite the prodigious development of Antwerp and Hamburg, London remains the great world marketplace, it is because news from overseas arrives there first. . . . In many places the London price is the only one known, being the only one transmitted by cables which have London as their origin.[10]

And Thomas Lenschau added:

> All important commercial and political news were known in England two to three hours before the Continent, a fact that one needs only say, in order to recognize what an incredible advantage it gives English firms over their competitors in international trade.[11]

Outside the Atlantic, Britain's main concern was the security of its communications with its empire. One issue that cropped up again and again was the protection of telegraph cables in wartime. In 1858, in his telegram of greetings to Queen Victoria over the first Atlantic cable, President Buchanan proclaimed:

> May the Atlantic telegraph, under the blessing of heaven, prove to be a bond of perpetual peace and friendship between the kindred nations, and an instrument destined by Divine Providence to diffuse religion, liberty, and law throughout the world.
>
> In this view will not all the nations of Christendom spontaneously unite in the declaration that it shall be for ever neutral, and that its communication shall be held sacred in passing to the place of their destination, even in the midst of hostilities?[12]

The idea of politically neutralizing cables was raised by France at the Paris conference of 1865, but nothing came of it. In 1871 Cyrus Field and Samuel Morse, echoing a common American sentiment, asked the Rome conference to neutralize cables; the plenary assembly decided that this suggestion was outside its competence, but agreed to communicate it to all interested governments.[13] A conference on the protection of submarine cables, held in Paris in 1884, succeeded in drawing up rules to protect cables against fishing trawlers and ships' anchors, but on the more troubling issue of cutting cables in wartime, Great Britain insisted on inserting an article that read: "It is understood that the stipulations of this convention shall in no wise affect the liberty of action of belligerents." Lord Lyons, British ambassador to France and delegate to the conference, explained: "Her Majesty's Government understands Article XV in this sense, that in time of war, a belligerent, a signatory of the convention, shall be free to act in regard to submarine cables, as if the convention did not exist."[14] As Great Britain had by far the most cables, the most cable ships, and the most powerful navy in the world, its wishes carried weight.

Though Article 15 plainly put cables outside the law in wartime, the legal issue continued to fascinate jurists, especially Germans and Frenchmen, who wrote many learned dissertations on the question.[15] There was a reason for the British position and a reason for the French and German concern, but they only became clear much later.

In the early years of cables, the British government worried about its communications with India, which were vulnerable not only to the hazards of an unreliable technology—as in the Red Sea cable fiasco of 1858—but also to the control exercised by the countries through which its lines ran: Prussia, Russia, and Persia for the Indo-European Telegraph Company; half of Europe and the Ottoman Empire for the Turkish line; and Portugal and Egypt for the first cable to India. Since there was no hope at the time for an all-British route to India, the next best solution was to have multiple routes. This was the recommendation of the Select Committee on communications with India appointed by the House of Commons in 1866.[16]

For that time on, multiple and all-British routes remained the two preferred means to ensure communications security. Because of the high cost of cables, it was fortunate that most strategic cables—that is to say, those serving the big British naval bases—followed the major trade routes, so that commerce made subsidies unnecessary. By the 1880s Cape Town, Singapore, Hong Kong, Halifax, Gibraltar, Malta, Alexandria, and Aden could cable to Britain. Exceptions like Mauritius and Bermuda made the strategists uncomfortable.[17]

In the nineteenth century, nothing stimulated British strategic thinking as much as a good Russian war scare. The scare of 1878 led to the appointment of a Royal

Commission on the Defence of British Possessions and Colonies, chaired by Lord Carnarvon. Its reports, issued in September 1881, emphasized anew the importance of cables to the trade and defense of the Empire.

Another scare, in 1885, led to some panicky decisions, such as the Admiralty's spending £85,000 for a cable from Shanghai to Korea, which later proved useless and was sold to John Pender for £15,000. But it also had more long-lasting results. At the behest of the Colonial Office, the cabinet set up a permanent Colonial Defence Committee that included representatives of the Admiralty and the Colonial, Foreign, India, and War offices.[18]

The Committee believed that British communications were basically safe because cables were hard to find at sea and their landing places were protected by shore guns.[19] Yet it was concerned with two areas: Bermuda, which was the only large British naval base without a telegraphic connection to Britain, and the West Indies, Jamaica in particular, which could only communicate with Britain via Cuba and the United States. As early as 1877 the Admiralty had recommended a cable from Halifax to Bermuda and on to the West Indies. The suggestion was renewed by the Carnarvon Commission in 1880, and by the Admiralty and the War and Colonial Offices in 1882, but each time it was vetoed on financial grounds, for it would have little commercial value to help defray its expense.[20] Upon the recommendation of the Colonial Defence Committee, however, the Cabinet finally signed a contract in 1889 for the Halifax–Bermuda section, with a subsidy of £8,100 per year.[21]

Two years later, the Colonial Defence Committee appointed a temporary subcommittee under the chairmanship of Juland Danvers to look specifically at the question of cables. Its seven members, representing the five ministries concerned with imperial defense, met six times in early 1891. On March 19, 1891, they issued a "Report of a Committee Appointed to Consider the Question of Telegraphic Communication with India in Time of War."[22] This report began with the following basic principles:

> 2. The telegraphic systems of the world are so closely interconnected that the Committee have found it impossible to deal with the question of telegraph communication with India, without taking into consideration the requirements of the Empire as a whole.
>
> 3. The ideal of telegraph communication for purposes of war would be fulfilled by cables landing on British territory only, following recognized trade routes, and not passing near the naval stations of a possible enemy.

Instead of considering each cable individually, the committee looked at communications between the vital points of the Empire in the event of a war with the two obvious potential enemies of the time, France and Russia. Unless Britain lost command of the sea—a remote possibility indeed—the committee did not think it likely that an enemy could cut British cables. Even if some cables were cut, it would not be for long, since the British Empire owned twenty-eight of the world's thirty-six cable ships. The committee also considered the possibility that Portugal might become an "unfriendly neutral," which would jeopardize the communications passing through the Eastern station at Lisbon. Some of the most important British cables landed in Portugal or its Atlantic islands (Madeira, Cape Verde, Azores), and the British government never lost confidence in its "oldest ally."[23] All in all, the report concluded that the ideal cable network would be unreasonably expensive, but that the network that Britain already owned was almost secure enough for any foreseeable war. It did, however, recommend two strategic cables to round out the existing network: a new cable to India and Australia, either around Africa or across the Pacific; and another from East Africa to the Seychelles and Mauritius. The former, a major project, was not implemented until the Boer War. The latter, however, was both feasible and urgent.

Mauritius was an important sugar island strategically located on the sea lanes between South Africa and India. Eager to communicate by telegraph with the rest of the world, the government of the colony had approached France about jointly subsidizing a cable linking Zanzibar with Mauritius via the French colonies of Madagascar and Reunion. This plan, while logical from a commercial point of view, horrified the British strategic planners. The director of military intelligence, H. Brackenbury, wrote a confidential memorandum that Secretary of State for War Edward Stanhope forwarded to the Cabinet:

> In the event of war with France, when our commerce will be obliged to go round the Cape instead of through the Canal, Mauritius becomes at once the naval outpost of India, and Seychelles the base from which operations would be undertaken by a naval and military expedition against the French coaling station of Diego Suarez, Madagascar.
>
> Unless immediate steps are taken to get this cable laid, an agreement will be come to between the French Government, the Colony of Mauritius and the Eastern Telegraph Company, for a cable from Zanzibar viâ Madagascar and Réunion, to Mauritius. Such a cable would be useless to us in time of war. . . .[24]

Soon thereafter, a War Office conference issued a melodramatic statement:

> Are we not only bound to defend the Colonies, but have we no power and no moral right to impose our veto to prevent a Colony, such as Mauritius, from making arrangements with a foreign Government which would be dangerous to us, and consequently to them also, in time of war? . . . If the contingency of war with France is to be considered at all, should it not be considered in the interests of the Colony as well as in the interests of England? Ought not a Dependency to bear in mind the same strategic considerations as the Empire to which it belongs?[25]

Their protests were heard, for two years later the Eastern and South African Telegraph Company laid a cable from Zanzibar directly to the Seychelles and Mauritius, toward which Mauritius contributed £7,000, the Seychelles £1,000, and Britain and India each £10,000.[26]

In 1896, when Great Britain and the United States got involved in a dispute over the border between British Guiana and Venezuela, the British government realized that all its communications with the West Indies passed through American land lines and the Key West–Havana cable. It therefore hastily prolonged the Halifax–Bermuda cable to Jamaica, at a cost of £8,000 per year.[27]

Telegraphic Delays and French Imperialism

In 1905 George Peel, a spokesman for British cable companies, wrote:

> From 1870 to the present time, Germany, Spain, Portugal, Morocco, Tunis, France, Italy, Austria, Greece, Tripoli, Crete, Cyprus, Turkey, and Russia have allowed British capital

and British enterprise to connect them with our system, in complete reliance upon the proved international uprightness and fair dealing of our citizens.[28]

Peel notwithstanding, there were complaints about the British cables even before the crisis of 1898, and a crescendo of recriminations afterward. The complaints fell into three categories: the content of the news they transmitted, the political advantage that Britain derived from its control over the world's cables, and its unfair commercial practices.

In the case of the French Antilles, the conflict had arisen between the colonial governments and the cable company; the French government was dragged in reluctantly, and Great Britain was not involved at all. In those parts of the world where the empires were still expanding, however, especially during military actions when important events happened fast, the timeliness of the news mattered a great deal. At those moments, the imperial governments were immediately involved, and even brief delays could be construed as national affronts.

From the mid-1880s on, France actively pushed on the frontiers of its empire in Africa and the Far East, leading to occasional disagreements with Great Britain, all of which were eventually resolved. Politicians and journalists were aware of the British cable monopoly and of an occasional delay in transmitting information, but their protests were rather muted. Only after 1898 did a chorus of delayed indignation arise concerning events that had taken place a decade or two before.

The first incident took place in March 1885, during an undeclared war between France and China, when Admiral Courbet was defeated at Langson on the Tonkin–Chinese border. News of the event traveled by the cables of the Eastern Extension and Eastern Companies; the British Foreign Office received the information and transmitted it to the British ambassador in Paris before the French government heard of it.[29]

Two years later, during the debates in the Chamber of Deputies on the French Antilles cable bill, Minister of Posts and Telegraphs Granet complained:

> After the Chamber voted to entrust the laying of the Tonkin cable to an English company, on more than one occasion dispatches have arrived late in the hands of the French government, because the English companies which transmitted them gave preference and priority to telegrams of news and speculation destined for London, so that the French government was informed after the fact of the most serious events.[30]

The next incident occurred during the Siam crisis of 1893. France had been pressing on Siam from the east, hoping to take Cambodia, if not the whole country. Great Britain was worried as always about the marches of its Indian Empire, and wanted to keep Siam independent as a buffer protecting Burma. In May 1893, after some border clashes, the French sent two gunboats to Bangkok, which the Siamese fired on. The French government thereupon authorized Admiral Humann to issue an ultimatum to the Siamese, demanding a large piece of territory and other privileges. The cable containing this authorization was held up by the Eastern Telegraph Company until the British Cabinet could read it.[31] In the end, the British tolerated the French action because they coveted some Siamese provinces in Malaya. In 1896 they came to an understanding with France that left Siam independent, but much smaller than it had been.

The following year another incident took place in a part of the world where both the French and the British were active. When the Sultan of Morocco died on June 11, 1894, the British consul in Tangier requisitioned the country's only cable for a day and a night in order to communicate with the Foreign Office. In its June 13 dispatch from Madrid, the French news agency Havas reported:

> Newspapers complain that the English cable, the only one working between Tangier and Europe after the break in the Spanish cable, was seized during the whole of last night by the English minister to communicate with the Foreign Office.
> The newspapers wonder what can be, under these conditions, the security of the interests of other nations if England, holding all sources of information, can thus suspend at will communications which are not its own.[32]

The following year saw another incident, this one in Madagascar, which France was coveting but where Britain had commercial and religious interests. On September 30, 1895, a French force attacked and captured the capital of Tananarive. News of the event, sent via Eastern, was held up in London for three days before the French were informed.[33]

In all these cases, the delays in transmitting the news to Paris did not affect the outcome of the French imperial expansion. They only revealed the hold that Great Britain had over other countries' information, and the fact that, while the British believed their behavior was characterized by "uprightness" and "fair dealing," other nations did not have the "complete reliance" that George Peel claimed they had.

Germany and the Azores Affair

All the cable incidents that occurred in the colonial empires in the nineteenth century involved France. Germany was far behind, both in its colonial expansion and in its cable enterprises. Until 1882, German communications with America went by cable under the North Sea, then crossed Britain on Post Office land lines to the Anglo-American transatlantic cable. In 1882, the Vereinigte Deutsche Telegraphengesellschaft (German Union Telegraph Company) had a cable laid to Valentia, Ireland, to connect directly with the Anglo cable. In spite of frequent breakdowns and poor service, the Germans did not begin to plan to lay their own cable across the Atlantic Ocean until the 1890s. Beyond the North Atlantic there was as yet no demand for German cables, and few complaints about the British. The only one of any significance concerned Kaiser Wilhelm's telegram of congratulations to President Kruger of the Transvaal in January 1896; according to one writer, it was leaked to the London papers, which printed it before it reached Pretoria. Other than that, when German authors wanted to back up their statements about British misdeeds in the nineteenth century, they had to choose examples from the French experience.[34]

Yet there was one case in which German ambitions ran up against British obstruction. Though at the time it was considered a commercial issue, in retrospect it took on a sinister political coloring; such was the evolution of Anglo-German relations between the 1890s and the early 1900s. This was the case of the German Atlantic cable project and its landing in England and in the Azores.

As German trade with North America increased in the 1880s and 1890s, so did the cable traffic. The main line of communication was the German cable to Valentia, where it connected to the Anglo-American Company's cable to America. By the early 1890s, this route was overcrowded and Germans complained that their telegrams were given a low priority by the Anglo. In 1891, therefore, the German government agreed in principle to the creation of a new line between Germany and North America. Since it was technically impossible to bridge that great a distance directly, it sought intermediate landing points where messages could be relayed. The best places seemed to be the Azores, one-third the way across the Atlantic, and Porthcurno at the western tip of Cornwall, where the Eastern cables landed.

This scheme immediately involved a lot of other parties. Portugal had long been eager for a cable to the Azores, and had given a concession for such a cable to the Telegraph Construction and Maintenance Company in February 1892. The French government managed to have the concession transferred to the Société Française des Télégraphes Sous-Marins, which hoped it would be the first step toward a cable from Europe to the West Indies, but the Chamber of Deputies refused to subsidize this cable, and the concession lapsed in April 1893. TC&M regained the concession and laid the cable for the Europe and Azores Telegraph Company, a new subsidiary of Eastern.[35]

Eastern looked favorably upon the German project. A German cable to Porthcurno would give the company direct access to Germany and Central Europe, bypassing the British Post Office. Furthermore, the landing in the Azores would provide a direct connection between North America and the Eastern domains of South America, Africa, and Asia, avoiding the older transatlantic companies. Thus Eastern agreed to share its Azores concession with the Germans.

On August 17, 1894, the German government signed a contract with the cable manufacturers Felten und Guilleaume of Cologne to lay and operate the new Atlantic cable. All that was needed was the landing license in Britain, which the German Post Office formally requested on August 20. The Anglo-American Company and its cartel-mates the Direct United States and the Western Union companies stirred up a press campaign against the project. On October 4, the General Post Office informed the Reichspostamt that its request had been denied on the basis of an 1888 agreement that all Anglo-German cables should be owned and operated by the two governments jointly.[36]

The refusal was, in the words of the French cable expert Charles Lesage, "a major event in the telegraphic world."[37] The reason officially given was transparently false, since the proposed cable would have carried no Anglo-German traffic. Nor was its purpose to protect the ailing Anglo-American Company and its cartel-mates. The real reasons are found in a memorandum dated October 26, 1894, from the General Post Office to Colonial Secretary Lord Kimberley: first, the establishment of a new telegraphic center in the Azores, and second, the loss to the British Post Office of valuable transit fees.[38] The British government evidently hoped, by its action, to prevent the emergence of a rival cable node between the Eastern and Western Hemispheres, one through which information would flow outside the control of Great Britain.[39] If it thought so, it was mistaken, for six years later Germany laid a cable to the Azores directly, one on which the British government could neither read nor delay the traffic. In 1901 Britain authorized the Commercial Cable Company to lay a cable from Nova Scotia to Ireland via the Azores, because it was obviously futile to prevent Atlantic cables from using the Azores as a stopping point. Yet Germans interpreted the refusal of 1894 not as a communications policy, but as an insult to Germany.[40]

The Spanish–American War

All of the incidents recounted above were of limited importance at the time they happened, noticed only by the telegraphic industry, the financial press, and an occasional political journalist. Only in retrospect did they seem like portents of far more dangerous confrontations. It was the events of the years 1898–1902 that changed the perceptions of the press and the politicians. It was then that the world learned that control over cables meant access to information, and that control over information was another form of political and military power. This revelation was the result of three events: the Spanish–American War, the Fashoda incident, and the Boer War. Let us look at them from a communications point of view.

For forty years, many jurists and politicians believed that telegraph cables ought to be declared neutral in time of war, but their opinion clashed with that of the British government. Yet the issue had never been tested, and it was a matter of some curiosity whether in an actual war, the belligerents would respect the cables. The question was divided into several parts: would belligerents cut cables on the open sea, or only in enemy waters? those linking an enemy to a neutral? those belonging to a neutral? those joining two neutrals but carrying information of value to the enemy? The Spanish–American War was to answer these questions.

Before 1898, many cables joined Cuba to the rest of the world. Two Western Union cables connected Havana with Key West and the United States; the West India and Panama Telegraph Company had cables from Santiago to Jamaica, from where another one ran to Bermuda, Halifax, and on to Great Britain; the Société Française des Télégraphes Sous-Marins had a cable from Guantanamo to Haiti and on to South America; and finally the Cuba Submarine Telegraph Company operated a cable along the southern coast of Cuba, from Batabano to Santiago.

When the war began, the United States had two objectives: to stay in touch with its armed forces and to prevent Spain from doing likewise. To communicate with its fleet blockading Havana, the navy brought up one of the Key West–Havana cables. Later in the war, when the U.S. Army invaded Cuba near Santiago, the British refused to allow the Americans to use their cables, claiming neutrality. The U.S. government had to requisition the French-owned New York–Haiti cable that the French, to avoid problems with landing rights, had obligingly put in the name of a dummy American corporation, the United States and Hayti Cable Company.[41]

Opening communications with the American forces, it turned out, was easier to achieve than cutting those of the enemy. When the war began, General Greely, Chief Signal Officer of the U.S. Army, came up with an elaborate list of actions to take vis-à-vis different cables in wartime: Cables connecting two points in enemy territory could legitimately be cut or seized; those connecting the enemy with a neutral could be cut but only in enemy waters; neutral cables near enemy territory that might carry enemy messages (e.g., the New York–Haiti cable) should be put under military censorship; and finally censorship on distant cables, like those across the Atlantic, could be left to the superintendents of the cable companies, "men of high character, whose good faith was guaranteed by the companies whose interests they likewise guarded." While the categorization was somewhat complex, the basic principle behind the American policy was simple. In Captain Squier's words: "In the absence of definite international law upon the many points involved, the United States was forced to take the initiative and use this powerful military weapon for the benefit of the cause of the United States."[42]

So much for the theory: what actually happened was not quite what Greely had expected. On April 23, 1898, the day before the United States declared war on Spain, he ordered censorship at the Key West cable station. A few days later, the Spanish in Cuba instituted military censorship at their end of the cable. Thus the cable remained open to private and commercial messages during the whole war. Elsewhere censorship failed dismally. Spain obtained information about the United States via Canada and Mexico, most of it written by American journalists; meanwhile the U.S. Navy learned the plans of the Spanish fleet from the Associate Press correspondent in Madrid, who got it from the Spanish papers.[43] Censorship was no more effective than it had been in the Crimean War half a century before.

To isolate Cuba from Spain, the United States would have had to cut five cables. The navy succeeded in cutting the coastal cable near Cienfuegos, but failed to find the cables to Jamaica and Haiti. Communications between Captain-General Blanco in Havana and Admiral Cervera in Santiago, at the other end of the island, were impeded though not prevented entirely. Cuba was not cut off from Spain until the Americans took Santiago.

The reasons for the failure were obvious. The British report noted that "the failure to sever the communication may have been due not to any respect for neutral property on the high seas, but to the lack of proper appliances for cutting in deep water."[44] And Captain Squier added: "The searching for deep-sea cables in the high seas in time of war, without an adequate chart of the location of the cable, is a difficult and very doubtful operation," and advocated that in the future, the United States acquire a "naval cable cruiser."[45]

In the Philippines, the situation was much simpler. The islands' only link to the outside world was the Hong Kong–Manila cable laid by the Eastern Extension Company under an exclusive concession obtained from Spain a few months before the war. On May 1, Admiral Dewey proposed to Captain-General Primo de Rivera that the cable be neutralized and used by both sides. When Primo de Rivera refused, Dewey ordered the cable cut in Manila Bay, and tried to use it to telegraph to Hong Kong. Instead of cutting the cable to Hong Kong, however, the navy had cut a local cable to Cavite. When the U.S. government discovered that Spain could still communicate with the Philippines, but the United States could not, it protested to the British, who ordered the Eastern Extension Company to seal off the Hong Kong end of the cable. Thus neither side got to use it.[46]

In order to contact the United States, Dewey had to send dispatch boats to Hong Kong, and send his telegrams from there. To maintain Britain's neutrality in the conflict, the company was only allowed to accept telegrams from the American consul, not from a cruiser, and it had to distinguish between "messages to direct or influence warlike operations" and "narrative of past operations . . . for general publication as news."[47] The company finally reopened cable service to Manila on August 22, ten days after the end of hostilities.

What were the consequences of all the cable cutting and censorship? In the short run probably none, since the war was so lopsided to begin with. The only telegrams that made a difference were the two sent by the Spanish Navy Minister Bermejo to Admiral Cervera at Martinique, informing him of coal supplies near at hand and permitting him to return to Spain. Cervera never got them. In Captain Squier's words, their "accidental non-delivery undoubtedly changed the whole history of the Spanish–American War," for had Cervera received them, he might have saved the Spanish fleet.[48]

In a longer perspective, the Spanish–American War was much commented on, not only by writers on telegraphic questions, but also by the British War Office, for it determined the fate of cables in wartime. It proved that, in order to sever an enemy's communications, a nation needed control of the sea and the know-how to cut cables; and the only nation that could do so was Britain.

The Fashoda Incident

In the same year, 1898, another event took place that illustrated even more forcefully the power of communications. This was the confrontation on the upper Nile between a French expedition under Major Marchand and the British under General Kitchener. While far less dramatic than a war, it was potentially more serious. The Spanish–American War, after all, pitted a major power against a lesser one, and the result was a foregone conclusion, whereas at Fashoda, two great powers came close to the brink of war and then pulled back.[49]

Marchand had started out from Gabon two years before, heading east toward Ethiopia. His was not just another exploring mission; the purpose of his expedition was to claim a swath of French territory across northern Africa, from Dakar on the Atlantic to Djibouti on the Red Sea. He reached the Sudanese village of Fashoda on the Nile in July 1898. An Anglo-Egyptian force under Kitchener, meanwhile, had been fighting the Sudanese, defeating them at Omdurman near Khartoum on September 7. The British also had ambitions in Africa, at the minimum, to control the whole course of the Nile in order to protect the security of Egypt—better yet, in the minds of the more ardent imperialists like Cecil Rhodes, to take all of East Africa from the Cape to Cairo.

While the ambitions were equally megalomaniacal, the means to carry them out were anything but equal. Kitchener, hearing of Europeans on the Nile, sailed up the river on four steamboats, arriving at Fashoda on September 19. Both parties claimed the area for their country, but neither intended to fire a shot, preferring to refer the issue to their respective governments. But how? At Omdurman, Kitchener had a telegraph that ran along the railway to Egypt, and from there to England by cable.

He was therefore able to send a telegram to London on September 24, which arrived the same day, and a longer report, a summary of which was sent from Cairo on the 29th. He described the Marchand expedition as being in desperate straits:

> He is short of ammunition and supplies . . . he is cut off from the interior and his water transport is quite inadequate. He has no following in the country and had we been a fortnight later in crushing the Khalifa nothing could have saved him and his expedition from being annihilated by the Dervishes. Marchand quite realises the futility of all their efforts and he seems quite as anxious to return as we are to facilitate his departure.[50]

This was an exaggeration, for Marchand's force was as numerous, as well fed, and as well armed as the British, although he lacked gunboats. However, Marchand had only two ways to communicate with France: by sending messengers back to the Atlantic coast, which would have taken nine months or more, or by asking the British for permission to use their telegraph. In Paris, meanwhile, the only news of Marchand came from the British. Upon receiving Kitchener's telegram, Prime Minister Salisbury had the British ambassador in Paris read it to French Foreign Minister Delcassé. On the 27th, the latter requested facilities to communicate with Fashoda.

The British would not let Marchand use the military telegraph at Omdurman. They did, however, allow one of Marchand's associates to travel to Cairo and cable from there. Thus it was not until October 22 that the French government received Marchand's report. During an entire month, the French government believed Kitchener's story about Marchand's predicament, and on this basis decided to back down. On October 25 Marchand himself went to Cairo, only to be chastised by Delcassé for his "incredible and unpardonable" conduct in apparently deserting his post.

While Delcassé sought a way to avoid war while saving the honor of France, the British government stepped up the pressure. The Home Fleet was concentrated, war orders were signaled to the Mediterranean Fleet, and the Channel Fleet was ordered to Gibraltar. At that same moment, the cable to Dakar, the main French naval base in the South Atlantic, suddenly fell silent. Fearing the worst, the governor of Senegal mobilized his native troops and armed the cannon overlooking the harbor. Five days later the cable was repaired. Was it, as Maxime de Margerie asked with a touch of irony, "a simple coincidence"?[51]

The French government felt it had no choice. Marchand was ordered back to Fashoda, and on December 11 his expedition left for Ethiopia and Djibouti, from where it returned to France in May 1899.

In these events, the relative strengths of the French and British expeditions counted for little. What mattered ultimately was the power of the Royal Navy. But more immediately, the British won the diplomatic confrontation because they alone could communicate with the Sudan, and they used their control over information to deceive the French.

The British Strategic Cable Report of 1898

The Fashoda crisis, while dramatic, was over quickly. It was followed by another much deeper crisis. In South Africa, relations between the British and the Afrikaners had been getting worse for years, and were clearly heading towards open conflict. In this crisis, Britain felt distinctly isolated. Relations with Russia were strained as usual, and so were those with France after Fashoda; furthermore, Germany, for the first time, showed a hostile face to Britain, while the United States was at best neutral. The British government and its strategic planners had to face the possibility of fighting a war alone against another major power.

Anxieties about Britain's diplomatic "splendid isolation" appeared in the press as well as in government circles. For example, in 1896 the influential *Contemporary Review* carried an article entitled "Our Telegraphic Isolation." It author, Percy Hurd, denounced the British cable network as "an excellent fair-weather system, but it is little more," and feared that in the event of a war, British communications would be cut in Portuguese territories, in the United States, or in the Mediterranean and Red seas. As proof, he pointed to the simultaneous interruption on both east- and west-coast cables to South Africa from December 30, 1895, to January 4, 1896, right after the Jameson raid, a particularly sensitive moment in British–Afrikaner relations. It seemed, indeed, an ominous portent. His solution, which was often to be repeated in later years, was to lay new cables to Australia and to the West Indies, touching only on British territory.[52]

In the fall of 1898, the Cabinet appointed a committee "to consider the control of communications by submarine telegraph in time of war." This committee included not only representatives of the Admiralty, the War Office, the Colonial Office, and the Post Office, but also J. Denison Pender, head of the Eastern group. Its report, dated October 22, 1898, touched on the same topics as the 1891 report, but at greater length and in a more adamant tone.[53] In minute detail, it prescribed what should be done to stock supplies, station cable ships, lay new cables, defend landing sites, and otherwise prepare for war. Like the 1891 committee, it recommended that strategic cables touch only on British soil, including some very long ones: from Gibraltar to South Africa, from South Africa to Australia, and from Jamaica to British Guiana. Unlike its predecessor, it emphasized the need and disregarded the cost entirely. This provoked a protest from Chancellor of the Exchequer Michael Hicks Beach, who was not represented on the committee: "I see no limit to the demands which may be initiated by a body like the Committee on the control of telegraphic communications in time of war."[54]

The committee drew up various contingency plans in the event of a war with France, Russia, Japan, or the United States, but especially France. (Evidently, the chance of a war with Germany was so remote it was not even considered.) It placed no faith in the possibility of neutralizing cables, which had been advocated by the Colonial Defence Committee of 1886:

> The present Committee are not aware that . . . there has been any advance towards the neutralization of cables in war. The experience of the recent war between Spain and America . . . points to the conclusion that a nation will not hesitate to cut a cable, even when belonging to the subjects of a neutral Power, if it anticipates that any military advantage will be derived from such action. . . . It seems doubtful whether an enemy would be in any way influenced in the direction of fairness and restraint by what this country might do.[55]

The committee fully expected that an enemy would try to cut British cables, but, like its predecessors, it believed that Britain's best defense was the multiplicity of its cables and its ability to repair them, protected by the superiority of the Royal Navy.

Freed of the need to worry about fairness and restraint, the committee proposed:

> Seeing that there are places which Great Britain would find it very desirable, for naval and military reasons, to isolate in war, especially against France, and bearing in mind the superior resources possessed by Great Britain for carrying out this nature of attack, the Committee, after full discussion, have come to the conclusion that we ought to cut an enemy's cables wherever necessary for strategic reasons.[56]

It made long lists of foreign cables to be cut, and British cables interrupted, in the event of war with France, with France and Russia, with Japan, or with the United States.

The committee did not advocate harming neutrals:

> The importance to Great Britain of retaining in the hands of British Companies the main cable communications of the world, is such as to render it desirable to minimise interference with the messages of neutrals and even with the private messages of the inhabitants of a hostile country in time of war.[57]

But it did advocate censorship of telegrams passing through British territory, and a discreet scrutiny of messages passing through British-owned cable stations on neutral territory. As for censorship of the news,

> [S]uch a policy, though it may be suited to a country like Spain, is antagonistic to the Anglo-Saxon spirit. . . . The case, however, is different as regards India, Egypt, and those Colonies which have mainly a native or foreign population, and in those a censorship, to be put into force at the discretion of the chief civil authority . . . should be instituted.[58]

While all of these suggestions seem reasonable, even mild by later standards, the report contains one item that cannot fail to astonish an inhabitant of the twentieth century: a recommendation for the appointment of a Chief Censor, under whom there would serve, among others, "an expert in deciphering." It is of course absurd to criticize the committee for not anticipating what we now know, namely that in two world wars to come, the fate of Great Britain would rest on the prowess of its cryptanalysts. What is surprising, however, is that Britain still had no code breakers at a time when the other European powers, in particular France and Russia, had elaborate "black chambers" to decrypt each other's codes and ciphers. Evidently before 1914, cryptanalysis was considered "antagonistic to the Anglo-Saxon spirit."

The Boer War

By September 1899, it was obvious that a war in South Africa was imminent. There were, at the time, two cables between South Africa and Europe, one up the east coast from Durban to Delagoa Bay, Mozambique, Zanzibar, and Aden, the other from Cape Town to Mossamedes, Loanda, Sao Tomé, and on up the west coast of

Africa. On October 3, in an effort to stop communications between the Afrikaners and their friends in Europe, the War Office imposed censorship on telegrams between the Cape and Natal on the one hand, and Transvaal and Orange Free State on the other. This was a stopgap measure, since the Afrikaners could still communicate via the Portuguese colonies. On October 14, two days after the war began, the War Office imposed censorship not only at Cape Town and Durban, but also at Zanzibar and Aden, forbidding all telegrams in code or cipher except those between foreign governments and their consuls in Africa. Five days later, the postmaster general of Great Britain broadened the ban to include government telegrams, and officially notified the International Telegraph Bureau in Berne.[59]

This was perfectly legal, for according to the agreement of the St. Petersburg Conference of 1875, every state had the right to suspend any message going through its territory, "subject to notification . . . to the other contracting governments." On October 25, in response to an inquiry by the German government, the ban on government code and cipher telegrams was rescinded. Then on November 17 the British government issued a new notification to the International Bureau, once again banning all code and cipher telegrams. Clearly the British did not trust other governments, although they secretly allowed Portuguese and American government cipher telegrams through.

The other powers were quick to protest. Both France and Germany complained that the British action hurt their legitimate commercial interests in southern Africa. At the request of the German ambassador, the British made an exception to their rule, allowing the German government to communicate with the governor of German East Africa in cipher; this was carried out secretly, in order to avoid antagonizing the French by seeming to favor the Germans.[60]

The British government took other actions. On January 6, 1900, the Home Secretary issued a warrant to the Post Office

> to produce, for the information of the Intelligence Department of the War Office, until further notice, any telegrams passing through the Central Telegraph Office [in London], which there is reason to believe are sent with the object of aiding, abetting, or assisting the South African Republic and the Orange Free State.[61]

It also scrutinized cables to and from the French base at Djibouti and censored telegrams in Sierra Leone.

Finally, on January 26, in response to French and German pressure, the British government announced that commercial codes could be used, provided that two copies of the relevant codebooks were deposited at the Aden cable office. This alleviated the complaints of foreign merchants who had resented having to pay the exorbitant charges for clear-language telegrams.[62] The ban against government cipher telegrams was not lifted until June 1900 for German communications with Southwest Africa, November for French communications with Zanzibar and Madagascar, and December for Reunion. Other forms of censorship continued past the peace treaty, and were only lifted in July 1902.

What were the results of the censorship? The secret report of the War Office Intelligence Department smugly claimed:

> On the whole it would appear that little secret intelligence succeeded in passing between the enemy and their agents in Europe or elsewhere. . . . This resulted, not so much from

the importance of the messages stopped by the censor, as from the mere fact that the censorship existed.[63]

As proof, it pointed out that shipments of canned food to Delagoa Bay for sale to the Boers stopped on December 1899; after that, the Boers were reduced to eating fresh food.

Yet censorship had another consequence, unanticipated by the short-sighted intelligence officers and, more surprisingly, even in the Foreign Office memorandum of November 1900. It proved that Great Britain was not only able to interfere with the communications between France, Germany, and Portugal and their overseas possessions, but was perfectly willing to use its control of the world cables to its own advantage. Fairness and restraint were no longer part of the vocabulary of European relations as they had been for most of the nineteenth century. It was the first lesson in twentieth-century ethics.

Notes

1. Robert J. Cain, "Telegraph Cables in the British Empire 1850–1900" (Ph.D. dissertation, Duke University, 1971), 189; Vary T. Coates and Bernard Finn, *A Retrospective Technology Assessment: Submarine Telegraphy. The Transatlantic Cable of 1866* (San Francisco, 1979), 89. See also R. A. Jones, *The British Diplomatic Service, 1815–1914* (London, 1983).

2. Coates and Finn, 89.

3. Ibid., 83.

4. Sir Horace Rumbold, *Recollections of a Diplomatist* (London, 1902), 2:111–12, cited in Stephen Kern, *The Culture of Time and Space 1880–1918* (Cambridge, Mass., 1983), 274.

5. Cain, 188.

6. Charles Mazade, *La guerre en France 1870–1871* (Paris 1875), 1:37, cited in Kern, 274.

7. Cain, 188.

8. Hugh Barty-King, *Girdle Round the Earth: The Story of Cable and Wireless and its Predecessors to Mark the Group's Jubilee, 1929–1979* (London, 1979), 101.

9. Charles Bright, *Submarine Telegraphs, Their History, Construction and Working* (London, 1898), 171.

10. Maxime de Margerie, *Le réseau anglais de câbles sous-marins* (Paris, 1909), 105–6.

11. Thomas Lenschau, *Das Weltkabelnetz*, Angewandte Geographie. I. Serie. 1. Heft. 2. Auflage (Frankfurt, 1908), 9.

12. P. M. Kennedy, "Imperial Cable Communications and Strategy, 1870–1914," *English Historical Review* 86 (1971), 730.

13. Keith Clark, *International Communications: The American Attitude* (New York, 1931), 126; George A. Codding, Jr., *The International Telecommunication Union: An Experiment in International Cooperation* (Leiden, 1952; repr. New York, 1972), 27.

14. Captain George Owen Squier (U.S. Army Signal Corps), "The Influence of Submarine Cables upon Military and Naval Supremacy," *National Geographic Magazine* 12, No. 1 (January 1901), 8; George Grafton Wilson, *Submarine Telegraphic Cables in their International Relations. Lectures Delivered at the Naval War College, August 1901* (Washington, D.C., 1901), 12–13; Clark, 156–61.

15. For example: J. Depelley, "Les câbles télégraphiques en temps de guerre," *Revue des deux mondes* (1 January 1900), 181; R. Hennig, "Die Seekabel im Kriege," *Zeitschrift für internationales Privat- und öffentliches Recht* 14, Nos. 3–4 (1904); Pierre Jouhannaud, *Les câbles sous-marins, leur protection en temps de paix et en temps de guerre (Thèse pour le doctorat)* (Paris, 1904); Kraemer, *Die unterseeischen Telegraphenkabel in Kriegszeiten* (Leipzig, 1903); Ludwig Schuster, *Landtelegraphen und unterseeische Kabel im Krieg. Inaugural-Dissertation der juristischen Fakultät der Friedrich-Alexanders-Universität zu Erlangen* (Bamberg, 1915); Hugo Thurn, "Das Recht der Seekabel in Kriegszeiten," *Militär-Wochenblatt*, 135–37 (1903).

16. "Report of the Select Committee appointed to Inquire into the Practical Working of the Present System of Telegraphic and Postal Communications between this Country and India," *Parliamentary Papers* 1866 (428), IX.

17. Vice-Admiral Arthur R. Hezlet, *The Electron and Sea Power* (London, 1975), 9–10.

18. Cain, 207–11 and 228.

19. "Protection of Telegraph Cables in Time of War," memorandum by G. S. Clarke, secretary of the Colonial Defence Committee, August 5, 1885, in Public Record Office (Kew) [hereafter PRO], Cab 8/1, No. 12M. See also Sir James Anderson, *Cables in Time of War* (London, 1886), 9; Anderson was one of the directors of the Eastern Telegraph Company.

20. Memorandum of May 12, 1885, on the Bermuda cable in PRO Cab 8/1, No. 4M; Cain, 212–13.

21. Charles Bright, "The Extension of Submarine Telegraphy in a Quarter-Century," *Engineering Magazine* (December 1898), 426; Cain, 213.

22. PRO, Cab 18/16/2.

23. Donard de Cogan, "British Cable Communications (1851–1930): The Azores Connection," *Arquipélago* (Ponte Delgada, Azores), numero especial 1988: *Relaçoes Açores-Gra-Bretanha*, 165–93.

24. Confidential memorandum from H. Brackenbury, Director of Military Intelligence, March 18, 1891, in PRO, Cab 37/29, No. 20.

25. War Office to Cabinet, April 1, 1891, in PRO, Cab 37/29, No. 21.

26. Margerie, 85; Cain, 214.

27. De Cogan, "Azores Connection," 178; Cain, 220–21.

28. George Peel, "The Nerves of Empire," in *The Empire and the Century: A Series of Essays on Imperial Problems and Possibilities* (London, 1905), 259.

29. Charles Cazalet, "Les câbles sous-marins nationaux," *Revue économique de Bordeaux* 12 (March 1900), 43; Charles Lemire, *La défense nationale. La France et les câbles sous-marins avec nos possessions et les pays étrangers* (Paris, 1900), 8; Margerie, 37.

30. *Journal officiel de la République française* (July 12, 1887), 1689.

31. Jacques Haussmann, "La question des câbles," *Revue de Paris* 7, No. 6 (March 15, 1900), 252–53.

32. Harry Alis (pseudonym for Henri Percher), article in *Journal des débats* (July 8, 1894), 2; see also Léon Jacob, "Les intérêts français et les relations télégraphiques internationales," *Bureau des questions diplomatiques et coloniales* (1912), 3–4; Haussmann, 252–53; Margerie, 37.

33. Cazalet, 43; Margerie, 37–38.

34. Artur Kunert, *Geschichte der deutschen Fernmeldekabel. II. Telegraphen-Seekabel* (Cologne-Mülheim, 1962), 205–209; R. Hennig, "Die deutsche Seekabelpolitik zur Befreiung vom englischen Weltmonopol," *Meereskunde* 6, No. 4 (1912), 7–8; Lenschau, 45–50; Charles Lesage, *La rivalité anglo-germanique. Les câbles sous-marins allemands* (Paris, 1915), 7–14; de Cogan, "Azores Connection," 182.

35. Lesage, 94–97; Haussmann, 261–69.

36. "Post Office Correspondence and Memorandum Relating to a Scheme for a Cable from Germany via the Azores to America (1894–1899)," British Post Office archives, POST 83/55; and "Correspondence with Government Departments and German Administration on scheme for laying a cable from Germany via the Azores to North America, 1899," POST 83/58; "Concession granted to Messrs. Felten & Guilleaume (Cologne), 17th August, 1894, by the Imperial German Government for Laying and Working a Submarine Telegraph Cable between Germany and North America via Great Britain and the Azores," Cable and Wireless archives, 1554/1. See also F. S. Weston, "Os cabos submarinos no Fayal," *Boletim do Nucleo Cultural da Horta* 3 (1963), 215–30; Kunert, 209–16; Margerie, 108–9; and Lesage, 42, 53–60, and 94–96.

37. Lesage, 46–47.

38. Memorandum of 26 October 1894 from G.P.O. to Lord Kimberley in Post 83/58 (1894), iii.

39. POST 83/58, x–xii; Margerie, 109.

40. This is the opinion of the French expert Charles Lesage, no friend of Germany (op. cit., 46–47), and of the German telegraph historian Artur Kunert, 216–17.

41. James A. Scrymser, *Personal Reminiscences of James A. Scrymser, in Times of Peace and War* (Easton, Penn., 1915), 92–97.

42. Squier, 10; see also Wilson, 23–25.

43. "Submarine cable communications in time of war: incidents during the Spanish–American War," report from the General Post Office to the War Office, April 1899, in PRO, WO 106/291, 30–34; Coates and Finn, 81.

44. PRO, WO 106/291, 23–24.

45. Squier, 11.

46. Leslie B. Tribolet, *The International Aspects of Electrical Communications in the Pacific Area* (Baltimore, 1929; repr. New York, 1972), 105 and 244–51; Scrymser, 98; Wilson, 17 and 26; Clark, 162. There is some discrepancy between Scrymser's account and the others on this point, but since Scrymser was personally involved in these events, I have followed his version.

47. PRO, WO 106/291, 6.

48. Squier, 1.

49. The story of the Fashoda crisis is told in great detail in George N. Sanderson, *England, Europe and the Upper Nile, 1882–1899: A Study in the Partition of Africa* (Edinburgh, 1965), 332–62; on the telegraphs in the Sudan, see Edward W. C. Sandes, *The Royal Engineers in Egypt and the Sudan* (Chatham, 1937), 279–87 and 415–16.

50. Sanderson, 337.

51. Margerie, 37–38; Haussmann, 253.

52. Percy A. Hurd, "Our Telegraphic Isolation," *Contemporary Review* 69 (1896), 899–908.

53. "Report of Committee Appointed to Consider the Control of Communications by Submarine Telegraph in Time of War (October 22, 1898)" in PRO, Cab 18/16/4; this report was reprinted for the use of the Colonial Office a month later: see PRO, Cab 17/92/32. Including its very detailed appendices, it is 112 pages long, in contrast to the 23-page report of 1891. See also Kennedy, 728–52, and Cain, 221–225.

54. Memorandum from Hicks Beach to Cabinet, May 6, 1899, in PRO, Cab 37/49/31.

55. PRO, Cab 18/16/4 (1898), 13, No. 2.

56. Ibid., No. 3.

57. Ibid., 5–6.

58. Ibid., 28–29.

59. Two collections of documents deal with censorship in the Boer War: Great Britain,

War Office, Intelligence Department, "Telegraphic Censorship during the South African War, 1899–1902. Secret" (June 1903), preface by W. G. Nicholson, D.G.M.I., in PRO, WO 33/280; and "Memorandum on the Censorship of Telegrams to and from South Africa on the Outbreak of Hostilities with the Transvaal and Orange Free State (November 1900)" in PRO, FO 83/2196, 108ff. See also Lieutenant Colonel Thomas G. Fergusson, *British Military Intelligence, 1870–1914: The Development of a Modern Intelligence Organization* (London and Frederick, MD, 1984), 215–23.

60. "Memorandum," 7–8.

61. "Telegraphic Censorship," 11.

62. In a standard business code like the *A.B.C.*, a code word represented, on the average, six clear words; in a private code book specifically compiled for a particular firm, the ratio could be 28 to 1. In other words, codes compensated for the high cost of cabling. "Inter-Departmental Committee on Cable Communications. Second Report (March 26, 1902)," PRO, Cab 18/16/5, 39–40.

63. "Telegraphic Censorship," 26.

6

The Great Powers and the Cable Crisis, 1900–1913

After the crises of the turn of the century, the attitude of the great powers towards communications changed perceptibly. No longer could anyone rely on the kindness of strangers. Every great power needed its own communications, independent of others, with those parts of the world where it had vital interests. Some succeeded better than others, as Table 6.1 shows.

The British Pacific Cable and the "All-Red" Routes

Let us now consider the major participants in the cable-laying boom of the first decade of this century: Great Britain, the United States, France, and Germany. As usual, the British were first. And their first consideration, after the shocks of the turn of the century, was to turn their cable network into an invulnerable global communications system. This took two forms: completing their network of strategic cables, and perfecting their contingency plans in preparation for war.

One very obvious gap remained in the world cable network that radiated out from Britain in 1900: the Pacific Ocean. The Pacific cable project did not originate in colonial defense committees concerned with strategic questions but among Australians and Canadians who felt isolated at the very edge of the British world. They could not do anything about it, however, without Britain's help.[1]

The idea of a Pacific cable was first suggested during the cable boom of the 1870s, but no commercial firm would even consider it. It was brought up again by Canadian railroad entrepreneur Sandford Fleming at the Colonial Conference of 1887, and received the verbal endorsement of the British Post Office, the Association of Chambers of Commerce of the United Kingdom, the Imperial Federation League, and J. Henniker Heaton, member of Parliament from Canterbury and the

Table 6.1.   Distribution of Cables, 1892–1908*

Nation	1892[a]		1908[b]		increase	
	km	percent	km	percent	km	percent
Britain	163,619	66.3	265,971	56.2	102,352	45.2
U.S.A.	38,986	15.8	92,434	19.5	53,448	23.6
France	21,859	8.9	44,543	9.4	22,684	10.0
Denmark	13,201	5.3	17,768	3.8	4,567	2.0
Germany and Netherlands	4,583	1.9	33,984	7.2	29,401	13.0
Others	4,628	1.9	18,408	3.9	13,780	6.1
Total	246,876	100.0	473,108	100.0	226,232	100.0

*Of the 29,401 km of German and Dutch cables in 1908, 5,328 belonged to a joint venture in the Pacific.

[a]U.S. Hydrographic Office, Bureau of Navigation, Navy Department, *Submarine Cables* (Washington, D.C., 1892), 41–59.

[b]Maxime de Margerie, *Le réseau anglais de câbles sous-marins* (Paris, 1909), 34–35.

leading Parliamentary advocate of imperial cables.[2] In 1891 Hawaii, then an independent kingdom, offered to help subsidize the segment to North America. The British Colonial Office and the Treasury, however, rejected the idea on financial grounds.

Two years later, at the other end of the world, the governments of Queensland and New South Wales awarded a contract to the Société Française des Télégraphes Sous-Marins to lay a cable from Bundaberg, on the Queensland coast, to the French colony of New Caledonia. Its promoters, especially Australian cable lobbyist Audley Coote, did not see it as just a short feeder to the Eastern network, but as the first link in a cable to Fiji, Samoa, Hawaii, and San Francisco.[3] That aroused the opposition of the government of Victoria and of British Colonial Secretary Lord Ripon, who insisted that the cable to Canada be all-British.[4] It was to be part of the "All-Red" route, so named after the color of the British Empire on world maps of the period.

Behind that patriotic British opposition lay another more commercial concern. In a memorandum to the Colonial Office on January 3, 1894, Sir John Pender protested that by subsidizing the New Caledonia cable, the governments of Queensland and New South Wales "were practically committing the Australasian colonies to the laying of a Pacific cable under French auspices and control."[5] Coote saw it in a different light:

> The aim has been for the last nineteen years to break a growing and ungenerous monopoly in the telegraph world and, now that we have so far succeeded by giving the contract to the French company, the secret allies of the Eastern Extension Telegraph Company are agitating in the press, and in the minds of public men in some parts of Australia, to try and prevent the Pacific Cable being a success. It is not because the cable touches at New Caledonia, it is because it is opposing the Eastern Extension Telegraph Company.[6]

Eastern was not interested in substituting an all-British Pacific cable for the French project, but in preventing entirely a Pacific line that would break its lucrative

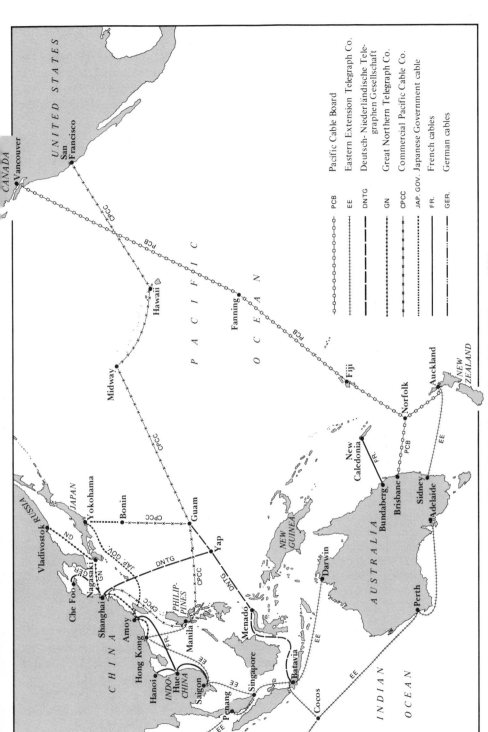

Figure 5. Pacific and East Asian Cables, c. 1905.

PCB	Pacific Cable Board
EE	Eastern Extension Telegraph Co.
DNTG	Deutsch- Niederländische Telegraphen Gesellschaft
GN	Great Northern Telegraph Co.
CPCC	Commercial Pacific Cable Co.
JAP. GOV.	Japanese Government cable
FR.	French cables
GER.	German cables

monopoly of the Australasian traffic. Together, the patriotic and the commercial oppositions postponed the project for another decade.

The Pacific cable issue brought out into the open the ambiguous position of the Eastern group in the British Empire. Eastern had served Britain well, laying cables to British colonies and spheres of interest, often without subsidies. The government's views were expressed in a memorandum of February 3, 1897, from the Treasury to the Colonial Office:

> [Eastern] represent a real British interest, and one entitled to great consideration from the Imperial Government. They have been the pioneers of Cable communication with the most distant parts of the Empire, and it is to their enterprise and skill that the establishment of these communications is due.
>
> In times of emergency they have always been ready to render to the Government any services which were in their power; and the advantages which have been secured from their cooperation could not in many cases have been obtained from any other body or in any other way.
>
> It is therefore a matter of no small importance that the Government should continue to maintain friendly relations with them.[7]

The good relations were demonstrated in 1892, when R. G. W. Herbert retired as permanent undersecretary of state in the Colonial Office to become chairman of Telegraph Construction and Maintenance, or when John Denison-Pender, chairman of Eastern, was appointed to the cable committees of 1898 and 1911.[8]

But if the British government appreciated Eastern, the Australians did not. Until 1895 telegrams between Australia and Europe cost 9s 4d per word, so much that all the Australian newspapers together could only afford a few hundred words a day, and most Australians could not afford to cable "home" at all. In order to get Eastern to reduce its rate to 4s 9d, the four Australian colonies had to bribe it with a subsidy of £32,400 a year until 1899, more than the interest on a new cable across the Pacific.[9] Henniker Heaton, himself owner of an Australian newspaper, expressed the feelings of many Australians when he spoke before the House of Commons on the Pacific Cable Bill:

> I know no monopoly in the world that is doing more injury to trade than the concentrated companies represented by the Eastern Telegraph Company and its six or seven satellites. . . . I once described John Pender and Co. as an octopus which, with its tentacles in every direction, is sucking the lifeblood out of the Empire. . . . I regard the scheme now before the House as a great step forward towards the breaking up of one of the greatest monopolies the world has ever seen, and towards the consolidation of the Empire.[10]

During the years of procrastination, the backers of the Pacific cable never ceased trying to revive it. The colonial conference at Ottawa in 1894 strongly endorsed the project. Sandford Fleming attempted to plant the British flag on Necker Island, a speck of land at the western end of the Hawaiian archipelago that would have served as a convenient cable station between Vancouver Island and British-owned Fanning Island. But Colonial Secretary Ripon made him back down, and the Hawaiian government, which had given exclusive cable landing rights to the United States, quickly sent a ship to annex the island instead.[11]

In 1895, the idea gained an important proponent in the new colonial secretary, Joseph Chamberlain, who advocated a Pacific cable "to communicate with one another without having to rely on the sufferance of foreign Powers."[12] In 1896 he appointed a Pacific cable committee with representatives of Canada, New South Wales, and Victoria, which recommended a state-owned Pacific cable. New South Wales, Queensland, Victoria, and New Zealand each agreed to pay one-ninth of the cost of the cable, and Canada five-eighteenths; that left five-eighteenths for Britain. In an attempt to block the project, Eastern offered to lay an all-British cable to South Africa and another from South Africa to Australia, on condition that Britain refrain from subsidizing any competitive venture.[13] To overcome the opposition of Chancellor of the Exchequer Hicks Beach and the Eastern group, Chamberlain took the issue to the Cabinet in February 1899. Hicks Beach accepted the argument that the cable represented a quid pro quo for Australasian and Canadian troop contributions to the Boer War. Parliament passed the Pacific Cable Bill in August 1901.[14]

Since Eastern would not cooperate even with a subsidy, the cable was entrusted to a new body, the Pacific Cable Board, representing Britain, Canada, the Australian colonies, and New Zealand. It signed a contract with TC&M in December 1900. The undertaking was difficult. Soundings had to be taken where none had ever been taken before. The section from Vancouver Island to Fanning Island, at 6,560 kilometers, was the longest single cable span on earth, so long that a new ship, the *Colonia,* had to be built to hold it. From Fanning the cable continued to Fiji and Norfolk Island, from which two lines ran to New Zealand and Queensland, respectively. The cable was finished in October 1902 and opened to the public on December 8.[15]

Great Britain had finally agreed to lay a Pacific cable because the tensions at the turn of the century had overcome fiscal and commercial considerations. Ironically, the cable turned out to be good business. Its first effect was to force Eastern to lower its England–Australia rate from 4s 9d in May 1900 to 3s in January 1902, to the great satisfaction of the Australians. It was also faster: a telegram took an hour instead of a day. In the long run, it carried enough traffic and accumulated enough profit to warrant the laying of a duplicate cable in 1921–22.[16] But was it all-British? Across the Pacific and Atlantic Oceans, yes, and also across Canada, where the telegraph ran alongside the Canadian Pacific Railway, "except for 270 miles when the line was diverted through the American state of Maine."[17] A minor omission.

The Pacific cable was not the only strategic cable laid in the immediate aftermath of the Boer War. Indeed, the armed forces and the Colonial Defence Committee developed what P. M. Kennedy called "a virtual fetish" for all-red cables.[18] Two were laid in the same years as the Pacific cable. The first of these was a new cable, completed in early 1900, from Cape Town to St. Helena, Ascension, and St. Vincent in the Cape Verde Islands; while not truly "all-red," since the Cape Verdes belonged to Portugal, it was considered much safer than the three that followed the African coasts, which were prone to natural breakdowns and vulnerable to foreign interference. A year later another cable was laid from Ascension to Sierra Leone.[19]

New cables were also laid across the Indian Ocean in 1901 and 1902: from Durban to Mauritius, from Mauritius to the Seychelles and Ceylon, from Mauritius to Perth via Rodrigues and Cocos islands, and from Cocos to Singapore. While duplicating existing lines, they provided an alternative route to India, the Far East, and Australasia in the event Britain lost control of the Mediterranean.[20] Finally in 1901 a cable was laid, at Admiralty request, from the British naval base at Weihaiwei to Taku in support of military operations against the Boxers in north China.[21]

British Cable Strategy, 1902-1914

By 1902, Great Britain possessed not only the world's major commercial cables, but also a set of strategic cables that made its communications with its major colonies and naval bases practically invulnerable to attack.

But having cables was not enough. In a world that was heading for war, strategists made ever more elaborate contingency plans and worried about defensive and offensive actions in minute detail. The first of the committees to concern themselves with cables after the Boer War was the Inter-Departmental Committee on Cable Communications. Its first report, dated August 8, 1901, dealt with the question of telegraph rates between Britain and India. Its second report of March 26, 1902, considered all the other issues.[22] It restated the basic principle behind British cable policy:

> We regard it as desirable that every important colony or naval base should possess one cable to this country which touches only on British territory or on the territory of some friendly neutral. We think that, after this, there should be as many alternative cables as possible, but that these should be allowed to follow the normal routes suggested by commercial considerations.[23]

It also repeated many of the recommendations of previous cable committees—the importance of completing the British network in the Indian Ocean, the contribution of the Eastern group to British security, and the need to maintain the profits of the private companies. In essence, the committee was satisfied with the security of British cable communications.

The strategists could now turn to offensive operations. In August 1904 the Admiralty issued a "Memorandum on the Protection of British Submarine Cables, and on the Destruction of an Enemy's Cables," which was mainly concerned with a possible war against France, with or without Russia.[24] In 1904 the War Office prepared a document entitled "Censorship of Submarine Cables in Time of War." Noting that the International Telegraph Convention of St. Petersburg required that other governments be notified before any telegraph service was suspended "except where the advice might be dangerous to the security of the State," it recommended that "wherever there was a suspension of service under that Article it would be held dangerous for the security of the State to advise the office of origin, and therefore no advice should be sent."[25] In other words, the British attitude toward state security was edging closer to that of Russia and Germany.

In 1908, with the "Report of an Inter-Departmental Committee appointed to draw up instructions for establishing a secret censorship of submarine cables at certain foreign stations in time of grave emergency," Britain moved yet another step further from peace[26]:

During a period of strained relations with a foreign Power, when war, though not inevitable, may break out at any moment, it may become necessary, at certain stations abroad, to take measures to prevent the disclosure of information regarding naval or military preparations and movements. The inauguration of the scheme of open cable censorship arranged to be put in force in time of war might in such circumstances precipitate hostilities; it is therefore necessary to resort to some form of secret censorship.

The last major report on cable strategy was "Submarine Cable Communications in Time of War," issued by the Standing Subcommittee of the Committee of Imperial Defence on December 11, 1911. On the issue of defense, the report noted with satisfaction that Britain now had an "all-red" system: "The dependence of the United Kingdom on cable stations situated upon foreign territory for the transmission of telegrams has been generally eliminated."[27] As to the offense, the report acknowledged for the first time the German threat and gave detailed instructions on how to cut Germany's communications without offending potential neutrals like the Netherlands and the United States. It was a much simpler task than isolating France: "Generally speaking, if France and Russia were in alliance with this country, it would be possible to isolate Germany from practically the whole world, outside Europe, by cutting the cables to the Azores, Tenerife, and Vigo and the three cable landings on Yap Island."[28] Finally, in another innovation, it recommended the construction of wireless stations to supplement cables at vulnerable places.[29]

Great Britain had finally achieved the ultimate goal of communications strategy: Its own cable network was invulnerable to attack or interference, and it had the ability to spy on its enemies or isolate them from the rest of the world. It was an important weapon in the world wars to come.

The American Cables

Laying a cable across the Pacific appealed to Americans as well as to Australians and Canadians. In the early 1870s Cyrus Field, promoter of the Atlantic cables, proposed cables to Japan and Russia, but had to abandon the scheme in the face of technical and political difficulties. Several times during the 1870s, Congress discussed the proposal, but appropriated no money. The government of Hawaii was more interested: It promised exclusive concessions to Cyrus Field and later to Audley Coote, but they lapsed before they could be carried out.

In the 1880s, President Grover Cleveland supported the idea, and in the early 1890s, the Hawaiian legislature, dominated by American businessmen, granted an exclusive concession and a yearly subsidy of $25,000 to General Hartwell. Several bills involving an American subsidy for a Pacific cable passed the Senate but were defeated in the House of Representatives.[30]

By 1895, as trade across the Pacific increased, the cable idea attracted the attention of several capitalists. One of them was Colonel Zephaniah S. Spalding, a businessman with interests in Hawaii, America, and Europe. Supporting Spalding secretly was none other than John Pender, who had fought so hard against the all-British Pacific cable. The president of Hawaii, Sanford B. Dole, promised Spalding an exclusive twenty-year concession and $40,000 a year on condition that the United States government also grant him a subsidy. Spalding then founded the

Pacific Cable Company of New Jersey, which was to have joined the Eastern Extension and the Great Northern companies in laying and operating the cable. The following year, the Western Union Telegraph Company became involved through J. Pierpont Morgan and James A. Scrymser, director of the Mexican and Central and South American Telegraph companies. The two men founded a rival firm, the Pacific Cable Company of New York, and attacked Spalding's company as a front for the Eastern interests. Both companies lobbied Congress for subsidies, but their mutual accusations only achieved a deadlock.[31] The Pacific Ocean and the Far East were still very peripheral to the interests of American politicians.

Then came the Spanish–American War and the annexation of Hawaii. Quite unexpectedly, the United States found itself in possession of an empire stretching across the Pacific Ocean. A cable was suddenly a strategic necessity. In a special message to Congress on February 10, 1899, President McKinley said:

> The necessity for speedy communication between the United States and all these Pacific islands has become imperative. Such communications should be established in such a way as to be wholly under the control of the United States, whether in time of peace or of war. At present the Philippines can be reached only by cables which pass through many foreign countries, and the Hawaiian Islands and Guam can only be communicated with by steamers, involving delays in each instance of at least a week. The present condition should not be allowed to continue for a moment longer than is absolutely necessary.[32]

In his annual messages to Congress on December 5, 1899, and December 3, 1900, McKinley repeated his pleas. After his assassination, his successor, Theodore Roosevelt, did likewise:

> I call your attention most earnestly to the crying need of a cable to Hawaii and the Philippines, to be continued from the Philippines to points in Asia. We should not defer a day longer than necessary the construction of such a cable. It is demanded not merely for commercial, but also for political and military considerations.[33]

Between January 1899 and December 1901, some eighteen Pacific cable bills were introduced in Congress. Some called for government construction, ownership, and operation of the cable; others would have entrusted it to private enterprise with a government subsidy. The leading proponents of the government cable were Rear-Admiral Bradford and Captain Squier of the Signal Corps, while Scrymser and E. L. Baylies of the Pacific Cable Company of New York, among others, lobbied for private ownership.[34] But it was all in vain, for Congress, deadlocked between the public and the private cable proposals and not yet convinced that an empire cost money to maintain, rejected them all.[35]

On August 22, 1901, the Pacific cable issue, which had been tossed about for twenty-five years, was suddenly resolved. John W. Mackay, president of the Commercial Cable Company and the Postal Telegraph Company, rival to Western Union, offered to lay a cable to the Philippines without a government subsidy. He also promised to lower the rate of a message from San Francisco to the Far East to a dollar a word from the $2.35 charged by Eastern. He founded the Commercial Pacific Cable Company, bought a cable from the India Rubber Company in England, and had it sent to the Pacific. Instead of requesting a landing license, he proceeded under the Telegraph Act of 1866, which "gives the right to any telegraph company organized under the laws of any state, and complying with its conditions, to construct and operate lines of telegraph throughout the domain of the United States, and over, under or across the navigable streams or water of the United States."[36] Now that Hawaii, Guam, and the Philippines were American, the Pacific Ocean had become a "navigable water of the United States." It was a wise move, since neither the executive branch nor Congress had any established procedure for granting landing licenses. The Commercial Pacific cable reached Manila on July 4, 1903. In 1906, it was connected to Japan and China.[37]

Mackay's enemies accused him of having made a secret deal with the Eastern conglomerate, but he stoutly denied it. Twenty years later, in the Cable Landing License Hearings before the Congress, his son Clarence Mackay admitted that the Commercial Pacific Cable Company was only one-quarter owned by the Commercial Cable Company; another 25 percent belonged to the Great Northern Company, and the remaining 50 percent to the Eastern and Eastern Extension companies. In other words, his father had lied.[38] On June 26, 1904, seventeen agreements were signed between the Eastern group, the Great Northern, Commercial, Commercial Pacific, German–Dutch, and Indo-European Telegraph companies, and the Chinese and Russian telegraph administrations. They formed a giant cartel to apportion all telegraph traffic in the Pacific, and to ensure that the rates from China to Europe would be lower via Russia or India than across the Pacific and America.[39] It was all done secretly, and did not appear in the reports of any of the companies involved.

The reason for the agreements was that the Eastern Extension and the Great Northern had exclusive concessions to land cables in China and Japan, and the Eastern Extension even claimed the exclusive right to land cables in the Philippines, based on a Spanish concession that the United States had rejected.[40] In theory, it should have been impossible to lay a cable from America to the Far East without their permission. But for the Eastern and Great Northern companies to have stood on their rights would have caused a furor in the United States, and they dared not risk such a confrontation. The solution was to back an American enterprise. It had to be done in the greatest secrecy, however, to avoid offending not only American but also British sensibilities, for it would have seemed in poor taste for Eastern to support an American Pacific cable after trying for so many years to prevent a British one. In exchange for providing most of the capital and—more importantly—the cables that could only be obtained in Britain, the Eastern and Great Northern got control of the rates, and thereby secured their stranglehold over communications in the Far East and the maintenance of their profits. In the nineteenth century, when governments had been relatively peaceable and cooperative, enterprises were exclusively of one nation or another. In the twentieth, ironically, just as peoples and politicians were entering an era of strident and bellicose nationalisms, private firms were becoming more international-minded. But they had to be rather discreet about it.

In the Atlantic, as in the Pacific, the United States government stayed out of the cable business and let private enterprise operate on its own. The result was a tremendous expansion of American cables at the expense of British interests. In 1909 AT&T, already a telephone monopoly, bought the Gould family holdings in Western Union. AT&T's president, Theodore Vail, hoped to consolidate America's telephone and telegraph lines into one giant network. Since Western Union owned some Atlantic cables, the government threatened to take the company to court on the grounds that the Atlantic cable pool violated the Sherman Anti-Trust Act. To avoid a suit, Vail pulled Western Union out of the pool. In 1911 the British members of the pool, the Anglo-American and Direct United States companies, suddenly found themselves cut off from Western Union's nationwide network of land lines and offices, and were about to lose all their business. To avoid bankruptcy, they were forced to lease their cables to Western Union. Three years later, AT&T sold its holdings in Western Union. Ironically, the government's legal threat had only created a more monopolistic situation than before.[41]

Internationally, the results were ambiguous. The cables were British owned but operated by an American company that employed British cable clerks. One British expert, the engineer Charles Bright, found it frightening that Great Britain no longer controlled a single Atlantic cable:

> Not a single one of the Atlantic cables . . . could at any time be relied upon as a genuinely All-British strategic connection in the event of trouble with the United States or with other countries interested in disturbing our Imperial communications.[42]

The British government, however, was not worried. If a German or French company had leased the cables instead of Western Union, it would no doubt have stepped in to prevent it. But the report of December 1911 on "Submarine Cable Communications in Time of War" did not even consider the possibility of a war with the United States. What mattered from a strategic point of view was neither ownership nor management of the cables, but their location. Since all the leased cables passed through Britain, the government could censor or scrutinize the traffic as easily as under British management. In effect, the British and American cable interests were not rivals, but close allies.

France and the Cable Crisis

In 1898, the United States was just beginning its imperialistic career outside North America, and American politicians were still rather naive about the dangers of global competition. Hence the American Pacific cable project was motivated more by financial than by political considerations. France, in contrast, already had a long history of overseas conquests and an even longer experience of European power politics. The French were thus acutely sensitive to their position in the world relative to other nations. The events of the turn of the century affected France directly and triggered a political reaction.

In certain ways, France was in an advantageous position with respect to global communications. It faced both the Atlantic and the Mediterranean; it had colonies on every continent, which provide both a demand for communications and convenient landing places for cables; and it was a rich nation, able to invest large sums abroad. In other ways, however, France was at a serious disadvantage compared with Britain. Its colonies were far poorer and, except for Algeria, none of them had white settlers. It had less industry and less overseas trade. Its politicians were preoccupied with the German threat and, with few exceptions, less interested in overseas questions. Its merchants did little trade with the French colonies, other than

Algeria. Only in the 1890s did public opinion begin to take pride in the empire. But worst of all was the fact that France had lagged behind in the first cable boom, and the British had seized all the profitable routes.

The result was visible in the fate of the French cable enterprises. The first of them, the Société du Câble Transatlantique Français (or Société Erlanger), was absorbed by the Anglo-American Company in 1873 after four years of operation. The second one, the Compagnie du Télégraphe de Paris à New York, or PQ, limped along from 1879 to 1895. Both were exclusively transatlantic, while a third firm, the Société Française des Télégraphes Sous-Marins, operated short cables with government subsidies in the West Indies and between Australia and New Caledonia. When the PQ company went bankrupt in 1895, the French government forced it to merge with the Société Française, creating the Compagnie Française des Câbles Télégraphiques, or CFCT. In contrast to British cable companies that treated the government of Britain as a valued customer and occasional collaborator, the French company was so deeply in debt to the government and so tightly controlled as to be essentially an official agency. This was to be the vehicle for France's cable policy.[43]

Before 1898 only a few voices in France called for more cables. In 1886 and again in 1889 the Chamber of Deputies had refused to vote credits. In 1894–95 the cable lobby, which was identical to the colonial lobby, tried again. The journalist Harry Alis, head of the Union coloniale, wrote a series of articles in the *Journal des Débats* in July 1894 calling attention to the fact that in every French colonial harbor there sat a British "agent" employed by a British cable company, watching the French ships; that the British used their power to withhold vital information, as in the Tangier case; and that France was spending 2,337,000 francs (£93,480) a year subsidizing British cables instead of laying its own.[44] The Société des études coloniales et maritimes, a colonial lobby, presented the following resolution to the Chamber of Deputies with the support of the ministers of war, navy, and colonies:

> Whereas it is necessary for a great country like France to have independent national telegraphic communications with its colonies, in order to avoid, on the one hand, the repetition of serious problems like those which were noticed during the Tonkin and Dahomey expeditions and the Siam affair, and, on the other, to guarantee to our overseas commerce advantages equal to those of our foreign competitors until now privileged, the Société des Etudes Coloniales et Maritimes expresses the wish that a sufficient sum be put into the budget each year to serve as a subsidy or guarantee of interest to French telegraph lines, in existence or to be created, destined to link the French colonies to the metropole.[45]

At the same time, J. Depelley, head of the Compagnie Française des Câbles Télégraphiques, spoke before the Union Coloniale Française on the subject of "Submarine Cables and the Defense of Our Colonies":

> The nation whose colonial interests are the most often in opposition and at war with ours is England. Is it not imprudent to leave our means of correspondence in its hands? It is already a mark of inferiority from the commercial and political point of view; it would be a danger if we had to defend our colonies.[46]

But their efforts were in vain, for the Chamber of Deputies was too parsimonious and too preoccupied with the defense of France against Germany to be swayed by such arguments.

What changed the situation was the Fashoda crisis and the Boer War. On November 27, 1899, a group of deputies, led by Deputy Henrique, presented the first cable project to the Chamber. In December Colonial Minister Decrais and Commerce Minister Millerand announced to the Chamber that the Council of Ministers was now convinced of the need for a French cable network. On January 30, 1900, the government presented a bill on "the establishment of a network of submarine telegraph lines destined to connect certain French colonies to the metropole and to extend the land lines in the French colonies of West Africa." It called, in the first place, for cables from Indochina to Hong Kong, from Madagascar to Reunion, from Marseille to North Africa and Senegal, and land lines from Senegal to the other West African colonies; and after that, for cables from France to Senegal, and from Gabon to Madagascar. This bill received the support of the committee on colonial affairs and of a number of influential deputies.[47]

The parliamentary debates were accompanied by a chorus of publicity by cable and colonial lobbyists. The Syndicat de la presse coloniale, the Groupe colonial des conseillers du commerce extérieur, and various business groups in Marseille and Bordeaux issued proclamations. Books and articles appeared in the press denouncing British companies, pointing out how vulnerable France would be in the event of a war with Britain, and demanding an all-French cable network.[49]

Finally in July 1901 the Chamber passed two laws: one "authorizing expenditures for the creation of a submarine network," which the government used secretly to buy the South American Telegraph Company; the other "authorizing the purchase of the cables of the West African Company," which ran along the West African coast from Senegal to Gabon. Two years later the Chamber authorized the laying of cables from Brest to Dakar, from Madagascar to Reunion and Mauritius, and from Indochina to Borneo.[49]

In the nineteenth century, France had acquired two cables across the Atlantic, several joining France to Algeria and Tunisia, a small network in the West Indies linked to New York since 1896, and short pieces linking Madagascar and New Caledonia to the British network. They now proceeded to expand their communications channels in two ways: wherever possible by buying or laying cables, and elsewhere by joining nations other than Britain in forming alternative routes.

The first objective was South America, where France had commercial and political interests. In 1901 the French government paid the India Rubber Company £365,000 for the shares of the South American Telegraph Company, which had operated a cable from Dakar to Pernambuco since 1892, but never paid a dividend. It was done secretly in order to avoid offending Brazil, which would not have tolerated a foreign government agency operating on its shores. The purchase created an anomalous situation: a company that was at the same time British and French, public and private. It was also a commercial mistake, since Pernambuco was a backwater, and Brazil had given an exclusive concession to the Western Telegraph Company, an affiliate of Eastern, for cables along its coast to Rio and beyond. Therefore, the French were just as subject to British power as before. In 1914 the firm was renamed Compagnie des Câbles Sud-Américains, and its headquarters were moved to Paris.[50]

In February 1902, the French government made its second major purchase. For £144,000 it bought from the West African Telegraph Company those sections of its cable that connected Dakar with Conakry (Guinea) and Grand-Bassam (Ivory Coast) with Cotonou (Dahoney) and Libreville (Gabon). Intermediate stops at non-French ports were cut out. The stretch from Conakry to Grand-Bassam was covered by a land line through the interior. Three years later France laid a cable directly from Brest to Dakar. From then on it had an independent all-French cable to its West African possessions. In 1912–13 it completed the line with a piece from Conakry to Grand-Bassam and an extension from Libreville to Pointe-Noire in the French Congo.[51]

More distant French colonies got less adequate service. It had always frustrated French colonialists that their richest possession, Indochina, could only communicate with France through the Eastern cables. In 1901, therefore, a cable was laid between the Vietnamese town of Tourane and Amoy in China, connecting with the Great Northern cable. Léon Mascart, the captain of the cable ship *François Arago,* which laid the cable, saw it as "a dazzling proof of the perfection of our industry," and proclaimed: "to cable from Indochina to Paris without being subject to the supervision of the English offices . . . the emancipation from English censorship. . . . Thanks to this new cable, Indochina has a route which, if not entirely French, is at least friendly and neutral."[52]

Five years later another cable was laid between Saigon and Pontianak in Borneo, where it joined the Dutch and German lines to the American Pacific cable at Guam. Now France had two non-British means of communicating with Indochina. There were even plans to lay cables from Java to Reunion, and from Madagascar to the French Congo, either by cable around Africa, or somehow across Tangayika and the Belgian Congo.[53] These grandiose schemes were totally unrealistic, as they would have required enormous subsidies and the cooperation of many other countries. Reality was also a matter of business. Both non-British routes to Indochina had to charge higher rates than those of Eastern. Hence all the business traffic continued to use Eastern, and the cables consistently lost money. When they broke a few years later, they were judged not worth repairing and were abandoned.

What then were the results of the French desire for cables after 1900? Only the cables to North America and to North Africa showed a profit; the rest were commercial failures. All in all, the French government paid between six and eight million francs (£240,000–320,000) per year for cables between 1900 and 1914.[54] But of course the cables were not laid for commercial reasons. Their ostensible purpose was strategic, more specifically because of the fear of a war with Great Britain. Although that fear evaporated when France and Britain signed the Entente Cordiale in 1904, the cable-laying momentum continued, impelled by the vested interests it had created and the continued efforts of the cable lobby.[55] This implies that the cables were not really strategic, either, for if there had been a war with Britain, they would have been cut. It is in peacetime that they served their purpose: to keep France among the great powers in the realm of global communications.

Germany and the Cable Crisis

Behind France lay Germany, a country with aspirations to greatness. A latecomer to the community of nations, it had missed the imperialist banquet and had to content itself with leftovers, minor colonies hardly commensurate with its swelling national ambitions. From the standpoint of communications, they were too distant and too far apart to be of much use in a cable network, and too poor to warrant a commercial investment. Even in the Atlantic, where Germany had serious business interests that fully justified direct cables, its location had long frustrated any telegraphic plans. When the German government at last determined to build its own cable network after the cable-landing incident of 1893–94, it found itself at a great disadvantage vis-à-vis other nations.

German submarine telegraphy was the product of a cooperative effort between three parties: the Felten und Guilleaume Carlswerk A.G., manufacturers of wire rope and cable, or more exactly their owners, the brothers Emil, Max, and Theodor Guilleaume; the Reichspostamt, or Imperial Post Office, especially the directors of its telegraph department, Dr. von Stephan until 1901 and Dr. Sydow after that; and the A. Schaaffhausen'scher Bankverein, a Cologne bank. In 1896 Felten und Guilleaume founded the Deutsche See-Telegraphengesellschaft, which operated a cable to Vigo in Spain, where it connected with the Eastern network.[56] Three years later, it started a cable-making subsidiary, the Norddeutsche Seekabelwerke, and bought three cable ships. The acquisition of cable technology posed no difficulty; by the 1890s Germany had the most sophisticated electrical industry in the world. The firms Siemens und Halske of Berlin and Siemens Brothers of London had long cooperated on technical matters, and many German cable experts–Wilhelm Siemens and Eugen Obach in particular—had worked in Britain. By the 1890s German shipbuilding was catching up with the British. As soon as the demand appeared, German industry was ready to supply the cables.

In the next few years, Felten und Guilleaume also founded the Deutsch–Atlantische Telegraphengesellschaft, or DAT, to operate cables to North America; the Deutsch–Südamerikanische Telegraphengesellschaft for Africa and South America; the Osteuropäische Telegraphengesellschaft for Eastern Europe; and the Deutsch–Niederländische Telegraphengesellschaft for the Pacific.[57] Felten und Guilleaume was thus in a good position to benefit from the sudden enthusiasm for cables that erupted in Germany in 1900.

What triggered the boom was a combination of economic demand and political indignation. The demand resulted from the growth of the Germany economy and of its overseas trade, as shown in Table 6.2. Much of this overseas traffic was transatlantic, and the number of telegrams exchanged between Germany and the United States also grew in this period, from 30,000 in 1880 to 343,292 in 1901 and 710,376 in 1910.[58] Thus, even had there been no political motives, the growth of trade would have fully justified laying cables from Germany to North America and even to South America. What politics did, in Germany as in France, was to divert cable investments to other less profitable routes, such as to Africa and in the Pacific, where German business interests were marginal at best.

As in France, it was British censorship in the Boer War that triggered the political indignation that led to a German cable policy. In November 1899 the government asked the Reichstag for credits to build a cable network. The first appropriation, an annual subsidy of 1,400,000 Reichsmark (£67,000), went to the DAT, founded by Felten und Guilleaume and A. Schaaffhausen'scher Bankverein earlier that year to lay a cable across the Atlantic.[59]

Table 6.2. German Commerce and Merchant Marine, 1882–1913[a]

Year	Commerce outside Europe	Merchant marine
1882	499,715,000 Reichsmark	458 steamships 251,648 tons net
1894	1,944,500,000 Reichsmark	1016 steamships 823,702 tons net
1913	7,277,000,000 Reichsmark	2098 steamships 2,655,000 tons net

[a]Charles Lesage, *La rivalité anglo-germanique. Les câbles sous-marins allemands* (Paris, 1915), 27–29.

Unlike in France, it is only after the political decision was taken that books and articles began appearing to justify the new policy.[60] The literature became more strident as Germany's naval and imperial ambitions grew and its relations with Great Britain deteriorated. In Germany, in contrast to France and Britain, the official mind usually preceded public opinion. On the subject of cables, as on so many others, German ideas at that time consisted of a mixture of feelings of persecution and self-assertion. Richard Hennig, a frequent writer on communications questions, complained:

> It was England itself which, in the nineties, suddenly sounded a fanfare before an unsuspecting world and repeatedly used its almost total power over cables for national-political purposes in a manner that was extraordinarily painful for the other European peoples. . . . A war between England and another European colonial power in the nineties would have been a . . . gruesome game of cat and mouse.[61]

And Thomas Lenschau asserted: "It is all the more important for us that Germany recently also entered into the ranks of states with their own substantial cable networks."[62]

Germany's first goal was to cross the Atlantic. Felten und Guilleaume made a deal with the Commercial Cable Company: In exchange for landing rights in the United States and access to the Postal Telegraph Company's American network, the DAT would share the German–American traffic with Commercial Cable, avoiding their mutual enemies, the Anglo-American and the Western Union Telegraph companies. The DAT also obtained landing rights in the Azores from the Europe and Azores Telegraph Company in exchange for a contract to TC&M to lay the DAT's cable from Borkum to Horta in the Azores, and from there to Coney Island, New York. Thus, the Germans were able to use to their advantage the fierce competition that divided the rival American and British cartels. The new cable, completed on September 1, 1900, was so successful and received so much traffic that it had to be duplicated two years later. The German Atlantic cable of 1902 was the first to be manufactured and laid by Norddeutsche Seekabelwerke.[63]

In the North Atlantic, Germany benefitted from the goodwill of Portugal and of the Eastern group—not exactly a liberation from British hegemony. To escape the British in other parts of the world—in particular the Middle East, the Western Pacific, and the South Atlantic—Germany needed allies.

The first objective under the new telegraph policy was the Ottoman Empire, where Germany had growing interests. Communications with Turkey went by one of two ways, neither of them efficient or secure: by Russian land lines to Odessa, then by British cable to Constantinople; or across Austria, Serbia, and Bulgaria. In July 1899 Felten und Guilleaume founded the Osteuropäische Tele-graphengesellschaft and quickly obtained the right to lay a land line across Hungary and Rumania. For the next five years, it sought landing rights for a cable from Constantsa in Rumania to Constantinople, but encountered Turkish procrastination and British intrigues, for this was a part of the world where the British did not relish German interference. Only by threatening to interrupt the Indo-European Telegraph Company lines across Germany in 1905 did the Germans obtain the landing rights they wanted.[64]

But this was only a first step, as observers realized. In the 1890s, Germany had obtained railway concessions from Constantinople to Ankara and on to Bagdad, which the British and Russians found most upsetting. It was clear that Germany also aimed to run a telegraph line along the railway and on to the Persian Gulf. In 1903 Thomas Lenschau wrote: "Perhaps after the completion of the Bagdad Railway the opportunity will arise to continue the connection to the Persian Gulf and thereby obtain a shorter path to India."[65]

In 1908, Germany planned a cable from Basra on the Persian Gulf to Goa and on to Sumatra, but neither Portugal nor Turkey granted the necessary concession. Since their refusal was partly inspired by a fear of British displeasure, the German government approached Foreign Secretary Sir Edward Grey in 1913, asking for "a declaration from His Majesty's Government that they will not oppose in principle the landing of a cable at such a point," that is, the Persian Gulf. The response of the British was that "Sir E. Grey is advised that Germany has no great commercial need for a cable such as that described and he is accordingly led to the conclusion that the object of their request is political." Thus was Germany blocked from the Indian Ocean.[66]

Germany was more successful in the Far East and the Pacific, even though it arrived there late. In 1898 it acquired Tsingtao and Kiaochow Bay in China; in 1899 it bought the Carolinas, Marianas, and Palao from Spain; and in 1900 it obtained part of Samoa. Connections between Tsingtao and Shanghai through Chinese land lines, unsatisfactory in the best of times, were interrupted during the Boxer Re-bellion of 1900. The German government therefore had the Great Northern Com-pany lay a cable from Tsingtao to Chefoo and Shanghai, without Chinese authoriza-tion.[67] France, Britain, Russia, and Japan were doing similar and worse things to China at the time.

The new cable joined Tsingtao to Germany through either British or Russian telegraphs; at the time there was no choice. In the Pacific, however, Germany could look for assistance to the Americans and the Dutch.[68] Throughout the nineteenth century, the Netherlands had lived in the shadow of Britain, and not without misgiv-ings. According to telegraph historian Jorma Ahvenainen, "concern for the safe transmission of cables was also felt in Dutch government circles and the censorship practiced by the British during the Boer War had left the Dutch considerably ill at ease."[69] Evidently the Dutch, like the French and Germans, chafed at their depen-dence on Britain for communication with their main colony, the Netherlands East

Indies. When Emil Guilleaume approached the Dutch Telegraph Administration in 1900 about a joint cable project in the Pacific, he found a warm reception, culminating in a treaty signed in Berlin on July 24, 1901. Its purpose was to connect the Dutch East Indies and the German possessions in the Pacific to an eventual American Pacific cable.

When the American cable reached Manila in July 1903, the Dutch and Germans were ready. On July 19, Felten und Guilleaume founded a new subsidiary, the Deutsch–Niederländische Telegraphengesellschaft. The next year their cable-manufacturing subsidiary, the Norddeutsche Seekabelwerke, laid three cables from the German island of Yap: to Menado on Celebes, connecting with the Netherlands East Indies cable network; to Guam, connecting with the American Pacific cable; and to Shanghai, linked by cable to Kiaochow.

Germany and the Netherlands were now connected to their eastern colonies by non-British cables. This was an expensive form of reassurance, one for which the German government paid 1,525,000 Reichsmark or £76,250 a year, and the Dutch £18,750. Nor was it ever likely to pay for itself, since the agreements of July 26, 1904, with the Eastern Extension, Great Northern, and Commercial Pacific Cable companies stipulated that telegrams via America cost more than via India or Russia. This ensured that business traffic, which constituted nine-tenths of the world's long-distance telegrams, would inevitably avoid the new lines. But no matter, as Richard Hennig explained: "The new lines do not meet any requirement of business nor any requirement of peace, their purpose is much more an eminently strategic one, and just laying them constitutes a move against British cable policy."[70]

The other part of the world that interested Germany before World War I was South America. Thousands of Germans had emigrated to Brazil, Uruguay, Paraguay, and Argentina, 1.5 billion marks were invested there, and hundreds of ships traveled to and from Germany every year, making South America Germany's third trading partner after Europe and North America. Here a direct cable could be justified on commercial grounds. Unfortunately, Brazil and all the Portuguese islands on the way had granted exclusive concessions to the Western and the South American Telegraph companies. But Spain was willing to allow a cable landing at Tenerife in the Canary Islands, and Liberia one at Monrovia. That left Brazil. The concession for a cable from West Africa to Brazil belonged to the South American Telegraph Company, in other words the French government. The Deutsch–Südamerikanische, founded in 1908 by Felten und Guilleaume, asked the South American for permission to lay a cable from Monrovia to Pernambuco. On February 4 and March 25, 1910, France and Germany signed the agreements on the South Atlantic cables. The Norddeutsche Seekabelwerke laid a Liberia–Brazil cable the following year and a Liberia–Cameroon cable in 1913.[71]

The German motives were logical enough. As German trade with South America grew, so did its need to communicate. There was also a political motive associated with the emigration of thousands of Germans to Brazil and Argentina. Charles Lesage, professor at the Ecole des Sciences Politiques in Paris and France's foremost expert on the German cable industry, commented: "A manifestation, legitimate up to this point, of German imperialism, the execution of the submarine network is an episode in the general struggle going on for the past twenty years between Germany and England for predominance in the world."[72] An arrangement with France was the only way to achieve this goal.

But why did France allow it? Partly, no doubt, for business reasons: In exchange for the concession, Norddeutsche Seekabelwerke completed the French West African network between Conakry and Grand-Bassam for half a million francs, a fraction of its value.[73] But this was also a political undertaking, for it was accompanied by an agreement to connect France and Germany by a direct Emden–Brest cable. The French public learned about the cable agreements in October 1911, in the midst of the Second Moroccan Crisis, when a German cable ship sailed into Brest with the end of the cable from Emden. The agreements were therefore misunderstood, not only by the press but even by specialists. Charles Lesage interpreted the French motives in a negative way. It was clear that "Germany had, at times, the support of France in its struggle against the telegraphic dominance of England."[74] He quoted the German nationalist Max Roscher, who wrote: "The new communication . . . was a public demonstration of the rapprochement between Germany and France in cable matters. . . . [O]n the question of submarine cables, the interests of Germany run parallel to those of France."[75] Since relations between France and Germany were otherwise hostile, Lesage concluded: "The French Administration at the time entertained with the German telegraph interests relations which were considerably more cordial than those which were painfully being maintained between the Wilhelmstrasse and the Quai d'Orsay."[76] This situation, he believed, arose because of a flaw in the French political system:

> This prolonged disagreement between the general principles of French diplomacy and the procedures of its telegraphic policies come, I believe, from the fact that in this country, each ministry has its own foreign policy: the Ministry of Foreign Affairs has one, the Ministry of Finance has another. . . . The Postal and Telegraph Administration also has, from time to time, a foreign policy; and it so happened, these past few years, that, without being entirely hostile to England, it demonstrated a strong inclination for Germany.[77]

It was, in Lesage's opinion, bad enough that Germany took advantage of the French Telegraph Administration's indulgence in its fight with the British; but this indulgence created a serious misunderstanding in the minds of Chancellor von Bülow and Foreign Minister Bethmann-Hollweg, and "led Germany into error on the true nature of France's relations with England, that is they incited her to believe that the Franco-English Entente was not worth much."[78]

In fact, the cable agreement was not a misguided policy on the part of the Postal and Telegraph Administration, but a byproduct of the fluctuating Moroccan situation. During 1905 and 1906, French and German imperialist ambitions had collided in Morocco. Germany's willingness in 1909 to give up its designs on that country in exchange for a piece of equatorial Africa paved the way for the cable agreements of 1910 that reflected their common interests against the British.[79] The fact that the two countries were once again at loggerheads over Morocco a year later did not affect the outcome of these agreements.

Conclusion

Between the Boer War and World War I, the world witnessed a second cable boom, comparable in its extent to the boom of the 1870s, but with a different mix of motives and protagonists. This expansion corresponded to a boom in world trade, and many of the new cables—the German Atlantic cables and the American and British Pacific cables in particular—were profitable commercial ventures. Yet in addition to the economic motivation to communicate, every great power felt it needed its own communications for national security reasons. The British, though well represented, no longer had the game to themselves, but had to face competition from the United States, France, and Germany.

Cable rivalry began in the 1880s and accelerated sharply in the 1890s. The increase in world commerce alone would have stimulated the laying of new cables, but the crises of the turn of the century, especially the Boer War, convinced governments of the urgency of having their own cables. Telecommunications was no longer just a business or a public utility but had become one of the pillars of national security. Yet France and Germany could not simply build their own national cable networks parallel to that of Britain, for they lacked the necessary landing licenses, acquired long ago by the British under exclusive concessions. Thus rivalries in telecommunications were not merely a consequence of political and economic rivalries, but contributed to the atmosphere of tension and misunderstanding that was beginning to build up at the turn of the century.

Since that time, technologies of communication have come and gone, but their role in national security, hence in international insecurity, has not diminished.

Notes

1. On the Pacific cable, see George Johnson, ed., *The All-Red Line: The Annals and Aims of the Pacific Cable Project* (Ottawa, 1903).
2. J. Henniker Heaton, "The Postal and Telegraphic Communications of the Empire," *Proceedings of the Royal Colonial Institute* 19 (1887–1888), 171–221, and "Imperial Telegraph System: Cabling to India and Australia," *Contemporary Review* 63 (1893), 537–49. See also Robert J. Cain, "Telegraph Cables in the British Empire 1850–1900," (Ph.D. dissertation, Duke University, 1971), 232–40.
3. Letter from French Consul General Biard in Sydney to Minister of Foreign Affairs Develle, November 22, 1893, and note to Secrétaire d'Etat des Colonies, December 13, 1893, in Archives Nationales Section Outre-Mer (Paris) [henceforth ANSOM] Affaires Politiques 1554 dossier 10: "Création du câble transpacifique, 1892–94."
4. French chargé d'affaires in London to Foreign Minister Develle, October 23, 1893, and Develle to Colonial Minister Boulanger, April 3, 1894, ibid.
5. Quoted in Hugh Barty-King, *Girdle Round the Earth: The Story of Cable and Wireless and its Predecessors to Mark the Group's Jubilee, 1929–1979* (London, 1979), 93.
6. Audley Coote to Colonial Office, May 13, 1893, ibid.
7. Memorandum from Treasury to Colonial Office, February 3, 1897, in Public Record Office (Kew) [henceforth PRO], CO 42/850, cited in Cain, 257–58.
8. Cain, 255–56.

9. Cain, 235; Barty-King, 95; K. S. Inglis, "The Imperial Connection: Telegraphic Communication between England and Australia, 1872–1902," in *Australia and Britain: Studies in a Changing Relationship*, eds. A. F. Madden and W. H. Morris-Jones (London, 1980), 21–38.

10. Barty-King, 137–38.

11. Leslie B. Tribolet, *The International Aspects of Electrical Communications in the Pacific Area* (Baltimore, 1929), 161; W. D. Alexander, "The Story of the Trans-Pacific Cable," *Hawaii Historical Journal* 18 (January 1911), 57–60.

12. Memorandum from Chamberlain to Cabinet, February 1899, in PRO, Cab 37/49/15.

13. Barty-King, 116; Cain, 253–64.

14. Memoranda from Hicks Beach, March 3 and 30, 1899, in PRO Cab 37/49, Nos. 15 and 23; Cain, 267; P. M. Kennedy, "Imperial Cable Communications and Strategy, 1870–1914," *English Historical Review* 86 (1971), 735; Barty-King, 133–38; Robert Kubicek, personal communication, December 1989.

15. G. L. Lawford and R. L. Nicholson, *The Telcon Story, 1850, 1950* (London, 1950), 84; Cain, 227–28 and 270; Barty-King, 138; Maxime de Margerie, *Le réseau anglais de câbles sous-marins* (Paris, 1909), 159.

16. Tribolet, 165; Barty-King, 141–42.

17. Barty-King, 195.

18. Kennedy, 733.

19. "Telegraphic Censorship," 1–3 in PRO, WO 33/280; Memoranda from George Goschen, First Lord of the Admiralty, to Cabinet, June 7, 1899, in PRO, Cab 37/50/37, and March 12, 1900, in PRO, Cab 37/52/35; Margerie, 88.

20. "Telegraphic Censorship," 1–3; George Peel, "The Nerves of Empire," in *The Empire and the Century: A Series of Essays on Imperial Problems and Possibilities* (London, 1905), 270.

21. Memoranda on cables in China, 1899–1901, in PRO Cab 37/52 and 37/53.

22. Both reports are in PRO, Cab 18/16/5; censored versions were published in *Parliamentary Papers* (1902), XI [Cd. 1056].

23. Ibid., Second Report, 16.

24. Draft sent to the Foreign Office August 9, 1904, in PRO, FO 83/2196, Nos. 294ff.

25. "Censorship of Submarine Cables in Time of War. Action to be Taken by Her Majesty's Government and by Different Government Departments concerned. Prepared by the General Staff, War Office," in PRO, FO 83/2196, Nos. 387–427. A similar document is in Cab 17/92.

26. In PRO, Cab 17/92.

27. In PRO, Cab 16/14, p. 2.

28. Ibid., p. 14.

29. We will return to the subject of radio in a later chapter.

30. Jorma Ahvenainen, *The Far Eastern Telegraphs: The History of Telegraphic Communications between the Far East, Europe and America before the First World War* (Helsinki, 1981, 158–59; Tribolet, 156–58 and 168–69; Alexander, 50–57.

31. Ahvenainen, 160–65; Tribolet, 168–79.

32. Quoted in "An American Pacific Cable. A paper presented at the one hundred and thirty-eighth meeting of the American Institute of Electrical Engineers, New York, December 27, 1899, by George Owen Squier," in U.S. Senate, 56th Congress, 1st Session, Document No. 88 [hereafter Squier (1899)].

33. Quoted in Alexander, 68, and Tribolet, 180.

34. See documents Nos. 85–89 referred to the Committee on Naval Affairs (January 19,

1900) in U.S. Senate, 56th Congress, 1st Session, in particular Squier, "A United States Government Pacific Cable" (Document No. 89) [hereafter Squier (1900)].

35. Ahvenainen, 166–70; Alexander, 68–80; Tribolet, 181.

36. Alexander, 69–71.

37. Alvin F. Harlow, *Old Wires and New Waves: The History of the Telegraph, Telephone and Wireless* (New York and London, 1936), 429–30; Ahvenainen, 172–73 and 187–89; Tribolet, 182–91 and 242; "Pacific Cable," pamphlet in Cable and Wireless archives (London), 1558/6.

38. U.S. Congress, Senate, Committee on Interstate Commerce, *Cable-Landing Licenses: Hearings* (December 15, 1920 – January 11, 1921); U.S. Congress, House, Committee on Interstate and Foreign Commerce, *Cable-Landing Licenses: Hearings* (May 11–13, 1921); "Memorandum on ownership of Commercial Pacific Cable Company, October 1, 1904," Cable and Wireless, D/137; Tribolet, 83–84.

39. The agreements of July 26, 1904, will be found in the Cable and Wireless, 921, D97, D98, D101, D126, and D130. See also Ahvenainen, 178–83, and Artur Kunert, *Geschichte der deutschen Fernmeldekabel. II. Telegraphen-Seekabel* (Cologne–Mülheim, 1962), 318–25. This was of course the peak of the cartel era, when shipping conferences, sugar and oil trusts, and other monopolies were busy staking their claims to large parts of the world.

40. Tribolet, 190–91.

41. Ivan S. Coggeshall, "Annotated History of Submarine Cables and Overseas Radiotelegraphs 1851 to 1934. With Special Reference to the Western Union Company and with an Introduction dated 1984," manuscript written 1934, cited with permission of the author. Ivan Coggeshall was general traffic supervisor of the Western Union cables from 1927 to 1936 and assistant vice president from 1936 to 1959.

42. Charles Bright, "Imperial Telegraphs," *United Empire* 2 (August 1911): 551. See also his "Inter-Imperial Telegraphy," *Quarterly Review* 220 (1914): 134–51.

43. Margerie, 179–81 and 189–95.

44. Harry Alis (pseudonym for Henri Percher), *Journal des débats*, July 8, 14, 16, and 23, 1894.

45. "Société des Etudes Coloniales et Maritimes, Résolution" (1894), in ANSOM, Affaires Politiques 2554: Services Publics, Comunications, dossier 4: "Organisation des liaisons télégraphies des colonies, 1890/97."

46. J. Depelley, *Les câbles sous-marins et la défense de nos colonies. Conférence faite sous le patronage de l'Union coloniale française* (Paris, 1896), 5. For similar views also published before 1898, see Henri Bousquet, *La question des câbles sous-marins en France* (Paris, 1895), and Lazare Weiller, "La suppression des distances," *Revue des deux mondes* 148 (July 15, 1898), 396–423.

47. Minister of Posts and Telegraphs A. Millerand, "Rapport du ler mai 1900 au Président de la République française," *Journal officiel* (May 12, 1900), 2984–3013; see also "Rapport 1900" in France, archives of the Ministry of Posts and Telecommunications (Paris), No. 2996; Charles Lesage, *La rivalité anglo-germanique. Les câbles sous-marins allemands* (Paris, 1915), 134–36; Margerie, 38–39; Camille Guy, *Les colonies françaises*, Vol. 3: *La mise en valeur de notre domaine colonial* (Paris 1900), 559.

48. Among others: H. Casevitz, "La télégraphie sous-marine en France," Société des ingénieurs civils de France, *Mémoires et comptes-rendus des travaux* 53, No. 7 (April 1900), 365–82; Charles Cazalet, "Les câbles sous-marins nationaux," *Revue économique de Bordeaux* 12, No. 71 (March 1900), 41–51; J. Depelley, "Les câbles télégraphiques en temps de guerre," *Revue des deux mondes* (January 1, 1900), 181–95; Guy, op. cit.; Jacques

Haussmann, "La question des câbles," *Revue de Paris* 7, No. 6 (March 15, 1900), 251–77; Charles Lemire, *La défense nationale. La France et les câbles sous-marins avec nos possessions et les pays étrangers* (Paris, 1900).

49. Pierre Jouhannaud, *Les câbles sous-marins, leur protection en temps de paix et en temps de guerre* (Paris, 1904), 302; Margerie, 38–39.

50. Lesage, 122–54.

51. "The West African Telegraph Company Ltd., Agreements No. 2," Cable and Wireless, 1096; "Arrangement Relating to the Sale to the French Government of the Cables Serving the Stations of Conakry, Grand Bassam, Kotonou and Libreville" (February 10, 1902), ibid., 924/243; C. Bouerat, "Les débuts du Service des Postes et Telégraphes en Côte d'Ivoire (1880–1905)," *Bulletin de la Société internationale d'histoire postale* 19/20 (1972), 11–93; *Les postes et télégraphes en Afrique occidentale* (Corbeil, 1907), 99–100; Lesage, 86–87, 136–42, and 224–26.

52. Léon Mascart, "Le câble sous-marin Tourane-Amoy," *Revue générale des sciences* 13, No. 1 (January 15, 1902), 27–35; Conseil supérieur de l'Indochine, "Note sur la situation et le fonctionnement du service des Postes et Telégraphes en 1902," No. PB332, and "Câbles en Indochine," No. FO90 bis 4460, in archives of the Ministry of Posts and Telecommunications, PB332; A. Berbain (inspecteur des Postes et Télégraphes), *Note sur le service postal, télégraphique et téléphonique de l'Indochine* (Hanoi–Haiphong, 1923), 6; Lesage, 184–85 and 213–15.

53. Lesage, 199–202, 228, and 235; Thomas Lenschau, *Das Weltkabelnetz*, Angewandte Geographie. I. Serie. 1. Heft. 2. Auflage (Frankfurt, 1908), 64–66.

54. Philippe Bata, "Les câbles sous-marins des origines à 1929," *Télécommunications: Revue française des télécommunications* 45 (October 1982), 62–69.

55. See, for example, Alfred Gay, *Les câbles sous-marins*, 2 vols. (Paris, 1902–1903); Jouhannaud (1904); Margerie (1909); "Câbles sous-marins et défense nationale," *Revue de Paris* (December 15, 1910), 877–903; Léon Jacob, "Les intérêts français et les relations télégraphiques internationales," *Bureau des questions diplomatiques et coloniales* (1912); and Lesage (1915).

56. Kunert, 206 and 224.

57. Lesage, 32–39, 75, and 244–45; Kunert 203–206 and 224.

58. Lesage, 27–29 and 81; also private communication from Donard de Cogan.

59. Margerie, 38–39; Lesage, 75; Kunert, 246.

60. For a sampling of this literature, see Lenschau, *Weltkabelnetz*, 1st edition, (Halle, 1903); Hugo Thurn, *Die Seekabel unter besonderer Berücksichtigung der deutschen Seekabeltelegraphie. In technicher, handelswirtschaftlicher, verkehrspolitischer und strategischer Beziehung dargestellt* (Leipzig, 1909); August Röper, *Die Unterseekabel* (Leipzig, 1910); R. Hennig, "Die deutsche Seekabelpolitik zur Befreiung vom englischen Weltmonopol," *Meereskunde* 6, No. 4 (1912); Max Roscher, "Der Staat und die Seekabel," *Jahrbuch für Gesetzgebung* 36 (1912), 1741–65.

61. Hennig, 5–6.

62. Lenschau, 72.

63. Kenneth R. Haigh, *Cableships and Submarine Cables* (London and Washington, 1968), 328–9; Lesage, 63–78; Kunert, 228–53; Lenschau, 19–20 and 50–52.

64. Kunert, 292–301; Lesage, 237–39.

65. Lenschau, 13–14.

66. "Germany: Telegraphic Communication with China, 1912–1913," in PRO, Cab 17/75; "History of telegraphic communications with India (1858–1872) and an account of Joint Purse from 1874" (1897), British Post Office archives (London), POST 83/56.

67. Kunert, 306–13.

68. On the German and Dutch cables in the Pacific, see Ahvenainen, 175–84; R. Hennig, "Die deutsche–niederländische Telegraphenallianz im Fernen Osten," *Grenzboten* 65 (April–June 1906), 289–93; Kunert, 319–36; Lenschau, 12–13 and 64–65; Lesage, 193–205; Günther Meyer, "German Interests and Policy in the Netherlands East Indies and Malaya, 1870–1914," in *Germany in the Pacific and Far East, 1870–1914*, eds. John A. Moses and Paul M. Kennedy (St. Lucia, Queensland, 1977), 45; and Peel, 278–79.

69. Ahvenainen, 1975.

70. Hennig, "Telegraphenallianz," 291–92.

71. Kunert, 261–74; Lesage, 101–22 and 155–60.

72. Lesage, 247–50.

73. Kunert, 270–71 and 345.

74. Lesage, xi.

75. Max Roscher, *Deutsche Erde* (1912), 6–7, quoted in Lesage, 86–88.

76. Lesage, 84–85.

77. Ibid., 257–58.

78. Ibid., xi–xv.

79. Jean-Claude Allain, *Agadir 1911: Une crise impérialiste en Europe pour la conquête du Maroc* (Paris, 1976), 133–35 and *Joseph Caillaux et la Seconde Crise Marocaine* (Lille, 1975), 2:1246–48. I am indebted to Professor Allain for clarifying the mystery of the Franco-German cable agreement of 1910.

7

The Beginnings of Radio, 1895–1914

The telegraph, appearing in an era of peace, was long thought to be peaceful by nature; it did not become an object of dissension until the turn of the century, when nations turned antagonistic for other reasons. The radio, in contrast, was born into a world of jittery jingoism and started life as a weapon in the commercial and military rivalries of the great powers. Thus do humans unfairly project their own virtues and vices upon the machines they create.

Two characteristics of radiotelegraphy (or wireless as it was then known) were apparent from the start. It could communicate with ships and other vehicles that had been incommunicado in the age of the telegraph, and it sprayed its messages in all directions and crossed national boundaries with impunity, making it far less secure than cables.

For many years, radiotelegraphy was seen as a potential rival of telegraphs and cables. It was much slower and less reliable than wire telegraphy, but its inferiority was simply due to newness; less than thirty years after its birth, it had become as fast and reliable as cables, and considerably cheaper. It also offered the promise, experimentally demonstrated in 1915, of carrying voices across the oceans, something cables could not do until 1956. In both its military and civilian guises, it was perceived as a means to further national ambitions and thwart other nations, but also as a dangerous interloper.

Thus the wireless was never simply a substitute for cables, but meshed with the cable networks in complicated calculations of economic costs and benefits and military risks and opportunities. The history of radio cannot be told simply in terms of devices, inventors, and manufacturers, but must be integrated with the history of political power and information.

116

Marconi and the Birth of Wireless Telegraphy, 1895-1899

Guglielmo Marconi did not invent radio all by himself. His contribution consisted in putting together pieces attributed to other men—Hertz's spark, Branly's coherer, Popov's antenna, Lodge's tuning circuit—thereby creating a device that not only sent and received electromagnetic waves, but used them to transmit information in the Morse code. Moreover—and in this he was unique among the many inventors of radio technology—he was a skilled and energetic entrepreneur backed by a wealthy family and shrewd advisers.[1]

Born of an Italian father and an Anglo-Irish mother, Marconi grew up and performed his first experiments in Italy. As soon as he thought his device was ready to demonstrate, he approached the Italian Ministry of Posts and Telegraphs, but was politely rebuffed. He and his mother then decided to move to London. Guglielmo, an avid sailor, recognized the potential of wireless for marine communications, and Great Britain was obviously where the customers were to be found. Furthermore, Annie Marconi, daughter of the Jamesons, purveyors of fine whiskeys, knew her son would receive the help he needed in starting his new enterprise.

Soon after their arrival in early 1896, Guglielmo was introduced to William Preece, chief engineer of the Post Office and one of Britain's foremost authorities on the telegraph. Preece had been working for some years on a form of wireless telegraphy using electromagnetic induction, but his experiments had reached a dead end, and he was willing to give Marconi the publicity he needed for his experiments. At Salisbury Plain in September 1896 and March 1897, Marconi convinced all witnesses that his was indeed the first true system of wireless telegraphy.

Reactions were mixed, however. Preece was angry when Marconi formed a company, the Wireless Telegraph and Signal Company, instead of giving the benefit of his invention to the Post Office, which had supported his demonstrations; for years thereafter the Post Office was to be one of Marconi's major antagonists, and refused to purchase his equipment.

Yet Marconi also made a friend at Salisbury Plain. Captain Henry Jackson, commander of the Royal Navy's torpedo school at Plymouth, had been experimenting with Hertzian waves but admitted that his apparatus, which only reached a distance of 3 miles, compared poorly to Marconi's 4½ miles. Throughout Jackson's distinguished career—he rose to First Sea Lord in 1916—he always maintained good relations with Marconi and, most important of all, made the Admiralty Marconi's first and best customer.

Soon after the success at Salisbury Plain, Marconi proved that he was as gifted at public relations as he was at technology. In the summer of 1898 he reported the Kingstown yacht races for the Dublin *Daily Express* and installed a wireless set on the royal yacht, which allowed Queen Victoria to communicate with the Prince of Wales. He demonstrated his equipment to the Italian and French navies; the French were noncommittal, but the Italians immediately ordered the Marconi apparatus.[2] This bestirred the Admiralty to install Marconi sets on ships that were to participate in the Naval Maneuvers of 1899; the results were so impressive that the First Lord of the Admiralty, George Goschen, congratulated Marconi "on having brought his invention to its present state of perfection."[3]

Marconi's first customer, it turned out, was the British War Office, then engaged in the Boer War, which shipped five Marconi sets to South Africa along with Marconi-trained operators. There storms created too much static and tore down the antennas, and the army finally handed over the sets to a Royal Navy squadron at Delagoa Bay, where they worked much better. This experience convinced the Admiralty of the value of wireless. In July 1900, after difficult negotiations in which Captain Jackson came to Marconi's defense against the Treasury and the Post Office, the Admiralty ordered six coastal and twenty-six ship's sets from Marconi at a cost of £3,200 apiece plus an annual royalty of £3,200. A year later, it ordered another fifty sets to equip all battleships and cruisers on the Home, Mediterranean, and China stations, and in 1903 it made Marconi's its sole supplier of wireless equipment for the next eleven years.[4]

Thus did Marconi acquire his two best customers, the British and Italian navies. It was no coincidence that Britain's chief rivals, France and Germany, did not follow suit. The French navy hesitated, waiting for a French Marconi to appear. The Germans reacted more energetically. Professor Adolf Slaby of the Charlottenburg Technical Institute near Berlin, who had witnessed Marconi's experiments at Salisbury Plain as a guest of Preece, went home to perform some experiments on his own. With the support of the giant Allgemeine Elektrizitäts-Gesellschaft (AEG), Slaby and Count von Arco developed a rival system that avoided infringing on Marconi's patents. Simultaneously, Professor Braun of Strasbourg produced another system that separated the spark and antenna circuits, and demonstrated it to the German navy at Cuxhaven in 1899; his experiments were backed by Siemens und Halske, manufacturers of telegraph and electrical equipment. The contrast with the inertia or hostility of the British electrical equipment firms (TC&M, Ediswan) is most revealing; from the very beginning, German radio was adopted by major corporations, with the approval of the state.[5]

Marconi's early successes and failures corresponded logically to the alignment of powers at the turn of the century. One potential customer, however, was still uncertain: the United States. After the Kingstown yacht races, the *New York Herald* invited Marconi to report on the America's Cup races. In September 1899 he sailed for New York, where he was welcomed by Captain George Squier, a personal friend. He also showed his apparatus to four officers of the U.S. Navy's Bureau of Equipment, and reluctantly allowed them to test his equipment on board the battleship *Massachusetts* and the cruiser *New York*. The Navy wanted to test several sets transmitting simultaneously. Marconi knew that they would interfere with one another because they lacked tuning circuits, for which he had not yet obtained a patent. He warned the officers that the equipment he had brought to America was incomplete. Admiral R. B. Bradford, chief of the Bureau of Engineering, nonetheless recommended that the Navy should buy Marconi equipment. But the Navy decided not to, in part because of the interference problem, but also because of Marconi's exacting conditions: He would only sell twenty sets for $20,000 plus another $10,000 a year in royalties.

Behind this refusal lay other reasons. The U.S. Navy was run by elderly officers hostile to the fast pace of technological change that was being foisted upon them. Inventors threatened the stability of their institution, and foreigners were worse yet.

Besides, in June 1899 General Greely reported that the Army Signal Corps had achieved a range of twelve miles; it was only a matter of time before America would have its own wireless system. In the meanwhile, a bit of procrastination was not unreasonable. It later proved to be critical to the future of radio and to the fate of the Marconi enterprise.[6]

The Marconi Monopoly and the Reaction of the Powers, 1900–1906

Marconi, never modest in his ambitions, wished to claim the electromagnetic spectrum as his private domain and create, in radio communications, a company as powerful as the Eastern group in cables. To achieve this goal, Marconi realized his firm had to do more than manufacture radio sets for sale to others; it had to enter the communications business. He was prevented from offering a radiotelegraph service within Britain by the Post Office monopoly on internal communications. Outside Britain, however, the field was open to private enterprise. In April 1900 he founded Marconi's International Marine Communication Company to operate ship and shore stations using Marconi equipment and employees. It soon acquired important customers, including the Cunard, P & O, White Star, Hamburg-Amerika, North German Lloyd, Compagnie Transatlantique, and Canadian Beaver lines. Most important of all, the Lloyd's marine insurance conglomerate leased sets and operators from Marconi's Marine. Marconi, who owned the sets, instituted a policy of nonintercommunication. Any ship that wished to communicate with Lloyd's worldwide marine intelligence network or with a Marconi-equipped ship or shore station—and these were the majority—had to agree to Marconi's terms. This was the keystone of his monopolistic scheme.[7]

Needless to say, not everyone was delighted with such a policy. Within Britain, Postmaster General the Marquess of Salisbury, First Lord of the Admiralty Lord Selborne, and the president of the Board of Trade, G. W. Balfour, discussed the idea of a State monopoly of international radiotelegraph communications. Lord Selborne even proposed to the Cabinet that the Post Office and Lloyd's take over international and marine wireless, respectively, leaving Marconi's to manufacture equipment, but nothing came of his suggestion.[8]

Foreigners were more emphatic. In early 1902 the Germans experienced the effects of the Marconi monopoly when Prince Heinrich, brother of the Kaiser, traveled to the United States on a Marconi-equipped ship, the *Kronprinz Wilhelm,* which had a large radio traffic. He returned to Germany on the *Deutschland,* which could not communicate with any Marconi station off New York or in the English Channel because it was equipped with a Slaby–Arco set. According to Marconi's biographer, W. P. Jolly, "the Germans considered that this was a deliberate slight to their Emperor's brother, while the Marconi Company maintained that they would certainly have communicated with the *Deutschland* if they had been asked."[9] The official biographer of the Marconi Company, W. J. Baker, offers an even more ingenuous explanation:

> Those [Marconi] stations had received specific orders to reply to any transmission from the German vessel because of the distinguished passenger she carried. . . . Although at

this distance of time it is impossible to establish the truth of the matter, there is no doubt that at that time the German equipment was not proving particularly successful and it is likely that on that run the *Deutschland*'s wireless was either partially or wholly out of action because of a technical fault.[10]

Whether or not Marconi stations made exceptions in the case of traveling princes was of course irrelevant, for the incident demonstrated to everyone the power of Marconi's to choose its correspondents.

The incident had immediate political repercussions. The German government ordered German stations to use only Slaby–Arco sets. In May 1903 it encouraged the two rival German firms, Slaby–Arco-AEG and Braun–Siemens–Halske, to merge and form the Gesellschaft für drahtlose Telegraphie, better known as Tele-funken. And that summer it invited Britain, France, Spain, Austria, Russia, Italy, and the United States to the first International Radiotelegraph Conference, held in Berlin August 4–13. There the German government proposed that "Radiotelegrams coming from and sent to ships shall be received and transmitted without regard to the system employed." Marconi's Wireless responded with a press campaign depicting the conference as an attack by Germany on a British industry. All the participants except Britain and Italy attacked Marconi's nonintercommunication policy. In the end, the participants decided that the technology was too new to be regulated, and the conference only passed resolutions, not a draft treaty. Britain simply ignored these resolutions.[11]

Despite this apparent victory for Marconi's, the British government was in fact vacillating on the issue. As always, the opposition to Marconi's was led by the Post Office. In March 1904 Postmaster General the Earl of Stanley recommended to the Cabinet that the government license all radiotelegraph stations and bring Great Britain into closer agreement with other governments.[12] Part of this plan became law in the Wireless Telegraphy Act of January 1, 1905, which gave the Post Office the power to grant licenses to all radio stations. The Post Office gave Marconi's an eight-year license for its shore stations, but then bought them in 1909.[13]

That did not settle the issue of nonintercommunication, however. In late 1906 Germany called a second International Wireless Conference at Berlin with the same agenda as the first. Again, Britain supported the Marconi policy, while the United Stated led the opposition. Of the thirty nations that attended, twenty-seven signed the resulting draft treaty, twenty-one of them voting in favor of free marine inter-communication, with Britain, Italy, Japan, Mexico, Portugal, and Persia opposed.

Another important issue was discussed, namely the allocation of the spectrum, which was becoming crowded, especially in Europe. By now there were so many transmitters operating at once that, despite tuning circuits, they were interfering with one another, and international cooperation was urgently required to prevent chaos on the air. Germany, supported by the United States, proposed reserving the longer waves (600–1,600 meters) for government and military uses, relegating companies like Marconi's to the shorter 300–600-meter waves where long distances were impossible.

The requirements of technology and international trade forced compromises on all the participants. In exchange for giving up the right of nonintercommunication, Britain preserved the longer waves for commercial uses. The participants signed the

Convention for the Regulation of Wireless Telegraphy on November 3, 1906, to come into force on July 1, 1908.[14]

In early 1907 it came up for ratification before the House of Commons. Postmaster General Sydney Buxton and First Lord of the Admiralty Lord Tweedmouth supported ratification, as did the Select Committee of the House of Commons to Inquire into the Convention on Wireless Telegraphy. An alternative report by a member of the Select Committee, Arthur Lee, opposed the convention on the grounds that it protected the spark system against competition from the more modern continuous-wave transmitters. There was opposition in the press as well; the influential *Edinburgh Review,* for instance, carried a long article objecting to Marconi's press campaigns and the falsehoods put before the House of Commons.[15] In July 1907, Parliament ratified the convention by a single vote and only after agreeing to subsidize Marconi's Wireless for three years as compensation for lost business.[16]

Though the American delegation had adamantly opposed the British position at the conference, it did not have much support back home. In the United States, popular and Congressional sentiment saw radio as a miracle of free enterprise and opposed regulation of any kind. Congress did cause a huge increase in the demand for radios in 1910 when it required sets on all ships carrying over fifty people; the Senate, however, did not ratify the convention until 1912.[17]

Technological Change and Commercial Rivalries, 1900–1907

Despite the setback, Marconi's Wireless Company had achieved a position of dominance in radio thanks to two markets: the Royal Navy and commercial marine service in the Atlantic and off the east coast of North America. Yet Marconi had a greater goal: to communicate across the Atlantic and compete with the cable companies. This goal eluded him for many years.

Marconi was given to making extravagant promises, which he later fulfilled to the astonishment of the world. In 1900 he promised to communicate by wireless across the Atlantic. Toward this end, he acquired land at Poldhu in Cornwall and installed a twenty-five-kilowatt set transmitting at 366 meters. He then traveled to St. John's, Newfoundland. In December 1901, he claimed to have picked out the letter S (three dots in Morse) over the background static. If his account is true (no one else was there to corroborate it), it was a remarkable technical achievement, but still far from commercially viable.

As always, Marconi had friends and enemies. The press either lionized him as a "genius," or vilified him for making a claim he could not prove to others. The Admiralty was interested in a system they hoped would allow them, should an emergency arise, to broadcast an order to all their ships in the North Atlantic at once. The cable companies, which until then had ignored radio in the hope that it would go away, reacted angrily. The Anglo-American Telegraph Company threatened to sue Marconi's Wireless, claiming a monopoly on all communications with Newfoundland. Marconi, with the air of a martyr, moved his equipment to Glace Bay, Nova Scotia.[18]

From 1901 to 1904 Marconi made repeated attempts to signal across the Atlantic, changing the position and shape of the antennas, the wavelength, and various elements in the apparatus itself. What these experiments proved, given the current knowledge of radio waves, was that a regular reliable transatlantic service would require much longer waves and more power. In 1905 he began construction of a huge station at Clifden in Ireland, and ordered a radical increase in the size of the Glace Bay installation. Commercial service finally opened in October 1907. It charged half the cable rate, but was plagued by electrical interference and poor transmission, especially during the day.[19] While transatlantic communications were still not flawless, Marconi's did provide service to ships all the way across the ocean.

In his obsessive determination to communicate across the Atlantic, Marconi brought the technology of spark transmission to its highest development, and, in so doing, he neglected two other directions in which radio technology was moving: continuous wave and shortwave. Scientists like Hertz, Righi, and Lodge, who had studied electromagnetic waves before Marconi, were fascinated to discover that waves could be refracted and reflected, proving that radio and light waves were variations of the same phenomenon. But this only held true for the shorter wavelengths. Marconi, who was interested in communication rather than in physics, discovered by trial and error that longer waves carried further. While waves in the meter range were reflected, refracted, or absorbed by objects in their path, long waves, those measured in kilometers, flowed around obstacles, even around the curvature of the earth. Marconi's aim, from the start, was to communicate over ever greater distances, and this meant producing ever longer waves. This in turn required huge antennas and vast amounts of power. A typical Marconi long-range station cost £60,000 to build, of which £32,000 went for the thirty 100-meter-high antenna masts. For over twenty years and at enormous cost, Marconi led radio in the direction of long-distance telegraphy. In 1927, after amateurs with low-power equipment had shown that short waves reflected off the ionosphere could be received across oceans and continents, Marconi looked back over his life's work and said: "I admit that I am responsible for the adopting of long waves for long-distance communication. Everyone followed me in building stations hundreds of times more powerful than would have been necessary had short waves been used. Now I have realized my mistake. . . ."[20]

Marconi's solutions after 1900, while not innovative, were nonetheless practical and based on extensive experimentation. Thus, in his receivers, he replaced the erratic coherer of the turn of the century with a more sensitive magnetic detector and finally with Fleming's valve. In the transmitter, he moved away from the staccato sparks of the early sets, so easy to confuse with the crackling of atmospheric static, towards the "musical frequency" produced by a disk discharger, which emitted a shrill whistle broken into dots and dashes. The musical note was not unique to Marconi but was used by every transmitter, thus allowing them to intercommunicate. Better yet, it permitted reception through earphones, which was faster than the paper tape used by the telegraphs.

The years 1900–1907 also saw the emergence of serious rivals to Marconi's dominance. The first of these were the Germans, who had nationalistic as well as commercial reasons to challenge anything British. In May 1903, as we have seen, the German government forced the creation of Telefunken and gave it every sort of encouragement, from military orders to patent protection. Telefunken immediately sought technological advances and foreign customers. It introduced the quenched spark, a musical-frequency transmitter, one of the first electrolytic detectors for receivers, and an alternator that produced a true continuous wave. It was also engaged in a race with de Forest in America and Fleming in Britain to develop tubes. Telefunken acquired the patent for the von Lieben receiver tube in 1911, and claimed to have developed the first transmitter tube two years later.[21]

Like Marconi, Telefunken was eager to achieve record-breaking distances. The German government realized that its overseas cable connections were vulnerable to British interference in the event of war, and that its communications with America and its African colonies would depend on radiotelegraphy. To reach that far, Telefunken began building a giant station at Nauen, near Berlin, in 1906.[22] It also specialized in mobile radio sets for army use, which were used in the Herero War of 1904 and in the Russo-Japanese War of 1904–1905. Finally, Telefunken aimed at foreign markets such as the United States, Latin America, and the Netherlands East Indies, where an alternative to Marconi's was as much appreciated as the quality of German manufactures.[23] It did not do so well in Marconi's special field, marine communications. This was less the fault of the equipment itself, as of a quirk of fate In the Russo-Japanese War, the Russian navy used Telefunken, while the Japanese had Marconi sets. At the Battle of Tsushima (May 27–28, 1905), the Japanese used radio much more skillfully than did the Russians, thus consolidating Marconi's reputation in naval circles.[24]

France had fallen far behind Britain, Germany, and the United States in the field of radio, and was a long time catching up. In 1897, when Eugène Ducretet, manufacturer of scientific apparatus, heard of Marconi's demonstration to the Italian navy at La Spezzia, he built a transmitter and a receiver with which he communicated over a distance of four hundred meters. A year later he was able to send a message from the Eiffel Tower to the Pantheon, four kilometers apart. Though it aroused much popular interest, there was no institutional setting for further research. Before World War I France had many small telephone and telegraph equipment manufacturers, none large enough to finance research. Nor were there any links, as in Germany, between industry and the universities, or between government and industry. The largest manufacturer, Société Industrielle des Téléphones, had a small laboratory where investors could come and demonstrate their inventions. This system had served well enough in the days of the telegraph, but was insufficient for the more complex and expensive field of radio.[25]

Nonetheless, the French performed some interesting experiments. In 1901 the Ministry of Colonies sent postal and telegraph inspector L. Magne to Africa to try out radio in the hot dry climate of Senegal and in the hot humid climate of Gabon and the French Congo. Communicating in Gabon was a difficult challenge, because of the constant electrical storms that drowned out the reception of spark transmissions, and Magne was only able to cover a distance of thirty-five kilometers. The following year, a more urgent crisis took Magne and Captain Gustave Ferrié of the army engineers to the Caribbean. When the volcano Mont Pelé erupted on the island of Martinique, it cut all cables. In the midst of the chaos Ferrié was able to establish communications with Magne on the island of Guadeloupe, the nearest cable landing point.[26] It was the beginning of research in tropical communications, which was of special interest in French colonial circles.

The U.S. Navy and Radio to 1908

In radio technology, as in many other fields, the United States was fast becoming a center of innovation and industry in the first decade of this century. In contrast to Germany, where inventors, industry, and government cooperated, the early history of radio in the United States was one of conflicts and rivalries among inventors, corporations, and the Navy.[27]

Numerous American inventors turned their attention to radio from the late 1890s on. Reginald Fessenden and Ernst Alexanderson were the first to design transmitters that would generate continuous waves. Lee De Forest invented the *audion,* an early version of the vacuum tube. Cyril Elwell built arc transmitters for the Federal Telegraph Company, which dominated marine communications on the West Coast and in the Pacific. Several other companies also got a foothold in American radio: Tropical Radio, a subsidiary of the United Fruit Company, which operated a marine radio service in the Caribbean and Central America; United Wireless, which operated ship and shore radio stations from 1906 to 1911; and, finally, American Marconi, founded by Marconi in 1902 to exploit his patents in the United States.

The U.S. Navy played an important but ambiguous role in the early history of American radio. A few officers saw radio not only as an important element in fleet operations but also as a means of expanding the role of the Navy into new spheres. At the same time, the leadership of the Navy hesitated to commit itself.

Before 1908, the two officers most interested in marine radio were Commander Barber and Admiral Bradford. Barber, retired and living in Europe, investigated various systems: the French Rochefort and Ducretet, the German Slaby–Arco and Braun–Siemens–Halske, and Marconi's. He particularly disliked Marconi's for its nonintercommunication policy. In December 1901, he wrote Bradford: "Such a monopoly will be worse than the English submarine cable monopolies which all of Europe is groaning under and I hope the Navy Department of the U.S. will not be caught in its meshes."[28]

In 1902 the Navy bought two sets each from Ducretet, Rochefort, Slaby–Arco, Braun, and De Forest. The next year it bought another twenty Slaby–Arco sets. Although radios were installed on several ships, they were seldom used, for the officers refused to change their ways. Until 1907, American warships at sea operated on their own as commerce raiders rather than in fleets, and officers saw radio as a threat to their freedom of action; as one historian of naval radio explained:

> The traditional power of a commanding officer to do as he felt best with his ship or command as soon as he got out of sight of land would have been completely wiped out if someone in the Bureau of Navigation or elsewhere could give him orders. So often the instructions to the wireless room were to shut down the wireless and not acknowledge calls from shore at all.[29]

If the Navy did not use radio to control its ships, this did not prevent it from trying to monopolize the new technology. Officers like Bradford and Barber shared the views of military men in Europe and put the interests of the armed forces and the government ahead of those of the private sector. In June 1904 President Theodore Roosevelt, dismayed at the squabbling over radio between the U.S. Navy, the Weather Bureau, and the Signal Corps, appointed an Interdepartmental Board of Wireless Telegraphy, which recommended that the Navy operate all coastal stations and provide free commercial ship-to-shore service. This was a blatant attack on private enterprise, not only on the American Marconi marine network but also on the various other companies then operating in the United States. Protests in the press prevented the Navy from establishing a monopoly. But already the battle lines were drawn between the Navy, the American Marconi Company, and the other private firms.[30]

The Continuous Wave, 1908–1914

Whatever modus vivendi might have come about between the contending parties was upset, again and again, by technological innovations. The most important of these, in the years before 1914, was the continuous wave. Spark transmitters, like lightning, produced not one but many electromagnetic waves of varying frequency and intensity, which caused a loud crackle in the receiver. Even advanced equipment, such as Marconi's disk discharger and Telefunken's quenched spark, merely produced a chain of sparks that were shorter and more frequent, thus sounding like a sharp whistle. These devices had two disadvantages: They took up a large slice of the spectrum, which was increasingly objectionable as the number of stations multiplied; and they could only transmit dots and dashes, not voice or music.

Reginald Fessenden, who worked at one time for the Weather Bureau and later for his own firm, the National Electrical Signaling Company, or NESCO, was probably the first person to envision a transmitter that could generate a pure continuous wave at one precise frequency. After much experimentation, he developed one of the three devices capable of producing such waves: the high-speed alternator. To produce very long waves for long-distance communication required an alternator turning at previously unheard-of speeds: for 6,000-meter waves the alternator had to rotate 50,000 times per second. Before 1911, only the General Electric Company, manufacturers of electric generators, could create such a machine, and then only thanks to the engineering genius of Ernst Alexanderson. Fessenden was the only customer for this machine, and GE the only supplier.[31]

This is not to say that there were no other alternators. Indeed, several European inventors, in particular von Arco, Goldschmidt, Latour, and Bethenod, built alternators that turned more slowly but multiplied the resulting frequency.[32] While not as good as Alexanderson's, they were all a step ahead of the spark transmitters that had dominated the field until 1910.

Another method of producing continuous waves was the electric arc, similar to the powerful arc lights used in public places. The original patent was held by the Dane Valdemar Poulsen. In 1909 Cyril Elwell, an Australian who had studied at

Stanford University, bought the rights to the arc for the United States and its territories and possessions. In 1911 he founded the Federal Telegraph Company with the intention of establishing a chain of stations from California to the Philippines. By January 1914 he had installed giant 100-kilowatt transmitters in San Francisco and Honolulu, which provided day and night service over the longest stretch of ocean anywhere at the time.[33]

A third method of producing continuous waves was the vacuum tube. It was a descendant of Lee De Forest's audion, improved by a third electrode and a higher vacuum. These developments, and the application of the tube to generating radio waves, were to await further research during the war.[34]

Continuous-wave transmitters did not replace the obsolescent spark machines until after World War I, because of the large investments in the older technology. In particular, continuous-wave transmissions could only be received with a heterodyne circuit, another Fessenden invention. More important, Marconi's Wireless, which had been so successful with spark, showed no interest in continuous wave until 1913; soon thereafter the war forced them to turn from research in long-distance wireless to manufacturing sets for the military.[35]

While Marconi's was no longer a technological pioneer, it achieved its goals through commercial power, a forerunner of the giant corporations that were to take over the field of radio during and after World War I. Until 1911, the company had refrained from suing for patent infringement, partly because its own position vis-à-vis Oliver Lodge's 1897 tuning patent was somewhat dubious. In 1910, however, Godfrey Isaacs, an expert financier and legal mind, became managing director of Marconi's Wireless, and the following year he decided to attack the company's rivals. He acquired Lodge's patent, giving the company a solid legal base. American Marconi then sued the United Wireless Company for patent infringement, won the suit, and thereby acquired United's assets, including seventy shore stations and several hundred shipboard sets. It then went after NESCO, putting it out of business. From 1912 to 1917 American Marconi had almost total control over American marine radio and handled much of the international press and commercial traffic as well. Its only rivals were Federal Telegraph in the West, Tropical Radio in the Caribbean, and two stations on the East Coast built to communicate with Europe: Telefunken's station at Sayville, New York, and a transmitter at Tuckerton, New Jersey, built by a German firm for the French Compagnie Universelle de Télégraphie et Téléphonie Sans Fil.[36] From a commercial point of view, what American Marconi had achieved was no different from what it had done in Britain or what RCA was to do later in the United States. The difference was that the nationalistic officers of the U.S. Navy perceived American Marconi as a foreign firm and an agent of British imperialism, and thus an enemy.

Until 1912 the Navy showed little interest in using radio on warships, while asserting grandiose claims to the technology everywhere else. After 1912, Secretary of the Navy Josephus Daniels fought to gain a complete monopoly of radio in America and almost succeeded. The Radio Act of 1912 required the Navy to increase its radio activities and to exchange messages with ships if there was no commercial station within a hundred miles. Congress also appropriated funds for a high-powered station at Arlington, Virginia, the first of a chain designed to keep the

Navy Department in communication with all its ships at sea. While this station was equipped with a rotary spark transmitter designed by Reginald Fessenden, the Navy also allowed Elwell to demonstrate a thirty-kilowatt arc transmitter. The results were so remarkable that the Navy ordered Federal arc transmitters for Darien (Canal Zone), Cavite (Philippines), Pearl Harbor, San Diego, El Cayey (Puerto Rico), Guam, and Samoa. After a decade of procrastination, the Navy jumped into the radio age with enthusiasm; as Hugh Aitken points out:

> This network far surpassed in coverage anything the British or any other government could claim and, because of the Navy's early and decisive commitment to continuous wave operation, functioned at a level of technical efficiency markedly superior to that of the Marconi or any other private system.[37]

The Navy also began incorporating radio into the procedures and tactics of the fleet, thanks to the efforts of Lieutenant Stanford C. Hooper. In 1912 Hooper became the first fleet radio officer, developed a tactical signaling code, and groomed a cadre of ensigns to become radio officers on ships in place of the enlisted men to whom the device had previously been entrusted. After maneuvers in 1913 proved that a fleet could signal by radio better than with flags, the radio finally began to be used in ways long familiar to the British, German, and Japanese navies.[38]

It is astonishing, in a country that prided itself on its technical ingenuity and great inventors, how poorly the pioneers of American radio fared. Fessenden, who lost his company to Marconi's in 1911, abandoned the field entirely. Elwell was bought out by the Navy and moved to Britain. De Forest, like many inventors, suffered a string of failures and lawsuits. By 1910 America had entered the era of corporate technology, much of it obtained through lawsuits and chicanery rather than honest research. Thus Fessenden saw one of his inventions, the electrolytic detector, copied by other companies for the Navy, which denied any moral obligation to respect patents if the price was too high.[39] In early 1913 De Forest sold his rights to the audion through an attorney who secretly represented the American Telephone and Telegraph Company.[40]

From an international perspective, the years 1911–1914 marked the emergence of the United States as a full-fledged challenger to Britain and Germany in the field of radiotelegraphy. Marconi's dominance of the industry was not to last; already by 1914 the U.S. Navy and the corporations (Federal Telegraph, GE, AT&T) were preparing to squeeze his company out of the United States.

French Colonial Wireless, 1908–1914

By 1908, France had fallen far behind Britain and Germany in radio technology. Until 1907, instrument makers like Eugène Ducretet made radio parts for military and amateur builders.[41] That year the government set up a technical commission on wireless telegraphy to coordinate policy. At the suggestion of Captain Ferrié, three small manufacturers of radio parts merged to form the Compagnie Genérale de Radiotélégraphie, which supplied the army, while the navy and merchant marine were equipped with Marconi sets.[42]

Meanwhile experiments continued. Minister of War de Freycinet, who had been following Marconi's work, assigned the task of radio experimentation to Captain Ferrié. During the French campaign in Morocco in 1907, Ferrié transmitted from the Eiffel Tower in Paris to Casablanca, two thousand kilometers away[43]; compared with Marconi's commercial transatlantic service, it was a small achievement.

In France, there was little interest in radio technology outside military circles because communications were a state monopoly and France had an excellent telegraph network and a conservative postal and telegraphic administration. But there had always been a crying need for better communications in the colonial empire, especially in equatorial Africa and Indochina, where the telegraphs were unsatisfactory. It is there that French radio developed.

Indochina offered interesting opportunities for radio. The large population, important business interests, and occasional frontier fighting created a strong demand that neither the coastal cables nor the vulnerable land lines could meet. In 1904 Captain Péri, head of the military telegraphic service, built three one-kilowatt wireless sets that he placed at Hanoi, Kien-An on the northern frontier, and Cap Saint-Jacques near Saigon; five years later these three stations were taken over by the Posts and Telegraphs Department.[44]

In equatorial Africa, meanwhile, Inspector Magne's early experiments in 1901 had proved disappointing because the sparks produced by ordinary fifty-Hertz alternating current were too easily confused with the emissions of electrical storms that occur almost continuously in the humid tropics. By 1909, however, musical-frequency transmitters operating at 400 to 1,000 Hertz had solved the problem of tropical static. That year the former army officer Emile Girardeau met A. Fondère, president of a riverboat company on the Congo, who complained of the frequent breakdowns on the Brazzaville–Pointe Noire telegraph line. Fondère introduced Girardeau to Governor Martial Merlin of the French Congo, who offered Girardeau a contract to establish a radio link between the two towns. With this contract, Girardeau founded the Société Française Radio-électrique, or SFR. The firm built two ten-kilowatt musical-frequency stations and erected them in the Congo the following year, the first of their kind in Africa. These radio stations replaced the land line and served not only French Equatorial Africa but the Belgian Congo as well. On the strength of that achievement, SFR got contracts to build several more sets for the Belgian Congo and French Africa.[45]

Other colonies also obtained radios in the years before 1914. Small marine stations were placed along the coasts of North and West Africa and Madagascar; they communicated not only with passing ships, but also with their neighbors, albeit inefficiently.[46]

Up to 1910, French colonial radio projects were all local and on a small scale. That year, however, grander plans arose. Colonial Minister Adolphe Messimy won the approval of the Council of Ministers, in principle, for an imperial radiotelegraph network, to include ten high-powered stations in the Caribbean, Africa, and the Far East, and scores of lesser ones in every colony. After the sinking of the *Titanic* in April 1912 had brought radio communications to the attention of the public,[47] Messimy began agitating for the implementation of his plan. His motivations were twofold: first, that Great Britain, Germany, Belgium, and Italy all had or were building superstations to communicate with their colonies, and France should not fall behind; and second, that a radio network was needed to spread French influence: "There is no corner of the world, except the northern Pacific, where we could not create a French center of electrical transmission, and therefore of diffusion of our thought as well as our economic activity. Are we going to neglect this opportunity to cut a figure in the world?"[48] In early 1913 the Chamber of Deputies debated a bill to build three radiotelegraph chains—to Madagascar, to Indochina and the Pacific, and to South America—but did not appropriate the funds.[49]

The trouble, as always, was matching the resources to the dreams. In 1911 Albert Sarraut, newly appointed governor general of Indochina, decided to go ahead on his own. First he ordered a medium-size station built at Hanoi, to supplement the often interrupted cables to Hong Kong and Saigon. A year later he proposed a huge 300-kilowatt station at Saigon, able to communicate directly with France; it was to cover, in a single bound, the longest distance ever attempted by radio, and free Indochina from its dependence on foreign cables. Hearing of this scheme, the Indochina desk at the Ministry of Colonies in Paris protested against "the absence of all study of the means to be employed, and especially the absence of any directing principle." In order to get his station, Sarraut had to agree to pay for it entirely out of the budget of the colony, without help from France.[50] In 1913 Péri went to France to order the necessary equipment from SFR. The following year it was completed and loaded on board a ship at Marseille bound for Indochina, when the war broke out. Sarraut immediately offered the station to the French government, which transferred it to Lyon, where it served during the war to communicate with Russia and the United States.[51]

German Long-Distance and Colonial Radio, 1906–1914

In spite of its industrial and scientific superiority, Germany was in a weak position in the field of long-distance radiotelegraphy. Its nearest colonial possession was Togo in West Africa, five thousand kilometers away; from there to Southwest Africa was another three thousand kilometers. The rest of its possessions were in Asia and the Pacific, on the opposite side of the globe. Germany had no territories in the Atlantic comparable to British Ireland and Nova Scotia.[52]

The German government and the Telefunken Company strove to overcome these obstacles through heavy investments in the latest technology. They realized that communications with the colonies were a political necessity, while only communications with Germany's trading partners, especially the United States, would ever be profitable.[53] Their efforts aimed in three directions: across the Atlantic, toward Africa, and in the western Pacific.

The first two projects required a station in Germany so powerful it could reach both the United States and Togo. In 1906 Telefunken began building its Nauen station. Unlike the French and British radio companies, Telefunken received the support of the Post Office, especially after 1908, when the postal official von Bredow, a supporter of a German global radio network, became its director. After 1910 a new technology, the continuous wave, permitted the company to achieve its goal. In 1911–12 it erected antennas covering two square kilometers at Nauen, and installed a 100-kilowatt von Arco alternator, soon replaced by a 200-kilowatt machine. This was then the world's most powerful station, and the Germans were justly proud of it. In late July 1914 a group of senior Marconi engineers were taken on a tour of Nauen and of Telefunken factories and laboratories. As soon as they left, the military took over the station, in preparation for war.[54]

In 1914 Telefunken was busy building a network of stations designed to complement or, if need be, replace Germany's cable network. Sayville, near New York, was working by August 1914, but not yet open to commercial traffic. Kamina in Togo began communicating with Nauen in July 1914, and from there, messages were to be relayed to smaller stations at Duala (Cameroon), Windhoek (Southwest Africa), and Dar-es-Salaam (Tanganyika). By the time war broke out, Germany was in radio communication with America and Africa.[55] In 1912 the cable expert Richard Hennig had predicted: "We have every right to say that the British cable monopoly is now a thing of the past."[56] He was right, but only for a few weeks.

Germany had no hope of communicating with its Pacific colonies directly; there, its objective was to supplement its cable network and connect it to the smaller possessions that did not warrant cables. In 1912, with German government subsidies, Telefunken and the Deutsch–Niederländische Telegraphengesellschaft founded a joint subsidiary, the Deutsche Südseegesellschaft für drahtlose Telegraphie, which built stations at Tsingtao (China), Yap (Carolinas), Apia (Samoa), Rabaul (Bismarck Archipelago), and Nauru (Marshall Islands). This network was completed in the early months of 1914.[57]

The British Imperial Wireless Chain, 1911–1914

In 1910 Marconi's Wireless was still pushing its system of longwave transmissions to ever greater distances. After installing a powerful new transmitter at Clifden, Marconi sailed south to measure its range, and found that he could receive it at a distance of 6,400 kilometers during the day and 10,900 at night. Another even larger station built at Coltano in Italy the next year was able to communicate with Eritrea and Nova Scotia. Two years later the firm built its largest transmitters of all at Caernarvon in Wales and New Brunswick, New Jersey, able to communicate between America and Britain day and night.[58]

The company had grow commercially. It operated shore stations throughout the British Empire, the United States, and Latin America. It had also penetrated the European market, where it dominated Italian radio and owned a substantial share of the French Compagnie Générale de Télégraphie Sans Fil (CSF) and the Belgian Compagnie (later Société Anonyme Internationale) de Telégraphie Sans Fils. In marine radio, despite the treaty ratified by both Germany and Britain in 1906–07, Marconi's and Telefunken persisted in refusing to intercommunicate, causing difficulties to shipping in the English Channel and in the approaches to German ports. These differences were resolved in 1910–1911 when the two firms jointly founded the Deutsche Betriebsgesellschaft für drahtlose Telegraphie, or DEBEG.[59] The issue was finally settled by the third International Radiotelegraph Conference in

London in 1912; moved by the *Titanic* disaster, even Great Britain accepted the principle of obligatory intercommunication between ship and shore stations and among ships at sea.[60]

But Marconi wanted a worldwide network of long-distance stations, the radio equivalent of the Eastern cable empire, and for that he needed the approval of the British government. In 1906, when he proposed to the Colonial Office to build a chain of stations one thousand miles apart throughout the Empire, the idea was rejected as much too radical. In March 1910 he presented a new proposal, this one to build eighteen stations at a cost of £60,000 apiece plus a royalty of 10 percent on the gross receipts for twenty-eight years.[61] The question of an Imperial Wireless Chain was discussed at the Imperial Conference in the spring of 1911. The Post Office presented a "Scheme for Imperial Wireless Stations" to be operated by the government. The Cable Landing Rights Committee made a counter-proposal for six stations to be built in England, Cyprus or Egypt, Aden, India, Malaya, and Australia.[62] The premier of New Zealand, Sir Joseph Ward, introduced a motion favoring a wireless chain to be built by Marconi's but operated by the Post Office. The Imperial Conference unanimously passed a resolution "that the great importance of wireless telegraphy for social, commercial, and defensive purposes renders it desirable that a chain of British State-owned wireless stations should be established within the Empire," but without specifying details.[63]

In March 1912, Marconi's submitted a new bid. A month later, after further negotiations, the Post Office and the Committee of Imperial Defence approved plans for stations in Egypt, Aden, India, and South Africa to be built by Marconi's and operated by the Post Office.[64] In July Postmaster General Herbert Samuel signed a detailed contract with Marconi's, subject to parliamentary approval.[65]

Before the scheme could be presented to Parliament, however, a scandal broke out. It was a case of insider trading involving shares of American Marconi sold by Godfrey Isaacs to his brother Rufus the solicitor general, Chancellor of the Exchequer David Lloyd George, Lord Murray the Liberal chief whip, and Herbert Samuel; the shares were then resold at a profit. Tory politicians and the press flung accusations of corruption and stock market rigging at the Liberals. An Advisory Committee on Wireless Telegraphy, which met from October 1912 to January 1913, recommended that "it is a matter of urgency that a chain of Imperial wireless stations should be established."[66] Although nothing illegal was ever proved, the scandal had postponed parliamentary approval for a year.[67]

Finally, on July 31, 1913, a contract was signed between the Post Office and Marconi's, providing for six stations to be built in England, Egypt, East Africa, South Africa, India, and Malaya or Singapore; Australia was to build its own.[68] Of the six, only one was under construction before World War I, a 110-kilowatt station at Abu Zabal near Cairo, which was to communicate with the Post Office's station at Leafield near Oxford.[69]

Compared with the American radiotelegraph chains in the Caribbean and the Pacific, Great Britain had slipped very badly, and was never to regain its advantage. The scandal and the squabbling between Liberals and Tories were partly to blame for this, but a more fundamental cause was a general spirit of lethargy regarding radio that prevailed in British official circles.

On June 29, 1914, when the tensions of imminent war were already palpable, the Sub-Committee on Empire Wireless of the Committee of Imperial Defence met to discuss the Empire's radio communications.[70] Present were representatives of the Board of Trade, the Post Office, the Treasury, the Foreign, Colonial, India, and War offices, and the Admiralty; only one member, Frank J. Brown of the Post Office, was a radio expert. The subcommittee noted a memorandum from the War Staff of the Admiralty to the Committee of Imperial Defence, dated February 19, 1914, which stated, ruefully:

> In the past Great Britain has had a principal share in the cable industry of the world but at present there is little indication of her having a corresponding preponderance in the wireless traffic. There are two main reasons for this unsatisfactory state of affairs:
> (1.) Wireless telegraphy being a Government monopoly.
> (2.) Foreign competition.
> Wireless telegraphy has provided a means to foreign nations of regaining lost ground, and Germany has been particularly active in this direction.

No one suggested attacking enemy radio installations in the event of war; neither the War Office nor the Admiralty had any information about the defenses of German radio stations. Instead the discussions centered around the defense of British stations, but at the most petty level: how to prevent "evil disposed persons" or raiding parties from scaling the fences and damaging radio stations, and whether the government or the station owners should pay for the fences. At the next meeting, on July 6, they discussed an Admiralty request for stations at Bermuda, Ascension, Bathurst, Cape Race, Jamaica, and Trinidad. A telling detail is that the Admiralty admitted that a station at Bathurst would be more useful than in Sierra Leone, despite the danger of French attack—this at a time when everyone was expecting a war with Germany!

The contrast between the wireless subcommittee of 1914 and the strategic cable committees of 1891, 1898, 1901, 1904, 1908, and 1911 is astonishing. Whereas the cable committees discussed in great detail how to strengthen Britain's cable communications and how to destroy those of any potential enemy, the wireless subcommittee seemed defeated from the start.

Conclusion

Among the documents studied by the Sub-Committee on Empire Wireless in June 1914 was a list of long-distance stations compiled by the Admiralty War Staff.[71] On this list were four French, nine German, eleven American, two Belgian, four Italian, four Spanish, and three other stations. This seemed irrefutable evidence that in radio communications the British had lost that "corresponding preponderance" they had gotten used to in the heyday of cables. But was this really the case?

To France and Germany, the radio promised to give them a national means of communication, a substitute for the cables they lacked. In fact they did not have true global networks but several regional networks scattered around the globe, linked by foreign (often British) cables. Other than Britain, only the United States had radio communications with its colonial empire and all its warships.

In the radio race, Britain had, if not a preponderance, at least a leading position. By 1914 the Admiralty and the British shipping companies could communicate with their ships everywhere but in the Pacific; only Singapore and Hong Kong were still without stations.[72] But more important, for Great Britain radiotelegraphy was not a substitute for cables, but a complement, part of an integrated system of communications. This explains the contrast between the enthusiasm with which the Admiralty and British shipping interests adopted Marconi's wireless, and the resistance encountered by Marconi in his plans for transatlantic and imperial radio communications.

Seen from this point of view rather than from that of a particular technology, Great Britain had what no other nation could boast: a choice. Between England and its possessions, messages could take multiple routes, going underwater if secrecy were required, avoiding broken cables or untrustworthy neutrals, dependent neither on other nations nor on the weather to provide reliable, secure, and cost-effective communications. Proof was to come just five weeks after the Sub-Committee on Empire Wireless issued its gloomy pronouncement.

Notes

1. On the early years of Marconi's career, see Rowland F. Pocock, *The Early British Radio Industry* (Manchester, 1988); W. P. Jolly, *Marconi* (New York, 1972), 32–49; W. J. Baker, *A History of the Marconi Company* (London, 1970), 25–28; and Hugh G. J. Aitken, *Syntony and Spark: The Origins of Radio* (Princeton, N.J., 1985), 218–227 and 286.

2. Rowland F. Pocock and G. R. M. Garratt, *The Origins of Maritime Radio* (London, 1972), 44; Pocock, 173.

3. Vice-Admiral Arthur R. Hezlet, *The Electron and Sea Power* (London, 1975), 28–31; Aitken, *Syntony and Spark*, 290; Jolly, 52–71; Baker 28–43; Pocock, 154.

4. G. E. C. Wedlake, *SOS: The Story of Radio Communication* (Newton Abbot, 1973), 89–94; Hugh Barty-King, *Girdle Round the Earth: The Story of Cable and Wireless and its Predecessors to Mark the Group's Jubilee, 1929–1979* (London, 1979), 127–28; Baker, 50–51 and 97; Hezlet, 34–37; Jolly, 85–91; Aitken, *Syntony and Spark*, 232; Pocock, 154–72; Pocock and Garratt, 34.

5. "Telefunken-Chronik," *Telefunken-Zeitung* 26, No. 100 (May 1953): *Festschrift zum 50 jährigen Jubiläum der Telefunken Gesellschaft für drahtlose Telegraphie m.b.H., gleichzeitig als 100. Ausgabe der Telefunken-Zeitung,* 149; Zenneck, ibid., 154; Hugo Thurn, *Die Funkentelegraphie,* 5th ed. (Leipzig and Berlin, 1918), 25–26; Pocock, 123 and 140.

6. Susan J. Douglas, *Inventing American Broadcasting, 1899–1922* (Baltimore, 1987), 110–12; Captain Linwood S. Howeth, *History of Communications–Electronics in the United States Navy* (Washington, 1963), 25–35; Aitken, *Syntony and Spark*, 247; Baker, 48–50; Jolly, 67–82.

7. Aitken, *Syntony and Spark*, 233–38; Pocock, 150–51; Jolly, 92–93; Baker, 59.

8. Memoranda of June 4 and 6, 1901, in Public Record Office [hereafter PRO], Cab 37/57, Nos. 55 and 56; Memoranda and proposals of December 10, 1901, in Cab 37/59, No. 129.

9. Jolly, 124.

10. Baker, 95–96.

11. John D. Tomlinson, *The International Control of Radiocommunications* (Geneva,

1938), 14–17; Leslie B. Tribolet, *The International Aspects of Electrical Communication in the Pacific Area* (Baltimore, 1929), 21; Keith Clark, *International Communications: The American Attitude* (New York, 1931), 170–71; Irwin Stewart, "The International Regulation of Radio in Time of Peace," *Annals of the American Academy of Political and Social Science* 142 suppl. (March 1929), 78; Douglas, *Inventing American Broadcasting*, 120–21; Howeth, 71; Baker, 96.

12. Memoranda of March 7 and 8, 1904, in PRO, Cab 37/69, No. 39.

13. Jolly, 139; Barty-King, 154–55.

14. Tomlinson, 19–27; Stewart, 78–80.

15. "The Politics of Radio Telegraphy," *Edinburgh Review* 424 (April 1908), 465–86.

16. PRO, Cab 37/85, No. 93 (December 4, 1906); Cab 37/89, No. 68 (June 13, 1907) and 72 (July 11, 1907); Douglas, 141; Baker, 115.

17. Tomlinson, 28; Howeth, 118 and 158–59; Clark, 171–73 and 219–25.

18. Jolly, 103–108; Baker, 61–73.

19. Jolly, 128–61; Baker, 117–24.

20. Speech to the Institute of Radio Engineers, quoted in Aitken, *Syntony and Spark*, 272.

21. Alfred Ristow, *Die Funkentelegraphie, ihre internationale Entwicklung and Bedeutung* (Berlin, 1926), 23–24; Zenneck, 155–57. Hugh Aitken disputes this claim (private communication, June 1989).

22. Johannes Zacharias and Hermann Heinicke, *Praktisches Handbuch der drahtlosen Telegraphie und Telephonie* (Vienna and Leipzig, 1908), 109–18.

23. Richard Hennig, "Die deutsche–niederländische Telegraphenallianz im Fernen Osten," *Grenzboten* 65 (April–June 1906), 292.

24. Eugen Nesper, *Die drahtlose Telegraphie und ihr Einfluss auf den Wissenschaftsverkehr unter besonderer Berücksichtigung des Systems "Telefunken." Mit einem Vergleichnis der Patente und Literaturaufgaben über drahtlose Telegraphie* (Berlin, 1905), 25 and 88–89; Thomas Lenschau, *Das Weltkabelnetz*, 2nd ed. (Frankfurt, 1908), 68–69; Peter Lertes, *Die drahtlose Telegraphie und Telephonie*, 2nd ed. (Dresden and Leipzig, 1923), 2–3; Mario de Arcangelis, *Electronic Warfare: From the Battle of Tsushima to the Falklands and Lebanon Conflicts* (Poole, Dorset, 1985), 11–18; "Telefunken-Chronik," 149; Baker, 103; Hezlet, 43–49; Tomlinson, 17.

25. Catherine Bertho, "La recherche publique en télécommunication, 1880–1941," *Télécommunications: Revue française des télécommunications* (October 1983), 2; René Duval, *Histoire de la radio en France* (Paris, 1980), 19–21.

26. L. Magne, "Télégraphie sans fil. Notes sur les expériences faites au Congo français et sur une installation de postes aux Antilles," *Revue coloniale* n.s. 11 (March–April 1903), 502–42 and 12 (May–June 1903), 654–93; Daniel R. Headrick, "Les télécommunications en Afrique équatoriale française, 1886–1913," *Recherches sur l'histoire des télécommunications* 2 (December 1988), 73–86.

27. There are two remarkable studies of American radio before 1922: For the technological and business aspects, see Hugh G. J. Aitken, *The Continuous Wave: Technology and American Radio, 1900–1932* (Princeton, N.J., 1985); for the cultural, military, and business side, see Susan J. Douglas, *Inventing American Broadcasting, 1899–1922* (Baltimore, 1987). In addition, the special, and often difficult, relations between the U.S. Navy and the pioneers of radio are analyzed in Douglas, "Technological Innovation and Organizational Change: The Navy's Adoption of Radio, 1899–1919," in *Military Enterprise and Technological Change: Perspectives on the American Experience*, ed. Merritt Roe Smith (Cambridge, Mass., 1985), 117–73; and Howeth, 133–51 and 193–203, which gives the Navy's viewpoint.

28. Quoted in Douglas, *Inventing American Broadcasting*, 112.

29. George H. Clark, "Radio in the U.S. Navy," Clark Collection, quoted in Douglas, *Inventing American Broadcasting*, 134–35.

30. On the U.S. Navy and wireless to 1906, see Douglas, *Inventing American Broadcasting*, Chap. 4.

31. Aitken, *Continuous Wave*, 85; Douglas, *Inventing American Broadcasting*, 252; Hezlet, 68.

32. Aitken, *Continuous Wave*, 251; Alexander Meissner, "Die Zeit der Machinensender," *Telefunken-Zeitung* 26, No. 100 (May 1953), 159–63.

33. Aitken, *Continuous Wave*, 122–51.

34. Douglas, *Inventing American Broadcasting*, 241–46.

35. Douglas, *Inventing American Broadcasting*, 254–55; Aitken, *Continuous Wave*, 138–40.

36. Aitken, *Continuous Wave*, 193–94 and 282–83; Jolly, 190–91.

37. Aitken, *Continuous Wave*, 94–95; see also Douglas, *Inventing American Broadcasting*, 254–59.

38. Douglas, *Inventing American Broadcasting*, 260–66.

39. Douglas, *Inventing American Broadcasting*, 128–30.

40. Ibid., 241–44.

41. Emile Girardeau, *Souvenirs de longue vie* (Paris, 1968), 52; Bertho, "La recherche publique."

42. Andrew Butrica, "The Militarization of Technology in France: The Case of Electrotechnics, 1845–1914" (paper read at the annual meeting of the American Historical Association, Cincinnati, December 1988); I am grateful to Mr. Butrica for allowing me to cite this paper.

43. Maurice Guierre, *Les ondes et les hommes, histoire de la radio* (Paris, 1951), 55–57.

44. André Touzet, "Le réseau radiotélégraphique indochinois," *Revue indochinoise* (Hanoi, 1918), 245/150; Lieutenant Colonel Cluzan, "Les télégraphistes coloniaux, pionniers des télécommunications Outre-Mer," *Tropiques* 393 (March 1957), 3–8; Indochine, Gouvernement général, *La télégraphie sans fil en Indochine* (Hanoi–Haiphong, 1921), 4.

45. Girardeau, 58–61; Duval, 25; Société Française Radioélectrique, *Vinqt-cinq années de TSF* (Paris 1935), 9–10 and 40; Guierre, 87–91; "L'appropriation de la colonie," *Afrique française* 23 (February 1913), 59; "Rapport de M. Tixier, Inspecteur Adjoint de la Colonie" (April 23, 1914), in Archives Nationales Section Outre-Mer, Travaux Publics 152, dossier 15; Headrick, "Télécommunications."

46. "Le réseau intercolonial de télégraphie sans fil," *Afrique française* 23 (February 1913), 59; *Les postes et télégraphes en Afrique occidentale* (Corbeil, 1907), 100–101; Major Jean d'Arbaumont, *Historique des télégraphistes coloniaux* (Paris, 1955), 159; Léon Jacob, *Les intérêts français et les relations télégraphiques internationales* (Paris, 1912), 3–4; Cluzan, 4–5.

47. On the role of radio in the *Titanic* disaster, see Baker, 138–40.

48. Adolphe Messimy, "Le réseau mondial français de télégraphie sans fil," *Revue de Paris* 19 (July 1, 1912), 34–44.

49. "Reseau intercolonial," 59.

50. "Note sur le réseau 'impérial de T.S.F.'" (December 27, 1911) and memorandum from Service du Secrétariat et du Contreseing to Service de l'Indochine (January 10, 1912), in Archives Nationales Section Outre-Mer, Colonies Série Moderne, Indochine NF 890.

51. Touzet, 3–6; *Télégraphie sans fil en Indochine*, 3–6; Girardeau, 76; *Vinqt-cinq années*, 40.

52. Smaller colonial powers had similar problems. Italy and Portugal relied on Marconi stations. Belgium ordered small stations for the Congo from the Société Française Radio-électrique, and built a superstation at Laeken near Brussels, which was no sooner completed then it had to be destroyed in the face of the German invasion. Robert Goldschmidt, "Les relations télégraphiques entre la Belgique et le Congo," in *Notes sur la question des transports en Afrique précédées d'un rapport au Roi*, ed. Count R. de Briey (Paris, 1918), 559–77; Leo Weinthal, *The Story of the Cape to Cairo Railway and River Route from 1887 to 1922*, 5 vols. (London, 1923–1926), 3:422.

53. Meissner, 159.

54. Baker, 158.

55. Ibid., 161; Lertes, 5; Telefunken-Chronik, 149; Hezlet, 77.

56. R. Hennig, "Die deutsche Seekabelpolitik zur Befreiung vom englischen Welt-monopol," *Meereskunde* 6 (1912), 32–33.

57. Artur Kunert, *Geschichte der deutschen Fernmeldekabel. II. Telegraphen-Seekabel* (Cologne–Mülheim, 1962), 339–40; Charles Lesage, *La rivalité anglo-germanique. Les câbles sous-marins allemands* (Paris, 1915), 210–211.

58. Jolly, 173 and 217; Hezlet, 76–77; Baker, 154–55.

59. Helmuth Giessler, *Die Marine-Nachrichten- und -Ortungsdienst. Techniche Entwicklung und Kriegserfahrungen* (Munich, 1971), 17–19; Baker, 130–35; Jolly, 190–91; Aitken, *Continuous Wave*, 355; Ristow, 17. It is interesting to note that the Anglo-German radio agreement coincided with the Franco-German cable agreement (see Chapter 7), just as German relations with Britain and France were deteriorating.

60. Ristow, 28–30; Tomlinson, 28–29 and 43; Stewart, 80–81.

61. Jolly, 172; Baker, 116; Barty-King, 156.

62. General Post Office, "Scheme for Imperial Wireless Stations" (May 26, 1911), in PRO, Cab 37/107, No. 63.

63. Imperial Conference, 1911, "Minutes of Proceedings of the Imperial Conference, 1911," in Great Britain, *Parliamentary Papers* 1911 (Cd. 5745), Vol. 54:307–15.

64. Committee of Imperial Defence, "Establishment of a Chain of Wireless Telegraph Stations throughout the Empire. Action Taken by the Post Office" (April 2, 1912), in PRO, Cab 38/20/4.

65. "Copy of Agreement between Marconi's Wireless Telegraph Company, Limited, Commendatore Guglielmo Marconi, and the Postmaster General, with regard to the Establishment of a Chain of Imperial Wireless Stations; together with a Copy of the Treasury Minute thereon," in Post Office Archive (London), POST 88/33–34; see also General Post Office, "Draft Specification of Imperial Wireless Installation. Copy of Draft Specification, Submitted by the Marconi Company, Descriptive of the Wireless Telegraph Installation under the Contract for Imperial Wireless Stations" and "Imperial Wireless Installation. Copies of Correspondence Relating to the Contract for Imperial Wireless Stations," in *Parliamentary Papers* 1912–13 (Cd. 6318 and Cd. 6357), Vol. 68.

66. Advisory Committee on Wireless Telegraphy (Lord Parker of Waddington, chair), "Report of the Committee appointed by the Postmaster General to consider and report on the merits of the existing systems of long distance wireless telegraphy, and in particular as to their capacity for continuous communication over the distances required by the Imperial Chain," *Parliamentary Papers* 1913 (Cd. 6781), Vol. 33:725.

67. Frances Donaldson, *The Marconi Scandal* (London, 1962); Jolly, 192–210; Baker, 143–45: Wedlake, 81–83.

68. "Copy of agreement between Marconi's Wireless Telegraph Company, Limited, Commendatore Guglielmo Marconi, and the Postmaster General, with regard to the Establishment of a Chain of Imperial Wireless Stations; together with a Copy of the Treasury

Minute thereon, and other Papers," (July 31, 1913), in Cable and Wireless archives (London), B2/1106; "Copy of Agreement" in POST 88/33–34, also in *Parliamentary Papers, 1912–13* (265), Vol. 49:465.

69. Baker, 160.

70. Committee of Imperial Defence, "C.I.D. Sub-Committee on Empire Wireless Telegraph Communications 1914" (June 29, July 6, and July 22, 1914), in PRO Cab 16/32.

71. "Memorandum no. WT3: List of Long-Distance Radio-Telegraph Stations in Foreign Countries which connect them to their Colonies and Dependencies or to other Countries. Prepared by Admiralty War Staff. June 17, 1914," in PRO Cab 16/32.

72. Wedlake, 84.

8

Cables and Radio in World War I

Whenever victory or defeat in war has hinged on information, the channels of communication have been as valuable as fleets and armies. In that great twentieth-century invention, the total war, every piece of information has represented a danger and an opportunity. What would have been news in peacetime was now either a secret or a propaganda item. Business communications became contraband. Personal letters were suspected of being tools of espionage. And the telecommunications channels, with their ability to carry vital information fast enough to affect the outcome of a battle in progress, turned into weapons.

Total war did not break out at once in August 1914. Despite years of planning, it took the belligerents a long time to learn what information was available, how to control it, and how to turn it against the enemy. And some nations learned the lessons better than others. At the beginning of the war, the authorities acted as though information were military supplies. Their first reaction was to cut off the enemy's flow of information by severing cables and destroying radio transmitters. To prevent their own information from falling into enemy hands, they constructed codes so elaborate they could never be broken (or so their authors believed). They also imposed measures such as postal censorship and the confiscation of radios to stop the export of information. Fear of espionage was the first reaction of a besieged officialdom.

Only after months of war did the belligerents realize that the most important information was not what spies might steal but what each side gave away free. The culprit was radio. Before radio the channels of communication were physical—letters, wires—and could be guarded. Radio released information from its physical bonds and sent it out into the ether in all directions. Hence the importance of tapping enemy communications and extracting information from it, even at the expense of giving up some of one's own. As secret interception and code-breaking were added to the arsenal of the warring powers, a new weapon was forged: communications intelligence. This, as has recently become clear, was as important to the outcome of the First World War as the strategies and tactics that were formerly emphasized. In this field, Great Britain was the clear winner, a position it kept in both world wars.

The Jitters of July 1914

World War I will be remembered not only as the most ghastly ever fought up to then, but also as the epitome of human incompetence. On the Western Front, generals sent millions of soldiers to be slaughtered in vain because they had neither the imagination to overcome enemy machine gun fire nor the wisdom to stop trying. Meanwhile, the world's most powerful fleets sat bottled up in harbors by the confusion and timidity of their admiralties. Not until 1917 did they begin adjusting to the imbalance between defense and offense.

Appropriately enough, a war so great directed by men so small began through misjudgments and indecision. The history of July 1914 is one of events sweeping men before them—not just ordinary citizens, but also rulers and strategists who had spent years planning for just such a moment. Much of the shock had to do with the speed of events for which statesmen were completely unprepared, having been raised in a slower age, before electrical communications had affected the relations between states. In his book *The Culture of Time and Space,* Stephen Kern blames the confusion, in part, on the telegraph:

> There is abundant evidence that one of the causes of World War I was a failure of diplomacy, and one of the causes of that failure was that diplomats could not cope with the volume and speed of electronic communications. Most of the aristocrats and gentlemen who made up the diplomatic corps in 1914 were of the old school in many respects, as wary of new technology as some generals were wary of newfangled weapons and strategies. . . . The diplomats failed to understand the full impact of instantaneous communications without the ameliorating effect of delay.[1]

He gives two examples. One is the series of ultimata that preceded the declarations of war. After debating and procrastinating for almost a month, Austria issued an ultimatum on July 23, giving Serbia exactly forty-eight hours to respond. When Serbian Foreign Minister Pacu replied to Austrian ambassador Giesl that some of the ministers were absent from the capital, Giesl replied: "The return of the ministers in the age of railways, telegraph and telephone in a land of that size could only be a matter of a few hours."[2] When Austria declared war on Serbia a few days later, it was done, for the first time in history, by telegram. And that was slow compared with what happened later. The German ultimatum to France on July 31 gave that country eighteen hours to respond; the one to Russia, that same evening, had a twelve-hour limit. And on August 4, Great Britain gave Germany five hours to answer its ultimatum. Though the statesmen were still going through the motions, the day was fast approaching when they would skip the formalities entirely.

The hasty ultimata covered up a breakdown in the process of decision-making. Nothing illustrates this better than Kaiser Wilhelm's futile attempts to control events by changing his mind. After having given Austria every encouragement in its hard attitude towards Serbia, Wilhelm suddenly got cold feet and tried to back down when Austria took this policy to its logical conclusion and declared war on July 28. He told Secretary of State Jagow that, since Serbia had accepted all of Austria's conditions, "every cause for war falls to the ground." Though the wires hummed with frantic telegrams, that message never got through to the Austrian government.[3]

Sensing the approach of war, Wilhelm turned to his cousin and fellow-emperor, Tsar Nicholas of Russia. On July 29 "Willy" and "Nicky" sent each other one of the most futile series of messages in the history of telegraphy. At 1:00 A.M. the Tsar urged the Kaiser to stop Austria from "going too far," and informed him that pressures in Russia were forcing him to "take extreme measures which will lead to war." In response, Wilhelm reminded Nicholas that the "dastardly murder" of Archduke Franz-Ferdinand had precipitated the whole trouble, and appealed to him to help "smooth over the difficulties that might still arise." That evening when Nicholas suggested to Wilhelm that the problem be resolved by a conference at the Hague, Wilhelm proposed that Russia "remain a spectator" in the Austro-Serbian conflict. The next day, after Nicholas had tried to justify Russian military prepared-ness, Wilhelm answered that "The whole weight of the decision lies solely on your shoulders now, who [will] have to bear the responsibility for peace or war." On July 31, Nicholas told Wilhelm that "It is technically impossible to stop our military preparations which were obligatory owing to Austrian mobilization." The following day, Nicholas asked Wilhelm to guarantee that "these measures [i.e., mobilization] do not mean war," and in a last telegram, Wilhelm informed Nicholas that he had ordered the mobilization of the German army.[4]

Thus ended the attempts of Wilhelm II and Nicholas II to control the destiny of the countries over which they thought they ruled as autocrats. As Kern points out,

> The telegrams exchanged between the Tsar and the Kaiser constituted a small fraction of the hundreds sent during the negotiations. Because they took place between the two monarchs of rival powers, they highlighted the strength and weakness of telegraphic communications. . . . This telegraphic exchange at the highest level dramatized the spectacular failure of diplomacy, to which telegraphy contributed with crossed messages, delays, sudden surprises, and the unpredictable timing. Throughout the crisis there was not just one new faster speed for everyone to adjust to, but a series of new and variable paces that supercharged the masses, confused the diplomats, and unnerved the generals.[5]

Allied Attacks on German Communications

The flurry of telegrams was the last attempt to use words to avoid war. As the inevitable approached, a more ominous series of messages appeared. On July 30, the British Admiralty sent all its warships to battle stations. A few days later, a radiogram broadcast by Nauen ordered all German merchant ships to make for the nearest neutral port. On August 4, when the German army marched into Belgium and Britain issued its ultimatum, the Admiralty warned the Royal Navy to stand by for a message; at 11 P.M. Greenwich Mean Time (midnight in Germany) it went out: "Commence hostilities against Germany."

Among Britain's first hostile acts was to sever Germany's communications with the outside world. At midnight on August 4, when the ultimatum expired, the German lines cleared their traffic and shut down. A few hours later, implementing the decision of the Committee of Imperial Defence of 1912,[6] the British cableship *Telconia* hauled up and cut the five cables that linked Germany to the outside world: two to the Azores and North America, one to Vigo, one to Tenerife, and one to Brest.[7] The next day, the French Compagnie des Câbles Sud-américains stopped all traffic between Central Europe and South America.[8]

The Russians were not quite so efficient. The German naval officer Franz Rintelen tells of his attempts to wire 2 million yen to the German naval attaché in Tokyo so that the latter could supply gold to Admiral von Spee, commander of the German Far East fleet. As early as August 2, the cable office in Emden reported that London was not replying to its messages. A few days later, though Germany and Russia were already at war, Rintelen managed to get a Danish bank to transfer the money via the Great Northern Telegraph Company's lines across Siberia.[9] When that route was cut, all cable communication between the Central Powers and the outside world came to an end.

Yet Germany still had radio stations and cables scattered around the world, and one by one these were attacked or neutralized. In early August, British warships destroyed the German radio stations at Dar-es-Salaam and Yap. Later that month, as French and British troops approached Kamina in Togo, the Germans blew up their own station. At the end of August, troops from New Zealand occupied Samoa, while a British ship cut the German cable linking Chefoo, Tsingtao, and Shanghai.

In September, the German radio stations at Rabaul and Nauru in the Pacific were destroyed, British forces seized Duala in Kamerun, Portuguese authorities shut down the Azores–New York cable, and Liberia closed down the cable from Monrovia to Pernambuco, which might have relayed radiograms from Germany onward to South America. By an Executive Order of September 5, 1914, the U.S. Navy took over the Tuckerton station and made it available for plain-language communication with Eilvese in Germany. It also shut down the station at Sayville until July 1915, then reopened it for commercial traffic with Nauen.[10]

In November 1914, Japanese forces captured Tsingtao, and the French cut the cable linking Tenerife to Monrovia. Windhoek in German Southwest Africa fell to a South African force on May 12, 1915, and the French navy cut the Monrovia–Pernambuco cable in November of that year.[11] With that, the last of Germany's worldwide communications facilities had fallen into foreign hands.

German Attacks on Allied Communications

Germany also tried to destroy Allied communications, but had a more daunting task. Not only did Great Britain, France, and Russia have far more links with the rest of the world, but they were also better able to prevent attacks and to repair the damage.

The British land lines to India via Russia and Turkey were the first to go, for cutting them required no military action. Then in September 1914, the Germans severed the Baltic cables of the Great Northern Company that connected France and Britain to Russia. All the traffic to India and the Far East that had once gone overland now had to be carried by the Eastern cables, causing serious delays.[12] When the Ottoman Empire joined the Central Powers in November, the Black Sea cables were also cut, reducing communications with Russia. Foreseeing just such an eventuality, Britain and Russia had built a radio link before the war, and the damage was quickly repaired when the British laid a new cable from Peterhead to Alexandrovsk in January 1915.[13]

More dramatic, though less important from a communications standpoint, were the three German attacks on distant cable stations. In Southwest Africa, German troops occupied the Eastern and South African Telegraph Company station and held the staff prisoner for almost a year; since the British cable companies no longer communicated with that station anyway, it made no difference.[14]

On September 7, the German cruiser *Nürnberg,* part of von Spee's Far Eastern fleet, arrived off Fanning Island in the mid-Pacific and landed a party of men who destroyed some machinery and interrupted the Pacific cable. By mid-October the station and cable were repaired and functioning again.[15]

The third attack was on the cable station on Cocos-Keeling Island. After having sunk various ships in the Indian Ocean and bombarded Madras, the German cruiser *Emden* appeared off Cocos at dawn on November 9, 1914. At 6 A.M. the station cabled to Singapore: EMDEN AT COCOS LANDING AN ARMED PARTY. Then the line went dead until 9:15 P.M., when Singapore received a feeble message: EVERYTHING SMASHED. WILL GET INSTRUMENT UP AT DAYLIGHT. REPORT US ALL WELL. EMDEN ENGAGED BY BRITISH CRUISER. RESULT UNKNOWN. LANDING PARTY COMMANDEERED SCHOONER AYESHA. GOOD-NIGHT! In the intervening hours, the Germans had destroyed some equipment and several dummy cables, but had missed the main cable to Singapore. Alerted by the first message, the Australian light cruiser *Sydney* appeared off Cocos and destroyed the *Emden.* Meanwhile the landing party escaped in a schooner to Arabia, and from there overland to Germany. It made an exciting story all around, with many heroes and few victims, a good yarn to relieve the deadly tedium of bulletins from the trenches.[16] But it made no difference at all to Britain's communications network, for the damage was repaired within twelve hours after the Germans had left.

With the destruction of their commerce raiders in the fall of 1914, the Germans turned to submarine warfare. Here they were more effective than with cruisers. Submarines were too small to shell coastal stations or land parties of marines, and grappling a cable from the deck of a submarine was much more difficult than from a properly equipped cable ship, yet they succeeded many times in the North Sea, and a few times in the Atlantic. On February 10–12, 1917, the *U-155* cut three cables off Lisbon, and on September 19–20 she cut the Canso–New York cable off Halifax.[17] Two more cables may have been cut by the *U-151* in May and June 1918 off Sandy Hook, New Jersey.[18]

Allied Communications during the War

By 1915, apart from the occasional message smuggled out by a friendly neutral, German overseas communications were reduced to the radio links between Nauen and Eilvese, on the one hand, and Sayville and Tuckerton, on the other, the latter two subject to American goodwill. The overseas communications of the Allied Powers, in contrast, not only survived, but increased considerably. One reason was the severed German cables, which were put to good use. One Borkum–Azores cable was diverted to Penzance, where it connected Britain to the Azores; its continuation to New York was cut by the British in 1917 after the United States joined the war, and diverted to Halifax to become the first Atlantic cable owned by the British government. The other German Atlantic cable was diverted to Brest at one end, while the other end was relaid to the French cable station at Coney Island, New York; it only opened for traffic in March 1919. In 1915 the German cable to Tenerife and Monrovia was turned into two French cables, one from Dunkirk to Cherbourg, the other from Brest to Casablanca and Dakar. Its continuation to Lome in Togo was used by the British to connect that town with Accra. German cables in European waters were used to link France and Britain, and, in the Far East, where the Japanese seized the German colonies of Tsingtao and Yap, they retained the cables from Yap to Guam and Menado, but relaid the Yap–Shanghai cable to link Okinawa with Shanghai and the Tsingtao–Shanghai cable to connect Tsingtao with Sasebo.[19] Thus the three Allies expanded their cable network considerably, and, in doing so, they created a subject for postwar quarrels.

In addition to their new cables, the Allies also increased their radio communications. Of the six Imperial Wireless Chain stations originally contracted for by Marconi, only the one at Leafield near Oxford was in operation when war broke out. A second one at Abu Zabal near Cairo was hurriedly completed. When Marconi asked for more money to build the rest, the government cancelled the contract and awarded Marconi £600,000 in damages.[20] Marconi's station at Caernarvon was taken over by the Admiralty; the Clifden–Glace Bay circuit continued to transmit commercial messages until 1917, when it was closed down at American insistence. Otherwise, the Marconi Company concentrated on building radio equipment for the armed forces, among which were thirteen new radio stations that the Admiralty ordered after the defeat at Coronel in November 1914.[21]

The French likewise built up their radio communications during the war. The powerful transmitter destined for Saigon was quickly set up at Lyon-la-Doua in September 1914, where it served to communicate with Russia. A series of smaller stations were erected in Africa, Madagascar, and Tahiti to form the nucleus of a colonial chain. At the end of 1918, France also acquired a powerful U.S. Navy station at Bordeaux. Thus France ended the war with far better international communications than in 1914.[22]

Before the United States joined the Allies in April 1917, the U.S. Navy took advantage of the 2½ years of neutrality to create the most modern and extensive radio-communications network in the world, with a series of high-powered stations covering the western Atlantic, the Caribbean, and the Pacific. The first in the chain was the Federal Telegraph arc transmitter installed at Arlington, Virginia, in December 1912, followed by a station at Darien (Canal Zone) in June 1915. The navy thereupon ordered a series of 200–500-kilowatt arc transmitters from Federal, which were erected at San Diego, Pearl Harbor, Cavite (Philippines), and Annapolis (Maryland) during 1917. The Navy's Office of Communications also operated a chain of maritime shore stations and all other government stations except those of the Army.[23]

In addition, the Navy also seized control of privately owned stations. The pretext was President Wilson's Neutrality Proclamation of August 5, 1914, which forbade the transmission or delivery of "unneutral" messages and prohibited stations from "in any way rendering to any one of the belligerents any unneutral service during the continuance of hostilities."[24] By executive order, the Navy took over the recently completed Tuckerton station on September 9, 1914. It also seized American Marconi's Siasconsett station on September 24, 1914, on the grounds that it had transmitted an "unneutral" message, and did not allow the station to reopen until January 17, 1915. Likewise the Sayville station belonging to Telefunken was taken over on July 9, 1915, on the grounds that the installation of a new alternator and antenna made it a "new" station operating without a proper license; the Navy then used it to operate a profitable commercial link with Nauen in Germany.[25] Although the American Marconi Company was also affected, the Navy's actions hit the German interests much harder than British interests. German protests that the British still had their cables and could send coded messages without censorship or interference fell on deaf ears. During the "neutrality period" the United States was not so much neutral as opportunistic.

As soon as the United States declared war on Germany on April 6, 1917, the Navy seized all radio stations except those of the Army. Among them were fifty-three commercial stations, most of them belonging to the American Marconi and Federal Telegraph companies. The Navy also acquired from the Alien Property Custodian the German stations it had controlled for over two years. Its next aim was to obtain radio sets for ships. Since Marconi's factory could not meet this sudden surge in demand, the Navy ordered sets from anyone else who could manufacture them and assumed liability for any patient infringement that might ensue; this brought dozens of new firms into the radio business, including such giants as General Electric, Westinghouse, and Western Electric.[26]

In spite of its ownership of Tuckerton and Sayville and its control of Marconi's New Brunswick station, the Navy was still dissatisfied with America's transatlantic communications. Not only were the cables overloaded and vulnerable and the existing ratio stations unreliable, but traffic was certain to surge as American troops poured into Europe. Joint Army–Navy and interallied conferences decided that more radio links were needed. The Navy, impressed with the performance of Alexanderson's 50-kilowatt alternator recently installed at New Brunswick, urged General Electric to build a 200-kilowatt alternator. When it opened for service at the New Brunswick station in September 1918, it provided the first continuously reliable twenty-four-hour transatlantic service and carried the bulk of the transatlantic radio traffic for the next two years.[27]

With that, the Navy had all the communications it needed for the successful conduct of the war. But Secretary of the Navy Josephus Daniels had other views. As he wrote in his diary in 1917: "Logic is: Communication is a governmental function and the government must own, control radio, waterways, telegraph and telephone."[28] He wanted the Navy to possess all radio communications in America, in peacetime as well as war. To prevent American Marconi from buying the Federal Telegraph Company and its precious arc-transmitter patents, the Navy purchased Federal in May 1918 for $1.6 million. In October it tried to buy Marconi's 330 ship stations, but had to take Marconi's 45 shore stations as well for $1.4 million. By war's end the Navy had almost completed the nationalization of radio in America, without Congressional approval. But one fear remained: that when peace returned, American Marconi, a company controlled by foreigners, would repossess its stations, especially New Brunswick with its state-of-the-art GE alternators, and return America to a state of subservience to Britain. Assertive nationalism and military socialism were closely allied in the mind of Secretary Daniels.[29]

Censorship

Besides trying to cut off their enemies' communication channels, the belligerents strove to deprive their enemies of useful intelligence by supervising very tightly the export of information. This effort took two forms: seizing all private means of communication and censoring the public media.

As early as 1903 the British government had been concerned about the dangers of private radio transmitters.[30] In the first days of the war, Parliament passed the Defence of the Realm Act, which stated: "No person without the permission in writing of the Postmaster General shall buy, sell, or have in his possession any apparatus for sending or receiving messages by wireless telegraphy, nor any apparatus intended to be used as a component part of such apparatus." Constables all over Britain went around confiscating or sealing up private wireless sets; by the end of August 2,500 licensed and 750 unlicensed sets were closed down.[31] In those days before sophisticated police methods, this led to a few ludicrous incidents. G. E. C. Wedlake recalls:

> One schoolboy known to the author possessed a 'receiving station' which consisted of a very crude crystal receiver hitched to an aerial hung from a short wooden mast. He duly declared this, and a few days later an army officer called to inspect it. The officer directed that the receiver should be placed in a drawer, which he proceeded to seal. Nor was this the end of it. For more than a year the officer called once a month to make sure that the seal was intact. Eventually it must have occurred to someone that the whole performance was an appalling waste of manpower, for one day the crystal set was taken away to be watched over in some central place of security and was never seen again.[32]

And Sir Basil Thomson tells a tale of hapless wireless chasers:

> On one occasion the authorities dispatched to the Eastern Counties a car equipped with a Marconi apparatus and two skilled operators to intercept any illicit messages that might be passing over the North Sea. They left London at noon; at 3 they were under lock and key in Essex. After an exchange of telegrams they were set free, but at 7 p.m. they telegraphed from the police cells in another part of the country, imploring help. When again liberated they refused to move without the escort of a Territorial officer in uniform, but on the following morning the police of another county had got hold of them and telegraphed, 'Three German spies arrested with car and complete wireless installation, one in uniform of British officer.'[33]

In spite of the spy mania that swept Britain (and every other country), no case was recorded of anyone transmitting a message to an enemy by radio, and for good reason: in those days the smallest transmitter capable of reaching a foreign country required a four-horsepower engine to power it, and let out a loud crackling sound. What the British authorities did not expect was the outcry from radio amateurs who wanted to keep their sets, not to transmit secrets to Germany but to intercept the flood of messages that the Germans were pouring forth in the course of their military operations. This aspect of communication, as we shall see, came as a complete surprise to everyone.

Much more important to the authorities were the public communication channels that linked Britain to other countries, channels upon which the nation's survival depended. In defense, Britain, like all countries at war, erected a complex censorship apparatus. Its original purpose was to prevent important information from being sent to the enemy disguised as innocent commercial or personal messages. Almost immediately another aim appeared. Since Britain had imposed a blockade on the Central Powers, the censorship stopped commercial messages to Sweden, Denmark, and the Netherlands that might have benefitted the German economy.[34]

Censorship began on August 2, 1914, even before Britain entered the war, when Colonel Arthur Churchill, head of M.I.8, a branch of Military Intelligence, took over the headquarters of the Eastern and Associated Companies in London; another censor was installed at the Porthcurno cable station two days later. Western Union handed over sacks of in-and-out cables to Naval Intelligence officers who returned them the next day; whether they were unopened, as the president of Western Union later told a Senate committee, is doubtful.[35] Naval Intelligence was also responsible for radio, and Commodore Sir Douglas Brownrigg was appointed chief censor of radio-telegraphy. The military men were aided by experts in trade, finance, and insurance to help spot suspicious telegrams.[36]

Over the next few months, censors were stationed at all the other British cable stations around the world, following plans devised before the war.[37] As the official report explained:

> The reason for this universality of censorship was that, apart from the possibility of enemy activities developing in unexpected quarters, the entire cable system throughout the world constitutes a single field which offers facilities for the use of circuitous routes apparently remote from the sphere of action.[38]

This power is exactly what other countries had feared and resented for so many years. The British made exceptions, however, when a British-owned line competed with a foreign one, for example between the United States and Latin America. There, in place of overt censorship, they used a discreet surveillance through which "the Government obtained a considerable amount of information from telegrams which actually passed, and which but for this concession would have avoided British territory altogether."[39]

Censorship involved a number of methods. At first all languages but English and French were forbidden, but that rule was gradually loosened; in January 1915 Spanish was allowed between Spain and Latin America; in July Italian could be used to and from Italy; and in June 1916 Portuguese was permitted between Portugal and its colonies. All codes were forbidden except between governments and their diplomatic representatives, but protests from the business community persuaded the censors to allow commercial codes that were deposited with the Board of Trade.[40]

Another weapon in the censors' arsenal was delay. They deliberately held back commercial telegrams to Europe for eighteen to forty-eight hours, despite protests from France, Italy, and the British public. Before major military operations the delays were as long as a week. This was done to ensure that any spy messages that might have escaped the censor's eye would arrive too late to be of use to the enemy.[41]

The application of censorship revealed other uses that had not been clearly foreseen by the British, though they were obvious to other countries. One was intelligence. This took some time. Before May 1915 the cable censors, who were Army men, had no contact with Naval Intelligence. As a result, 175 cablegrams from German naval attachés in the Americas passed through England and European neutrals on their way to Germany without being decoded; only later was it discovered that these messages contained information about German cruisers and supply ships overseas.[42] But as the censorship bureaucracy became organized, it began supplying copies of intercepted messages in ever-widening circles. Eventually 212 different ministries, departments, commissions, branches, and sections of the government were on their mailing list, and a total of 2.1 million telegrams were distributed in 10 million typed copies.[43] While most were concerned with the war effort, the U.S. State Department received reports that some business telegrams sent to the Board of Trade ended up in the hands of British firms.[44]

Britain used censorship to reinforce its control over world trade. Neutral shipping became an adjunct to the British war effort by the simple expedient of denying instructions, insurance, and fuel to any ship carrying cargo that might be of use to the enemy, the so-called "war contraband." From there the power spread: any bank or business that engaged in transactions with the enemy was cut off from the world's cable network. Britain eventually used its power to coerce a whole country. To stop the Germans from shipping sand and gravel to the Western Front via the Netherlands, Great Britain banned cable traffic with the Netherlands and its colonies on October 2, 1917. The embargo was only lifted on November 9, 1918, after the Dutch prohibited the transit trade.[45]

How effective was British cable censorship? The official report only gives it modest credit. As Major Anson of M.I.5 (British counterintelligence) wrote to Chief Cable Censor Colonel Arthur Browne: "As the censorship of cables organised by your section came fully and effectively into operation, there was a marked decrease in the use of code telegrams by enemy agents, and a corresponding development of the technique, and general use, of writing in invisible ink."[46] But in a modern war no amount of invisible ink, bound to paper letters and subject to the scrutiny and delays of the postal censorship, could have replaced telegraphic information.[47] In the final analysis, while cable censorship was of some use in catching spies and obtaining information about the enemy, its real value lay in halting the trade between the Central Powers and the world outside Europe and in alienating neutrals from the Central Powers. The only countermeasure Germany could devise was the desperate gamble of unrestricted submarine warfare.

Propaganda

World War I was the first war in which propaganda played a major role. All belligerents used it to keep up the fighting spirit of their own people, to sap that of their enemies, and to enlist the sympathy and aid of neutrals. Here the Allies had a great advantage, since they controlled the world's cables.

Before the war, four news agencies had divided up the world: Asia and the British Empire were reserved for Reuters, southern Europe and Latin America for Agence Havas, northern Europe for Wolff, and North America for the Associated Press. Reuters' vaunted independence from the British government vanished when the war broke out. It received government subsidies to distribute official Allied war communiqués to neutral countries, and its managing director, Sir Roderick Jones, also served as director of propaganda in the Ministry of Information.[48]

The Havas news agency, always an organ of the French government, continued to transmit Allied communiqués to Latin America. In the early years of the war, when the United States was still neutral, Havas refused to let the Associated Press, its cartel-mate, sell German communiqués to Argentina. In spite of this, the AP resisted official pressure to take over Havas' territory in order to avoid becoming a vehicle for U.S. government propaganda.[49]

The most important, and controversial, use of propaganda was to sway public opinion in neutral countries, especially the United States. Here the Allies, Britain in particular, used both a steady flow of news items and an effective censorship of the news from the opposite side. According to one journalist, three-quarters of the dispatches from American correspondents in Central Europe were eliminated by the British censors.[50] An authoritative study of the news reaching America from the war concluded:

> During the first year of the war, never more than 4 per cent of the front-page news [in the *New York Times*] came directly from Germany, while 70 per cent came from Entente origins, chiefly London. The direct German proportion never exceeded 12 per cent. . . .
>
> The tendency of the news was always in favor of the belligerent furnishing the greater amount. Most of the tendentious news was directed against a belligerent, rather than in favor of a belligerent. For several months after August, 1914, the news was not much more favorable to the Entente than to the Central Powers, but following the sinking of the *Lusitania* antipathy toward Germany rapidly mounted. . . .
>
> Under modern conditions, neutrality tends to terminate in favor of the belligerent which supplies the largest amount of news . . . the advantage of the belligerent in command of the means of communication is tremendous.[51]

There was more to propaganda than the sheer quantity of words transmitted; there was also a certain subtlety the British possessed, and the Germans lacked, as Franz Rintelen admitted. In 1915, he wrote,

> everybody in Germany was raging. Large packets of newspapers had been received from America, and there was not a word of truth in the reports that were being made about the military situation. We were particularly indignant at the numerous stories of atrocities which had found their way into the American papers. With this kind of journalism it was inevitable that not only the mass of newspaper readers, but gradually also official circles in America, would assume an anti-German attitude. . . .

I . . . was frequently the center of a whole group of foreign journalists. Eventually we succeeded in making it clear to them that the military situation was not unfavourable for Germany at all. When they were finally convinced of this they were honest enough to cable impartial reports to their papers in America. But no sooner had these articles appeared than our rooms were veritably stormed by the foreign correspondents, who protested that the British were no longer transmitting their wires. The British controlled the international cables, and were naturally exercising a strict censorship in their own favour. . . .

I was on good terms with Major Langhorne, the American Military Attaché in Berlin, who too had his difficulties owning to the English control of the foreign cables. He was in search of a way to send his telegrams to Washington without London reading or intercepting them. . . . I proposed to him that he should give us the code telegrams and that we should have them sent via Nauen to the American wireless station, which had just been completed. In this way they would speedily reach his Government at Washington. . . .

When we gained those great victories in Russia . . . I re-wrote Major Langhorne's telegrams so that they gave a clear account of our military position, and added the whole extent of the enemy defeats in such a way, of course, that the American Government was bound to believe that these telegrams came from its own Military Attaché.

Things went on well for weeks. When the next batch of American newspapers arrived a certain change of view was already noticeable in the more serious journals. Germany's strategic position was regarded and criticised more favourably, and I rejoiced at this success. Suddenly, however, . . . I overdid matters by sending a telegram which allowed a certain pro-German attitude to be apparent between the lines, and the end came soon. Without warning and without reason Major Langhorne received laconic instructions from Washington to return to America. . . . when [he] was shown his telegrams on his arrival in Washington he of course immediately denied that he had ever sent them, and little acumen was required to realise from whom they had come.

I was pricked by conscience at the way in which I had acted, but I consoled myself with the thought that Germany was facing a world in arms, a vastly superior force, which would perhaps crush her if she did not use every means in her power to defend herself.

Every means in her power![52]

Conclusion

What was the impact of communications on the conduct of the war? By 1917, Allied cable communications were strained beyond the limit just through the huge increase in wartime traffic. In 1918 the British government alone was cabling 30,000 words a day, ten times more than in 1913.[53] German cable cutting may have exacerbated the pressures that led to the construction of transatlantic radio stations, but, while press and private telegrams were backed up for days, sometimes for weeks, official messages always got through on time and safe from German espionage.

For the real weapon was not the ability to cut cables or damage radio stations, but to repair them. Germany's cables, once cut, were lost for good. Germany's ability to communicate overseas by radio was also damaged in the first months of the war, and its last remaining link, the radio transmitters at Nauen and Eilvese, were vulnerable to code-breaking.

In contrast, Allied cables did not remain out of commission for more than a few weeks. Britain and France never lost for long the ability to communicate by cable and in secrecy with Russia, India, the Far East, or the Americas. The United States did much better: It developed a true imperial chain stretching from Paris to Manila, the first serious rival to Britain's globe-girdling cable network. In the battle over cables and radio in a war in which so much hinged on good communications, the Allies won a total victory.

Notes

1. Stephen Kern, *The Culture of Time and Space 1880–1918* (Cambridge, Mass., 1983), 275–76.
2. Ibid., 263.
3. Ibid., 266–67.
4. Ibid., 267–68.
5. Ibid., 268.
6. "Committee of Imperial Defence. Submarine Cables in Time of War. Note of Action Taken upon the Report of the Standing Sub-Committee (June 1, 1912)," in Public Record Office [PRO], Cab 38/21/21.
7. Most authors say the *Telconia* cut the cables off the German coast; see, for example, Christopher Andrew, *Secret Service: The Making of the British Intelligence Community* (London, 1985), 87; Patrick Beesly, *Room 40: British Naval Intelligence, 1914–18* (London, 1982); and Barbara Tuchman, *The Zimmermann Telegram* (New York, 1958), 14–15. However, the German cable expert Artur Kunert says it was the *Alert* in the English Channel; see *Geschichte der deutschen Fernmeldekabel. II. Telegraphen-Seekabel* (Cologne–Mülheim, 1962), 349–51; so does J. Bourdeaux, "Submarine Cable Work during the War," *Post Office Electrical Engineers Journal* 13 (1920–21), 237.
8. "1914–1918 War Crisis. Correspondence concerning & instructions to stations re censorship and operations during the war," in Cable and Wireless archives (London), 1490.
9. Captain Franz Rintelen von Kleist, *The Dark Invader: Wartime Reminiscences of a German Intelligence Officer* (New York, 1933), 35–37. This book, like all the reminiscences of spies, must be treated with great circumspection, for it contains as much swashbuckling derring-do as believable information.
10. Sayville was officially confiscated in 1917 when the United States entered the war; Hugh G. J. Aitken, *The Continuous Wave: Technology and American Radio, 1900–1932* (Princeton, N.J., 1985), 285–86.
11. While numerous authors mention these events, there are many variations in the dates. See W. J. Baker, *A History of the Marconi Company* (London, 1970), 160; Albereto Santoni, *Il primo Ultra Secret: L'influenza delle decrittazioni britanniche sulle operazioni navali della guerra 1914–1918* (Milan, 1985), 104–6; Arthur R. Hezlet, *The Electron and Sea Power* (London, 1975), 84; Hugh Barty-King, *Girdle Round the Earth: The Story of Cable and Wireless and its Predecessors to Mark the Group's Jubilee, 1929–1979* (London, 1979), 166; W. Schmidt and Hans Werner, *Geschichte der Deutschen Post in den Kolonien und im Ausland* (Leipzig, 1942), 79–88; Aitken, 257; and Kunert, 240–42 and 249–57.
12. Barty-King, 173–75.
13. "Telegraph Communications in Time of War: Direct Wireless Telegraph Communications with Russia" (March 7, 1913), in PRO, Cab 4/5/2/173B; G. L. Lawford and L. R.

Nicholson, *The Telcon Story, 1850, 1950* (London, 1950), 90; Hezlet, 85; Kunert, 359–60 and 709.

14. Gerald R. M. Garratt, *One Hundred Years of Submarine Cables* (London, 1950), 33.

15. *The Great War: The Standard History of the All Europe Conflict* (London, 1914–19), 11:213–16; S. A. Garnham and Robert L. Hadfield, *The Submarine Cable: The Story of the Submarine Telegraph Cable from its Inception down to Modern Times. How it Works, how Cable-Ships Work, and how it Carries on in Peace and War* (London, 1934), 188–91; Barty-King, 164.

16. Kenneth C. Baglehole, *A Century of Service. A Brief History of Cable and Wireless Ltd. 1868–1968* (London, 1969), 24–25; *Great War*, 11:217–19; Santoni, 140–52.

17. Graham Storey recounts an incident in which "an Admiralty repair ship found attached to one of the ends of a severed cable a bottle in which was a slip of paper saying: 'This is the work of U-Boat No. 26 and puts a stop to Reuters' damned anti-German lies.' " *Reuters: The Story of a Century of News-Gathering* (New York, 1951), 166. Unfortunately, I have found no confirmation of this delightful story.

18. The sources differ widely. Here I have followed the account of F. Birch and W. F. Clarke, *A Contribution to the History of German Naval Warfare 1914–1918*, 3 vols. (compiled c. 1920), 1:649 and 657; Vols. 1 and 2 are unpublished, Vol. 3 is secret; I am indebted to Donard de Cogan for this information. But see also Kunert, 709–12, who lists numerous Allied cables damaged or destroyed in the course of the war: five off Canso in September 1918 and possibly one off Vigo (January 1915) and one off Brest (February 1915); all the rest were in the North Sea, the Baltic, or the Black Sea. On the cables off Sandy Hook, see Captain Linwood S. Howeth, *History of Communications-Electronics in the United States Navy* (Washington, D.C., 1963), 235; R. H. Gibson and Maurice Prendergast, *The German Submarine War, 1914–1918* (New York, 1931), 307; and Robert M. Grant, *U-Boat Intelligence 1914–1918* (London, 1969), 151–52.

19. Kunert, 349–58; Garnham and Hadfield, 177–79; Barty-King, 172–75.

20. "Imperial Wireless Chain," memorandum from Postmaster-General C. E. Hobhouse, September 5, 1914, in PRO, Cab 37/121; Baker, 160; Barty-King, 162.

21. *Report on Cable Censorship during the Great War (1914–1919)* prepared by Colonel Arthur Browne, chief cable censor, in PRO, DEFE 1/130, 65–66; Baker, 159–61; Hezlet, 95.

22. Jean d'Arbaumont, *Historique des télégraphistes coloniaux* (Paris, 1955), 43; René Duval, *Histoire de la radio en France* (Paris, 1980), 25; Emile Girardeau, *Souvenirs de longue vie* (Paris, 1968), 77; Maurice Guierre, *Les ondes et les hommes, histoire de la radio* (Paris, 1951), 107–8; Société Française Radio-Electrique, *Vingt-cinq années de TSF* (Paris, 1935), 47.

23. Susan J. Douglas, *Inventing American Broadcasting, 1899–1922* (Baltimore, 1987), 266–67; Aitken, 153–58; Hezlet, 136; Howeth, 222–24.

24. Douglas, 269.

25. Douglas, 270–73; Howeth, 225–29; Aitken, 285.

26. Paul Schubert, *The Electric Word* (New York, 1928), 150–52; Aitken, 286; Douglas, 276.

27. Aitken, 312; Schubert, 155–56; Douglas, 278; Howeth, 235–41. This is the station that carried President Wilson's Fourteen Points speech on January 8, 1918; see Howeth, 295, and Douglas, 280.

28. Aitken, 254.

29. Aitken, 286–87; Douglas, 279; Schubert, 152–63.

30. "Use by private persons of wireless telegraph stations in war-time" (November 18, 1903), in PRO, Cab 38/3/72.

31. Nigel West, *GCHQ: The Secret Wireless War 1900–86* (London, 1986), 20–21.

32. G. E. C. Wedlake, *SOS: The Story of Radio Communication* (Newton Abbot, 1973), 101.

33. Sir Basil Thomson, *Queer People* (London, 1922), 39, quoted in Christopher Andrew, *Secret Service,* 178.

34. The most valuable source on British censorship is the *Report on Cable Censorship during the Great War.*

35. Aitken, 260–61.

36. *Report on Cable Censorship,* 301; Andrew, 176; Barty-King, 163; West, 26–27.

37. The prewar censorship plans are to be found in "Censorship of submarine cables in time of war" (1904), in PRO, Cab 17/92; "Censorship of submarine cables in time of war. Action to be taken by Her Majesty's Government and by different government departments concerned. Prepared by the General Staff, War Office" (May 30, 1905), in FO 83/2196, Nos. 387–427; "Report of an inter-departmental committee appointed to draw up instructions for establishing a secret censorship of submarine cables at certain foreign stations in time of grave emergency" (1908), in Cab 17/92; and "Regulations for censorship of submarine cable communications and frontier land lines throughout the British Empire and radio-telegraphy in the Overseas Possession and Protectorates" (1913), in WO 33/610.

38. *Report on Cable Censorship,* 9–10.

39. *Report on Cable Censorship,* 60–61.

40. *Report on Cable Censorship,* 51.

41. *Report on Cable Censorship,* 16–18 and 59–60; "War Crisis," in Cable and Wireless, 1490; Barty-King, 163; West, 28.

42. Beesly, 129.

43. *Report on Cable Censorship,* 351.

44. Aitken, 261.

45. *Report on Cable Censorship,* 19–23 and 40–45.

46. *Report on Cable Censorship,* 103–4.

47. On secret ink, see Herbert O. Yardley, *The American Black Chamber* (New York, 1931, reprinted 1981), 26–39.

48. Jonathan Fenby, *The International News Services* (New York, 1986), 45; Storey, 160–71.

49. Vary T. Coates and Bernard Finn, *A Retrospective Technology Assessment: Submarine Telegraphy. The Transatlantic Cable of 1866* (San Francisco, 1979), 82; Fenby, 45–46.

50. Walter Millis, *The Road to War* (Boston, 1935), 147.

51. Harry S. Foster, Jr., "Studies in America's News of the European War" (Ph.D. dissertation, University of Chicago, 1932), abstract, 7–11.

52. Rintelen, 57–60.

53. Barty-King, 175.

9

Communications Intelligence in World War I

War brings with it a great urge to communicate. Armies on the move and fleets of ships soon disappear from the line of vision of their commanding officers. Before the twentieth century, this was one of the frustrations of command, part of what Clausewitz called "the fog of war," which prevented even Napoleon and Nelson from engaging in battles covering more than a few square miles.

With the industrial age, all that changed. The telegraph, the telephone, and especially the radio finally allowed commanders to control enormous forces spread over hundreds of square miles. Yet the outcome was a complete surprise: instead of Napoleonic battles on a gargantuan scale, war once again became medieval, each alliance an impregnable fortress besieged by invincible enemies. There are many reasons for this that military strategists and historians will no doubt debate forever. But in the mix of causes, communications played a significant part. For the new communications not only allowed each side better command and control of its own forces, they also permitted the enemy to penetrate and partially neutralize those very advantages. In modern warfare, as the belligerents belatedly realized, communication was inseparable from its nemesis, communications intelligence.

Communications intelligence belongs to the secret world of intelligence and espionage. Indeed, *comint* (to use its military name) is the most secret part of that world, more vital even than "human intelligence" or cloak-and-dagger espionage. Governments and the military have willingly tolerated leaks about the exploits of traditional spies as a smokescreen hiding the humdrum but more productive work of those who capture signals from the ether, decrypt messages, and analyze radio traffic. Thus, in our own time, the American public is much more familiar with the CIA than with the far larger National Security Agency, and in Britain, M.I.6 is much better known than its shadowy cousin the Government Communications Headquarters.

Cryptology, the science of codes and ciphers, is an essential part of communications intelligence. Though its origins can be traced back to the dawn of civilization, its modern history is intimately bound with that of communications technologies. The telegraph led to the development of new forms of codes and ciphers and methods of creating them: the science of cryptography. Because the national land telegraph systems were relatively safe from espionage and because the telegraph appeared in an era of European peace, little attention was paid to methods of breaking codes and ciphers. Radio, by scattering its signals in all directions, made codes and ciphers far more vulnerable than they had been in the days of the telegraph; hence it led to cryptanalysis, the art of cracking codes and ciphers. This was not the result of an orderly process of logic, but of trial and errors, of victories and defeats in war.[1]

Government Cryptology before 1914

Commercial codes, while invaluable, offered no security, which is why the British had tolerated them during the Boer War. For official correspondence requiring secrecy, governments preferred ciphers or number codes that could be superenciphered as an additional precaution. The British Foreign Office began encrypting its transatlantic telegrams as an economy measure in 1867, but continued the practice for security reasons.[2] After some embarrassing leaks to the press in the *Alabama* claims negotiations of 1872, the U.S. State Department developed its Red Code for sensitive telegrams, which it used until 1918.[3]

While every government created new codes and ciphers, historians of intelligence agree that there was little code breaking or cryptanalysis. Britain closed its "black chamber" in 1844; Germany and the United States never had one. Christopher Andrew writes: "By abandoning cryptanalysis at a time when the electric telegraph . . . was about to make both the transmission and interception of diplomatic messages much easier, the Foreign Office deprived itself of what was to become the most valuable form of diplomatic intelligence gathering."[4] After the Boer War, Colonel Edmonds, head of Section H (later M.O.5, now M.I.5), the military intelligence branch of the War Office, tried to compile a list of experts in deciphering and intelligence, but with little success.[5] Lieutenant Colonel Thomas Fergusson, historian of British military intelligence, writes: "The available evidence indicates that, although officers of MO5 studied foreign codes and ciphers, they did not engage in an organized code-breaking operation against the encrypted communications of any foreign power before the beginning of the Great War."[6] Naval historian Arthur Hezlet concludes: "Before the outbreak of war, no government department in Great Britain had contemplated trying to decipher secret enemy messages even if war should break out."[7]

The same was true of Germany. Heinz Bonatz, historian of German naval intelligence, notes that the German navy began intercepting British radio communications from 1907 on, but only to keep abreast of British technical progress, not to decrypt the messages.[8] As David Kahn explains, "The 1870 victory may have convinced the Germans that they were doing things right and did not need to change. . . . Their writers occupied themselves with cryptography to the virtual neglect of cryptanalysis."[9]

In those crucial years before the war, only France and Austria–Hungary kept alive the art of cryptanalysis.[10] The French government, stung by the humiliation of 1871, sought to compensate for military weakness through superior intelligence. It employed talented cryptologists like Auguste Kerckhoffs, author of *La cryptographie militaire,* and Etienne Bazeries, who worked at the Bureau du Chiffre (or "cabinet noir") of the Ministry of Foreign Affairs. Using copies of telegrams furnished by the Ministry of Posts and Telegraphs, the Bureau du Chiffre "was successful in at least partially breaking the diplomatic codes and ciphers of Italy, England, Germany, Turkey, and Japan, and probably those of the United States and Spain as well."[11] As war approached, the French government shared some of the results of its espionage with Britain, just as Austria–Hungary did with Germany, but without giving away the methods.[12]

Communications Intelligence on Land

No war was ever so precisely prepared as was World War I. Each side drew up detailed mobilization timetables, strategic plans, and marching orders. The most precise of all were the Germans. Their General Staff had planned in great detail not only how they would win, but also exactly when and where the enemy would lose. And their plan almost succeeded.

To control the hundreds of thousands of men involved in the attack on France, the General Staff developed an impressive communications network. The attacking armies were to use the telegraph lines in Belgium and France and, as a backup, they had thirty transportable radio stations and twenty-two light radios. In Belgium the resistance was greater than anticipated, and much of its telegraph network was damaged. In the offensive of August 1914, the attacking Germans had to use the radio more than they had planned, even between the General Staff headquarters at Koblenz and the armies in the field. As a result, messages were delayed for hours, sometimes days, by overload, inefficiency, and French jamming from the Eiffel Tower.[13]

In terms of radio equipment, the Western allies were worse off. When the war began, the entire British army had exactly ten radio sets, only one of which was in France in early August.[14] However, the French and British had the inestimable advantage, in communications terms, of falling back, for retreat gave them access to telegraph and telephone networks that were not yet damaged in battle.

The worst off were the Russians. Faithful to their obligations, they invaded East Prussia in mid-August 1914 to relieve the pressure on France. General Samsonov, on the offensive in enemy territory, committed one of the greatest blunders in military history: To ensure that his orders reached his corps commanders more rapidly and more accurately, he ordered that they be transmitted in plain language. The Germans, listening to the radio, had the pleasure of hearing the Russian plans laid out before them. The result was the massive German victory of Tannenberg (August 26–30), at which Samsonov's army was surrounded, 100,000 men were taken prisoner, and Samsonov himself committed suicide.[15]

By September the offensives were exhausted, and armies on both sides sank into the mud. On the Western Front, the communications picture changed. Behind the German lines, the telegraph and telephone lines were repaired, and radio was no longer used between the General Staff and the various army headquarters. Near the front, however, the situation was reversed. Artillery barrages forced army corps headquarters back, and broke the lines linking them to the forward trenches. On both sides, the armies demanded field wireless sets, mass produced from 1916 on using the newly developed vacuum tubes.[16]

One area in which there was no substitute for radio was artillery spotting. Heavy guns hurled their shells so far, the only way to see where they landed was from an airplane far above the battlefield. To communicate the observations back to the gunners, spotter planes were equipped with radios. At first, interference between the airborne transmitters limited their use to one for every two thousand yards of front, but from 1916 on continuous-wave transmitters made it possible to send up ever greater numbers of planes; with radiotelephones squadron commanders could even stay in touch with their units during dogfights. By the fall of 1918, the British Royal Flying Corps alone had some six hundred planes and one thousand ground stations at the Western Front.[17]

Radio, however, was easily intercepted, and thus a precious source of intelligence. Field ciphers were never fully secure, and even changes in the frequency or direction of transmissions alerted the enemy to an impending attack. In August 1914 the French and British military intelligence services began intercepting and analyzing German radio traffic. In October two former Marconi engineers, C. S. Franklin and H. C. Round, went to France to set up the first direction-finding stations. From these beginnings there grew up, on both sides of the front, chains of intercept and direction-finding stations able to locate the positions of aircraft, dirigibles, and ground stations.[18]

France had long had sophisticated code-breaking agencies in the Ministries of War and Foreign Affairs. When the German armies overran northern France and began using radio, the military Bureau du Chiffre under Colonel François Cartier took advantage of German inexperience in secret communications. Breaches of security committed by German signal corpsmen—repeating messages in several codes, mixing code and plain language, using stereotyped phrases—gave the French an opportunity to break German codes time and again.[19]

The French also benefitted from the German ignorance or disdain of cryptanalysis. While some German radiomen stationed in northern France were able to penetrate a low-grade British naval code in the fall of 1914, there is no evidence that German cryptanalysis had much impact on the fighting until the end of the war.[20]

By 1916, both sides began avoiding the tactical use of radio and returned, whenever possible, to more secure methods: the telegraph and the telephone. Yet these devices, which used a wire and an earth return, were known to leak currents that could be picked up with the appropriate device. In early 1915 Captain Stanley and Sergeant Nesbitt-Hawes of the British Expeditionary Forces developed a device with an earth antenna and a three-tube amplifier that could monitor German telephone conversations across the front. They discovered that the Germans already had such devices and were learning of Allied offensives ahead of time. Thereafter, both sides banned the use of field telephones within three kilometers of the front and replaced the earth returns with a two-wire system. This alleviated the problem somewhat, but did not solve it entirely.[21]

Not until the offensive in the spring of 1918, the first real movement on the Western Front since the summer of 1914, did the Germans use field radios once again. This time they used a new cipher, the ADFGVX, the most complicated ever used in battle. From the start of the Ludendorff Offensive on March 21, 1918, it was clear that the Allied defense depended on breaking this system. When Captain Georges Painvin, France's most gifted cryptanalyst, finally cracked it in early June, it revealed the location of Ludendorff's final plan of attack, which the French were thus able to thwart.[22] But by then the Germans had also made some progress in cryptanalysis: on September 12, 1918, the American army attacking the St. Mihiel salient found that the Germans had already evacuated it, because they had broken the rather simple American cipher and knew the attack was coming.[23] Though both sides had made great strides in cryptanalysis, the science that told the French where to counterattack only told the German army when to retreat.

British Naval Interception and Direction-Finding

On the Western Front the belligerents were evenly matched in every respect, including their communications, and intelligence did not affect the outcome. At sea, however, intelligence was as important as strategy and armaments. As recent studies have shown, British command of the sea, hence the security of Britain, hinged on superior naval intelligence as well as on a bigger fleet.[24]

Part of the credit for the success of British naval intelligence in World War I must go to the German navy. When the war broke out, German battleships, flagships, and coastal stations were equipped with Poulsen–Lorenz arc transmitters, and smaller vessels with Telefunken musical-frequency spark transmitters.[25] The navy had long stressed the value of good communications, especially in combat, where tightly coordinated fleet operations were seen as the key to victory and ships were expected to maneuver with the precision of eighteenth-century infantrymen. Naval historian Helmuth Giessler sums up the attitude of the navy with these words: "They were just happy finally to be able to communicate with one another without wires!"[26]

To avoid enemy jamming—their great fear—radio operators were taught to repeat messages at different frequencies. For security, they relied on two techniques: low-power transmission and secret codes. The naval high command had such faith in these precautions that it had issued orders before the war forbidding participants in maneuvers to intercept and try to decrypt each other's messages.[27] Korvettenkapitän Bindseil expressed the smug self-righteousness of the Kriegsmarine in these words: "An iron radio discipline ensured the military efficiency of this important communications medium."[28] Thus protected by a feeling of security that only self-delusion can provide, the German navy confronted an enemy with no moral compunctions about spying.

When the war began, the British were perhaps as disorganized as the Germans were self-deluded. The Royal Navy had only one listening station at Stockton and no experience in communications intelligence. In the inimitable manner of which the British are so proud, it was amateurs who came to the rescue of a torpid officialdom. When the call went out confiscating all privately owned radio receivers, two were somehow overlooked. One belonged to Russell Clarke, a barrister and friend of Sir Alfred Ewing, Director of Naval Education; the other to Richard Hippisley, retired Royal Engineers colonel and former director of the South African telegraphs. With their sets they intercepted a flood of radio messages from Germany, all of them in code, which they passed on to Naval Intelligence.

Rear Admiral H. F. Oliver, Director of Naval Intelligence (and later Chief of Staff under First Sea Lord Jacky Fisher), gave the intercepts to Ewing, who had expressed an interest in cryptology. Ewing assembled a team of linguists, mathematicians, and other academic types, and set them to work trying to crack the coded messages that were piling up. This team later moved to room 40 in the Admiralty's Old Building in Whitehall, and have ever since been referred to as "Room 40."[29]

Meanwhile, Hippisley and Clarke were set up in a radio station at Hunstanton in Norfolk to obtain more intercepts. A dozen other stations were later added to form the Y (intercept) Service with direct lines to the Admiralty.

By 1916 the great majority of German naval signals from the Heligoland Bight (where the German High Seas Fleet was stationed) were being intercepted, and by 1917 all signals were being heard, even low-power ones between ships in harbor. In addition, the Y Service intercepted some German signals from the Baltic and, in cooperation with the French, German and Austrian signals from the Mediterranean.[30]

Intercepting enemy signals, of course, was only the beginning. The other elements in communications intelligence included direction-finding (to locate the origin of the signal), traffic analysis (to extract information from a pattern of signals), decryption, and, finally, analysis or drawing the right conclusions about enemy forces and intentions from the raw data.

For direction-finding purposes, Britain had an advantage over Germany: While the Germans were restricted to a short piece of coastline stretching from the Danish border on the north to Ostende in the south, the British could place stations all along their coasts. With a longer baseline, they could locate enemy transmitters more precisely than could the Germans.

In September 1914 Lieutenant Round of Military Intelligence suggested to Rear Admiral Oliver that Bellini–Tosi directional antennas be used in pairs to locate enemy transmitters by triangulation. After having erected a chain of direction-finding stations along the Western Front, he returned to Britain to set up six stations stretching from the Shetland Islands to southern England, and later others in southern Ireland and in the Mediterranean.[31] These so-called B Stations were equipped with vacuum tube receivers, which were much more sensitive than the older crystal sets, and could determine the position of a transmitter in the North Sea within twenty miles, and within fifty miles in the Atlantic. Even without decrypting the messages, British Naval Intelligence was able to learn a great deal about German ships, U-boats, and Zeppelins just by observing the frequency, location, movement, and call signs of their transmissions. Not until 1916 did the Germans realize how sensitive and accurate the British receivers were; after that they became much more circumspect in their use of the radio.[32]

German Codes and British Cryptanalysis in 1914

Direction-finding served another and more subtle purpose in the game of intelligence: it provided a cover for the work of Room 40, which was the most closely guarded secret of the war. The German navy, like all others, used codes enciphered with a key that changed periodically. By one of the strangest twists of fate in military history, the British obtained three of the most precious German codebooks right at the start of the war. On August 11, 1914, the Australian navy seized the German freighter *Hobart* off Melbourne. The captain, unaware that war had started, did not have time to destroy his codebook, which fell into Australian hands. The *Handelsverkehrsbuch,* or HVB, was the code used by German merchantmen, U-boats, and Zeppelins. The Australians sent a copy of HVB to Britain, where it arrived in October.

On August 26, during an engagement with Russian cruisers in the Baltic, the cruiser *Magdeburg* was sunk and the Russians captured its codebook, the *Signalbuch der Kaiserlichen Marine,* or SKM, along with its current superencipherment tables. This was the most secret of all the naval codes, the one used in battle. The Russian navy, in a rare gesture of generosity, sent this material to Britain, where it arrived on October 10.

Finally, on November 30, a British fishing trawler recovered a lead-lined chest from the German destroyer *S-119,* which sank off the Dutch coast on October 17. This chest contained the *Verkehrsbuch,* or VB, used at sea by flag officers.[33]

It was the capture of these three codes that allowed Room 40 to decrypt the radio messages of the German navy and gave the British, in Beesly's words, "better information about the movements and intentions of their opponents than any other military command had ever possessed."[34] Or, as Heinz Bonatz put it more bluntly: "The Imperial Navy waged war in the first three years of World War I with an open hand of cards."[35]

Recently, however, Italian naval historian Alberto Santoni has cast some doubts on this version. At the outbreak of war, two German warships, the battle cruiser *Goeben* and the light cruiser *Breslau,* found themselves in the Mediterranean. On August 4, the German Admiralty radioed to Admiral Souchon, commander of the two ships, ordering him to sail for Constantinople. The next day, he was told that Turkey would not allow him to enter. Two days later, the Turks changed their minds. On August 10, after a wild chase around the Mediterranean with the British in hot pursuit, the *Goeben* and the *Breslau* entered the Dardanelles, where their presence helped bring Turkey into the war on the German side.

During those events, the messages between the German Admiralty and Souchon, encoded in the VB code, were decrypted by the British within hours; and this before there was a Room 40, and long before the VB code was miraculously fished out of the sea. In fact, the British had been cracking this code since March 1914, months before the war began. They were also able to decrypt messages in SKM and in HVB from mid-August on, even though they did not obtain the codebooks until two months later.[36] In Santoni's words:

> We must therefore conclude that the Naval Intelligence Division of the British Admiralty, from the very first days of the war and even when Room 40 was not yet officially founded, was able to "read" correctly the three German naval codes HVB, SKM, and VB and even the diplomatic code ABC. And this thanks to a timely work of analysis and reconstruction that in many cases preceded the material possession of these secret documents.[37]

Deception, which is the very essence of intelligence work in wartime, does not stop when the war ends, but continues in the documents upon which historians rely when reconstructing the past. Faced with a tale of deception, the historian can only ask: What motives lie behind it?

Santoni provides a plausible explanation. The British, and in particular Winston Churchill, who was First Lord of the Admiralty during these events, wanted it believed that their cryptological achievements in World War I were the result of good fortune cleverly exploited by a handful of amateurs. This story would reassure future potential enemies that such fortuitous circumstances were unlikely to happen again, and that there was nothing inherently superior in British Naval Intelligence. Both during and after the war, the Germans refused to believe that the British had a better cryptanalytic service than their own, and attributed British successes to better direction-finding and sheer blind luck. Lulled by an overoptimistic faith in their own communications security, they fell into the same trap in World War II. Deception served a useful purpose.[38]

While the question of British cryptanalytic achievements in the first months of war was to have long-run consequences, it had no short-run impact because of flaws in the command structure. For it is not enough to know an enemy's forces and intentions; one must also act on that information. And here, unfortunately, the admirals who commanded the Royal Navy—Fisher, the First Sea Lord, and Jellicoe, commander of the Grand Fleet—were little inclined to piece together the scraps of information from intercepts and decrypts, or to listen to the advice of subordinates and civilians. During 1914 the Admiralty therefore acted as if secret codes and decrypts hardly existed. A faulty staff system explains why the Royal Navy, despite its overwhelming superiority in the Mediterranean and its knowledge of Admiral Souchon's intentions, was not able to stop the *Goeben* and the *Breslau*.

A more serious incident took place in December. On the 14th, Room 40 decrypted radio messages indicating that the German battle cruisers, commanded by Vice Admiral Hipper, were about to make a sortie against the east coast of England. Though warned, the Admiralty reacted too slowly, and Hipper was able to shell the seaside towns of Hartlepool, Whitby, and Scarborough and escape back to Germany. Meanwhile, the German High Seas Fleet had also come out, but it kept radio silence, hoping to trap the British. Hipper's battle cruisers, Jellicoe's Grand Fleet, and von Ingenohl's High Seas Fleet all slipped past each other in the North Sea fog, and everything returned back to normal. It was the first of a series of stalemates in the North Sea.[39]

The most important naval battles of 1914 did not take place between the great fleets poised to strike at each other across the North Sea, but far away, off the southern tip of South America. Here too, communications and the lack thereof played an important role.

In early August the German East Asiatic Squadron, commanded by Admiral von Spee, left Tsingtao in China, headed for the South Pacific. von Spee had no means of communicating with Germany except by stopping off at a neutral port and sending a cable. At the end of August he dispatched the cruiser *Nürnberg* to Honolulu to organize, with the help of the German consul, a supply service for the fleet off the west coast of South America. Having accomplished that mission, the *Nürnberg* then proceeded to Fanning Island to cut the British Pacific cable.

For over a month the British lost track of the fleet. Then on October 4 the Australian Naval Office at Melbourne decrypted a radio message in code HVB between von Spee's flagship the *Scharnhorst* and the light cruiser *Dresden* and cabled the decrypt to London. The Admiralty ordered Rear Admiral Craddock, based in the South Atlantic, to intercept von Spee.

Off the coast of Chile, both fleets had great difficulties communicating with their governments. The Germans communicated by radio with the German merchantman *Yorck* interned at Valparaiso, where the German consul transmitted messages by cable to neutral countries in Europe, from which they were retransmitted to Germany. Due to poor relations between the Admiralty and the War Office, which ran the cable censorship, the British, who controlled the cables, did not systematically intercept or decrypt these German naval telegrams disguised as neutral messages until several months later.[40] The British Admiralty used much the same routes, and messages took days to reach their destination.

Locally, von Spee was kept well informed of the location and strength of Craddock's fleet by the *Yorck* and by Chilean coastal stations. His radio operators also intercepted messages between the British cruisers *Good Hope, Monmouth,* and *Glasgow.* On October 31, Craddock learnt that he faced the entire German East Asiatic Squadron. Knowing himself outnumbered, he requested reinforcements. On November 3 the British Admiralty received his request and dispatched the cruiser *Defence* to his support. By that time, however, Craddock and his fleet had been sunk for two days already. The battle of Coronel on November 1, 1914, was the worst British naval disaster in over a century, and it was due in part to the attempts of the Admiralty in London to control events thousands of miles away, well beyond the reach of effective communications.

When the Admiralty learned the news of Coronel on November 4, it reacted quickly to repair the damage. On November 19 Room 40 decrypted a telegram in the ABC diplomatic code from the German consul in Valparaiso relating von Spee's intention to sail for Germany via the South Atlantic. The Admiralty sent Admiral Sturdee with a larger fleet, including the battle cruisers *Invincible* and *Inflexible,* to the Falklands to intercept von Spee. This time it took some elementary precautions to safeguard its communications. The cruiser *Vindictive,* equipped with a powerful transmitter, was stationed at Ascension Island to act as a relay. As Sturdee maintained radio silence, von Spee believed he had sailed for South Africa to put down a Boer revolt. And so on December 8 von Spee's fleet headed for the Falklands, fell into Sturdee's trap, and was destroyed.[41]

British Naval Intelligence, 1915–1916

The battles of Coronel and the Falklands are important from a communications as well as a naval point of view. In them, the British learned the importance of getting accurate decrypts, of receiving information and issuing orders on a timely basis, and of maintaining radio silence. While the Admiralty still had a great deal to learn about integrating communications intelligence into operational practice, the events off South America constituted a major step forward in this learning process. And a large part of the credit must go to Captain William "Blinker" Hall, named Director of the Intelligence Division in November 1914 when Admiral Oliver became Chief of Staff. Although his relations with Ewing and Room 40 were never officially clarified, Hall, unlike Oliver and Ewing, had a gift for conspiracy and espionage, and understood the intricate relations between intelligence and operations. He was able to make full use of this gift in late 1916 and early 1917, after Ewing had returned to academic life.[42]

From a naval point of view, the year 1915 was uneventful. The German fleet stayed bottled up in its North Sea harbors, its admirals afraid to confront the more powerful Royal Navy, and waiting for the German army to bring about victory on land. The Royal Navy, for its part, was content to maintain the blockade of Germany and averse to risking its tenuous superiority in an all-out battle. Even when the Germans risked themselves in a sortie, as at the Dogger Bank on January 22–24, 1915, the encounter was indecisive. Warships were so precious and irreplaceable that the officers on both sides preferred a stalemate to the dangers of a costly encounter.

Part of the indecisiveness on the British side was a reluctance to do anything that would betray their knowledge of German codes, and this in turn meant passing up opportunities to use this information operationally. So successful was this policy that the Germans, already complacent in security matters, were slow to take the necessary precautions. The German Admiralty, aware of the loss of SKM after the sinking of the *Magdeburg*, did not think it would have serious consequences and did not distribute a new edition of the key table for two months. Similarly, it suspected the loss of the HVB code as early as November 1914 and received confirmation from a survivor of the Falklands battle who was able to communicate to Germany that the British had broken the German codes, but did not reduce its radio traffic until June 1915. Even then, the German Naval Staff blamed the leaks on British direction-finding rather than on cryptanalysis.[43] It also concluded, after a careful investigation, that the German codes were unbreakable and that the British must have received their information from spies and traitors, "some of them going as far as to suspect Admiral von Tirpitz himself."[44] As a result, the German navy did not get new codes until very late in the war. These were the *Funkverkehrsbuch* (FVB), which replaced the old HVB for U-boats in the summer of 1915, and the *Allgemeines Funkspruchbuch* (AFB) issued in early 1916. The British broke the AFB in September 1916 after the codebook was found in a Zeppelin shot down over England.[45]

The most important naval engagement of World War I, the battle of Jutland on May 31–June 1, 1916, also enjoys the dubious distinction of being the most hotly disputed in naval history. Heinz Bonatz and Alberto Santoni consider it to have been a German victory, and, tactically, it was: The German fleet, though smaller, sank fourteen British ships, three of them battle cruisers, for a total of 113,580 tons, while losing only eleven ships, of which one battle cruiser, totalling 61,760 tons.[46] Yet neither side won, since the balance of power after Jutland remained exactly what it had been before, with the German fleet blockaded in its harbors by the Royal Navy. But that situation, in itself, was favorable to Britain, for it made the Germans use submarines, hence antagonizing the United States.

The battle brought out the strengths and weaknesses of the communications and intelligence capabilities of both sides. On May 29, before the German ships had even weighed anchor, Room 40 had decrypted the first German messages in both the new AFB and the old SKM and VB codes. The following day, when Admiral Scheer ordered the High Seas Fleet to assemble in the outer Jade estuary, Room 40 decrypted his signals, and the direction-finding stations observed the ships moving out to sea. However, the Germans had exchanged call signs between their flagship and a shore station at Wilhelmshaven. Despite the temporary confusion this created in the British Admiralty, the Grand Fleet and the battle cruisers were ordered out to sea in time to intercept the High Seas Fleet off Jutland the next day.

When the two fleets met, they erupted in radio traffic. While the Germans used direction-finding, traffic analysis, and air reconnaissance to good effect, the British had the decrypts of German signals almost as soon as the Germans themselves. Unfortunately Admiral Oliver and the Naval Staff hesitated to send all the relevant information to Jellicoe and Beatty, who in turn hesitated to believe what they received. Thus it was the Germans, not the British, who had the advantage of surprise.[47]

Jutland was awkward and embarrassing for both sides, just as the Western Front, indeed the whole war, was devoid of military glory. There is a reason for this, besides an amazing coincidence of small minds on both sides. This was the first war in which communications were sufficiently powerful for central headquarters to command an entire theater of war at once with knowledge gleaned from myriad sources, including radio interception. Yet the military leaders had been educated in an era of poor communications, when battlefield commanders made decisions based on historical precedents, intuition, and local information, and intelligence was something that spies did and military men regarded with disdain. Despite evidence to the contrary, the German admirals could not get themselves to believe that enemy code breakers consistently decrypted their messages. Neither Jellicoe and Beatty at sea nor Oliver in London were prepared to let the results of a great battle hinge on decrypts produced by lowly civilians. Santoni, a critic of the British Admiralty, concluded: "Never in the history of preceding wars did one of the contenders enjoy such extraordinary advantages with impunity, without however using them to achieve the results one would expect."[48] Not until the next world war would the Admiralty have an Operational Intelligence Centre.

The U-Boat War, 1917–1918

After Jutland, the Germans gradually became suspicious of British communications intelligence, and more circumspect in their use of radio. In May 1917 they introduced a new code, the *Flottenfunkspruchbuch,* or FFB, which replaced the SKM, but was partially broken by Room 40 by September of that year.[49] Key changes every seven to ten days took Room 40 two or three days to crack, which provided some measure of security. More important, the Germans learned to practice radio silence, more out of fear of direction-finding than of cryptanalysis. In October 1917, the cruisers *Brummer* and *Bremse,* sailing under radio silence, surprised a British convoy between Norway and Scotland, sinking nine of its twelve freighters and two escorting destroyers. Similarly the last sortie of the High Seas Fleet, on April 23, 1918, was also carried out in complete radio silence until the cruiser *Moltke* broke down and radioed for help; by then, however, it was too late for the Grand Fleet to attack the German ships before they reached safety.[50]

These minor sorties notwithstanding, the German government had decided after Jutland to stop confronting the Grand Fleet, but instead to defeat Great Britain by using U-boats to cut off its vital supplies.

To operate effectively, submarines needed to communicate by radio even more than did surface craft. They were vulnerable when surfaced, and when submerged to periscope depth they moved slowly. Without help, they had difficulty locating merchant ships, enemy warships, minefields, and escort vessels. The *Führer der U-Boote* (commander of the submarines) in Germany required them to receive orders and to report whenever they sank a ship, got into trouble, or were headed home so that they could be escorted through the minefields to their bases. In 1917, in response to the Allied convoy system, the Germans tried to direct several U-boats from a central command post at sea, a forerunner of the wolf-pack tactic used in World War II; this too required frequent radio messages. Despite the dangers of British direction-finding, U-boats used the radio a great deal.[51]

Their equipment was not up to their requirements, however. Not until 1913 was it even possible to install a radio set in a submarine, because of the dampness on board. During the war, U-boats were equipped with two kinds of radios. Their receivers were designed to hear the powerful longwave transmitters at Nauen, Bruges, and Eilvese, as well as smaller transmitters at Pola, Damascus, and elsewhere in the Mediterranean. At the beginning of the war, messages from home often had to be relayed from submarine to submarine, taking several days to reach American coastal waters. In 1917 Nauen's power was boosted to 400 kilowatts, and submarines with improved receivers could hear it far out in the Atlantic, once even from the Cape Verde Islands. Submarines even discovered that under certain conditions they could receive Nauen while submerged up to thirty meters.[52]

Transmission was quite a different problem. On board a submarine there was no room for a longwave transmitter, let alone the large antennas it required. Until 1916 U-boats were limited to small 500-watt middlewave spark sets with collapsible antennas that could only reach three to five hundred kilometers. Captain Schwieger of the *U-20*, which sank the *Lusitania* in the Irish Sea in May 1915, could not boast about his kill until he had returned to the North Sea and was within three hundred kilometers of Ludwigshaven. In 1917 and 1918, one-kilowatt vacuum tube receivers were installed in U-boats, allowing them to radio home from as far away as Iceland and the Canary Islands. This helps explain why the submarine war shifted from the vicinity of the British Isles to the open sea.[53]

All this radio talk let the British locate U-boats by direction-finding to within twenty miles in the North Sea and fifty in the Atlantic. This was a risk the Germans were willing to accept, since a U-boat could submerge before destroyers could find it. They did not realize that Room 40 also decrypted the messages, and therefore knew the U-boats's plans as well as its location.[54]

Until 1917, however, the British made poor use of this information because of the lack of coordination between Room 40 and the Admiralty's Transport Division. Not until the renewal of unrestricted submarine warfare in the early months of 1917 did the mounting losses of merchant ships force the British to adopt the convoy system and to integrate the Enemy Submarine Section and Room 40 into a new unit called Intelligence Division (or ID) 25. The number of "special telegrams" to naval commanders at sea, giving them information about U-boats in their vicinity, rose from 39 a month in early 1917 to 66 a month in late 1917, and to 172 a month in 1918. Convoys could now be diverted away from the U-boats, and the U-boats hunted down by destroyers.[55] The threat of starvation in Britain, which had seemed imminent in the spring of 1917, receded and with it went the Germans' last hope of victory.

German Communications Intelligence

Communications intelligence was by no means a one-way street, and Germany also made efforts in that direction. This was inevitable, since the Allies used the radio, and U-boats especially needed information about merchant ships.

In the course of the war, British radio equipment evolved in parallel with that of the Germans. When the conflict began, most ships were still equipped with musical-frequency spark sets. Gradually these were replaced by Poulsen arc sets, and, toward the end of the war, vacuum tubes made their appearance on ships. In addition to the many shore stations that served the merchant marine, auxiliary patrol boats scoured the British home waters searching for U-boats.[56] As a result, there was more than enough radio traffic for the Germans to intercept.

When the war began, Germany had three intercept stations: one on Heligoland Island, and two on board ships. Vice Admiral Hipper ordered the regular interception of enemy radio traffic by his ships. The *Bord-B-Dienst* (on-board interception service) attempted to estimate the distance from an intercepted transmitter by its loudness, an unreliable method. The service did traffic analysis of land transmitters, but had little success with ships at sea, and did not decrypt messages. It did, however, obtain information on minefields and convoy routes.[57]

The Germans were not much more successful with direction-finding. Technically, their equipment was on a par with the British.[58] But their coastline, while long enough to locate transmitters in the North Sea, was too short for direction-finding west of the British Isles, where most of the merchant ships were. The German direction-finding stations at Sylt, Borkum, Nordholz, and Bruges (and later at Cleve and Tondern) served to guide German ships through the minefields and Zeppelins in bad weather, rather than to track enemy ships.[59]

German efforts at cryptanalysis were even less successful. In the fall of 1914, Hipper ordered the regular interception of all British naval radio traffic. A central decryption office was established on board the *Kaiser Wilhelm II*, flagship of the High Seas Fleet.[60] It evidently had no success, for the first cryptanalytic breakthrough we hear of came not from the navy but from the radio communications unit of the Sixth Army, stationed in northern France. In October 1914, with little to do once the front had stabilized, the radiomen began to listen to British naval radio traffic and succeeded in decrypting some of it, probably the low-grade communications of the Dover Patrol. These decrypts were sent to the naval radio station at Bruges, and from there to the Admiralty in Berlin and the High Seas Fleet in Wilhelmshaven.[61] German and Austrian decryption of the simple British and French merchant marine codes, along with the reports of spies in neutral ports, explains the success of German U-boats in the Mediterranean.[62]

In May 1915, when the British submarine *E15* sank in the Dardanelles, the Germans were able to retrieve the current key to the British cipher, along with maps of the minefields in the Channel and the North Sea and a list of call signs. Reports from the army cryptanalysts in France, formerly sporadic, began to appear monthly. In June, reports of enemy ship movements were sent directly to the commander-in-chief of the U-boats, instead of through the Admiralty. In July, the navy sent officers to learn from the army, then set up its own cryptographic center in Bruges. It even placed cryptanalysts on board U-boats, but with little effect.[63]

Not until February 1916 did the navy establish an official headquarters for the B-Dienst and E-Dienst (Entzifferungsdienst, or deciphering service) at Neumünster in Holstein. It controlled lesser cryptanalysis stations at Bruges (for the Channel), Tondern (for the North Sea), Libau (for the Baltic), and Skopje and Pola (for the Adriatic and Mediterranean), which reported every fourteen days.[64] By May this service was beginning to make headway with the Royal Navy code, but not enough to affect the battle of Jutland, for Heinz Bonatz writes: "The English radio messages at the battle of Jutland could only be decrypted by Neumünster *after the fact*. Their tactical application during the battle was out of the question."[65]

By October 1917, the Neumünster cryptanalysts had broken the British convoy code, allowing the *Brummer* and *Bremse* to sink a convoy in the North Sea. According to Heinrich Walle, Neumünster decrypted 36 percent of intercepted messages entirely, and another 30 percent partially.[66] The Grand Fleet code, however, was never cracked.

By breaking the British merchant marine codes and those of countries other than

Britain, the Germans were able to wage a submarine campaign that was quite successful for a time, and always dangerous. They had no success, however, with the more difficult naval and diplomatic codes. There are several reasons for this.

The first is the extraordinary achievements of Room 40. By decrypting German messages, the British soon realized how much of their own secret communications the Germans could read. This persuaded the Royal Navy to maintain radio silence whenever possible; at all other times, they were extremely cautious, used many different codes, and changed keys frequently. After mid-1917, for example, ships on the Atlantic convoys communicated with one another using radios of such low power that they could not be intercepted beyond the horizon.[67]

The German system also suffered from two internal weaknesses, however. First, they lacked trained personnel and did not recruit enough educated people. As Bonatz notes: "Only after the end of the war was it determined that the lack of success was not caused by the difficulty of the code or key systems, but by the inexperience of the personnel."[68] Second, they made little use of the information that came from communications intelligence because Neumünster was far from both the Admiralty in Berlin and the naval headquarters in Wilhelmshaven, where operations were conducted.[69] This problem was, of course, not unique to the Germans, as Patrick Beesly points out: "On neither the British nor the German side was there adequate liaison between the code-makers and the code-breakers, but as has been said of war in general, victory comes to the side that makes the fewest mistakes, and the Germans made many more in the Wireless War than the British."[70]

The Zimmermann Telegram

Nothing illustrates the value of communications security quite as forcefully as the story of the Zimmermann Telegram, which contributed to the entry of the United States into the war against Germany. When the British cut the DAT cable on the morning of August 5, 1914, Germany lost its only secure channel of communication with America. From that moment on, it relied on the security of its codes and the willingness of neutrals to act as intermediaries with the Western Hemisphere.

Diplomatic codes can be made more complex than naval codes because the messages are not as urgent as those sent to ships in battle. Since 1909 Germany had been using a code called 13040, with variations, for much of its diplomatic traffic. At some point in late 1914 or 1915, Room 40 began to decrypt messages in this code. It was Captain Hall who directed the attention of Room 40 to the German diplomatic codes; this reflected both his own eagerness to move beyond tactical naval matters into the realms of strategy and foreign policy, and the reluctance of the Foreign Office to undertake anything so ungentlemanly as espionage.

Much confusion surrounds this achievement. Code 13040, or parts of it, may have been found in the luggage of Wilhelm Wassmuss, a German agent in Persia whose baggage fell into the hands of the British in early 1915. Or it might have been leaked to the British, piece by piece, by Alexander Szek or Czek, a young man of British and Austro-Hungarian parentage who worked at a German radio station in Brussels. Or, possibly, Room 40 cracked the code bit by bit, without the help of luck and secret agents.[71] In any event, the code did not give up its secrets in one day, but yielded to a patient accumulation of words and code groups over a period of many months.

For their most important transatlantic communications, the Germans developed a new codebook, known as 0075, one copy of which they sent to their ambassador in Washington, Count Johann von Bernstorff, on the submarine *Deutschland* in November 1916. This code was considerably more difficult to penetrate than 13040.[72]

The second problem the Germans faced was finding a channel of communication. They could only use plain language on the radio between Nauen and Sayville. For encoded diplomatic traffic, they needed the help of a complaisant neutral, and this turned out to be Sweden. German diplomatic telegrams to Washington were first sent to Stockholm, where the Swedish Foreign Office reenciphered them in the Swedish cipher to hide them from the British over whose cables they had to travel. In 1915, the British saw through the subterfuge and protested to the Swedish government against this breach of neutrality, threatening to bar Swedish diplomatic telegrams from the British cables. The Swedes expressed sincere regrets and gave firm assurances that they would cease transmitting German messages to Washington. After that they sent the German telegrams to the Swedish ambassador in Buenos Aires, where the German ambassador retransmitted them on American lines to Washington. This seven-thousand-mile detour was known as the Swedish Roundabout. German telegrams between Bernstorff and the German ambassador in Mexico City, Heinrich von Eckhardt, were handled by the Swedish chargé d'affaires in Mexico, Folke Cronholm, to avoid restrictions on coded telegrams by belligerents. In March 1916 Captain Hall discovered that Sweden was once again serving as a conduit for German telegrams, but rather than protest, he decided it was wiser to say nothing and decrypt the messages.[73]

In 1916, the German government looked for another route, not for fear of British cryptanalysts, but because the Swedish Roundabout was very slow, requiring up to a week for an answer to a message. On December 27, Ambassador Bernstorff asked Colonel Edward House, President Wilson's special adviser on foreign affairs, to let him communicate with Berlin through American diplomatic channels in the German code. Despite protests from Secretary of State Lansing, President Wilson agreed to this request.[74]

On January 16, 1917, German Foreign Minister Arthur Zimmermann sent a long telegram to Ambassador Bernstorff, using both channels. One copy went via the U.S. Embassy in Berlin to the U.S. Embassy in Copenhagen, and from there by cable to Washington. According to David Kahn, "Room 40 was 'highly entertained' at the sight of the German code in an American cable, but again did not protest."[75] This cable was in code 0075, which Room 40 could only partly decrypt, but it showed that a part of the message was to be forwarded to Eckhardt in Mexico. Hall guessed that Eckhardt did not have 0075, and that Bernstorff would have to retransmit the telegram in code 13040. On February 19, he obtained from a British agent in Mexico a copy of the retransmitted telegram, which cryptanalyst Nigel de Grey was able to decrypt in full.

The telegram instructed Eckhardt to incite Mexican President Carranza to join

Germany in a war on the United States, promising him Texas, New Mexico, and Arizona. Here at last was a provocation that President Wilson could not ignore. Hall arranged to have it leaked to U.S. Ambassador Page, who transmitted it to Washington, where it eventually found its way into the press and forced the hand of Wilson and the isolationists.

In order not to compromise the British ability to decrypt the German codes, the telegram was presented as having been stolen at the Mexican telegraph office. In Washington, the State Department also looked for a plausible story to present to Congress and the American public. After two days of arm-twisting (February 25–27), Acting Secretary of State Frank Polk persuaded the president of Western Union, Newcomb Carlton, to release, in violation of Federal law, a copy of Bernstorff's telegram to Eckhardt, to show that it was really obtained in the United States and not concocted by the agents of some foreign power.[76] The whole issue of its authenticity was made moot on March 2 when Zimmermann himself, challenged to deny the whole story, said: "I cannot deny it. It is true."[77]

The British penetration of the German diplomatic codes, which the Germans had thought secure, was not revealed until much later. So tight was Britain's grip on world communications that it could not only block or read, at will, the most secret messages of its enemies, it could even use that information without revealing its sources. Never before or since in history has communications power been so concentrated and so effective.

Notes

1. A *code* is the use of words (existing or artificial) as substitutes for plain text words or sentences; its use requires a dictionary-like codebook. A *cipher* substitutes letters or numbers for plain text letters or numbers, often in a shifting pattern requiring a key. Ciphers are more complex but usually more secure than codes. *Cryptology* refers to the science of codes and ciphers, *cryptography* to the creation of new codes and ciphers, and *cryptanalysis* to systems of penetration or decryption. The entire subject has been covered in David Kahn's magnificent work on cryptology, *The Codebreakers: The Story of Secret Writing* (New York, 1967).

2. Robert Cain, "Telegraph Cables in the British Empire, 1850–1900" (Ph.D. dissertation, Duke University, 1971), 106.

3. Vary T. Coates and Bernard Finn, *A Retrospective Technology Assessment: Submarine Telegraphy. The Atlantic Cable of 1866* (San Francisco, 1979), 90.

4. Christopher Andrew, *Secret Service: The Making of the British Intelligence Community* (London, 1985), 6.

5. Nigel West, *GCHQ: The Secret Wireless War, 1900–86* (London, 1986), 12–13.

6. Thomas G. Fergusson, *British Military Intelligence, 1870–1914: The Development of a Modern Intelligence Organization* (London and Frederick, Md., 1984), 219–20.

7. Arthur R. Hezlet, *The Electron and Sea Power* (London, 1975), 89.

8. Heinz Bonatz, *Die deutsche Marine-Funkaufklärung 1914–1945* (Darmstadt, 1970), 13.

9. Kahn, 239–40.

10. Mario de Arcangelis, *Electronic Warfare: From the Battle of Tsushima to the Falklands and Lebanon Conflicts* (Poole, Dorset, 1985), 19.

11. Fergusson, 218–19; see also 230–31 and Kahn, 230–39, 259, and 262.

12. Fergusson, 216; Bonatz, 13–14.

13. Hauptmann Vos and Hauptmann Nebel, "Das Nachrichtenwesen," in Max Schwarte, ed., *Kriegstechnik der Gegenwart* (Berlin, 1927), 318–23; G. E. C. Wedlake, *SOS: The Story of Radio Communication* (Newton Abbot, 1973), 118; West, 33.

14. W. J. Baker, *A History of the Marconi Company* (London, 1970), 164; Wedlake, 93 and 116–17; West, 29–30.

15. Barbara W. Tuchman, *The Guns of August* (New York, 1962), 290–309; Bonatz, 26; Kahn, 622–28.

16. Guy Hartcup, *The War of Invention: Scientific Developments, 1914–18* (London, 1988), 76; Vos and Nebel, 318–23; Wedlake, 118–20.

17. Wedlake, 121–24; Baker, 169–70.

18. West, 30–33; Fergusson, 189; Baker, 164; de Arcangelis, 22.

19. Kahn, 299–309.

20. Kahn states (p. 313) that "Germany had no cryptanalysts on the Western Front for the first two years of the war." This is not so, for the radiomen of the Sixth Army practiced cryptanalysis; rather it seems the German high command did not pay any attention to them.

21. Major Ammon, "Fernsprecher und Fernschreiber," in Max Schwarte, ed., *Die Technik im Weltkriege* (Berlin, 1920), 256–60; Peter Lertes, *Die drahtlose Telegraphie und Telephonie,* 2nd ed. (Dresden and Leipzig, 1923), 7; Fergusson, 189; Andrew, 138; Hartcup, 76–78; West, 30–31; de Arcangelis, 22–23.

22. Kahn, 340–47; Andrew, 138 and 172; Vos and Nebel, 303.

23. Herbert O. Yardley, *The American Black Chamber* (Indianapolis, 1931, reprinted New York, 1981), 17–19.

24. The three fundamental works on naval intelligence in World War I are Patrick Beesly, *Room 40: British Naval Intelligence, 1914–18* (London, 1982); Heinz Bonatz, *Die deutsche Funkaufklärung, 1914–1945* (Darmstadt, 1970); and Alberto Santoni, *Il primo Ultra Secret: L'influenza delle decrittazioni britanniche sulle operazioni navali della guerra 1914–1918* (Milan, 1985).

25. Korvettenkapitän Bindseil, "Signal- und Fernsignalwesen," in Schwarte, *Die Technik im Weltkriege,* 463–64; Kapitän zu See Bindseil, "Signal- und Fernsignalwessen," in Schwarte, *Kriegstechnik der Gegenwart,* 493–95; Bonatz, 12 and 18.

26. Helmuth Giessler, *Die Marine-Nachrichten- und -Ortungsdienst. Technische Entwicklung und Kriegserfahrungen* (Munich, 1971), 23.

27. Heinrich Walle, "Die Anwendung der Funktelegraphie beim Einsatz deutscher U-Boote im Ersten Weltkrieg," *Revue internationale d'histoire militaire* 63 (1985), 123; Giessler, 23–24. Johannes Zacharias and Hermann Heinecke, *Praktisches Handbuch der drahtlosen Telegraphie und Telephonie* (Vienna and Leipzig, 1908) asserted (pp. 174–75) that directional antennas and changes of frequency could prevent unauthorized interception; this misguided advice seems to have been heeded as late as 1914.

28. Bindseil (1920), 463.

29. On Room 40, see Beesly, Chap. 2; Kahn, Chap. 9; Santoni, 52; Andrew, 86; and Hezlet, 89–94.

30. Andrew, 87; Beesly, 9–13, 31, and 44; Hartcup, 124–26; Santoni, 50; West, 33.

31. When the United States entered the war, the U.S. Navy also set up direction-finding stations to track U-boats, including one near Brest; see Linwood S. Howeth, *History of Communications–Electronics in the United States Navy* (Washington, 1963), 264–65.

32. Baker, 150 and 163–66; Beesly, 69–70; Hartcup, 123–26; Hezlet, 87 and 98; Wedlake, 112 and 127–28.

33. For detailed accounts of these events, see Beesly, 3–7, and Santoni, 58–60.

34. Beesly, 7.

35. Bonatz, 31.

36. Santoni, 59–61 and 71–76; he bases his contention on documents found in the Public Record Office under ADM 137/4065: "Log of intercepted German signals in Verkehrsbuch (VB) code from various sources. March 1914–January 1915." This contradicts David Kahn's assertion (p. 267) that the British were not able to decrypt the German messages. [For an abbreviated English version of Santoni's thesis, see his "The First Ultra Secret: The British Cryptanalysis in the Naval Operations of the First World War," *Revue internationale d'histoire militaire* 63 (1985), 101.]

37. Santoni, 61.

38. Santoni, 53–54. The mystification continued well after World War II. Heinz Bonatz, writing in 1970, insisted that the information the British had was not based on their ability to *break* the German codes (*entziffern*), but only to *decode* them (*entschlüsseln*), the implication being that, without the good luck of having captured the German codebooks, the British cryptanalysts would have been no better off than their German counterparts; see Bonatz, 28 and 44–45.

39. Santoni, 87–91; Bonatz, 21 and 36–37.

40. F. Birch and W. F. Clarke, *A Contribution to the History of German Naval Warfare 1914–1918* (3 vols. compiled c. 1920, in Naval Historical Library, Ministry of Defence, London), 2:968.

41. On von Spee's expedition, see Santoni, 60 and 100–25; Bonatz, 62–63; and Beesly, 73–76.

42. Beesly, 129, 169, and 313.

43. Andrew, 92; Bonatz, 39; Walle, 117.

44. Hezlet, 147. German paranoia about traitors in World War I, while completely unfounded, was nonetheless a premonition of what hapened in World War II, when Admiral Canaris, head of the Abwehr (military intelligence), passed on secrets to the British.

45. Walle, 118; Giessler, 24–26; Beesly, 24–26; Santoni, 59–60; West, 52–53.

46. Santoni, 250–51; Bonatz, 45–60. Characteristically, Jutland is known in German as *Skaggerakschlacht*, the Battle of the Skaggerak, a point further from Germany and closer to Britain than Jutland.

47. For a detailed account of the communications intelligence aspects of the Battle of Jutland, see Santoni, Chap. 6; Beesly, Chap. 10; and Hezlet, 116–28.

48. Santoni, 303.

49. Beesly, 24–25 and 274; Santoni, 59–60.

50. Andrew, 123–24; Beesly, 283; Bonatz, 56; Giessler, 28–29; Hezlet, 139–40; Santoni, 303.

51. Andrew, 92 and 122; Hezlet, 141–42; Walle, 112, 127–30, and 134–37; de Arcangelis, 24.

52. Walle, 131–33; Giessler, 29–30.

53. Beesly, 109; Bindseil (1920), 468–69 and (1927), 497; Hezlet, 141; Lertes, 7; Walle, 123–24 and 131–33.

54. Beesly, 90; Hezlet, 142–43; Santoni, 169.

55. Andrew, 122; Beesly, 254–62; Santoni, 170 and 282–84.

56. Hartcup, 128; Hezlet, 88–89 and 129; Wedlake, 113.

57. Bonatz, 17–21 and 40–41; Walle, 119–122 and 128.

58. Alfred Ristow, *Die Funkentelegraphie, ihre internationale Entwicklung und Bedeutung* (Berlin, 1926), 25; Walle, 111.

59. Bonatz, 22; Vos and Nebel, 324; Bindseil (1920), 470 and (1927), 499; Walle, 135–36.

60. Bonatz, 19; Walle, 122.

61. Bonatz, 23, and Giessler, 24, say it was in Roubaix; Walle, 124–25, says Lille.

62. Beesly, 29; Kahn, 277; Walle, 128.

63. Bonatz, 23 and 72; Walle, 124–34.

64. David Kahn, *Hitler's Spies: German Military Intelligence in World War II* (New York, 1978), 38; Bonatz, 15, 24, and 41–42; Beesly, 32; Walle, 124–26.

65. Bonatz, 49. Kahn, however asserts (p. 278) that German cryptanalysis at Jutland helped their warships escape after the battle.

66. Walle, 128.

67. Bonatz, 25; Wedlake, 109; Santoni, 55.

68. Bonatz, 26.

69. Bonatz, 52–53; Birch and Clarke, 2:1008–9.

70. Beesly, 33; this is also the opinion of Birch and Clarke, 2:972–73.

71. The story of Wassmuss is told in Santoni, 61 and 272, Beesly, 130, and Barbara W. Tuchman, *The Zimmermann Telegram* (New York, 1958), 22–25. The Szek affair is from Tuchman, 21–22, Beesly, 129–30, and Santoni, 61. David Kahn concludes, on the basis of cryptological evidence, that the British reconstructed the code, and says: "I have excluded the romantic stories of Wilhelm Wassmuss and of Alexander Czek"; see *Codebreakers*, 1026, No. 289.

72. Kahn, *Codebreakers*, 282; Santoni, 273–75.

73. Beesly, 208–10; Kahn, *Codebreakers*, 284 and 289; Santoni, 274; Tuchman, *Zimmermann Telegram*, 95–98.

74. Tuchman, *Zimmermann Telegram*, 120–26; Beesly, 213–14; Kahn, *Codebreakers*, 284–85.

75. Kahn, *Codebreakers*, 285.

76. Tuchman, *Zimmermann Telegram*, 135–37 and 145–58; Beesly, 210–11; Kahn, *Codebreakers*, 285–94; Santoni, 275–77.

77. Tuchman, *Zimmermann Telegram*, 169; Beesly, 223.

10

Conflicts and Settlements, 1919–1923

No sooner did the guns go silent on the Western Front than the old conflicts over world communications reappeared. Great Britain, still dominating the world's information flow, was once again challenged by nations that resented its power. Yet in communications, as in every other field, the postwar world differed radically from the prewar. The changes were of three kinds: political, economic, and technological.

Defeat had eliminated Germany from world communications, and the Allies were determined not to let Britain's erstwhile competitor return to the field. In the process of defeating a dangerous enemy, however, Britain had acquired a much bigger rival. While the American people turned isolationist after the war, important sectors of the American establishment—President Wilson, the Navy, the State and Commerce departments, the bigger banks and corporations—were eager to expand American influence and trade around the world, and resented the lingering British presence, which hampered their expansion.

That in itself was nothing new, for the United States had been pushing at the edges of British power since it was born. What had changed was the relative economic strength of the two rivals. Britain, once the workshop and banker to the world, was now exhausted and living on credit. In the four years of European war, the United States had become an industrial and scientific giant and had replaced Britain as the world's creditor. The disproportion between the economic and the political power of the two nations made any residual British influence, especially in the Western Hemisphere, galling to expansion-minded Americans. This fact alone would have ensured that the United States would challenge Britain's cable hegemony.

What complicates the story is the progress of technology. The 1920s were an era of tremendous creativity in communications, witnessing four major advances in rapid succession. The best known is broadcasting, which revolutionized public information and entertainment, but had little impact on international relations. More significant for our purposes was the development of longwave radiotelegraphy, which finally became efficient and reliable on a global scale. In reaction to this challenge, cable technology improved more radically than it had since the 1870s. No sooner did these two technologies reach a rough balance than a third one, shortwave, upset all calculations and threw the global communications industry into disarray.

Each advance in technology reopened the political and economic questions surrounding communications, giving new opportunities to bypass the old cable network on which British influence had rested. By the time the Depression arrived, the British hegemony was broken. In the history of telecommunications, the 1920s were anything but an age of normalcy.

The Paris Peace Conference of 1919

All parties to the Paris Peace Conference were aware of the importance of communications, not only in a geostrategic sense, but also personally, in their everyday communications with their home governments. Since the American entry into the war, the military, the diplomats, and the press had generated an enormous volume of words, straining transatlantic communications beyond overload, and delaying commercial and private telegrams for days on end. The U.S. Navy's answer, the huge Lafayette radio transmitter at Bordeaux, was not completed until after the Armistice.

Yet the lack of efficient and reliable communications was not the main concern of the statesmen and diplomats who assembled in Paris in early 1919. What worried them was the national security aspect of communications. Each nation tried to maximize its own means of communications, even at the expense of global efficiency. The difference between them was that Britain, France, and Japan did so brazenly, while the United States enveloped its national interest in a cloud of high-minded rhetoric.

The first bone of contention was the German cables severed in 1914. One of the two Borkum–Azores–New York cables had been seized by the British, who diverted one end to Penzance (Cornwall) and the other to Halifax (Nova Scotia) in 1917. The other one was taken by the French, who brought one end into Brest, and diverted the other end to their cable station at Coney Island (New York), but only began using it in March 1919. Germany's South Atlantic cables also became French, while the German–Dutch cables in the Pacific were seized by Japan, along with the important island of Yap connected by cables to Guam, Okinawa, and Menado in the Dutch East Indies. All in all Germany lost 4,744 kilometers of cables, or 88 percent of its network.[1]

As the Americans were eager to reopen direct communications with Central Europe, discussion of the cable question began in early March 1919. In President Wilson's absence, Secretary of State Lansing proposed that the cables be given back to Germany. When Wilson returned to Paris, he received two memoranda on the cable question. One, dated March 14, was from Postmaster General A. S. Burleson, who argued:

> Our ships and merchant marine now have to depend upon the courtesy of foreign-controlled means of communication to get home connections. The world system of international electric communication has been built up in order to connect the old world commercial centres with that world business. The United States is connected on one side only. A new system should be developed with the United States as a centre.[2]

To achieve this goal, he argued, the British system of exclusive landing rights should be forbidden in the future, thus giving American companies the opportunity to compete.[3]

The other memorandum was from Walter S. Rogers, a member of the Committee on Public Information (American's propaganda organ during the war) and the communications expert with the U.S. delegation. He too was opposed to the British:

> Fraught with danger is a situation in which the commerce of some nations languishes through lack of means of communication, while the commerce of others is subventioned through control of communication facilities. And there must be direct, unhampered communication lest suspicion lurk that intermediaries profit by trade information passing through their hands.[4]

Rogers advocated government ownership of radio in every country, including the United States. As for the German cables, he recommended returning them to Germany or putting them under some sort of international control.

Wilson's advisers saw the question of communications as much broader than just a matter of the German cables. Their views, which shaped the United States position for the next few years, were twofold. First, they denounced the British stranglehold on communications through exclusive landing rights and Britain's habit of using this control to favor British commerce at the expense of others; it was the same argument the French and Germans had used twenty years before. To this they added a uniquely Wilsonian touch, advocating open and free communications for all nations under international control, in effect transforming telecommunications from an instrument of national power to a global public utility.[5]

At meetings of the Council of Ten in March and April 1919, Lansing and Wilson proposed that the cables should either be returned to Germany or come under the control of the Allies as a group; as for the island of Yap, which Japan had acquired along with all other German Pacific territories north of the equator, it should be internationalized and administered by an international commission.[6] To the British, French, and Japanese, however, the cables and the island were prizes of war that they had no desire to relinquish, let alone return to Germany.

The British in particular did not see themselves as monopolists with a stranglehold over world communications, but as victims of those bad American monopolies, Western Union and Commercial Cable. As Foreign Secretary Lord Balfour pointed out, except for one French and two German cables, all Atlantic cables were owned by or leased to American companies, for the British companies had been "forced to give them up by 'freeze out,' by discrimination in land rates on the part of the American telegraph companies."[7] The German cable that the British had seized and diverted to Halifax was thus the only British-controlled cable to North

America and Canada's only state-owned link with Europe. In the atmosphere of nationalistic suspicions and recriminations that pervaded the Peace Conference, even the victors felt sorry for themselves.

What Wilson and Lansing advocated was in fact an entirely new way of organizing world telegraphy, one that could hardly be decided in the middle of a peace conference. Faced with the obstinacy of Britain, France, and Japan in defending their fait accompli, Wilson finally yielded. In the end, the German cables were placed in the trust of the Allied and Associated Powers until another conference, to be held in the near future, could determine their final disposition. Yap became a class-C mandate of Japan, leaving the cable situation to future negotiations. The United States, having asked for too much, had gained only a promise to discuss the matter again sometime. The incident proved once again that possession is nine-tenths of negotiation.

The Washington Conferences of 1920–1922

In Paris, the United States, France, Britain, Italy, and Japan had agreed to hold a preliminary conference to deal with the communications issues left pending, to be followed by a conference open to all nations to establish a new world communications system. Britain, France, and Japan, who preferred the fait accompli, tried to postpone the meeting, but it was finally held in Washington from October 10 to December 14, 1920.[8] The attitude of the two sides had not changed since Paris. The United States still proposed to return the German cables, to ban exclusive landing rights, and to internationalize the island of Yap. The Admiralty summed up the British side in a letter of July 5, 1919, to the Imperial Communications Committee:

> The ex-German cables are prizes of war, and their capture was 'a legitimate application of the use of Sea Power.' . . . International control might hamper our communications with the outlying portions of the Empire. . . . No reason is seen why we should agree to any international control by which our present strong position would be weakened or our communications hampered in any way.[9]

The two sides were so irreconcilable that the only agreement between them was to operate the disputed cables as a joint purse or cartel. The argument revealed how little American businessmen and the U.S. government trusted the security of their messages on British lines.[10] This suspicion was summed up in a memorandum prepared by Elihu Root, Jr., son of the former secretary of state and attorney for the Western Union Company:

> It is a matter of common knowledge that the highly efficient cable system of Great Britain is so closely co-ordinated with the diplomatic and commercial interests of that country that no message which might be of value to either the British Foreign Office or to the British Board of Trade is assured of secrecy if at any point in its journey it passes over a British line.[11]

In response to a letter from British Ambassador Geddes pointing out that no complaint about leaks or delays on British cables had ever been substantiated, Assistant Secretary of State Alvin Adee referred to further rumors:

These complaints indicate the reasons that cause American business interests to consider it important to have cable facilities operated by Americans free from foreign censorship or control. . . . While this Government has not implied that the British Government has been guilty of such practices, the sentiment does exist. Furthermore, this sentiment is going to be difficult to dispel as long as the British Government exacts from the cable companies operating in England the delivery of all the messages which they handle.[12]

The British reacted angrily to these aspersions cast on their integrity. Foreign Secretary Lord Curzon wrote to Geddes in February 1921:

Reports of this nature were notoriously spread by enemy agents on several occasions during and after the war, with the sole object of creating friction between His Majesty's Government and the United States. The continued dissemination of such reports, based only on vague insinuations made some two years ago, show that their authors are still inspired by that object and that they can produce no evidence in support of their allegations.

Clearly the two sides were separated by more than a squabble over the spoils of war or some leaks of business information. The British government saw the United States as a threat to the Empire, and the U.S. government viewed Britain as an obstacle to free trade and fair competition. Once again, as happened twenty years before, conflicts over cable networks were a metaphor for the clash between an old and satiated empire and an upstart rival.

The United States, having failed to make any headway in 1920, insisted that communications, including the question of Yap, be placed on the agenda of the Conference on Naval Armaments Limitation to be held in Washington in November 1921. Although the issue of the German cables in the Atlantic was once again postponed, the United States had better luck with Japan, itself an upstart imperialist. On February 11, 1922, the United States recognized the Japanese possession of Yap in exchange for the right to land cables and operate radio and telegraph stations there without restrictions.[13]

The Struggle over Cables to Latin America

While the diplomats were wrangling over the former German cables, a more serious conflict was building up between the United States and Great Britain over communications with South America. Before the war two cable routes led to South America. One, through Central America and down the west coast, was dominated by All-America Cables through its affiliates, the Mexican Telegraph Company and the Central and South American Telegraph Company. The east coast of the continent was the territory of the Western Telegraph Company, one of the Eastern companies, which held an exclusive concession in Brazil.

The attitude of the U.S. government towards this situation was decidedly two-faced. On the one hand the United States had long been opposed in principle to monopoly concessions and advocated an "open door" to communications; as historian Joseph Tulchin explains: "Breaking the stranglehold of British and French exclusive cable privileges became an unchanging and unyielding United States goal from 1919 until it was achieved in 1923."[14] But as communications expert George Schreiner admitted in 1924: "The anti-monopolistic policy of the government of the United States, in so far as cables owned by foreigners were concerned, continued meanwhile. There can be no doubt that in the main this policy was highly inconsistent."[15] Indeed it was, for All-America extracted monopoly concessions from Mexico, Nicaragua, El Salvador, Peru, Colombia, and Ecuador, and admitted to the U.S. Senate in 1920:

> It is true that All-America Cables (Inc.) has monopolies on the west coast, but this fact does not lessen the injury which will be done to American commerce and American diplomacy if they are to be denied communication with northern Brazil except over British lines. . . . We must either fight with every resource diplomatic and commercial against the preponderance of British communications wherever encountered or we must give up all hope of making headway against it.[16]

All-America had been pushing against Western Telegraph for many years. The Central and South American Telegraph laid a line to Buenos Aires in 1892 and obtained permission from the Argentine government to lay a cable from there to Rio de Janeiro. Two years later, however, the Brazilian government granted an exclusive twenty-year concession to the Western Telegraph Company for cables to Uruguay and Argentina. When this concession expired in January 1914, All-America proposed to lay a cable from Buenos Aires to Rio and another one to Santos; it could not connect Rio and Santos because Western held an exclusive concession until 1933 on cables between points in Brazil. The Western Company was not about to let an American competitor onto its exclusive turf without a fight, and challenged the Brazilian government's right to grant a landing license to the Central and South American. In 1916 the Supreme Court of Brazil ruled against the Western Company, opening up Brazil to the American firm.

Despite this legal victory, further obstacles barred the Americans from Brazil. During the war, the British government would not allow the Telegraph Construction and Maintenance Company, All-America's sole source of cables, to export this strategic material. Later, minor Brazilian officials friendly towards the Western Company held up the landing license with red tape. It took pressure from Acting Secretary of State Frank Polk in July–August 1919 before the cable could actually be laid.[17]

By 1920 Brazil and the United States were connected by an American-owned cable. But it went the long way around South America, down to Argentina, across the Andes to Chile, up the west coast, and across Mexico. Quicker routes to Brazil, used by most businesses, went via London or the Azores. It was obvious to everyone that the growing commerce between the United States and Brazil required a more direct route. Wilson's treasury secretary, William McAdoo, complained to Newcomb Carlton, president of Western Union, about "the paucity of cable connections to South America" and told him: "We want you to extend your system to South America."[18] In 1919 Western Union proposed to do just that. It made a deal with the Western Telegraph Company whereby Western Union would lay a cable from Miami to Barbados and channel all telegrams between South America and its 25,000 U.S. offices via the Western Telegraph cables from Barbados to Brazil.

This would have reinforced the position of the Western Telegraph Company and ruined All-America Cables, which did not have a network of offices all over the United States like Western Union. The State Department, influenced by All-America Cables, did not look upon this scheme with favor, and in March 1920 it refused a landing license to Western Union. When Carlton, who had already ordered the cable, decided to lay it anyway, the Navy deployed a warship off Miami, chased the cableship out to sea, and cut the cable. Western Union sued the government, claiming that the president had no right to bar a cable landing without the authorization of Congress. Before the Supreme Court could decide the case, Congress got involved.[19]

The cable question was taken up by a subcommittee of the Senate Interstate Commerce Committee from December 15, 1920, to January 11, 1921, and then by the Committee on Interstate and Foreign Commerce of the House of Representatives from May 10 to 13, 1921. During the Senate hearings, which were by far the more important of the two, Congress and the public learned not only about the South American cable business, but also a number of other interesting facts. Clarence Mackay, president of the Commercial Cable and Postal Telegraph companies, revealed for the first time that the Commercial Pacific cable was in fact half owned by the Eastern group, one-quarter by the Great Northern Company, and only one-quarter by Americans, notwithstanding which "I want to make it emphatically clear, that the policy and administration of the Commercial Pacific Cable Co. have been 100 per cent American."[20] Newcomb Carlton of Western Union told them something even more disturbing:

> Great Britain is practically the only nation in the world that has turned out cable operators; so that wherever you will go you will find British subjects operating the cables. This fact negatives the idea in many people's minds that American ownership guarantees secrecy regardless of who operates the cable. . . . 95 per cent of our cable employees are British subjects. They are practically all British subjects.[21]

Mackay also told the committee about the British scrutiny of cables, as required by the Official Secrets Act of 1920: "Since censorship ceased the British Government have required us to turn over all messages 10 days after they have been sent or received. This is a right which they claim under the landing licenses they issue to all cable companies."[22] Carlton, embarrassed by this amazing revelation, tried to explain it away. He told the senators that the British government "gave us their assurance that the messages would not be deciphered; the reason why they wanted to keep track of who was cabling; and furthermore, they guaranteed that no information of any kind would be issued." He went on to explain:

> The messages were then placed in large bags, sealed I believe, and put in wagons. These wagons were driven away under the custody of the Admiralty and lodged overnight in a storehouse and returned to the cable offices the next morning. So that they were kept— they had actual custody of the messages but for a few hours, and so far as the United States messages were concerned, only as a matter of form to make the custom uniform for all countries. We have further investigated and are satisfied that during that period not a single message, commercial, diplomatic, or otherwise, has been actually handled by the Naval Intelligence Bureau, and that their contents are unknown to the British Government because of that fact.[23]

Whether Newcomb Carlton was the most naive person ever to testify before Congress, or the most deceitful, is not known.

All this testimony was hardly designed to make Congress look favorably upon the Western Union–Western Telegraph deal. As a result, Congress passed the Kellogg Bill (S.535, Public Law No. 8, 67th Congress), and President Harding signed it into law on May 27, 1921. It gave the president the power to grant cable landing licenses and forbade American companies to associate with foreign firms that held monopolistic concessions.[24]

Later that year, the Western Telegraph, All-America, and Western Union companies agreed to surrender their exclusive privileges in South America, and most of the countries concurred. In August 1922 the U.S. government granted the Miami landing license, All-America Cables merged with the Commercial Cable-Postal Telegraph conglomerate and two years later it bought out the French-owned United States and Hayti Telegraph Company with its cables to the Caribbean and Venezuela.[25] American companies could now encircle the continent with their cables.

The Radio Corporation of America

While the British were slowly giving way to American pressure in cable telegraphy, in radio there was no contest. By the end of World War I, the United States was well ahead of the rest of the world both in advanced technology and in the financial power to invest in new equipment. Nonetheless, the American radio industry was born amidst political strife.

At the end of the war, radio telegraphy underwent several technological advances in quick succession. The first was the introduction of huge continuous-wave generators. In mid-1918, General Electric erected a 200-kilowatt alternator for the Navy at New Brunswick, New Jersey, while the Société Française Radio-Electrique built a 125-kilowatt alternator at Lyon-la-Doua. A year later the Navy equipped its Bordeaux–Lafayette station with two giant 1,000-kilowatt Federal arcs. The last and most powerful arc station was the one built at Malabar (Java) in 1923 by Cornelius de Groot. Although arcs and alternators remained in use for many years, no new ones were built after 1923, as vacuum tubes proved to be reliable and cost-effective for both receivers and transmitters.[26] Within two years (as we shall see in Chapter 11) the new technology of shortwave made the huge longwave stations obsolete.

Brief as it was, the era of arcs and alternators left an important legacy: it contributed to the decline of the Marconi Company. For too long, Marconi had clung to the rotary-spark transmitter, letting others take the lead in continuous-wave equipment. In Hugh Aitken's words, "The technological leadership that the Marconi enterprises had once been able to claim was short-lived. Already shaky by 1914, by 1919 it was gone; and with it went any hope of basing a world monopoly of radiocommunications on exclusive control of the necessary technology."[27] The American Marconi Company, well aware of its technical lag, had tried to buy alternators from General Electric in 1915, but demanded an exclusive contract that

GE was not willing to give. The two companies reopened negotiations in 1919 and were close to concluding an agreement when the U.S. Navy intervened.[28]

During the war, the Navy had operated all American radio stations except those of the Army. It greatly expanded its own network by building stations, purchasing some private ones, and requisitioning others. When the war ended, it tried to retain its monopoly. In late 1918 Navy Secretary Josephus Daniels asked Congress to make the monopoly permanent. Congress, annoyed at governmental mismanagement of private industries during the war, refused. By early 1919 the Navy's budget was shrinking, its trained radiomen were returning to civilian life, and its proposal was again turned down by Congress.[29] Having failed to achieve a naval monopoly of radio, certain officers began thinking of an alternative, one that would have to be private yet "national" in a way no company had ever been before.

To imbue that corporation with a properly national aura required a presidential blessing. And for that a story—a sort of creation myth—arose to explain the origins of the Radio Corporation of America. It seems that at the Peace Conference in Paris in early 1919 Woodrow Wilson thought about telecommunications. Communications expert Keith Clark, writing in 1931, said that Wilson authorized the Navy to take over radio.[30] Historian Robert Sobel wrote that Wilson, aware of the dangers of foreign ownership of American communications, told his physician, Admiral Cary Grayson: "I wish you would remind me today to get in touch and communicate with the Navy Department officially or with Admiral Bullard. I have an important message that I want to send to Mr. Owen D. Young [of General Electric] relative to the protection of American rights and possibilities in radio communications."[31] And Kenneth Bilby, biographer of David Sarnoff, stated that Wilson specifically wanted to block the sale of GE alternators to Marconi.[32]

Probably the most accurate version of Wilson's role in the creation of RCA is that given by Hugh Aitken. At a breakfast meeting with Wilson, an aide brought Lloyd George a radiogram, and "some comment was passed about the probable importance of wireless in the postwar world." Wilson asked Admiral Grayson to convey a message to Admiral William Bullard, director of naval communications, "that he counted on him to keep a careful watch on American interests in radio." But, as Aitken points out, "There is no reference to this event in the diaries of Woodrow Wilson or of Cary Grayson."[33]

The story of Wilson's intervention may be true, or it may be apocryphal. In either case, the reason that it has been widely repeated is because it legitimizes an important shift in American history. In Robert Sobel's words, "What was involved in 1919 was nothing less than the creation of . . . "the military–industrial complex," the first element of which was to be a national wireless corporation."[34]

The real founders of that national wireless corporation were Admiral Bullard and Lieutenant Commander Stanford C. Hooper, head of the Radio Division of the Bureau of Steam Engineering.[35] Their goal was to get rid of the American Marconi Company, which they wrongly perceived to be controlled by Marconi's Wireless of Britain, and thus, wrongly again, thought to be a tool of the British government.

At the beginning of April 1919 they received word from Owen Young, vice president and acting counsel of General Electric, that GE was negotiating with

American Marconi. On April 8, Bullard and Hooper met with the senior GE executives in New York. There, Bullard made a patriotic plea to GE not to sell alternators to Marconi, and advocated "a policy of wireless doctrine similar to the greater Monroe Doctrine, by which control of radio in this country would remain in American hands." Privately, he told Young as a "state secret" that the president had personally asked him to dissuade GE from selling alternators to Marconi. Hooper then persuaded the GE executives to help found a new and entirely American company that would obtain the Navy's and GE's radio patents. American Marconi, deprived of alternators, would have to sell out to this upstart rival, which would thus win control of all of America's international radio communications.[36]

There followed months of long and complicated negotiations, first with the Navy, then with American Marconi, and finally with Marconi's of Britain. In November, the British sold their holdings in American Marconi and agreed to divide the world: the British Empire for Marconi's, Latin America for the Americans, Canada to be shared between them, and the rest of the world open to both. The purchaser was the new company first discussed at the April meeting, the Radio Corporation of America, incorporated on October 17. Its chairman was Owen Young of GE, and its president was Edward Nally, who came from American Marconi, as did most of the company's staff and equipment. In March 1920 the Navy handed over to the new company the transmitters requisitioned during the war. In short order RCA signed agreements with General Electric, AT&T–Western Electric, Westinghouse, and United Fruit–Tropical Radio. Though it did not obtain a government guarantee, RCA nonetheless had a de facto monopoly on America's international radio communications.[37]

No sooner was RCA founded than Nally sailed to Europe to sign exclusive traffic agreements with the various national radio systems. These agreements specified the correspondent stations, their frequencies, hours, and division of revenues, and included the cross-licensing of patents. They differed from the Marconi policy of operating both ends of the circuit like a cable company, a policy that had caused so much resentment before the war. They also removed the barriers to the transfer of technology that had hampered the spread of radio in its early days. Thus every country that could afford it, even new nations like Poland and Czechoslovakia, could get the very latest technology.

By the end of 1920, RCA had exclusive traffic agreements with the Compagnie Générale de Télégraphie Sans Fil, British Marconi's, Telefunken, and the Japanese government. In the next two years Poland, Italy, Norway, Sweden, the Netherlands, Brazil, and Argentina signed up, soon followed by almost every other country. As soon as transmitters could be built, circuits were opened and countries around the world began communicating directly with one another. Congestion on the cables and RCA's lower rates (e.g., 18¢ a word from New York to London, compared with 25¢ by cable) quickly gave radio a large share of the intercontinental telegraphy market: By 1923 RCA had captured 30 percent of the Atlantic traffic and 50 percent of the Pacific.[38] Even after cable and radio rates had been equalized, America's international radio traffic continued to grow, from 7 million words in 1920 to 23 million in 1922 and 38 million by 1927.[39] RCA served two purposes. It met a booming demand for communications that the cables, operating near capacity, could not meet. But it also fulfilled a national need, as J. H. Dellinger, chief of the Department of Commerce's Radio Laboratory, explained in 1925: "America approaches independence of the cables for communication with nearly every important country of the world."[40] What he meant by independence of cables was independence from British interference.

British Radio, 1919–1924

While Americans were struggling to free themselves from British communications, what were the British up to? Mainly, it seems, discussing the matter in endless committee meetings. As in America and many other countries, the aftermath of World War I saw a tug-of-war between the private and public sectors. In Britain, unlike elsewhere, both sides lost. Marconi's had obtained its monopoly of Britain's international radio communications not from the government but through its participation in the international cartel of traffic agreements. Throughout the 1920s, however, the government vied with Marconi's for the right to control Britain's imperial communications. The uncertainty this produced delayed the modernization of Britain's telecommunications facilities and allowed other nations to move into a field that had once been dominated by Britain.

In March 1919 Godfrey Isaacs, managing director of Marconi's Wireless Telegraph Company, wrote to the Imperial Communications Committee, proposing to build an Imperial Wireless Chain. Marconi's offered to erect the latest high-powered transmitters capable of communicating directly with Canada, South Africa, India, and Australia, and to do so without a subsidy.[41] The company was convinced that such a scheme was feasible, for its Caernarvon station had reached Sydney. But it was in poor financial shape, and it needed the business that an Imperial Chain would provide.[42]

In November 1919, in response to Marconi's offer, Lord Milner, chairman of the Imperial Communications Committee, appointed an Imperial Wireless Telegraphy Committee under Sir Henry Norman. Its report, issued on May 28, 1920, rejected Marconi's plan, and proposed instead a chain of eight smaller stations two thousand miles apart that would relay messages. It also recommended that these stations be built and operated by the British Post Office and the Dominion governments.[43] The committee disapproved of Marconi's request for a monopoly contract; it worried that high-powered stations would be too costly and unreliable; and it feared that, if successful, the Imperial Chain would threaten the cable companies. Behind those technical and economic reasons there lurked a personality clash, on which the *Electrical Review* commented: "The decision of the Marconi Company, owing to a personal quarrel between its managing director and the chairman of the committee, to abstain from giving evidence before the committee was a strategical blunder of the first magnitude."[44]

Neither side won that dispute, for Australia disliked the Norman plan, which would have put it at the end of a chain of four links, and contracted with Marconi's to build a high-powered station able to reach England directly. Canada and South Africa did likewise.[45] At the Imperial Conference of 1921, the Norman plan was damned with faint praise, and Winston Churchill, then colonial secretary and chairman of the Imperial Communications Committee, "refused to have anything further to do with its outmoded proposals."[46] In 1922 the Cabinet appointed a Wireless Telegraphy Commission under Lord Milner to look further into the matter. In July of that year, the government accepted the idea of high-powered direct links to the dominions, but refused to contract with Marconi's. Since Marconi's held the patent rights for Britain, neither the government nor any other company could build the stations, and thus the stalemate persisted.[47]

1923 and 1924 were years of confusion and vacillation. In late 1922 the conservative Unionists had replaced the coalition government of Lloyd George, and it was some time before they could develop a coherent communications policy. In March 1923 Prime Minister Bonar Law announced to the House of Commons that the principle of state monopoly in imperial communications was to be abandoned. When Marconi's applied for a license, however, its request was turned down as too monopolistic. The Post Office then offered to work together with Marconi's, but the two old antagonists could not resolve their differences and quarreled for the next year.

By mid-1923 it was clear to all that Great Britain was slipping badly behind its rivals. While the United States had twenty-one stations of 200 kilowatts or more and France had twelve, Britain only had the two stations at Leafield and Abu Zabal begun before the war, and Marconi's Caernarvon transmitter. In terms of power, the contrast was even starker: Compared with America's 3,400 kilowatts of high-powered stations and France's 3,150, the British Empire had only 700 kilowatts, hardly more than Germany's 600.[48] The Post Office decided to built a superstation at Rugby able to reach all the colonies and dominions, a project that would take three years to complete.[49]

In early 1924 Britain's first Labour government led by Ramsey MacDonald appointed the Imperial Wireless Telegraphy Committee chaired by Robert Donald, the sixth in a dozen years to investigate the imperial wireless question.[50] This committee did not ask Marconi's to present evidence. In its report to Parliament on February 24, 1924, it noted "a certain measure of impatience if not irritation [in the dominions] at the delays in the construction of the Empire Wireless Chain."[51] It characterized the deadlock between Marconi's and the Post Office as "a continuation of the misfortunes which have dogged the footsteps of Empire Wireless and caused the lamentable delays which have placed the Empire behind other nations in the use of wireless telegraphy as an indispensable means of communication throughout the world."[52] It recommended state ownership and operation of high-powered stations to communicate with the Empire, company communications outside the Empire, and competition in communications with Canada.[53]

This report and two others prepared for the Cabinet and the Committee of Imperial Defence that same year noted three obstacles to the development of British wireless in this period. The first was organizational: every decision involved the Cabinet, the Committee of Imperial Defence, the Imperial Communications Committee of the C.I.D., and the Wireless Telegraphy Sub-Committee of the I.C.C., each of them with representatives of the Post Office, the War Office, the Admiralty, the Treasury, the Board of Trade, the Air Ministry, the Colonial Office, and/or the India Office. When the British government had at last made up its official mind, it had to negotiate with the newly assertive governments of Canada, Australia, New Zealand, South Africa, and India.[54] Under those circumstances, it was amazing that anything ever got done.

The second obstacle was the feud between the General Post Office and Marconi's Wireless Company, which went back to 1897 and which only got worse as time went on. The goal of the Post Office sometimes seemed to be to block Marconi's even at the expense of British communications, while Marconi's, by insisting on monopoly concessions, overplayed its hand time and again. This antagonism stood in sharp contrast to the American view of RCA as the "chosen instrument" of the nation's destiny in telecommunications, or the wholehearted backing of Telefunken by the German government.

The biggest obstacle of all, however, was the glaring disproportion between Britain's resources and its imperial obligations, which had become painfully apparent after World War I. This is clear from the list of radio stations that Britain simply could not do without, according to the report of the Wireless Sub-Committee of May 28, 1924: for commercial purposes, Rugby, Cape Town, Agra, Melbourne, Vancouver, Montreal; for the Navy, Gibraltar, Malta, Ceylon, Singapore, and Hong Kong; for the Air Force, Malta, Jerusalem, Bagdad, and Ismailia; and others.[55] Even in the relatively simple matter of radio communications where it had once led the world, Great Britain was now suffering from what historian Paul Kennedy has called "imperial overstretch."[56]

German and French Radio to 1924

At the end of the war, the Germans found themselves bereft of cables and isolated from the Allies. At the Paris Peace Conference, the Allies ignored their protests against the "theft" of their cables and the news blockade imposed upon Germany.[57] The obvious solution was radio. The Treaty of Versailles bound Germany to obey any international radiotelegraph convention that might come into force in the next five years; but since no conference was called until 1927, Germany was free of any restrictions in this field.[58] In 1920 Telefunken installed a 400-kilowatt alternator at Nauen and founded a subsidiary, the Drahtlose Übersee-Verkehrs Aktiengesellschaft, or "Transradio," to operate it. In 1920–21 it signed a patent-pool and traffic agreement with Marconi's, CSF, and RCA, and thus became the fourth member in a cartel known as the Radio International Committee. To the great dismay of the British government, it also obtained a contract to build a superstation at Monte Grande in Argentina.[59] With no colonies left, Germany could concentrate on purely commercial radio.

Not so the French. They ended the war with only two high-powered stations: the obsolete one at Lyon-la-Doua, in use since 1914, and the U.S. Navy's Lafayette station, completed in late 1919 and renamed Bordeaux-Croix-d'Hins. Both were used by the government for military and colonial purposes. Research was conducted mainly by Colonel Ferrié at the Eiffel Tower in Paris and by the engineers Joseph Béthenod and Marius Latour, whose alternators rivaled Alexanderson's.[60] But France still lacked a powerful commercial station.

At the time, the only significant private company in the field was the Société Française Radio-Electrique, founded by Emile Girardeau in 1910. During the war SFR had manufactured equipment for the army, and in 1918 it found itself with a number of valuable patents but no capital. Marconi's Wireless, the Compagnie Française des Câbles Télégraphiques, and a consortium of banks founded a rival firm which was well capitalized but short on new technology. In 1919 the two firms merged under the name Compagnie Générale de Télégraphie sans Fil, or CSF for short. In September 1919 CSF signed a traffic and patent-pooling agreement with Marconi's, General Electric, and RCA, later joined by Telefunken. By joining the cartel, CSF obtained the exclusive concession to communicate with the United States, Latin America, and the Near and Far East.[61]

Although CSF was clearly the French equivalent of RCA, its entry into the communications business did not take place without a fight. The Ministry of Posts, Telegraphs, and Telephones had long enjoyed a monopoly of French communications and intended to keep it. Yet it was still attached to the use of wires and cables; as one administrator said to Girardeau: "So, you believe in radio, do you?"[62] CSF had some major advantages that the PTT lacked; not only did it have the will, the funds, and the know-how to operate high-powered radio stations, but it also had a traffic agreement with RCA on the vital North Atlantic circuit, and RCA refused to talk to the PTT. CSF's request for a license provoked intense debates in the Chamber of Deputies, for many deputies believed in state operation of communications or feared the appearance of "trusts" in France. The national union of PTT employees declared:

> We want everyone to remain in his role. . . . If the military and industrial groups have tried to deprive our administration of the monopoly of commercial radiotelegraphy in order to engage in profitable financial operations, if their secret agents have tried to eliminate us from colonial wireless in order to gain jobs and orders, there is no other motive for it than our unfortunate reputation as excessively upright civil servants.[63]

The government ignored these protests and signed an agreement with CSF on October 29, 1920. Prime Minister Aristide Briand declared: "Thanks to this agreement, the new means of international communications are not totally abandoned to foreign firms who fight over them with the help of their respective governments."[64]

As soon as it had its license, CSF set out to build a radio station capable of reaching Indochina, 20,000 kilometers away. When it opened for business in 1921, the Sainte-Assise station near Paris with its two 500-kilowatt Latour–Béthenod alternators and sixteen 250-meter-high antenna towers was the most powerful in the world, and carried as much traffic as France's cables. To operate it, CSF founded an affiliate called Radio-France.[65]

The French also built radio stations in their colonial empire. Indochina was the second-richest of France's colonies, yet, unlike Algeria, it was poorly served by cables. In 1914 it had almost obtained a radio station capable of reaching France when the war intervened. During the 1920s Indochina built a series of small stations in all the towns, to supplement its vulnerable wire network. In October 1921 Governor Maurice Long, unwilling to wait for the French government to act, contracted with CSF to build and operate a 500-kilowatt station in Saigon. When it was completed in January 1924, it communicated not only with Bordeaux-Croix-d'Hins, but also with Argentina, China, Japan, the Dutch East Indies, Singapore, Madagascar, New Caledonia, Tahiti, Hawaii, and ships at sea; in other words, French radio now covered another one-third of the world.[66]

The other French colonies, even very poor ones in Africa, obtained radio stations during the 1920s. By 1925 almost every colony could receive messages directly from France and could send radiograms to the next colonial station. Three high-powered transmitters—Beirut (operated by Radio-Orient, a branch of Radio-France), Bamako in the French Soudan, and Tananarive in Madagascar—could communicate directly with France. A fourth was under construction in Brazzaville in the French Congo.[67] As one officer put it in late 1925:

> France will have in 1926 or 1927 at the latest, direct communications with its main colonies and secure communications with only one relay with all its secondary colonies. It will thus be at the head of the European nations as far as setting up its imperial network.[68]

In colonial matters, France had always compared itself unfavorably with Britain. In the mid-1920s, thanks to French energy and British procrastination, France finally had a better radio network than that of its rival. Of course Britain still had its cables, which France lacked, and therefore had not really fallen behind in communications. But in this instance, efficiency mattered less than pride. André Touzet, professor at the University of Hanoi, expressed a common feeling when he wrote: "No matter how profound is our friendship with the English, the subjection to which we were reduced in having to turn to foreign intermediaries for our communications with the metropole was somewhat humiliating for our national self-esteem." From this perspective, the new radio station at Saigon marked "the end of a servitude, one might even say the end of an isolation."[69]

Radio in Latin America and China

So far we have considered only the major countries and their colonies. For countries that were independent but underdeveloped and wanted to obtain radio communications, the choices were limited: either to become a vassal of the great powers, or to play them off against each other. The Latin American republics fell into the first category, China into the second.

At the end of March 1919, the British learned to their horror that President Irigoyen of Argentina had personally awarded the concession for a major radio station to the Siemens Schuckert Company of Germany, "notwithstanding all the efforts of the British Minister to avoid it."[70] What was a shocking national affront to the politicians was a matter of competition to the businessmen, and businessmen, when faced with a competitive situation, naturally thought of forming a cartel. In October 1921, RCA, Transradio, CSF, and Marconi's agreed on a common policy towards Latin America, to be known as the AEFG (America–England–France–

Germany) Consortium. In order to avoid building duplicate radio transmitters in every Latin American country, the Consortium agreed that one transmitter would serve to communicate with all four members, hence with the world.[71] This was not quite what U.S. Secretary of State Lansing had in mind when he spoke in 1915 of opposing the ownership of radio "in European or Asiatic hands" and advocated instead "a broad and beneficient Pan-Americanism," but it was close.[72] The Consortium had nine trustees: two from each member company, plus a ninth appointed by RCA (though not connected with that company) who had veto power in cases where a majority sought to impose its will on the minority. In each Latin American country the Consortium formed a national radio company (e.g., Transradio Argentina) with a native of that country as president, but retained 60 percent of the voting stock. In other words, the Consortium members got most of the profits, while the American trustees made all the decisions. The Consortium began by taking over Argentina and Brazil's radio stations, then built a new station in Chile, and gradually extended its services to the rest of the continent and to Central America. It was what Admiral Bullard had called "a doctrine similar to the greater Monroe Doctrine."[73]

The Chinese case contrasts sharply with that of Latin America. Instead of an orderly cartel, there was intense political competition, as outsiders sought to profit, as always, from China's weakness. Back in 1900, when China was in the throes of the Boxer Rebellion, Western forces occupied Peking, and there was no responsible central government to speak for the nation, the Eastern Extension and Great Northern companies had extracted thirty-year monopoly concessions on China's external communications from the Chinese Telegraph Administration. At the end of World War I, when China was again in a time of troubles, foreigners came looking for concessions, this time for radio.

On February 21, 1918, the Japanese firm of Mitsui Bussan Kaisha signed an agreement with the Chinese Ministry of the Navy to build a high-powered station for overseas communications; a supplementary agreement signed on March 5 prohibited the construction of any other "wireless station in China for the purpose of communicating with any foreign country."[74] On August 27, 1918, and May 24, 1919, the Chinese Ministry of War signed agreements with Marconi's Wireless Company giving that firm the exclusive right to provide radio equipment and to set up a factory to manufacture and repair such equipment. Finally on January 8, 1921, the Chinese Ministry of Communications signed a ten-year exclusive contract with the Federal Telegraph Company of California to build a high-powered station in China to communicate with the United States, and four medium-powered ones for national and Asian communications.[75]

Needless to say, all these exclusive contracts signed by different branches of the Chinese government conflicted with one another. The Danish and British governments protested the Federal contract, claiming a monopoly on China's external communications until 1930. The British and Marconi's Wireless claimed a monopoly on all radio equipment in China until 1929. The Japanese government and Mitsui claimed a monopoly on China's overseas radio communications until 1948. Wrote an American official: "It has been said that the Chinese Government is taking advantage of the present situation to secure better terms for itself from one or the other of the companies."[76] The United States government rejected all these claims as violations of the principle of the Open Door.[77]

Federal Telegraph, too weak to fight all these foreign interests by itself, sought the help of RCA, and together they founded the Federal Telegraph Company of Delaware to defend their rights in China. Owen Young, chairman of RCA, turned to the State Department. Thus the question of radio communications with China was put on the agenda of the Washington Conference on Naval Armaments of 1921–22. There was some discussion of "internationalizing" China's external communications and creating a consortium like the one that was operating so successfully in Latin America, but Japanese hostility and Chinese procrastination succeeded in blocking the construction of the Federal superstation. Instead, RCA built a superstation in the Philippines and relayed telegrams to China through Hong Kong. As for the Japanese superstation, it was built but evidently never worked satisfactorily.[78] Throughout the 1920s, China's overseas communications continued to be dominated by the British.[79]

At that same time another issue surfaced that revealed the weakness of China vis-à-vis those who preyed upon it. The Chinese delegation to the Washington Conference asked for "the immediate abolition or surrender of all electrical means of communication, including wireless stations, now maintained on Chinese soil without the consent of the Chinese government." These included fifteen Japanese, three French, three American, and two British stations in the various legations, in the concessions at Shanghai and elsewhere, and along the Manchurian Railway.[80] While not intercontinental superstations, they were nonetheless powerful enough to reach Japan, Hong Kong, the Philippines, or Indochina. The foreign governments concerned all pointed to some clause in some treaty or contract that could be interpreted to give them the right to operate radio stations in China. In the end, China did not obtain their removal, but only a promise that they would only be used for official purposes and more promises to negotiate further.[81] China was even more helpless towards the invasion of foreign radio communications than it had been towards the telegraphs fifty years earlier. In the 1870s, at least, there was one central government of China, and it could always threaten to let "peasants" cut the wires. In the 1920s, radio stations could be concealed in foreign-controlled areas, and the Chinese government was too weak to do anything but complain.

Conclusion

The early 1920s were an era of American assertiveness in telecommunications as in other fields. Before the war, few voices had been heard in defense of an American communications network, the most prominent being George Squier of the Signal Corps and the cable entrepreneur James Scrymser. The war demonstrated what had long been suspected, that Britain's cable hegemony gave it powerful strategic and commercial advantages. While public opinion in the United States quickly turned isolationist after the end of the war, a few influential figures—military men like Hooper and Bullard, propagandists like Rogers, businessmen like Young and Sarnoff—saw a world full of opportunities, with Britain as an obstacle. They succeeded in involving the United States government for the first time in supporting American telecommunications overseas.

In some ways, American telecommunications policy followed very familiar lines. In the traditions of the Monroe Doctrine and Dollar Diplomacy, the United States government actively supported American corporations extending their influence southward from the Caribbean and Central America into South America, replacing the reluctant British wherever possible. In China, following the traditional Open Door policy, the United States did not seek to replace the other great powers but to join them; there, American interests being much weaker, so was the official support and so were the achievements.

Yet the American challenge to the British hegemony had two advantages compared with the prewar challenges by France and Germany. The war had impoverished Britain and enriched the United States, so that America was much wealthier compared with Britain in 1920 than France or Germany had been in 1900. Just as important was the emergence of radio as a competitor to cables. In its challenge to Britain, America had a choice of means. In the long run, these technological and financial advantages proved to be much more effective than any official support.

Notes

1. Kenneth R. Haigh, *Cableships and Submarine Cables* (London, 1968), 330; Artur Kunert, *Geschichte der deutschen Fernmeldekabel. II. Telegraphen-Seekabel* (Cologne–Mülheim, 1962), 349–60.

2. Ray S. Baker, *Woodrow Wilson and World Settlement,* 3 vols. (Garden City, N.Y., 1922), 2:468–69. On the United States position on submarine cables at the Paris Peace Conference, see Baker, Vol. 2, Chap. 47, and Hugh G. J. Aitken, *The Continuous Wave: Technology and American Radio, 1900–1932* (Princeton, N.J., 1985), 262–79.

3. Aitken, 263.

4. Quoted in Aitken, 265–66.

5. Aitken, 263–67; Baker, 2:475–79; John D. Tomlinson, *The International Control of Radiocommunications* (Geneva, 1938), 47–48.

6. Leslie B. Tribolet, *The International Aspects of Electrical Communications in the Pacific Area* (Baltimore, 1929), 232; Keith Clark, *International Communications: The American Attitude* (New York, 1931), 165; Baker, 2:480.

7. Clark, 150–51.

8. On the Washington Conference of 1920, see Joseph S. Tulchin, *The Aftermath of War: World War I and U.S. Policy toward Latin America* (New York, 1971), 211–20; Walter S. Rogers, "International Electric Communications," *Foreign Affairs,* 1, No. 2 (December 15, 1922), 152; Clark, 197–98; and Kunert, 363–65.

9. C.I.D., Imperial Communications Committee, Memoranda, 1919 in Public Record Office (Kew) [hereafter PRO], Cab 35/2/87. The Admiralty's views were echoed in the instructions to the British delegation; see C.I.D., Imperial Communications Committee, "Proposed International Congress at Washington, Report of the Washington Congress Sub-Committee of Imperial Communications Committee (30 June 1920)," in Cab 35/14.

10. Tulchin, 207.

11. Ludwell Denny, *America Conquers Britain: A Record of Economic War* (London and New York, 1930), 367; Tribolet, 5.

12. Great Britain, Foreign Office, "Correspondence Respecting Alleged Delays by British Authorities to Telegrams to and from the United States," in *Parliamentary Papers* 1921, Vol. 43 (Cmd 1230).

13. Clark, 165; Tribolet, 234; Tulchin, 224.

14. Tulchin, 210–11.

15. George A. Schreiner, *Cable and Wireless and their Role in the Foreign Relations of the United States* (Boston, 1924), 97.

16. U.S. Congress, Senate, Committee on Interstate Commerce, Cable-Landing Licenses: Hearings before a Sub-Committee of the Committee on Interstate Commerce, the United States Senate, Sixty-Sixth Congress, Third Session on S. 4301, a Bill to Prevent the Unauthorized Landing of Submarine Cables in the United States" (December 15, 1920–January 11, 1921), Frank B. Kellogg, chairman (Washington, 1921) [henceforth Senate Cable-Landing Hearings], 87–91. See also Eugene W. Sharp, *International News Communications: The Submarine Cable and Wireless as News Carriers* (Columbia, Missouri, 1927), 12–13.

17. The best account of these events is in Tulchin, 208–17; but see also Denny, 370; Tribolet, 46–48; and Schreiner, 78.

18. Clark, 155.

19. Ivan S. Coggeshall, "Annotated History of Submarine Cables and Overseas Radiotelegraphs 1851 to 1934. With Special Reference to the Western Union Telegraph Company" (manuscript written in 1933–34, with an introduction dated 1984, cited with kind permission of the author), 183–89; U.S. Federal Communications Commission, "Report of the Federal Communications Commission on the International Telegraph Industry submitted to the Senate Interstate Commerce Committee Investigating Telegraphs," in United States Senate, Appendix to Hearing before Subcommittee of the Committee on Interstate Commerce, 77th Congress, 1st Session, Part 2 (Washington, 1940), 476; "Sub-Chaser's Shot Stops Cable Ship; Crew Are Arrested," *New York Times* (March 6, 1921), 1; "Second Sub Chaser on Guard at Miami," ibid. (March 7, 1921), 15; Clark, 155; Tulchin, 217–22; Schreiner, 66–68; Tribolet, 49–56; Denny, 370–71.

20. Senate Cable Landing Hearings, 269–70.

21. Ibid., 108.

22. Ibid., 275. (The law is 10 & 11 Geo. 5.: Official Secrets Act, 1920; An Act to Amend the Official Secrets Act, 1911.)

23. Ibid., 186–87 and 312–14. See also Aitken, 261. Amazingly, public awareness of British cable scrutiny in peacetime disappeared after the hearings, only to be rekindled in 1967 by Chapman Pincher, defense correspondent of the *Daily Express;* see Peter Hedley and Cyril Aynsley, *The D-Notice Affair* (London, 1967).

24. Coggeshall, "Annotated History," 188–89; Tulchin, 222; Clark, 156.

25. Tulchin, 225–29; Schreiner, 218; Denny, 272.

26. Aitken, 94, 359, and 515–16; Paul Schubert, *The Electric Word: The Rise of Radio* (New York, 1928), 157–58; W. J. Baker, *A History of the Marconi Company* (London, 1970), 177; Emile Girardeau, *Comment furent créées et organisées les radio-communications transocéaniques internationales* (Paris, 1951), 2; Pascal Griset, "La naissance de Radio-France," *Revue française des télécommunications* 49 (October 1983), 86; Maurice Guierre, *Les ondes et les hommes, histoire de la radio* (Paris, 1951), 124; Société Française Radio-Electrique, *Vingt-cinq années de TSF* (Paris, 1935), 60–68.

27. Aitken, 357–58.

28. Aitken, 208–9 and 321–26; Clark, 242.

29. Aitken, 281 and 386; Susan J. Douglas, *Inventing American Broadcasting, 1899–1922* (Baltimore, 1987), 280–84; Schubert, 185–87; Robert Sobel, *RCA* (New York, 1986), 22–23; Captain Linwood S. Howeth, *History of Communications–Electronics in the United States Navy* (Washington, 1963), 313–16. The latter, like Josephus Daniels, confused the interests of the American Marconi Company with those of Great Britain, and the Navy's with those of the United States.

30. Clark, 242–43.

31. Sobel, *ITT: The Management of Opportunity* (New York, 1982), 34; *RCA, 27.*

32. Kenneth Bilby, *The General: David Sarnoff and the Rise of the Communications Industry* (New York, 1986), 46.

33. Aitken, 280–81. This is also the version told by Captain Howeth, based on testimony given by Admiral Grayson before a Senate committee in 1929, ten years after the event; see p. 354.

34. Sobel, *RCA,* 26.

35. Aitken, 328.

36. Aitken, 328 and 338–44; Bilby, 46–47; Howeth, 355–56.

37. For a very detailed account of these negotiations and their results, see Aitken, Chapters 6–8; but see also Schubert, 204–8; and Howeth, 356–60.

38. Aitken, 425, 461–62, and 481; Schubert, 250–54.

39. G. Stanley Shoup, "The Control of International Radio Communication," *Annals of the American Academy of Political and Social Sciences* 142 suppl. (March 1929), 101; Bilby, 48 and 64.

40. *American Year Book* for 1925, 593, quoted in Tribolet, 215.

41. PRO, Cab 35/2/4.

42. Baker, *Marconi,* 178–81 and 206–7; Aitken, 422–23; Vice Admiral Arthur R. Hezlet, *The Electron and Sea Power* (London, 1975), 156.

43. Imperial Wireless Telegraphy Committee, 1919–1920, Report (May 28, 1920), in PRO, Cab 35/12; also in *Parliamentary Papers* 1920 [Cmd. 777].

44. *Electrical Review* (July 16, 1920), quoted in W. P. Jolly, *Marconi* (New York, 1972), 243.

45. Baker, *Marconi,* 206–9; Schubert, 266–67; Hugh Barty-King, *Girdle Round the Earth: The Story of Cable and Wireless and its Predecessors to Mark the Group's Jubilee, 1929–1979* (London, 1979), 183–84; D. H. Cole, *Imperial Military Geography,* 7th ed. (London, 1933), 186–87.

46. Baker, *Marconi,* 207.

47. "Report of the Wireless Telegraphy Commission" (Viscount Milner, chairman), in *Parliamentary Papers* 1922 [Cmd. 1572]; Schubert, 266–67.

48. Sir Charles Bright, "The Empire's Telegraph and Trade," *Fortnightly Review* 113 (1923): 457–74.

49. Baker, *Marconi,* 210–11; Jolly, 243–44; Cole, 187.

50. Tomlinson, 55; Baker, *Marconi,* 211; Schubert, 268.

51. "Imperial Wireless. Report of the Imperial Wireless Telegraphy Committee, 1924" (Robert Donald, chairman), 2–3, in *Parliamentary Papers* 1924, Vol. 12 [Cmd. 2060].

52. Ibid., 4–5.

53. Ibid, 19.

54. "Cabinet Committee on the Report of Imperial Wireless Service, 1924," in PRO, Cab 27/240. In addition to this report, the radio question generated, between 1919 and 1928, reports by seven subcommittees of the C.I.D.'s Imperial Communications Committee, three

reports by a parliamentary Wireless Telegraphy Commission, and the report of the Imperial Wireless and Cable Conference of 1928.

55. Committee of Imperial Defence, "Colonial Wireless System, No. 203: Draft Report of the Wireless Sub-Committee of the Imperial Communications Committee," (May 22, 1924); and No. 205: "Revised Draft Report," in PRO, Cab 35/11.

56. Paul Kennedy, *The Rise and Fall of the Great Powers: Economic Change and Military Conflict from 1500 to 2000* (New York, 1987).

57. Kunert, 361; letters from Reichspostministerium, April 6, 1919, and Auswärtiges Amt, April 14, 1919, to Herrn Vertreter des Reichs-Marineamt bei der Deutschen Friedenskommission (microfilm in Ministry of Defence [London], Naval Historical Branch, Foreign Documents Section, GFM 32/20, 663-71).

58. Tomlinson, 47–49.

59. Alfred Ristow, *Die Funkentelegraphie, ihre internationale Entwicklung und Bedeutung* (Berlin, 1926), 43; "Telefunken-Chronik," *Telefunken-Zeitung* 26, No. 100 (May 1953), 150; Peter Lertes, *Die drahtlose Telegraphie und Telephonie*, 2nd ed. (Leipzig and Dresden, 1923), 8–9.

60. Catherine Bertho, "La recherche publique en télécommunication, 1880–1941," *Revue française des télécommunications* (October 1983), 8; Maurice Deloraine, *Des ondes et des hommes: Jeunesse des télécommunications et de l'I.T.T.* (Paris, 1974), 15–20; Griset, 86.

61. Girardeau, *Comment furent créées*, 6–9, and *Souvenirs de lonque vie* (Paris, 1968), 102–5; René Duval, *Histoire de la radio en France* (Paris, 1980), 28–29; Griset, 85–86; Société Française Radio-Electrique, 11.

62. Girardeau, *Souvenirs*, 100–101.

63. Duval, 28.

64. Paul Charbon, "Développement et déclin des réseaux télégraphiques: 1840–1940," *Recherches sur l'histoire des telécommunications* 1 (November 1986), 63; Griset, 85–88.

65. Griset, 88; Guierre, 131; Lertes, 181.

66. L. Gallin, "Renseignements statistiques sur le développement des communications radiotélégraphiques en Indochine," *Bulletin économique de l'Indochine* 32, No. 199 (1929), 369–81; Indochina, Gouvernement général, *La télégraphie sans fil en Indochine* (Hanoi–Haiphong, 1921), 7–12; André Touzet, "Le réseau radiotélégraphique indochinois," *Revue indochinoise* 245 (Hanoi, 1918), 7–12; J. de Galembert, *Les administrateurs et les services publics indochinois*, 2nd ed. (Hanoi, 1931), 516–20; "La T.S.F. en Indochine," *Annales coloniales* (special supplement, April 15, 1924).

67. "Poste intercolonial de Bamako," in Archives of the Ministry of Posts and Telecommunications (Paris), F90 bis 1690; "Poste intercolonial de Brazzaville," ibid., 1694; "Le réseau colonial de télégraphie sans fil," *Afrique française* 36 (May 1926), 274–76.

68. Commandant Metz in *Revue du Génie militaire* 23 (December 1925), 497.

69. Touzet, 21. The same motivation may have inspired Cornelius de Groot to build a powerful arc station in Java to communicate with the Netherlands; see Aitken, 94 and 516.

70. Letter from Godfrey Isaacs, managing director of Marconi's Wireless, to the Imperial Communications Committee, March 31, 1919, in PRO, Cab 35/2/20; letters from Reginald Tower, British ambassador in Argentina, to the Foreign Office, April 2 and 4, 1919, in Cab 35/2/58.

71. "Transradio Consortium (AEFG Trust)," in National Archives (Washington), Record Group 259, Box 13.

72. Clark, 239.

73. Schubert, 254–57; Tomlinson, 57–58; Tribolet, 57–69; Clark, 197; Denny, 382–83.

74. Westel W. Willoughby, *Foreign Rights and Interests in China,* 2nd ed. (Baltimore, 1927), 2:952.

75. Ibid., 948–61. See also Denny, 383–84; Schubert, 258–59; and Tribolet, 86–99.

76. Memorandum from P. E. D. Nagle, Communications Expert, Department of Commerce, June 29, 1923, in National Archives (Washington), Record Group 173, Box 356, file INT-6 China.

77. Willoughby, 962–64; Tribolet, 103–4; Schubert, 259–60; Denny, 385.

78. Willoughby, 962–67; Schubert, 261–64.

79. Denny, 387–88.

80. "Wireless telephone, telegraphic and wireless-telegraphic communications in China" (February 22, 1922), in National Archives, RG 173, Box 356, File INT-6 China.

81. Tribolet, 109–35; Willoughby, 970–71.

11

Technological Upheavals and Commercial Rivalries, 1924–1939

By the mid-1920s, cables and radio had reached a rough equilibrium. High-powered radio stations, though costly, were less expensive than laying new intercontinental cables; however, the demand for long-distance telegraphy was growing so fast that radio stations could be built all over the world without threatening the profitability and political value of cables.

The Distribution of Cables in the World in 1923

The distribution of cables among the different companies and nations as of 1923 is shown in Tables 11.1 to 11.3 and in Figure 6.

Table 11.4 shows the changes that occurred between 1892 and 1923, based on the figures from Tables 3.2 to 3.4 (for 1892) and 11.1 to 11.3 (for 1923).

As Table 11.4 shows, the world cable network underwent a number of changes between 1892 and 1923: It more than doubled in length, from 246,871 to 589,228 kilometers. While two-thirds of the world's cables had been British in 1892, by 1923 only half were British. The biggest gainers were the United States, whose share rose from 15.8 to 24.2 percent of the world total, and Japan, which went from nothing to 2.5 percent. Cables owned by governments went from 10.4 to 23.9 percent of the world total; while the Eastern and Associated Companies declined from 45.5 to 39.9 percent of the world total, the other British companies almost vanished, largely by leasing their cables to American firms. The general trend up to 1923, therefore, is unmistakable: the rise of American cable companies and foreign government cable networks at the expense of British firms.

Table 11.1. Distribution of Private Cables in the World in 1923[a]

	No. of cables	Length (km)	Percent of world total
Eastern and Associated Companies			
Eastern Telegraph Co.	153	97,144	16.5
Western Telegraph Co.	37	53,380	9.1
Eastern Extension . . . Telegraph Co.	31	51,194	8.7
Eastern & South African Telegraph Co.	15	19,252	3.3
African Direct Telegraph Co.	8	5,339	0.9
West Coast of America Telegraph Co.	7	3,780	0.6
West African Telegraph Co.	8	2,730	0.5
Europe & Azores Telegraph Co.	2	1,967	0.3
River Plate Telegraph Co.	4	409	0.1
Subtotal	265	235,195	39.9
Other British Companies			
West India & Panama Telegraph Co.	22	8,065	1.4
Cuba Submarine Telegraph Co.	12	2,746	0.5
Direct West India Cable Co.	2	2,346	0.4
Halifax & Bermudas Cable Co.	1	1,578	0.3
Direct Spanish Telegraph Co.	2	1,307	0.2
Indo-European Telegraph Co.	4	355	0.1
Subtotal	43	16,397	2.8
Total of British Companies	308	251,592	42.7
American Companies			
Western Union Telegraph Co.	33	40,397	6.8
All-America Cables, Inc.	36	33,527	5.7
Commercial Cable Co.	16	32,410	5.5
Commercial Pacific Cable Co.	6	18,550	3.1
Mexican Telegraph Co.	5	5,815	1.0
Commercial Cable Company of Cuba	2	2,870	0.5
United States & Hayti Telegraph Co.	1	2,577	0.4
Subtotal	99	136,146	23.1
Other Companies			
Compagnie Française de Câbles Télégr.	25	28,234	4.8
Compagnie des Câbles Sud-américains	4	5,145	0.9
Great Northern Telegraph Co.	26	15,590	2.6
Société Anonyme Belge des Câbles Télégr.	2	113	
Cía. Telegráfico-telefónica del Plata	3	156	
Subtotal	60	49,238	8.4
Total of all Company Cables	467	436,976	74.2

[a]George Schreiner, *Cables and Wireless and their Role in the Foreign Relations of the United States* (Boston, 1924), 229–60.

Cable Technology in the 1920s

In response to a revival of international trade and investments, the early 1920s were a seller's market for telecommunications services, and the changes occurring over time were gradual enough so that all concerned (except the Germans) were able to adjust smoothly. In the opinion of most experts, radio and cables were destined to

Table 11.2.   Distribution of Government Cables in the World, 1923[a]

	No. of Cables	Length (km)	Percent of world total
British Empire			
Britian and Ireland	276	20,776	3.5
Pacific Cable Board	7	17,398	2.9
India	14	4,324	0.7
Others	190	3,712	0.6
Subtotal	487	46,210	7.8
France and French Empire	79	31,554	5.4
Japan	214	14,463	2.5
Netherlands East Indies	34	12,706	2.2
Spain	34	6,603	1.1
United States and Philippines	48	6,475	1.1
Italy	97	5,823	1.0
Norway	1,294	4,013	0.7
Germany	88+	3,270	0.6
USSR	11	2,683	0.5
Others	706	7,180	1.2
Total government cables	3,092	140,980	23.9

[a]Same as for Table 11.1.

complement each other rather than compete. Only radio could transmit voices, communicate with ships, and broadcast to many receivers at once. Also, radio cost less: In the mid-1920s, two transatlantic stations cost between two and four million dollars, while a cable cost seven million.[1] Cables, however, were more secure and worked twenty-four hours a day, regardless of the weather. Thus the advent of radio did not give the executives of cable companies any sleepless nights. All over the world, international communications were better than they had ever been. Though Britain no longer dominated the cable business and still lacked an imperial wireless chain, all in all, the communications needs of the Empire were better served than ever before.

Table 11.3.   Private and Government Cables Combined in 1923[a]

	No. of Cables	Length (km)	Percent of world total
British Empire cables	795	297,802	50.5
French cables	108	64,933	11.0
American cables	147	142,621	24.2
Japanese cables	214	14,463	2.5
Danish cables	26	15,590	2.6
Others[b]	2,276	53,819	9.2
Total world cables	3,566	589,228	100.0

[a]Same as for Table 11.1

[b]Includes the ex-German cables, their status still undefined.

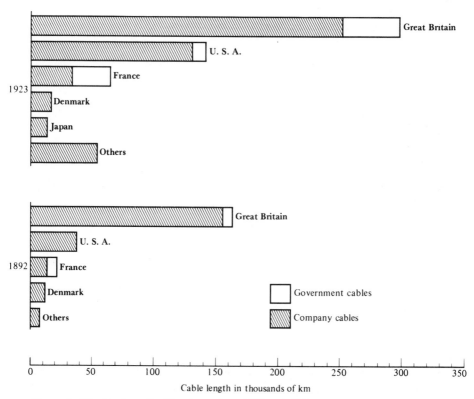

Figure 6. Distribution of cables by nation, 1892 and 1923.

At that very moment, two major technological innovations in quick succession were about to transform international telecommunications and upset the delicate balances between cables and radio and between Britain and its rivals. The first of these occurred in cables.

Until the mid-1920s, advances in long-distance telegraphy were all due to improvements in the sending and receiving equipment. Already before the war there had been attempts to speed up transmissions and reduce the number of clerks relaying messages from one line to the next. In the 1910s, cable companies had installed automatic relays that amplified and retransmitted signals, but amplified the distortions along with the signal. After 1923 the companies installed regenerative repeaters that could sample a distorted incoming signal and from it reconstruct the original signal. This allowed an unlimited number of automatic retransmissions and increased the accuracy and speed of long-distance telegraphy; a message from London to Sydney, which once would have been received and retransmitted eighteen times en route and taken twenty-one hours, now took only thirty minutes on the average, and in some cases less than a minute. At the end point automatic printers produced Roman characters on a gummed tape.[2]

The cables themselves had not changed since the 1870s, however. Stagnation in cable technology was due to the conservatism of the British manufacturers who

Table 11.4.   Comparative Cable Statistics, 1892 and 1923

	1892		1923		Changes	
	length	%	length	%	in length	in %
Company cables						
Eastern and Associated	112,711	45.5	235,195	39.9	122,484	−5.6
Other British cos.	43,103	17.5	16,397	2.8	−26,706	−14.7
All British companies	155,814	63.1	251,592	42.7	95,778	−20.4
American companies	38,987	15.7	136,146	23.1	97,159	+7.4
Other non-British cos.	26,343	10.8	49,238	8.4	22,895	−2.4
All non-British cos.	65,330	26.5	185,384	31.5	120,054	+5.0
All company cables	221,144	89.6	436,976	74.2	215,832	−15.4
Government cables						
British Empire	7,804	3.2	46,210	7.8	38,406	+4.6
French Empire	8,432	3.4	31,554	5.4	23,122	+2.0
Other governments	9,492	3.8	63,216	10.7	53,724	+10.7
All government cables	25,728	10.4	140,980	23.9	115,252	+13.5
Company and government cables combined						
British Empire	163,619	66.3	297,802	50.5	134,183	−15.8
French Empire	21,859	8.9	64,933	11.0	43,074	+2.1
United States	38,986	15.8	142,621	24.2	103,635	+8.4
Japan	—	—	14,463	2.5	14,463	+2.5
Denmark	13,201	5.3	15,590	2.6	2,389	−2.7
Others	9,206	3.7	53,819[a]	9.2	44,613	+5.5
All cables combined	246,871	100	589,228	100	342,357	

[a]Includes the ex-German cables, their status still undefined.

Note: Lengths are in kilometers; percentages are of the world total.

dominated the industry and to the cost and longevity of cables, which discouraged the cable companies from seeking improvements that might make their investments obsolete. It is not surprising, therefore, that, when an innovation appeared, it came from outside the industry.

Cables were slow compared with land lines. The average cable could transmit 150 letters (or thirty words) per minute, and a few up to 300. The reason was a phenomenon called *capacitance,* which blurred the signals. Electricians had long known that one way to decrease capacitance was to reduce the resistance of the core by making it heavier; in 1923 the Commercial Cable Company laid a cable from New York to England with a core that weighed 269 kilograms per kilometer, over six times as much as prewar cables. Though it was, for a short time, the fastest transatlantic cable, this heavy-handed approach did not find any imitators.[3] Instead, electrical engineers found a more elegant solution: loading.

In 1885–1887 British physicist Oliver Heaviside had demonstrated theoretically that it was possible to compensate for capacitance by adding inductance to the cable. This could be done either by placing coils at certain points along the cable (lump-loading) or by wrapping the core in soft iron (continuous loading). The first continuously loaded cable was laid in 1902, and the first lump-loaded one in 1906, but they were both short, and further technical advances had to await the end of the war. In 1921 the Western Electric Company, a subsidiary of AT&T, patented Permalloy, an alloy of nickel and iron that had a magnetic permeability thirty times that of soft iron. By wrapping a thin tape of Permalloy around the core of a cable, they found it would carry signals far more sharply, hence three to five times faster than ordinary cables. Two years later, Telegraph Construction and Maintenance, the world's leading cable manufacturer, patented Mumetal, a copper–nickel–iron alloy that had the same properties as Permalloy and was easier to work.

The capacity of loaded cables was far beyond the ability of the most skilled telegraph clerk to transmit or receive messages. To handle the flood of information that could flow through loaded cables, engineers introduced time-division multiplexing, which divided the flow into channels. Thus one cable could act like many, sending up to eight messages at once.[4]

The New Cables, 1924–1929

The first Permalloy cable was manufactured by TC&M for the Western Union Company and was laid between New York and Horta (Azores) in 1924. Obtaining a landing license was an accomplishment in itself, for the British, well aware that any cable through the Azores would escape their control, put heavy pressure on the Portuguese government to refuse; as the anglophobic American expert George Schreiner explained: "Portugal herself has been for almost a century little more than a vassal state of the British empire."[5] In the end, Portugal granted the license, perhaps for simple business reasons or perhaps, as the German Artur Kunert believed, because "already soon after the World War the United States designated the Azores as the limit of their sphere of interest."[6] The new cable was a technical success, able to handle 1,900 letters (or 380 words) per minute, five times more than previous cables.[7]

The Azores cable was only the first part of a complex deal worked out between Western Union, Commercial Cable, the Compagnia Italiana dei Cavi Telegrafici Sottomarini ("Italcable"), and the Neue Deutsche Kabelgesellschaft, bypassing Britain.

Italcable was Mussolini's instrument to spread Italian influence around the world. In addition to the Azores connection, the company also laid cables to Belgium and Brazil. In 1924, with technical assistance from Western Union, it laid a loaded cable from Anzio (near Rome) to Horta via Malaga (Spain). Western Union's British ally, the Western Telegraph Company, shared the same building at Horta and was thus connected to the United States and the Mediterranean.[8]

As early as 1921 German cable traffic to the Americas had surpassed the prewar figures, and the German Post Office, finding both the radio and the British cables unreliable and insecure, began negotiations with the American companies for a more direct cable link. While a first agreement was signed in January 1922, the German hyperinflation of 1923 and the collapse of the Neue Deutsche Kabelgesellschaft postponed its implementation for several years. Finally in 1926 the Norddeutsche Seekabelwerke laid a loaded cable from Emden to Horta for the

Deutsch-Atlantische Telegraphengesellschaft, the firm that had lost its cables in the war. Direct service to New York was inaugurated in April 1927, and was improved by the laying in 1928 of another Western Union cable, this one from Horta to Newfoundland.[9]

Great Britain, increasingly squeezed out of the American market, turned more and more to the Empire. In addition to the German cable seized in the war and diverted to Newfoundland, the British government bought another old cable from the Direct United States Cable Company in 1922 and relaid it to Halifax as well. When traffic filled its Pacific cable to capacity, the Pacific Cable Board used its ample reserves to duplicate it with a loaded one that could handle 250 words per minute, ten time more than the old one. The Eastern group, also enjoying the communications boom of the mid-1920s, laid new cables fro Gibraltar to Rio de Janeiro and to Bombay and from Cocos Island to Freemantle (Australia), reaching its peak in 1927 with 252,000 kilometers of cables.[10]

What can we learn from the cable boom of the mid-1920s? Very clearly, radio was no threat to cables, both because demand was rising fast enough for both industries to thrive, and because in loaded cables the cable industry had found an answer to its technological challenge. But in cables, as in radio, the United States had more capital and more important innovations than did Britain. The consequences of the shifting power of the two nations were first felt in Latin America, but the American tentacles were also beginning to reach out into the oceans, from the Azores to China.

ITT and the Telephones

The power of capital and technology to expand American influence was also evident, and spectacularly so, in another medium of communications. The telephone had long been used locally, but not until after World War I did long-distance calls become common. For reasons both technical and political, telephony was everywhere considered a public utility rather than an international business.[11] All this changed in the 1920s with the advent of ITT.

The International Telephone and Telegraph Company was an example of a firm that grew by mergers and acquisitions rather than by expansion. It was founded in 1920 by the brothers Sosthenes and Hernand Behn on the basis of their control of the Porto Rico and Cuban Telephone companies. The Behns combined a vision of the telephone as the communications medium of the future with an extraordinary financial wizardry. They also profited from the fragmentation of Latin America, the economic weakness of Europe after the war, and the restrictions on the expansion of American Telephone and Telegraph outside the United States.

In 1924, with the financial backing of New York banks and the diplomatic support of the American government, ITT bought up some small Spanish telephone companies and merged them into the Compañía Telefónica Nacional de España. AT&T, meanwhile, was under Justice Department pressure to give up its foreign interests in exchange for monopoly rights in the United States. In 1924 ITT, excluded from the United States, bought AT&T's foreign manufacturing subsidiary, the International Western Electric Company. Thus the two American firms divided up the world between them.

With the acquisition of International Western Electric, which it renamed International Standard Electric, ITT came into possession of the most up-to-date technology and numerous national telephone equipment manufacturing firms, including Standard Telephones & Cables of Britain, Le Matériel Téléphonique of France, Bell Telephone of Belgium, and others in Italy, the Netherlands, Japan, China, and Australia.

At this point Sosthenes Behn, not satisfied with telephones, expanded into cables and radio. In 1926 ITT acquired the Mexican Telephone and Telegraph Company, and a year later it merged with All-America Cables, which had meanwhile acquired the French cables in the Caribbean. In 1928 ITT bought out the Mackay interests, including the Commercial Cable, Commercial Pacific, Postal Telegraph, and Mackay Radio companies. The more Behn bought, the more eager were the Morgan Guaranty and National City of Bank of New York to lend him money. With their help, Behn set out on the greatest shopping spree in history. In quick succession he bought (mostly from British investors) telephone companies in Uruguay, Chile, Brazil, and Argentina, and linked them up with long-distance lines. By 1929 ITT controlled two-thirds of the telephones and half the cables in Latin America, one-third of the Atlantic cables, the Spanish telephones, and factories throughout the world.[12] And all this on borrowed money! It was a dazzling demonstration of American financial muscle. Not for nothing did the economist Ludwell Denny entitle his book about the 1920s *America Conquers Britain: A Record of Economic War*.

The Shortwave Revolution

In 1924–24, just as the cable companies were introducing new cables that would give them back their competitive advantage, long-distance radio underwent its first real change since Marconi came to England in 1897. That innovation was shortwave, and the man who made it happen was none other than the Commendatore himself. His work on shortwave put him in the most select company of all: people who have changed the world twice.

To be sure, shortwaves (defined as waves of 100 meters or less) were nothing new. In fact, nineteenth-century physicists who discovered that "Hertzian" waves behaved like light and thereby established the continuity of the electromagnetic spectrum had been experimenting with relatively short waves. One of Marconi's greatest achievements in those days was to discover that longer waves did not act like light but followed the contours of the land, and if sufficiently long and powerful, could travel around the earth. For that reason he, and everyone else, concentrated on the longer waves and neglected the short ones.

Shortwaves were not totally forgotten, however. In 1916 Marconi did some experiments for the Italian navy using two-meter waves and reflectors, hoping to develop secure line-of-sight communications between warships that could not be intercepted beyond the horizon; this proved to be a dead end, however, because the tubes then available could not generate such high frequencies.[13]

In 1919 the British and American governments, convinced that shortwaves had no practical value, allowed amateurs to experiment with the "useless" bandwidths under 200 meters. That year tubes became available, and amateurs using one-kilowatt transmitters discovered that they could communicate across the United States. Two years later they made contact across the Atlantic Ocean. These links, however, were erratic and unpredictable.

Marconi and his research engineers Charles Franklin and H. J. Round were also looking into the matter. They knew that radio waves could be reflected, but that the reflector had to be proportional to the wavelength, hence practical only for short-waves. With a parabolic reflector they could direct much more of the transmitter's energy toward the receiver, a system they called the "beam." After some inconclusive short-range tests, Marconi and Franklin built a twelve-kilowatt station at Poldhu, with a parabolic reflector. In 1923 Marconi sailed toward West Africa on his yacht *Elettra* and discovered that the signals from Poldhu, which had faded out soon after his departure, reappeared and could be heard at distances of 2,300 kilometers during the day and 4,000 kilometers at night. He had discovered the "skip" effect, by which shortwaves do not curve around the earth like longwaves, but bounce off the ionosphere to reappear far from their origin. What mattered was not the power of the transmitter but the distance between it and the receiver.[14]

In February 1924, just when the Donald Committee Report was being debated in Parliament, Marconi announced to the public that his shortwave experiments had been successful. In April and May he send a voice message to Australia. His signals were also heard in North and South America, South Africa, and India. At extreme distances, the little shortwave transmitter at Poldhu was heard better than the gigantic longwave stations at Caernarvon and Leafield. By the fall, using thirty-two-meter waves, Marconi was being received in Sydney twenty-three and a half hours a day. Not only was "beam" radio a technical success, it was also incredibly cheap, costing one-twentieth as much as long-distance longwave station. And finally, it was faster than longwave, faster even than loaded cables.[15]

There is a general trend in technology towards greater size, complexity, and cost, for instance when ocean liners replaced sailing ships or jets replaced propeller planes. For twenty-five years, long-distance radio had been following this trend towards ever larger, more powerful, and more expensive equipment concentrated in the hands of a few giant companies. Shortwave broke this cycle, making global communications simple and cheap, and threatening to make all previous telecommunications systems obsolete in short order. This was not just a technical innovation; it also promised some major political repercussions. They were not long in coming.

The British Reaction

In early 1924 Marconi's Wireless offered a new Imperial Wireless Scheme to replace its old longwave proposals. The new one, using shortwave, was to cost one-twentieth as much, use one-fiftieth the power, and transmit at three times the speed of longwave. The company informed the governments of Australia and South Africa that the longwave stations it was building for them were already obsolete.[16] The British government reacted defensively. In a memorandum dated April 29, the Admiralty rejected shortwave on the grounds that "The stations must transmit equally in all directions. Stations utilizing 'reflection' systems . . . are of little value for Naval purposes."[17] By May, the Admiralty was softening its proposition:

> The Admiralty felt that . . . the erection of High Power Stations in the Dominions was now subject to a certain amount of doubts. . . . The directional stations were unable to broadcast their messages and consequently were not suitable for all strategical purposes, but it was possible that owing to their cheapness [£20,000 instead of £500,000] some of the Governments of the Dominions might decide to adopt this type of station.[18]

On July 4 the Postmaster General wrote to the Cabinet that shortwave was too experimental, that it only worked at night and in one direction.[19] Despite all these objections, the government decided to adopt Marconi's beam system, but without giving up the Rugby station. On July 28, it signed a contract with Marconi's, by which the company promised to erect shortwave stations in twenty-six weeks. Stations for use within the Empire would be owned and operated by the Post Office, while Marconi's would communicate with foreign countries.[20] Later that year, the Imperial Communications Committee was still racked with doubts: on the one hand, it feared that amateurs would interfere with shortwave stations, but on the other, it was afraid that, in the event of war, the cables would be cut and radio would be needed; obviously, the days when British officials saw the world in terms of opportunities and advantages had long since passed.[21]

Marconi's set to work building shortwave stations in Britain and in the principal dominions. By October 1926 the circuit to Canada was ready and in the hands of the Post Office. Not only was it cheaper, but it was also able to carry far more traffic than any other radio circuit in the world.[22] Soon thereafter shortwave stations began operating in South Africa, Australia, India, and South America. While the British ends of the circuits were in the hands of the Post Office, the dominion ends were operated by local companies owned in part by Marconi's. So successful was it that the BBC decided in 1927 to begin broadcasting on shortwave to the Empire.[23]

The government meanwhile pressed ahead with the construction of its Rugby longwave station. It was enormous: the antennas, supported by twelve 250-meter-high towers, covered ten square kilometers; the tubes had an output of 500 kilowatts; and it cost £490,000 ($2.4 million). Though it was no longer as indispensable as it had once been, it still had advantages that shortwave lacked: It alone could broadcast to the entire Royal Navy at once and transmit to submarines underwater; also it made possible the first commercial transatlantic telephone service in October 1926.[24]

And so, fifteen years after it was first proposed, Britain finally had its Imperial Wireless Chain. It was certainly not to the government's credit. The British government was pushed, reluctantly, into the age of long-distance radio by the force of technology and the unflagging vision of Guglielmo Marconi.

French Colonial Shortwave

Because it was a small-scale, low-cost technology, shortwave radio had a double impact. On the one hand, it made long-distance communication affordable even to the poorest and most remote regions that had previously depended on the major cable and longwave companies, or had done without. On the other hand, the new technology caused an upheaval in the communications industry, especially in Great Britain. Let us consider these impacts in order.

It would be futile to list all the new shortwave stations and circuits that sprang up around the world in the late 1920s and early 1930s. The impact was greatest in those places most poorly served by the older technologies, such as French Africa and Indochina. In 1926 the French colonies had three big longwave stations at Saigon, Bamako, and Tananarive. When an experimental shortwave station at Sainte-Assise demonstrated the feasibility of this new medium, the Ministry of Colonies decided to build 1–5-kilowatt shortwave stations in New Caledonia, Tahiti, Martinique, Djibouti, Senegal, Soudan, Madagascar, and the Congo. To these transmitters, which could reach thousands of kilometers, were added dozens of small transmitters throughout the colonies that could communicate with the nearest long-range station; these cost one-thirtieth as much as longwave stations of equivalent reach, and one-tenth as much as telegraph lines over distances of 100 kilometers or more. The smallest of these sets were so cheap and simple that they were entrusted to Africans, in those days a real sign of an "intermediate" technology.[25]

In Indochina, the great Saigon longwave station, while providing a welcome alternative to the British cables, was costly and unreliable, especially from May to October when the monsoons created static. As early as January 1926 CSF opened a shortwave station in Saigon and another one in Hanoi in November 1927. The new system was both cheaper and more reliable than any previous connection, and the colony's radio traffic soared from 4,484 words per day in 1924 to 11,007 in 1928.[26] In 1930 CSF offered direct telephone service between France and Indochina, and by 1938 radio had captured 97 percent of the traffic between the two countries.[27]

The International Impact of Shortwave

As soon as shortwave was demonstrated to be technically efficient, its use spread around the world, thanks to the patent-pooling arrangements between the major companies. From the point of view of the radio industry, it represented an innovation and a substantial improvement rather than a threat. The United States government somewhat belatedly recognized the importance of radio when it established the Federal Radio Commission in February 1927.[28] One of its first important decisions was to deal with requests from the major consumers of international communications—the wire services, newspapers, banks, and brokerage houses—to operate their own shortwave circuits; the FRC rejected these requests in order to protect the existing companies.[29]

The U.S. government's recognition of radio truly became official when it called the International Radiotelegraph Conference at Washington in October and November 1927. This was the first such conference since 1912, one that had been postponed repeatedly since 1920 because of disputes over cables. Though Russia had signed the Convention of 1912, the U.S. government refused to invite the Soviet Union on the grounds that it was not recognized by the United States. In other respects, the conference went smoothly, concerning itself mostly with maritime radio and spectrum allocation. Unlike the prewar conferences, which were the scene of strong disagreements between Britain and Germany, this one was dominated by the United States, which wanted the Convention and General Regulations to be as vague and flexible as possible in order not to hinder experimentation and technical innovation. The United States also insisted that the question of rates be placed in separate Additional Regulations, which it refused to sign, along with Canada and Nicaragua.[30] If the Convention that resulted was, in the words of radio historian Paul Schubert, "a masterpiece of international concord and problem solving," that was in part because it required so few adjustments on the part of the signatory nations.[31]

The real victims of shortwave were the cable companies. The British Post Office's shortwave service to Australia charged 4d per word to Australia, one-sixth as much as the full cable rate.[32] Though Eastern lowered its rates, it could not match the shortwave rates without a loss. More and more traffic switched to shortwave radio. In 1927 the cable companies lost almost half their traffic to shortwave. Within six months of opening for business, the Post Office Beam Service to India and Australia captured 65 percent of Eastern's traffic and over half the traffic of the Pacific cable. On the France–Indochina circuit, where cables had handled all the traffic in 1921, by 1928 radio had captured almost 70 percent.[33] Final proof of the effectiveness of shortwave radio was to come in November 1929; when a seismic upheaval on the bed of the Atlantic broke thirteen out of twenty-one transatlantic cables, the rupture was hardly noticed, for the traffic simply moved over to radio.[34]

The British Communications Merger

The British government had always been of several minds about radio. Before the war, there had been two factions: Marconi and the Admiralty against the Post Office. In 1924–25 the shortwave revolution finally forced the Post Office to accept radio. By 1927, proliferating shortwave circuits, including the Post Office's own Imperial Beam Service, threatened that pillar of the British Empire, the Eastern and Associated Companies. In short order, a technological innovation had turned into a commercial upheaval and that, in turn, created a political problem of the first magnitude.

In late 1927 the Committee of Imperial Defence called a special Sub-Committee on Competition between "Beam" Wireless and Cable Services.[35] In the interim report issued on October 27, it considered the possibility that shortwave might be jammed in wartime, and concluded that "[t]he Power which had obtained command of the sea will be able to maintain its own cable communications and will be in a position to interrupt those of its enemies." The Admiralty informed the committee that "ample proof exists that a properly trained cryptographic bureau can in course of time break down the security of practically any code of cypher." For this reason, in its final report of December 8, the Sub-Committee concluded: "We have assumed that all Governmental communications of a secret or confidential nature will be transmitted by cable, as well as any communications of a quasicommercial character which might, if intercepted, convey information of use to an enemy." Yet, because of the limited capacity of cables to the east, the Sub-Committee also insisted that there must be wireless communications "under effective British control."

While the strategists wanted it all, the business world had a different view. Marconi, whose aversion to the cable companies is said to have been "akin to that attributed to the devil for holy water,"[36] was now in a position to undercut them. In this situation, the cable companies had a choice: either to lower their rates and gradually lose money until they went bankrupt; or to sell their assets, distribute their £20 million reserve fund to their shareholders, and go out of business.

Sir John Denison-Pender, chairman of the Eastern group, threatened to do the latter, raising fears, as *The Times* noted, that "if the Eastern Telegraph and its associated companies were to be forced into voluntary liquidation portions of the system might pass into foreign control."[37] Eastern was, in effect, holding the British Empire to ransom.

This time the British government did not appoint a mere committee but called the Imperial Wireless and Cable Conference, with delegates from the whole Empire, to meet on January 16, 1928. While the administrative machinery of government was slowly getting underway, Denison-Pender and his counterpart at Marconi's Wireless, Lord Inverforth, came up with their own solution to the crisis. On December 18, 1927, they agreed to negotiate the merger of their two firms, announcing their intention on January 10.[38] Merger talks and the Imperial Conference went on at the same time. On March 16, the two companies informed the conference that they had agreed to form a holding company with 56.25 percent of the shares to be held by the cable interests and 43.75 by Marconi's.[39]

After long deliberation, the Imperial Conference issued its report on July 6.[40] What it recommended was truly revolutionary: the merger of all British communications interests, including Marconi's, the cable companies, the Post Office shortwave system (to be rented for £250,000 a year), the Pacific Cable Board, and the government's transatlantic cables.[41] It envisioned a "merger company" to acquire all shares of Marconi's and Eastern, and a "communications company" to acquire all British communications assets, leaving the patent and manufacturing assets to the merger company. The companies were to have the same directors, two of whom were to be named by the British government. No more than 25 percent of the shares could be foreign owned. As a final precaution, the companies were to be supervised by an Imperial Communications Advisory Committee with representatives of the British and dominion governments.

The era of procrastination was over. The merger and formation of the two companies was approved by Parliament in August, and by Canada, Australia, India, and South Africa later that year. On April 8, 1929, the two companies were founded under the names Cables and Wireless Ltd., the holding company, and Imperial and International Communications Ltd., the communications company.[42] The latter owned 253 cable and radio stations and over half the world's cables, and could communicate with almost every point in the Empire by two or more channels.[43] Yet it could not operate like a normal business, for it was under orders from the Imperial Communications Advisory Committee to keep its strategic (and now unprofitable) cables operating.[44] What had emerged was a new form of enterprise, nominally private but in fact government regulated and monopolistic, a pillar of the Empire in the image of Imperial Airways and the P&O–British India Line. It was not just a company: it was the All-Red network, the most secure global communications system imaginable.

Responses to the British Merger

The merger of cables and radio as a response to shortwave competition was not restricted to Britain. French experts interpreted the British merger and the expansion of ITT as Anglo-Saxon threats to French telecommunications. To counter them, the two French companies, Radio-France and Compagnie Française des Câbles Télégraphiques, formed an Electrical Communications Committee in June 1928. With the approval of the government, they agreed to create a joint purse to avoid competition and handle their relations with the public. The mid-Atlantic earthquake of November 1929, which severed CFCT's Atlantic cables, made Radio-France the senior partner in the pool. Because of France's small overseas trade during the Depression, the arrangement had little impact on international relations.[45]

Much more important, from an international standpoint, was the American response. Americans reacted sharply to the news of the British communications merger, but not in any coherent fashion. Instead, each interested party saw this as an opportunity to pursue its own agenda, while the Hoover administration looked on. The government, meanwhile, still held to the traditions of free enterprise and competition.

The parties most interested in the merger were RCA, Western Union, and ITT. RCA, riding the boom in domestic commercial broadcasting and home receiver manufacturing, was the least affected; in 1927 transoceanic and marine radio provided $4.8 million, or 7 percent, of its $65 million in gross revenues. Western Union was in far worse shape, for its reserves were depleted by huge investments in Permalloy cables, and its president Newcomb Carlton withdrew to a defensive strategy. ITT was still vigorous and expansionistic, and Sosthenes Behn liked to talk about merging America's telecommunications interests, but ITT's subsidiary Commercial Cable, like Western Union, was feeling the competition from shortwave.[46]

In February 1928, when the Marconi–Eastern merger was still only a rumor, General James Harbord, president of RCA, sent his managing director David Sarnoff to London to limit the damage. Traveling on the same ship was Newcomb Carlton, on the same mission for Western Union. While on board ship, the two men discussed merging their companies' international communications, but Carlton hesitated. In June, ITT began negotiating with RCA for the sale of its communications business, with RCA spun off in January 1929 into a wholly owned subsidiary, RCA Communications, Inc., but ITT was too heavily in debt.[47] Besides, the Radio Law of 1927 prohibited the same company from owning both radio and cables, in order to prevent a monopoly. Any merger would require a special Congressional dispensation.

Those who favored a merger therefore started a campaign to persuade the public and Congress to change the law. General Harbord, speaking to the Harvard Business School in April 1928, said: "The American answer to this challenge can only be made by submitting the great communication companies, both cable and radio, to proper government regulation as to rates while exempting them from the operation of the anti-trust laws and permitting unification here and thus meeting the thrust of unification from abroad."[48]

The British response to American merger rumors was properly horrified. Roland Belfort, a Marconi executive, wrote in the magazine *United Empire:* "The British Empire is today fighting for the retention of its traditional supremacy in world communications against powerful competitors, the strongest, richest and most resolute being the Americans, who, from the telegraphic standpoint, are strongly entrenched in the heart of the Empire." A merger of ITT with RCA and Western Union, he calculated, would create a company with a capital of $1.6 billion, compared with $600 million for the British conglomerate. "Adding to this the probable support of American State diplomacy and prestige throughout the world, one obtains a clear conception of the puissant, world-embracing Combination with which the modest [sic] British amalgamated enterprises have to compete in the future."[49]

In 1929 and early 1930, at the request of RCA, the Senate Interstate Commerce Committee held hearings on the proposed merger of American communications companies.[50] G. Stanley Shoup, chief of the Communications Section of the Transport Division of the Department of Commerce, testified:

> I believe that the British merger was a result partly of competition; that is true, but there was another reason which was political. We have made rapid strides in this country in international communications, and the British feared the lead which the United States was taking, and unquestionably one of the main factors in determining a merger of British cables and radio was aimed directly at the United States.[51]

Owen Young, chairman of RCA, made an impassioned plea:

> If you have any hesitation about unifying our external communications in the hands of a private company under government control, then I beg of you in the national interests to unify them under government ownership in order that America may not be left in the external communications field to the dictatorships and control of foreign companies or governments.[52]

In the end, the urgings of RCA and ITT were not enough to overcome the opposition of Western Union and the reluctance of Congress to tolerate another monopoly, and the matter was shelved.

Rumors of an American merger revived in 1933 and 1934. The new president, Franklin D. Roosevelt, was known to be interested in communications, and some assumed his administration would be easier on mergers and conglomerates than Hoover's had been. Imperial and International Communications Ltd. kept a careful watch on events in America. In October 1933 Sosthenes Behn and Newcomb

Carlton visited London to talk to Denison-Pender of I&IC and Normal Leslie of the Imperial Communications Committee about matters of common interest, such as sharing traffic, amalgamating offices, and raising rates. Denison-Pender telegraphed David Sarnoff: TAKING ADVANTAGE OF THE PRESENCE IN LONDON OF BOTH CARLTON AND BEHN A MEETING TOOK PLACE HERE TODAY BETWEEN THE THREE OF US WHEN A SCHEME WAS DISCUSSED WHICH WOULD BENEFICIALLY AFFECT ALL OUR INTERESTS STOP I WILL LET YOU KNOW AS SOON AS ANYTHING DEFINITE EMERGES FOR SUBMISSION TO YOU.[53] For a while, I&IC and Western Union came close to an agreement on pooling traffic and sharing offices, but once again Carlton backed down. In November Sarnoff arrived in London to consult with I&IC about their mutual complaints against Behn. Sarnoff's plan, as confided to Denison-Pender, was to use his close friendship with President Roosevelt to bring about a merger of American communications companies in which RCA would have the controlling interest and Sarnoff would be the director.[54] In spite of Sarnoff's friendly attitude towards the British, Denison-Pender showed deep anxiety when he wrote the Treasury a week later:

> With the consummation of the American Merger . . . the position of London as the centre of the world's telegraph system will thus be challenged by the emergence of New York as an effective rival enjoying special privileges not available to my Company. . . . [T]he predominant position hitherto held by British communications will be seriously jeopardized by the creation of such a Merger.[55]

The Imperial Communications Advisory Committee, chaired by Sir Campbell Stuart, fully agreed: "A merger of American external services based on control of internal communications in the USA would be a much more dangerous opponent of Imperial and International than the present competing American companies."[56]

Despite British apprehensions, the merger never took place. While both Behn and Sarnoff were eager to merge their companies, each wanted to do so on his own terms: Behn wanted to absorb RCA Communications into ITT, while Sarnoff wanted RCA to acquire Postal Telegraph's offices throughout America. Carlton abstained.

When Behn and Sarnoff turned to the U.S. government, Roosevelt set up an Interdepartmental Committee that reported to him on January 23, 1934, endorsing the idea of a merger under close Federal supervision. In spite of this advice, Roosevelt did nothing to promote a merger; indeed his administration was just as hostile to the idea as was his predecessor's, and the Justice Department even charged the Western Union and Postal Telegraph companies in 1937 with conspiring to monopolize the telegraph industry.[57]

The merger idea was briefly revived in 1940 in a report by the Federal Communications Commission to the Senate Interstate Commerce Committee. Noting the rise of radio and the importance of cables to national security (the same arguments used by the British in 1928), the majority of the FCC commissioners recommended a merger: "The greatest guarantee of an efficient, broad, and secure American international communication system lies in the combination of a strong, thoroughly sound, and financially successful concern operating under strict governmental regulation in the light of national needs."[58] But once again, the merger failed to take place, mainly because the need was not urgent, as it had been in the British case. While arguments could be made for rationalizing America's overseas communications or for improving corporate profits through mergers, the nation's communications needs were well met by the existing competitive structures.

The British Dilemma: Profits versus Security

Imperial and International Communications Ltd. was born at the worst possible moment in the history of telecommunications, the beginning of the Great Depression. For the next ten years the company's records are full of complaints and fears, most of them well founded. As international trade shrank, so did the telecommunications business. While the decline was mainly due to the business slump, other pressures added to the company's woes. Some were technological, as the increasing use of the radiotelephone—a Post Office monopoly—cut into international telegraphy, while airmail was beginning to make inroads into the cheaper telegraphic services such as night-letter telegrams.[59]

But many of I&IC's problems were political. In June 1929 the Labour Party returned to power, and, when Ramsay MacDonald's Cabinet decided that the Post Office's Rugby station was better suited for transatlantic radio-telephony than I&IC's proposed shortwave service, it was widely interpreted as a political decision favoring a government enterprise over a private company established under Conservative auspices.[60] I&IC complained that the Foreign Office did not support the company in its dealings overseas as the State Department did for American companies, and that Americans were allowed to open offices in Britain and deal with the public directly, "a facility which the United States would never dream of granting to any foreign Company in America."[61] And finally, a sense of alienation between the government and the company is evident in a number of documents. Thus in 1934 the Admiralty admitted that at the time the company was set up, the Treasury made "a very good bargain with the company, under which the Company are still smarting." I&IC complained that there was too little communication between the Imperial Communications Committee, the government's policy-making board, and the Imperial Communications Advisory Committee, which supervised the company, resulting in long delays in getting decisions approved.[62]

In addition to its domestic troubles, I&IC also faced foreign pressures, as other nations increasingly bypassed the British network. Even the dominions, autonomous since the Statute of Westminster of 1931, sought their own direct connections, for instance between India and China, Canada and East Asia, Australia and Japan.[63]

Most threatening of all was the United States. In British eyes, American companies seemed big and wealthy and not tied to an obsolete technology. As the company wrote in August 1931:

America is endeavoring to dominate the telegraph communications of the world, with the full and active support of its Government and National Institutions. The recent extraordinary development of the International Telephone and Telegraph Corporation of America is probably well known to the Committee.[64]

The Imperial Communications Advisory Committee concurred: "The tendency must be, in the end, for wireless to supersede the cable system. Can we contemplate leaving foreign countries such as the USA to the mastery of the radio art, while the British group remains tied to what may become an outworn cable system?"[65]

And why was I&IC tied to an "outworn cable system"? Because it was not just a business but an instrument of British policy and that very special status, which had served the Eastern and Associated Companies so well in an age of British ascendancy, was now a heavy burden in the twilight of the Empire. For the real purpose of the merger had been to preserve the anglocentric cable network for strategic reasons, and to support it out of the revenues of radio. When radio revenues stopped rising, the political and the business goals of the company inevitably clashed.

This became apparent in October 1929 when Norman Leslie, secretary of the Imperial Communications Advisory Committee, sent the chairman of I&IC, Sir Basil Blackett, a list of cables "deemed essential on strategic grounds."[66] In July 1930, when I&IC proposed to rationalize its cable network by closing down unprofitable cables, the Imperial Communications Committee noted with dismay: "We have formed the impression, from various statements in their report, that the company are looking to wireless as their mainstay in the future, and we think that their energies will be oriented more and more away from the direction of cables." The Committee forbade the closing of cables on the grounds that most of the cables in question (e.g., Ascension–Sierra Leone, Zanzibar–Mombasa, Lagos–St. Vincent) were needed for defense.[67]

Two years later, hurt by the Depression, the company requested either permission to close down cables, or a £450,000 subsidy to keep them operating.[69] In response, the Imperial Communications Committee set up a Strategic Cables Sub-Committee to investigate the question. Its chairman, Oliver Stanley, warned that the company should not be allowed to abandon strategic cables, because they were much more secure than radio. British policy, then as always, was that "the Power which has obtained command of the sea should be able to secure comparative immunity for its cable services." If this entailed a sacrifice for the company, it might apply for a reimbursement; however, "it would be most unwise, if, in the meanwhile, anything was done to stir up the Company. It was very important . . . not to put ideas into their heads."[69] The Sub-Committee's report, issued in March 1933, listed Britain's strategic cables and reiterated the familiar security concerns. It did yield slightly to the company's demands, however, by placing strategic cables on a "care and maintenance" basis, meaning that they could be closed down if they were ready to be brought back on line with a month's notice, or one or two days' notice where there was no radio connection.[70] Two years later, when Italy asserted its power in Ethiopia, the Committee of Imperial Defence negotiated with the company for alternative cable routes to the British Empire in the event the Mediterranean cables were cut.[71]

Conclusion

Much happened between the world wars in the field of telecommunications, most of it surprising. The era began with a squabble over the spoils of war, with the United

States and Great Britain as the main contenders. While the German cable question faded away, their rivalry did not, for it had deeper roots. The real issue was the same one that had stirred up so much acrimony before the war: the British hegemony over world communications. This time, however, the challenge did not come from a self-conscious nationalism as it had in the case of France and Germany. While American were quite as capable as any other people of cloaking expansionistic ambitions in the rhetoric of self-pity, government policy, in the end, played almost no role in the rise of American power in telecommunications. Instead, it was America's wealth, aided by a changing technology.

The United States did not merely grow to a position of influence, but benefitted from the decline of its rivals. Germany and Russia were defeated and ruined by the war, France was wounded, Britain badly weakened. The United States first challenged Britain in Latin America, which the British rather grudgingly conceded by the mid-1920s. Elsewhere, Britain still kept its grasp on most of the world's information flow. What finally destroyed the British hegemony was shortwave, an invention brought to fruition, ironically, by Guglielmo Marconi, a man who loved Great Britain.

Since the turn of the century, there had been tensions between Britain's government and its telecommunications firms. For a long time, Marconi's entrepreneurship had clashed with the government's technological conservatism and economic statism. The tension persisted into the 1930s, but on a different basis. Both sides now had much less room to maneuver: the government was more insecure, hence more security minded than ever, while the company faced serious economic problems. In the clash between political and economic needs, Britain traded profitability for security.

Notes

1. Eugene W. Sharp, *International News Communications: The Submarine Cable and Wireless as News Carriers* (Columbia, Missouri, 1927), 25.

2. Cable & Wireless, Ltd., *The Cable and Wireless Communications of the World: Some Lectures and Papers on the Subject 1924–39* (Cambridge, 1939), 215–19; Vary T. Coates and Bernard Finn, *A Retrospective Technology Assessment: Submarine Telegraphy. The Transatlantic Cable of 1866* (San Francisco, 1979), 159–62; I. S. Coggeshall, "Abridgment of Submarine Telegraphy in the Post War Decade," *Journal of the American Institute of Electrical Engineers* 49 (March 1930), 217–20; K. L. Wood "Empire Telegraph Communications," *Journal of the Institution of Electrical Engineers* 84 (December 1938), 638–71; Gerald R. M. Garratt, *One Hundred Years of Submarine Cables* (London, 1950), 36–42 and 51–52; Hugh Barty-King, *Girdle Round the Earth: The Story of Cable and Wireless and its Predecessors to Mark the Group's Jubilee, 1929–1979* (London, 1979), 200–202; S. A. Garnham and Robert L. Hadfield, *The Submarine Cable: The Story of the Submarine Telegraph Cable from its Inception down to Modern Times. How it Works, how Cable-Ships Work, and how it Carries on in Peace and War* (London, 1934), 166–67.

3. H. H. Haglund, "Ocean Cable Crossroads, Horta, Azores Islands," *Western Union Technical Review* 7 (July 1953), 108–9. The insulation of the cables was also improved; see Daniel R. Headrick, "Gutta-Percha: A Case of Resource Depletion and International Rivalry," *IEEE Technology and Society Magazine* 6, No. 4 (December 1987), 12–16.

4. Ivan S. Coggeshall, "Annotated History of Submarine Cables and Overseas Radiotelegraphs 1851–1934. With Special Reference to the Western Union Company" (manuscript written in 1933–34, with an introduction dated 1984, cited with kind permission of the author), 133; Frank J. Brown, *The Cable and Wireless Communications of the World: A Survey of Present Day Means of International Communication by Cable and Wireless, Containing Chapters on Cable and Wireless Finance* (London, 1927), 76–79; G. L. Lawford and L. R. Nicholson, *The Telcon Story, 1850, 1950* (London, 1950), 89–96; Garnham and Hadfield, 161–65; Garratt, 31 and 47–49.

5. George A. Schreiner, *Cables and Wireless and their Role in the Foreign Relations of the United States* (Boston, 1924), 64, See also pp. 216–19, and Joseph S. Tulchin, *The Aftermath of War: World War I and U.S. Policy toward Latin America* (New York, 1971), 230–31.

6. Artur Kunert, *Geschichte der deutschen Fernmeldekabel. II. Telegraphen-Seekabel* (Cologne–Mülheim, 1962), 374.

7. Garnham and Hadfield, 165; Garratt, 49; Lawford and Nicholson, 95–96.

8. Donard de Cogan, "British Cable Communications (1851–1930): The Azores Connection," *Arquipélago,* numero especial 1988: *Relaçoes Acores–Gra-Bretanha* (Ponta Delgada, Azores, 1988), 187–88; A. L. Osti, "Italy's Submarine Cable System," *The Electrician* 104 (January 24, 1930) 90–92; Coggeshall, "Annotated History," 113–18; Kunert, 381–82; Haglund, 106–9; Tulchin, 231–32.

9. De Cogan, "Azores," 187–88; Coggeshall, "Annotated History," 122–23, and "Abridgment of Submarine Telegraphy," 217–19; Kunert, 372–94; Garratt, 31 and 49.

10. "Agreement between Pacific Cable Board and Telegraph Construction and Maintenance/Siemens Brothers re New Pacific Cable (1925)," in Cable and Wireless archives (London), D11 and D31; G. Stanley Shoup, "Transpacific Communications," *Commerce Reports* (October 17, 1927); Brown, 5, 17, and 80–82; Barty-King, 173, 188, and 201; Garratt, 37.

11. Short submarine telephone cables, e.g., across the English Channel, had existed since the 1890s, but for technical reasons the first transatlantic telephone cable was not laid until 1956.

12. Robert Sobel, *ITT: The Management of Opportunity* (New York, 1982), passim. But see also Ludwell Denny, *America Conquers Britain: A Record of Economic War* (London and New York, 1930), 369–402.

13. W. J. Baker, *A History of the Marconi Company* (London, 1970), 172–73 and 216–17; W. P. Jolly, *Marconi* (New York, 1972), 226–27.

14. Hugh G. J. Aitken, *The Continuous Wave: Technology and American Radio, 1900–1932* (Princeton, 1985), 512, Vice Admiral Arthur R. Hezlet, *The Electron and Sea Power* (London, 1975), 157–59; Baker, 217–19; Jolly, 239–45.

15. Barty-King, 192–93; Baker, 219–22; Hezlet, 157.

16. Baker, 211–13; Jolly, 245; Hezlet, 157–58.

17. "Joint Memorandum by the Representatives of the Admiralty, Colonial Office and General Post Office" (April 29, 1924), in Public Record Office (Kew) [hereafter PRO], Cab 35/11, No. 202.

18. Minutes of the meeting of the Wireless Sub-Committee of the Imperial Communications Committee, May 6, 1924, in PRO, Cab 35/9, No. 31.

19. Memorandum from Postmaster General to Cabinet, July 4, 1924, in PRO, Cab 270/240.

20. Baker, 214; Barty-King, 195; Jolly, 248–49.

21. Committee of Imperial Defence, Imperial Communications Committee, Report of the Sub-committee to Consider the Strategical Importance of 'Beam' Stations" (September 30, 1924), in PRO, Cab 35/14.

22. Baker, 224.

23. Paul Schubert, *The Electric Word: The Rise of Radio* (New York, 1928), 265 and 273; Krishnalal J. Shridharani, *Story of the Indian Telegraphs: A Century of Progress* (New Delhi, 1956), 126–27; Leslie B. Tribolet, *The International Aspects of Electrical Communications in the Pacific Area* (Baltimore, 1929), 216; Baker, 201–2 and 224.

24. "Second Report of the Wireless Telegraphy Commission, 1926" (Viscount Milner, chairman), in *Parliamentary Papers* 1926, Vol. 15 [Cmd 2781], 969; National Archives (Washington), Record Group 173, Box 351: FCC Radio Division, File INT-2: Beam Transmission; Maurice Deloraine, *Des ondes et des hommes: Jeunesse des télécommunications et de l'I.T.T.* (Paris, 1974), 24–43; G. E. C. Wedlake, *SOS: The Story of Radio Communication* (Newton Abbot, 1973), 144–45 and 220.

25. "Postes radio-télégraphiques coloniaux," in archives of the Ministry of Posts and Telecommunications (Paris), F90 bis 1690 and 1695; Conseiller du commerce extérieur Maigret, "Les communications par T.S.F. entre la France et les colonies. Rapport (Conférence du commerce colonial, 18–20 mai 1933), in Archives Nationales Section Outre-mer (Paris), Br. 9677 B; Agence économique de l'A.O.F., *Postes, télégraphes, téléphones, télégraphie sans fil en A.O.F.* (Paris, 1931), 13–15; Henri Staut, "La radiotélégraphie coloniale et les ondes courtes," *Bulletin du Comité d'études historiques et scientifiques de l'A.O.F.* 7 (1926), 517–20, and "L'application des ondes courtes à la radiotélégraphie commerciale en AOF," ibid. 9 (1928), 19–29; "Le réseau colonial de télégraphie sans fil," *Afrique française* 36 (May 1926), 274–76; Lieutenant Colonel Cluzan, "Les télégraphistes coloniaux, pionniers des télécommunications Outre-Mer," *Tropiques* 393 (March 1957), 3–8.

26. L. Gallin, "Renseignements statistiques sur le développement des communications radiotélégraphiques en Indochine," *Bulletin économique de l'Indochine* 32 (1929), 369–99.

27. Indochina, Gourvernement général, Direction des services économiques, *Annuaire statistique*, Vol. 8, *1937–1938* (Hanoi, 1939), 132–36; Maigret, "Les communications par T.S.F. entre la France et les colonies. Rapport. Conférence due commerce colonial, 18–20 mai 1933," in Archives Nationales Section Outre-Mar (Paris); André Touzet, "Le réseau radiotélégraphique indochinois," *Revue indochinoise* 245 (Hanoi, 1918). Despite the clear advantages of shortwave, the big colonial longwave stations were not scrapped but kept as aircraft radio beacons and as backups; "Rapport sur l'état de fonctionnement du poste à ondes longues et sur l'utilité de celui-ci pour la Défense Nationale," in PTT archives, FO90 bis 1690.

28. Keith Clark, *International Communications: The American Attitude* (New York, 1931), 227–28; Tribolet, 217–18.

29. Schubert, 302; Tribolet, 219.

30. Irwin Stewart, "The International Regulation of Radio in Time of Peace," *Annals of the American Academy of Political and Social Sciences* 142 (March 1929), 78–82; John D. Tomlinson, *The International Control of Radiocommunication* (Geneva, 1938), 58–66; Captain Linwood S. Howeth, *History of Communications–Electronics in the United States Navy* (Washington, 1963), 506–11; Tribolet, 23–24; Clark, 178–85 and 217–18.

31. Schubert, 302.

32. Barty-King, 197 and 203; deferred telegrams cost half as much by radio as by cable.

33. Baker, 229; Gallin, 370–744; Barty-King, 203.

34. Coggeshall, "Annotated History," 73–74; Baker, 233; Lawford and Nicholson, 106–7.

35. C.I.D., "Sub-Committee on Competition between 'Beam' Wireless and Cable Services (Brigadier General Sir S. H. Wilson, chair), Interim Report," in PRO, Cab 35/45; "Reports, Proceedings and Memoranda," in Cab 35/43.

36. Baker, 223.

37. Barty-King, 209–10.

38. Barty-King, 203–5.

39. W. J. Baker, historian of Marconi's (pp. 230–32) considers the merger to have been a great defeat for the radio company, caused by the lack of competent leadership; see also Jolly, 261.

40. Imperial Wireless and Cable Conference, 1928 (Sir John Gilmour, chairman), Report, in *Parliamentary Papers* 1928, Vol. 10 [Cmd. 3163].

41. The Post Office, however, kept its hold on international telephony, including the Rugby station. See Baker, 232; and Barty-King, 226.

42. Baker, 229–31; Barty-King, 210. In the 1930s their names were changed, respectively, to Cables and Wireless (Holding) Ltd. and Cable and Wireless Ltd.

43. Garratt, 43; Barty-King, 216.

44. Letter from Sir Normal Leslie, chairman of the Imperial Communications Advisory Committee, to Basil Blackwell, chairman of Imperial and International Communications Ltd., October 14, 1929, in Cable and Wireless archives, B1/112.

45. Pascal Griset, "De la concurrence à la complimentarité: Câbles et radio dans les télécommunications internationales pendant l'entre deux guerres," *Recherches sur l'histoire des télécommunications* 2 (December 1988), 55–70.

46. Sobel, *ITT,* 60–69.

47. Coggeshall, "Annotated History," 80; Sobel, *ITT,* 63–64.

48. G. Stanley Shoup, "The Control of International Radio Communication," *Annals of the American Academy of Political and Social Sciences* 142 (March 1929), 103.

49. Roland Belfort, "Outlook for Cable-Radio," *United Empire* 20 (January 1929), 19–23.

50. U.S. Congress, Senate, Committee on Interstate Commerce, "Hearings before the Committee on Interstate Commerce of the United States Senate, May 1929–February 1930 on S.6, a bill to provide for the regulation, by a permanent Commission on Communications, of transmission of intelligence by wire or wireless" ("Couzens Bill").

51. Quoted in Denny, 396. Shoup's views, very favorable to the merger, were repeated in his article, "The Control of International Radio Communication," published in March 1929.

52. Clark, 247.

53. "America—1933–1934. Impending merger of American communications companies. Negotiations between I&IC and WU, RCA & Col. Behn (ITT, CCC, PTC)," in Cable & Wireless archives, B1/157.

54. "Meeting held at Electra House, W.C.2, between Messrs. Sarnoff and Winterbottom, of the R.C.A. (Communications) and Mr. J. C. Denison-Pender, Sir Normal Leslie, and (part of the time) Mr. J. J. Munro of I.&I.C. Ltd, on Monday, 6th November 1933," in Cable and Wireless archives, B1/157.

55. Letter from Denison-Pender to the Treasury, November 14, 1933, ibid.

56. Barty-King, 222–23.

57. Sobel, *ITT,* 78.

58. U.S. Federal Communications Commission, "Report of the Federal Communications Commission on the International Telegraph Industry submitted to the Senate Interstate Commerce Committee Investigating Telegraphs," in the United States Senate, Appendix to Hearings before Subcommittee of the Committee on Interstate Commerce, 77th Congress, 1st Session, Part 2 (Washington, 1940), 473.

59. Barty-King, 224–25.

60. Articles in *The Times, Daily Mail, Financial Times, Daily Telegraph,* and other papers, February 26–March 1, 1930.

61. Letters and Memoranda re Imperial Communications Inquiry Committee, August 1931, in Cable & Wireless archives, B1/153 and B1/141.

62. C.I.D., Imperial Communications Committee, papers, 1933–1934, in PRO, Cab 35/32.

63. "Agreements and Commitments with North American Companies," in Cable & Wireless archives, B1/157.

64. Imperial and International Communications Limited, Memorandum from the Court of Directors to Imperial Communications Inquiry Committee (August 31, 1931), 45.

65. Barty-King, 236.

66. "Strategical requirements in regard to cable communications," letter dated October 14, 1929, in Cable and Wireless archives, B1/112.

67. Committee of Imperial Defence, Imperial Communications Committee, "Report on the Scheme Submitted by Imperial and International Communications, Limited, for the External Communications of the Colonies, Dependencies and Protectorates" (July 28, 1930), in PRO, Cab 35/14.

68. Committee of Imperial Defence, Imperial Communications Committee, "Report on inquiry into affairs of Imperial and International Communications Limited" (October 19, 1932), in PRO, Cab 35/45.

69. CID, Imperial Cable Committee, Strategic Cables Sub-Committee, Minutes of the First Meeting (December 15, 1932), in PRO, Cab 35/45.

70. CID, Imperial Communications Committee, Strategic Cables Sub-Committee, Report (March 8, 1933), in PRO, Cab 35/45.

71. Letter form J. Denison-Pender to Maurice Hankey (October 25, 1935), in Cable and Wireless, B1/112.

12

Communications Intelligence in World War II

In many ways, the Second World War was a replay of the First. Once again, Germany attacked and nearly conquered all of Europe. Again, German submarines came close to defeating Britain. And for the second time, the entry of the United States doomed the German hopes of dominating the world.

The differences, however, overshadowed the similarities. World War II was the first truly global war, with battles and belligerents spread throughout the world. It was also a war of movement, in contrast to the trench warfare of World War I. Both aspects required communications technologies on a scale never seen before.

These technologies were of two kinds. One was radio, and particularly short-wave radio. So small and inexpensive were transceivers that they could be installed in trucks and tanks and airplanes and submarines. Indeed, without small transceivers there would have been no Blitzkrieg, no U-boat tactics, no massive bombing raids and fighter defenses. The very nature of warfare had changed. Even long distances that formerly had required transmitters as large as railroad yards could now be bridged by a small device packed in the suitcase of a spy. Not surprisingly, nations went to war with thousands of radios, and the military filled the ether with their chatter.

If the new radios enormously increased the volume, speed, and coverage of communications, they were also—as everyone realized—vulnerable to interception. To provide the security that cables naturally possessed and radio lacked, the major powers turned to another invention, electromechanical cipher machines. Those sophisticated devices were considered almost completely secure, not only throughout the war but for thirty years thereafter.

If communications and cyptography had progressed enormously since World War I, so had their nemesis, communications intelligence. No longer was comint the serendipitous invention of clever amateurs: it had become an industry. Its achievements and failures, long hidden by a veil of official secrecy, have recently been made public, and the results are astonishing: Communications intelligence, it turns out, was as important in the course of the war as any other weapons system, and more important than most generals.

Here, too, there are similarities with the First World War. While the technology had changed dramatically, the balance of power between the nations had not. Through a combination of tradition, motivation, and skill, the British retained their mastery of communications even when they were closest to defeat, while the Germans, masters of warfare, lost the battle of information. The war in Europe was paralleled by another war in the Pacific. Like the Germans, the Japanese trusted their codes and ciphers and neglected the art of communications intelligence, failings that hastened their defeat. A third war, the one between Germany and the Soviet Union, is still shrouded in mystery, for the Soviets are silent about their communications intelligence.

The parallel between the wars in Europe and in the Pacific was no simple coincidence, for the British and American advantage in communications intelligence was the result of a carefully nurtured cooperation. No two nations in history had ever collaborated as fully and closely as did the United States and Great Britain in World War II. Like all good alliances, this one was mutually beneficial, although the benefits differed. In exchange for protection and a chance at survival, Great Britain allowed the United States access to the Empire and sacrificed its dominance over the global flow of information.

In communications, as in every sphere, Germany and Japan lost the war, Britain survived, and the United States won. As blessings go, improvements in communications were hardly unalloyed: like all other technological changes, they benefitted some nations at the expense of others.

British and German Communications Intelligence to 1936

The British, who had made the best use of communications intelligence in World War I, were aware of its power in peacetime, too. On February 27, 1919, the Admiralty, the War Office, and the Foreign Office recommended that NID-25 (naval cryptology) and MI-1b (military cryptology) combine their resources into a Government Code and Cypher School (GC&CS) responsible for ensuring communications security and also (secretly) for decrypting other nations' messages. The proposal was accepted in April, and the "school" officially opened on November 1, 1919, under Commander Alastair Denniston, a veteran of Room 40. Two years later, in April 1921, the school was transferred to the jurisdiction of the Foreign Office.[1]

How did GC&CS obtain foreign messages to decrypt? The intelligence establishment was reluctant to give up its wartime advantages, and for a time official censorship provided a continuing flow of messages. But before it ended in July 1919, the director of naval intelligence convinced the government to replace censorship with secret scrutiny. The Official Secrets Act of 1920 made the cable companies secretly deliver to the government copies of all cables and wireless messages entering or leaving Britain within ten days of transmission.[2]

Other sources of information included copies of cables passing through British cable stations at Gibraltar, Hong Kong, and elsewhere; radio intercept stations operated by the Coast Guard in Britain and by the Royal Corps of Signals throughout the Empire; and, in very rare instances, secret agents abroad.[3]

While intercepts were available, GC&CS lacked the staff and the government lacked the motivation to read more than a fraction of them. During the 1920s, the British government was interested in the Far East, specifically the French in Indochina and the Japanese in China. American and French diplomatic codes were also of some interest, especially during the Washington Naval Conference of 1921–22.[4] Germany was ignored, as the War Office noted in 1924: "Doubtless German messages would be useful if time and staff could be found to break the books."[5]

The main concern of the British government at the time was subversion, more specifically the threat of labor troubles fomented (or so the Conservatives believed) by Soviet agents. In the early 1920s the Soviets were still amateurs at cryptography, and GC&CS had the good fortune to employ the refugee Russian cryptanalyst Fetterlein, who cracked their simple codes with ease. Three times, in 1920, 1923, and 1927, the British cabinet denounced Soviet subversion, brandishing decrypted intercepts as proof. While this thereby gained some short-run political advantages for the British, in the long run it taught the Soviets the value of secure communications, a lesson they have never forgotten.[6]

The history of Germany's communications intelligence between the wars parallels that of foreign policy. From 1919 to 1929 the navy's B-Dienst (Beobachtungs-Dienst, or observation service) was a small bureau with only one officer and two cryptanalysts. In 1929 it was separated from the Admiralty, moved to Kiel, and treated in a "stepmotherly fashion."[7]

When Hitler came to power in 1933, things began looking up for all military and espionage organizations. By the summer of 1939, B-Dienst had grown to over five hundred men. Several other communications intelligence and decryption services sprang up, in accordance with Hitler's divide-and-rule policy within his government. The Foreign Ministry had its Pers Z, which concentrated on foreign diplomatic messages. The Oberkommando der Wehrmacht (military high command) created OKW/Chi, or cryptanalytic service. The Post Office had a Forschungsstelle (research department) that tapped telephone lines. Hermann Goering had his own Forschungsamt (research bureau) that tapped telephones, intercepted radio, and decrypted foreign military and diplomatic traffic. These bureaus sometimes cooperated, especially B-Dienst and OKW/Chi, but more often competed for manpower and funds and kept their secrets from each other.[8]

To obtain messages, the navy set up intercept stations on the Baltic and North seas and in southern Germany, while the Wehrmacht had stations along the borders; because of Germany's geographic position, these were too few and poorly placed to follow events in other European countries. To remedy this weakness, B-Dienst began cooperating with its counterparts in Finland, Italy, and after 1936, Spain. It could not, however, intercept American signals.[9]

These efforts were moderately successful. B-Dienst broke several British, Polish, and Russian naval codes, and followed British and French maneuvers in the Atlantic and the North Sea and Soviet ones in the Baltic. For a time the Abwehr had the French "code d'alerte." Pers Z successfully read many French and some Italian, American, and British messages, but no Soviet ones. The most successful was Goering's Forschungsamt, which cracked numerous lesser codes.[10] They had little influence on policy, however, since policy was made by Hitler, and Hitler could not be swayed from his vision of world domination by "facts" unearthed by his supine subordinates. As a general rule, nations on the offensive are less interested in intelligence about their potential victims than are defensive nations, whose very existence depends on knowing their enemies' intentions.

Cipher Machines

In the mid-1920s a new technology threatened to make cryptanalysis obsolete. In an age when everything else was becoming mechanized, it was inevitable, especially after the experience of World War I, that inventors should seek ways to encipher and decipher quickly and securely. Several inventors developed cipher machines with rotors that contained a maze of wires and could be set in different positions. These machines turned one letter into another in a way that could only be reproduced with an identical machine using identical rotor settings. A cipher clerk typed in the plaintext and read off the ciphertext before transmission, or typed in a ciphertext and read off the plaintext. Such machines were small and portable and could be used with radio as well as with line telegraphs. Two of them were commercially successful: one, the Hagelin, made in Sweden by Aktiebolaget Cryptoteknik; the other, known as Enigma, made in Germany by Chiffriermachinen A.G.[11]

The first nation to acquire cipher machines for its armed forces was Germany. In 1926 the navy adopted the Enigma Model C, later replaced by the more secure Model M. The Wehrmacht followed in 1928 and the Luftwaffe in 1933. By the end of 1935 the German government had acquired twenty thousand Enigmas for the armed force, the Abwehr (military intelligence), and the Sicherheitsdienst (Nazi Party security service), each with a different design. Since the rotors and plugboards on the Enigmas could be set in an almost infinite number of ways, cryptographic experts considered their output almost unbreakable, at least impossible to break quickly enough to be of use to an enemy in wartime.[12] As late as 1970 Heinz Bonatz, former head of the B-Dienst, asserted that the Allies could not have broken the German ciphers even after capturing several of the machines.[13]

Other countries followed the German example. The U.S. Signal Corps bought an Enigma as early as 1927, but ended up designing its own machine, the M-209, based on the Hagelin. The Japanese also bought one, and by the mid-1930s had devised an improved version of it for their naval and diplomatic communications. France purchased machines based on the Hagelin, but continued to use manual codes and ciphers.[14]

Britain held out the longest of all the great powers. Not until 1935–36 did the Royal Air Force adopt the Typex machine made by the Creed Teleprinter Company. The Royal Navy rejected the Typex as too delicate and complicated, and continued to use a manual system of codebooks and reciphering tables until well into the war. Thanks to mistakes made by British code clerks, the B-Dienst was able to break the

British naval code by 1938.[15] This helps explain the success of the German submarines in the first years of the war.

The Approach of War, 1936–1939

Unlike World War I, which surprised many people, the Second World War was seen coming a long way off. Germany reoccupied the Rhineland in 1936 and soon joined Italy in helping the insurgents in the Spanish Civil War. In 1937 Japan attacked China. The following year Germany annexed Austria. Until September 1938, optimists could still believe that Hitler only sought to revise the Versailles Treaty. The Munich Conference and the subsequent dismemberment of Czechoslovakia, however, signaled the unmistakable approach of war.

This did not mean that the military and intelligence communities all reacted with maximum efficiency. In France and Britain they were restrained by their own fears and ineptitudes and by civilian politicians who feared to hasten the coming of war by hostile actions, while Americans hid their heads in the sands of isolation. In the democracies, preparations for war were few and inadequate, if not entirely lacking.

Although the British government had insisted that Cable and Wireless maintain its strategic cables rather than switch to radio, the company had equipped its cable stations with shortwave radio sets in case the cables were damaged; the government belatedly ratified this decision in January 1939. Starting in August 1937 the government pressured the company to dismiss all foreigners employed at its cable stations in the British Empire. The company's buildings in London, Porthcurno, and Gibraltar were to be reinforced or alternatives found in case of bombardment. Officials were warned not to use the telephone to communicate with central and eastern Europe, because the lines went through Germany. In August 1939 the armed forces were ordered to test their communications under simulated wartime conditions.[16] When war broke out, they believed their communications were secure.

Britain also, somewhat belatedly, began improving its radio intercept and direction-finding networks. New intercept stations were built and old ones refurbished in Britain, Bermuda, Malta, Aden, Ceylon, Hong Kong, and Australia.[17] In the mid-1930s, naval intelligence had fallen dangerously behind and relied on the months-old reports of naval attachés to keep track of foreign warships; it had no cryptanalytic staff and only tenuous relations with GC&CS. By September 1939 the Royal Navy still had only six high-frequency direction-finding stations and nine medium-frequency ones, three of which were in the Mediterranean and two in the Far East. Yet it did create an Operational Intelligence Centre that received all available information about foreign as well as British warships and allowed a more precise conduct of naval operations than had ever been possible before.[12] The effective integration of intelligence with decision making was to be Britain's greatest strength in the coming war.

One lesson of World War I was not lost on the British government, namely that it was more important to read than to hinder an enemy's communications. To be sure, the government planned to impose censorship on all messages entering or leaving the country; but messages transiting over British-owned cables to other destinations were not interfered with, so as not to drive customers away. Instead the Foreign Office and Cable and Wireless worked out a "scrutiny scheme." First proposed in early 1937, it was revived at the time of Munich and finally implemented in August 1939, extending to the whole world the powers implicit in the Official Secrets Act of 1920. The company was to recruit retired telegraphers and send them out to its cable stations to read cable slip and retransmit interesting-looking items to London; eventually it planned to acquire direct printers that printed out the incoming telegrams in Roman characters, obviating the need for expert telegraphers.[19] Between censorship, cable scrutiny, and radio interception, the British government had access to much of the world's communications, except for the most dangerous: the German armed forces' machine-encrypted traffic.

The Outbreak of War, 1939–1940

The outbreak of war in September 1939 distorted the normal flow of information in ways both overt and secret. Ordinary civilian communications between nations were censored and replaced by propaganda. Governmental and military communications took over existing channels and spawned a proliferation of new ones. The enormous increase in the use of radio, caused by the global nature of the conflict and the mobility of military forces, stimulated the growth of communications intelligence and its offspring, espionage and deception. Its successes and failures, in turn, affected the outcome of the war in surprising ways.

A few statistics will illustrate the extent of the impact. During the war France lost thirty-seven of its forty-two broadcast stations and nine hundred kilometers of land lines; Greece lost 65 percent of its lines and 90 percent of its telecommunications equipment; Japan lost half its telephone lines.[20] Britain, in contrast, suffered little damage to its telecommunications plant, and the United States none at all. Traffic on the Cable and Wireless network more than doubled from 1938 to 1944, increasing from 231 million words to 705 million; the largest component of that increase was official messages, which rose twentyfold, from 12 million to 266 million. Some stations had to cope with a twelvefold increase in traffic with little additional manpower or equipment.[21] To encode and decode all of their communications, the American armed forces employed sixteen thousand cipher clerks, one for every eight hundred people under arms, compared with four hundred clerks (one for every ten thousand) in World War I.[22]

Like all belligerents, Britain imposed censorship on all postal and telegraphic communications. Hundreds of former telegraph clerks, retired or laid off in the Depression, were recalled as censors; a hundred worked at Cable and Wireless headquarters in London, and another fifty at Aden. Commercial codes were first forbidden, than gradually allowed again. The censors allowed coded telegrams to and from neutral embassies in London, but those transiting Britain on their way to and from neutral embassies in Eire were held up for twenty-four hours. Telephone communications with the European continent were severely restricted: Press calls could only be read by a government clerk after censorship, business calls had to be booked twenty-four hours in advance, and private calls were forbidden.[23]

Outside the British Isles, the policy of secret scrutiny was put into effect as rapidly as clerks could be hired and sent out; Malta and Aden were staffed in September 1939, Singapore, Barbados and Jamaica in October, Hong Kong in November. In Latin America British cable companies had to permit codes and deny allegations by their American competitors All-America Cables and RCA that they were censoring traffic. Yet the results were most satisfactory, for Britain obtained much more information this way than it could have by censorship.[24]

After smoldering for six months, the war burst out again in the spring of 1940 with the German invasion of Denmark, Norway, Holland, and Belgium, followed by the attack on France in May and June. The Blitzkrieg campaign revealed the appalling unpreparedness of the French army and its ally the British Expeditionary Force. While German tanks and planes were guided by an efficient system of tactical communications, the British had only begun installing radios in their tanks, and few French tanks were so equipped.[25] Even intelligence favored the Germans, who broke the French War Ministry and naval codes in 1939 and could read the most important military traffic. What few German messages the French and British read during that brief campaign hardly compensated for the overwhelming German superiority.[26]

When Germany conquered the Netherlands and Belgium, the Cable and Wireless Company was quick to open direct radio links with the Dutch East Indies and Belgian Congo. On June 15, before France even signed the armistice, the company presented the British government with a "proposed scheme for working French colonies." For a month, many French colonies communicated with Cable and Wireless, but then they broke off the contact under orders from Vichy. On August 29, London received a telegram from Brazzaville in French Equatorial Africa, asking to reopen the circuit; it was the first French colony to join de Gaulle's Free France.

British Communications Intelligence in Wartime

In September 1939 the British government recruited amateurs, as it had twenty-five years before, into the Radio Security Service to monitor the airwaves for secret spy transmissions. By March 1940 they had heard not a single spy lurking in the United Kingdom, but much German military radio traffic.[27] The British had expected that, once war began, the Germans would impose radio silence, but instead German radio traffic increased enormously. The British quickly built intercept stations throughout the United Kingdom and the Middle East, and in Malta, Gibraltar, and Iceland as well. The U.K. stations, which watched the German traffic across the Channel, were connected by teleprinter landline to the Government Communications Headquarters (GCHQ), successor to the Government Code and Cipher School, which had moved to Bletchley Park, north of London, in September 1939; less urgent intercepts traveled in a motorcycle dispatch-rider's pouch.[28]

Most of the German military traffic was encrypted with Enigma machines, but there was intelligence to be gathered from enemy radio signals even without decrypting them. Traffic analysis, aided by direction-finding, revealed which station was where and talking to whom. Knowing only the call signs and locations of enemy transmitters, radio analysts could reconstruct each division or army's network. Changes in volume or direction indicated an imminent operation; radio silence, a deliberate deception. The British even developed a device that "fingerprinted" radio operators and their sets and could to a certain extent see through a change of call signs.[29]

Yet the information that could be extracted by traffic analysis was limited. The real challenge was to decrypt the messages and make use of the information they revealed. Documents released by the British government since 1974 and memoirs of the participants have shown that the British codebreakers were more successful than anyone had imagined, and far more than the Germans. This is the story of Bletchley Park and its production of secret intelligence called Ultra. Fortunately, historians have published several excellent books on the subject and are likely to write many more.[30] Our purpose here is merely to sketch the outlines of this British achievement, stressing the role of communications in the process.

In the course of the war, the German government bought one hundred thousand Enigmas and placed complete confidence in them, thinking that the number of key settings was so enormous, there was no chance of a key being broken in time to be of any use to an enemy. This confidence encouraged careless mistakes and security lapses that could be exploited by enemy cryptanalysts. Radio operators practiced by repeating familiar nursery rhymes. Army commanders reported their situation to OKW every evening, often using stereotyped massages ("Nothing to report") that gave a clue to the day's key. Weather reports, being very standardized, were another source of breaks. The Luftwaffe, which sent out three hundred signals a day by August 1940, was especially sloppy in its procedures.[31]

Yet no amount of sloppiness would have helped the British cryptanalysts if they had not possessed the technique to attack the encrypted messages in the first place. This they got from Poland. A weak country caught between two dangerous giants, Poland had from the beginning of its independent existence devoted great efforts to penetrating its neighbors' communications. Until 1926 Polish cryptanalysts had succeeded quite well against both Germany and the Soviet Union. When the Germans switched to Enigmas, the Poles attempted to reconstruct the machine mathematically. They built fifteen replica Enigmas and were able to read 75 percent of the German intercepts until 1938, when the Germans added two more wheels to their Enigmas. The Polish cryptanalysts under Major Maksymilian Ciezki got in touch with Captain Gustave Bertrand of the French military intelligence. With the help of documents obtained from a German officer and a model of the new Enigma made by a Polish mechanic who had been employed in the Enigma factory, the Poles built a "bomba," or electromechanical decrypting machine. Though it was not very effective at first, it nonetheless contained the answer to the problem posed by the Enigma: the incredible number of different rotor settings could only be tried out, one after another, by a high-speed electromechanical decryption machine.

On January 9 and 10, 1939, Captain Bertrand, Gwido Langer of the Polish Cipher Bureau, and Alastair Denniston and Dyllwyn Knox of GC&CS met in Paris to exchange information. Denniston, Langer, and Colonel Braquerie, head of French military cryptology, met in Warsaw at the end of July. Knowing that war was but a few weeks away, the Poles gave their French and British counterparts a replica

Enigma and drawings of the bomba. It was the biggest contribution that Poland could have made to the Allied cause at that fateful moment. In October, Langer and fifteen other Polish cryptanalysts escaped to France with two more Enigmas and joined Bertrand's staff. Shortly thereafter they began decrypting the Luftwaffe's messages and communicated with Bletchley Park by teleprinter.[32] When the German army swept through France, the French cryptanalysts evidently succeeded in covering their traces, for the Germans found nothing to indicate that the Enigma had been compromised.[33]

The bomba (renamed "bombe") did not do the cryptanalysts' work, it only made it possible. As the war went on, their workload kept increasing, partly because the volume of intercepted traffic grew, partly because the Germans kept adding features and complications to their Enigmas—plugboards, new wiring, more rotors, different procedures—all of which forced the cryptanalysts to start over. There were even cases, especially involving the more complex naval Enigmas, that left the British completely in the dark for months at a time. And some ciphers were never cracked.

The enormous and unexpected volume of intercepts made Bletchley Park recruit more staff in a hurry. The day Britain entered the war, Denniston wrote: "For some days now we have been obliged to recruit from our emergency list men of the Professor type." Among them were linguists, mathematicians, chess experts, and of course experts on Germany. GCHQ even recruited "ladies whom it has found necessary to take in owing to the prevailing conditions." By the spring of 1942 Bletchley Park had a staff of 1,500 handling some forty thousand German military intercepts a month. While the Germans employed hundreds of people in cryptanalysis and preferred military signal corpsmen, Allied communications intelligence had thousands of employees chosen mainly among civilians on the basis of IQ tests.[34]

Intelligence and technique alone were often not enough, and luck was needed as well. In some cases, the solution to a particular Enigma model depended on the capture of the machine or some part of it. The first German naval ciphers were broken only after the British sank the submarine *U-33* in February 1940 and recovered three of its rotors. An Enigma with its operational keys was taken from a plane shot down off Norway in April 1940. The capture of the *U-110* in May 1941 was another major breakthrough.

In addition to the portable Enigmas, the Germans also used a much heavier and more complicated cipher machine with ten rotors, the *Geheimschreiber*, for the most secret strategic messages between Hitler and his army headquarters. This machine automatically encrypted the typed-in message and transmitted the ciphertext at sixty-two words per minute; at the other end, it printed out the cleartext on paper tape. While this device was designed to be used only with secure landlines, there were occasional security lapses. In 1941–42 the landline across Sweden between Germany and Norway was tapped by Swedish intelligence and the messages decrypted and leaked to the British. During the fighting in North Africa, messages between General Rommel and Germany, encrypted with a more advanced Geheimschreiber, went by radio for lack of a submarine cable. In December 1942, with the help of these messages and two machines captured in North Africa, British

Post Office engineer E. H. Flowers built the Colossus, an electronic computer able to decrypt Geheimschreiber messages.[35]

The Germans trusted their machines to a fault but distrusted one another, and when they discovered that the Allies had obtained secret information, they looked first for spies and traitors. The paranoia of the Nazis does not preclude the possibility that they may have been right, for German society was full of potential traitors, if not to their country then to National Socialism. Of all the Germans who might have helped British communications intelligence, the most interesting candidates are General Erich Fellgiebel, chief signals officer of the Wehrmacht, and his deputy General Fritz Thiele. Before the war, it was Fellgiebel who recommended that Enigmas be used by the Wehrmacht. He and Thiele controlled the creation and distribution of keys. They were also both active members of the Schwartze Kapelle, a conservative anti-Nazi conspiracy, and participated in the attempt on Hitler's life on July 20, 1944, for which they were both executed by the Gestapo.[36] The idea that these high-ranking generals in OKW could have been helping British intelligence is certainly appealing, but until the archives divulge evidence to prove it, we can only call it a tantalizing hypothesis.

If interception was the beginning of communications intelligence, cryptanalysis was the middle. After that came translation, then analysis. Unlike the German system, which separated these functions, Bletchley Park handled most of them in house. The interaction between cryptanalysts, translators, and intelligence analysts enhanced the effectiveness of all three and was one of the great strengths of British communications intelligence in World War II, in contrast to the situation in World War I.

Just as important was the system for making the resulting intelligence available to those who needed it, without revealing it to the enemy. For that purpose teleprinter lines were installed between Bletchley Park and the most important command centers in Great Britain—the Admiralty's Operational Intelligence Centre, the Royal Air Force's Fighter Command, the Chiefs of Staff, the Joint Intelligence Committee, Major-General Menzies (head of the Secret Intelligence Service or MI6), and, of course, Winston Churchill in his War Room. Most of the recipients accepted processed intelligence, but Churchill liked to read the actual decrypts himself, while the Admiralty insisted on doing its own analysis in the OIC.

Much of the fighting took place at sea or overseas, and that required special handling. The OIC sent messages derived from Enigma decrypts in its most secure ciphers and codes, and always took care that the information seemed as if it came from some source other than decrypts, such as direction-finding or air reconnaissance. Group Captain Winterbotham of MI6 in London was in charge of distributing Ultra (as Enigma decrypts were called) to army and RAF units fighting overseas. To do it safely, he developed Special Liaison Units or SLUs, teams of radio operators and cipher clerks posted to the major headquarters. At first these units communicated with London using one-time pads, a list of random numbers known only to the sender and the recipient and only used once; this was the only theoretically unbreakable encryption system known. Later they began using the Typex, a complicated encryption machine that the Germans never cracked. The SLU officer in the field showed the message to its intended recipient, and then destroyed it. Neither SLUs nor anyone aware of Bletchley Park or Ultra was allowed near enemy lines.[37] Knowing their enemy's weak point, the British used intelligence to the maximum extent possible but with the utmost prudence.

German Communication Intelligence in Wartime

During the war, the job of communications intelligence and cryptanalysis was divided up among many organizations in Germany. Some of them were quite successful for a while, in limited areas. We will see the successes of the navy's B-Dienst against Allied shipping, and that of the army cryptanalysts against the British tactical codes in North Africa. The OKW/Chi and the Foreign Ministry's Pers Z also broke the U.S. diplomatic codes until 1943. On the eastern front, military cryptanalysts broke low-grade Soviet tactical codes, but not their high-grade ones. The Luftwaffe's radio intercept service monitored Allied bomber raids with a fair degree of success.

From March 1942 to February 1944 the Forschungsstelle of the German Post Office succeeded in unscrambling intercontinental telephone messages scrambled with Bell Laboratory's A-3 Scrambler, including conversations between Roosevelt and Churchill. But the Germans obtained little information from that source, for the officials who used the radiotelephone, Churchill most of all, were aware that scramblers were insecure. In 1942 Churchill wrote: "The one secure way of conducting a radio telephone conversation on a secret matter is first to telegraph in cypher a memorandum in short numbered paragraphs, and then to conduct the conversation by reference to those paragraphs."[38]

Elsewhere, the Germans obtained considerable help from their Italian and Hungarian counterparts. They did not, however, succeed in breaking any high-grade codes and ciphers such as the ones used by the Royal and U.S. Navies, the British SLUs, or the Soviet diplomats. Even though the British lost two Typex machines during the evacuation of Dunkirk in June 1940, German cryptanalysts made no progress against this machine or its American equivalent, the Sigaba. Much of the fault lay in the schisms between cryptographers and cryptanalysts, between the latter and other intelligence specialists, and between intelligence and operations.[39]

The Battles of Britain and North Africa, 1940–1942

Even with the help received from the Polish cryptanalysts, Bletchley Park was unable to break into the German Enigma traffic until April 1940 because there were not enough intercepts to go on. That month, however, the beginning of the Blitzkrieg provided ample material, and the British penetrated the Luftwaffe traffic. The key changed every day, but the British became so well versed in the German procedures that they usually had it broken before breakfast. In the process, they learned a great deal about joint operations with the army and navy. Although the Germans changed their keying procedures on May 1, by the 22nd Bletchley Park was again reading Luftwaffe messages.

The breakthrough proved extremely valuable in July and August during the Battle of Britain. By early August a direct teleprinter line connected Bletchley Park and Fighter Command at Stanmore. "Eagle Day" (August 15, 1940) was to be Hermann Goering's day of victory with massive formations of German fighters sweeping the Royal Air Force from the skies. Instead, it turned into a major defeat, for the RAF was amply forewarned, first by Ultra decrypts and then by radar. Though his planes were vastly outnumbered, Air Chief Marshall Hugh Dowding was able to husband his forces and direct them efficiently, and only lost thirty-four to the Luftwaffe's seventy-five.[40]

Communications intelligence was also decisive in North Africa, where for 2½ years the tide of battle ebbed and flowed across the desert between Libya and Egypt. In those desperate struggles the most important factors were, as in every war, the leadership abilities of the generals, the fighting qualities of the soldiers, and the quantity of material and supplies; and so the battles for North Africa have been described in the military histories. But recently a new factor has been added to the equation: information. Was it a coincidence that the flow of information correlated well with the successes and failures of the two sides?

In a mobile war, both sides had to communicate by radio. The British cable to the Middle East was quite inadequate to carry the flood of information they required. So SLUs were stationed in Lebanon, Malta, and Egypt, and those channels seem to have been secure. The British also used radio to communicate between the armies in the field and headquarters in Cairo and among the units: by 1942 the British army had some six thousand transceivers.[41] Those were much less secure, and from them German intercept units, in particular Captain Alfred Seebohm's Radio Intelligence Unit, supplied General Rommel with a great deal of tactical information.[42]

The Germans also used the radio, perhaps more efficiently than the British; at least that was the impression given by the press, as the *New York Times* reported in June 1942:

> Many [London newspapers] are publishing tomorrow long dispatches from correspondents at the front attributing the German success at least partly to the red tape of the British system of communications, contrasted with the German system of split-second decisions and radio communications, regardless of the risk, a greater degree of initiative, resourcefulness and adaptability on the part of the German commanders.[43]

However, the most secret communications of the Germans and Italians were often known to the British thanks to Ultra. This information was the decisive factor at the Battle of Matapan (March 28, 1941), where the British surprised and sank the Italian battle fleet.[44] At other times, good information could not compensate for other weaknesses, as a British intelligence officer explained about the German attack on Greece in April 1941: "We had the German Order of Battle every evening, but unfortunately we could not do anything about it, having virtually nothing to hit back with."[45] In such cases, while Ultra did not help the British defeat the Germans, it did allow them to husband their limited resources.

A third channel of secret military information was the one used by the American military attaché in Cairo, Colonel Bonner Fellers. So eager were the British to befriend the Americans that they gave Colonel Fellers every facility. From September 1941 to August 1942, he radioed details of British strengths and plans to Washington every day, using the Black Code of American military attachés. Unfortunately for the British, this code was known to the Italians, who had borrowed and photographed the codebook from the U.S. Embassy in Rome, and to the Wehrmacht's OKW/Chi, which had reconstructed it analytically. Every day Colonel Fellers's transmissions were picked up by two German intercept stations, sent on the OKW/Chi in Berlin to be decrypted and translated, and retransmitted to Rommel, who called them "my good source."[46]

In June and July, 1942, just before Rommel's final offensive, luck switched sides, and once again the flow of information preceded the tide of battle. The Americans, having learned that the Germans had cracked the Black Code, changed to another code that the Germans could not break.[47] Meanwhile, the British had located Captain Seebohm's intercept post at Tel el Eisa, just one kilometer from the front lines, and on July 10, before dawn, a brigade of Australian infantrymen attacked and destroyed it.[48]

Suddenly Rommel's two main sources of information had dried up, and with them went much of his amazing skill. A recent historian of that campaign, Janusz Piekalkiewicz, notes: "The captured documents demonstrate that the many important operations of the legendary 'Desert Fox' were mostly due to the achievements of Seebohm's intercept company."[49] As Rommel's picture faded, Generals Alexander and Montgomery learned more and more about the Afrika Korps thanks to Ultra and local radio intercepts. The British also knew the sailings of the Italian ships that came to supply Rommel with fuel and sank most of them, leaving much of Rommel's equipment stranded in the desert. Rommel's last desperate offensive, launched on August 31, quickly turned into a defeat. By October the Afrika Korps was reeling back.[50] Writes Piekalkiewicz: "Ever since the attack on the intercept company, luck had abandoned Rommel, and the field marshal reminds one more and more of a man with bandaged eyes who has to maneuver across a dark room full of dangerous obstacles."[51]

German Spies and Allied Radio Deception

Espionage dates back to the dawn of history, but until recently, spies who discovered important information in wartime found it difficult to communicate with their masters. In 1914, paranoid British authorities had vainly seached their island for spies with secret radios. By World War II, such fears had become more realistic, for radio technology had advanced to the point where a radio transceiver could be hidden in a suitcase.

The first such sets were just barely portable, for they weighed some thirty kilograms, and were weak and unreliable. But technology moved rapidly, and by 1943 the British Radio Security Service had developed transceivers small enough to be hidden in a record player or the false bottom of a suitcase. The German Abwehr also built small transceivers, but often equipped their agents with captured British sets. Radio-equipped spies inevitably called forth their own nemesis, radio counterespionage by direction-finding vans. If the British were masters at sending agents into enemy territory with secret radios, the Germans were skilled at stalking them, because they had a lot of practice. But they were in good company, as the United States and the Soviet Union also played the game of spy–counterspy.

The Abwehr sent agents into Britain even before the war began. In January 1939 Arthur Owens, code-named SNOW, informed the police that he was working for the Abwehr and expected to receive a transmitter from Germany. When it arrived, MI6 agents had to fix it before he could transmit. When the war broke out, several other agents were either arrested or turned themselves in. Some of them were "turned" by British Intelligence, in other words they transmitted, under the supervision of MI6, information carefully chosen to deceive the Germans. During 1940 and 1941 the control of enemy agents had crystallized into two organizations: B1A and London Controlling Section, which was charged with deception in general. Since disinformation required a judicious mix of truth and falsehood, the Twenty (XX or Double-Cross) Committee was created in January 1941 to select secret information that would impress the Abwehr with its authenticity yet give away nothing of importance. All in all, B1A controlled 120 double agents who transmitted such information to the Germans.

The Abwehr had created an elaborate radio network to communicate with their agents, with stations at Hamburg and Ulm, and outlying stations at Oslo, Bordeaux, Madrid, Istanbul, and elsewhere. They were linked to headquarters at Hamburg by teleprinter landlines, but also by radio using special Abwehr Enigma machines. Although the British had captured many spies, they still feared that some spies might have slipped through and were sending real information. In the winter of 1941, however, the Bletchley Park cryptanalysts broke the Abwehr cipher and discovered that all German spies in Britain were under British control.

The elaborate double-cross system depended not only on the exquisite subtlety of the British deceptions, but also on the Abwehr's need to believe the information they received. The Abwehr unconsciously cooperated with the scheme, either because the controllers' jobs depended on the credibility of their agents, or because enough real information came through to justify keeping the scheme alive. Radio, unverified by other sources, blurred the distinction between truth and fiction.[52]

In the course of the war, the double agents controlled by the British transmitted a vast amount of information. The most brilliant result, without a doubt, occurred during the invasion of Normandy in June 1944. The Allies had devised elaborate plans to deceive the Germans about the date and place of the landing. In East Anglia and southeastern England, opposite the Pas de Calais, they erected decoys of tanks, airplanes, trucks, and other military materiel to fool German reconnaissance planes. Intense radio traffic indicated the existence of the First U.S. Army Group (FUSAG), which was totally fictitious except for its commander, General Patton, who was frequently reported in the area. Meanwhile the real forces concentrating in southwestern England communicated by landline. Radio messages from General Montgomery's headquarters at Portsmouth were relayed by wire to Dover and transmitted from there to deceive the German direction-finding.[53] In the spring of 1944, communications intelligence had alerted the Germans that an Allied landing was imminent. But they lacked two pieces of information: the date and, more important, the place where the Allies would land.[54]

The reports of German "spies" contributed to the general picture, one that Hitler instinctively believed, that the Anglo-Americans were planning an attack on the Pas de Calais. The most important of the agents was a Spaniard code-named Garbo. He had been smuggled into England by MI6 in April 1942 and had built up a team of agents (all of them imaginary) who funneled important information (all of it selected by the British) to his Abwehr controller in Madrid. In the early hours of the Normandy invasion, Garbo sent a detailed report to the Abwehr—too late to be of much use but accurate enough to establish his credibility. In the next two days General Rommel, commanding the Normandy sector, appealed to Hitler to release the Fifteenth Army, which was guarding the Pas de Calais, without which he could not push back the Allies. Hitler hesitated, then acceded to Rommel's demand. Just after midnight on June 9, Garbo radioed to Madrid:

> The present operation, though a large-scale assault, is diversionary in character. . . . The fact that the massive concentration of forces in east and south-east England remains inactive suggests that these forces are being held in reserve for other large-scale operations. The constant aerial bombardment which the sector of the Pas de Calais has been undergoing and the disposition of the enemy forces would indicate the imminence of an assault in this region.[55]

The message caused Hitler to rescind his order and stop the Fifteenth Army, and gave the Allies time to consolidate their beachhead. So important and persuasive were Garbo's reports that Germany rewarded him with the Iron Cross, and Britain, equally grateful, made him a Member of the Order of the British Empire.

In Latin America Germany also ran a network of agents, with no better luck than in Britain. Before the Italian entry, some messages reached Germany via Italcable, and, when those cables were cut, messages still got through via the ITT cables.[56] After Pearl Harbor, the Latin American countries except Argentina and Chile broke diplomatic relations with the Axis powers. Deprived of cables, Axis agents had to transmit their reports by radio.

Efforts to close down the spy rings varied from country to country. Brazil was most cooperative. It put censors in the Transradio Brasileira office and captured the German agent Jacob Starzicny in Rio along with two hundred other agents and Axis sympathizers. Argentina and Chile resisted the American pressure to join the war. Transradio Argentina was managed by Henri Pincemin, a pro-Vichy Frenchman, until August 1942. Even after he was replaced by a nominee of RCA, the station continued to communicate with the Axis countries, and German spy rings flourished until January 1944, when American pressure finally made Argentina break diplomatic relations with Germany.[57]

The task of ferreting out agents was carried out by the FBI, which claimed jurisdiction over the entire Western Hemisphere, and the FCC's Radio Intelligence Division, which specialized in intercepting and direction-finding. The RID sent a monitoring officer, John Debardeleben, to Chile and Argentina to locate Axis spy transmitters, often against the opposition of local government officials, who were more anti-American than anti-German.[58] In Chile, Frederick von Schultz Hausmann and Wilhelm Zeller operated until November 1942. Police raids failed to find Zeller's transmitter until American radio monitors helped them locate it. Two other stations were not smashed until February 1944.[59]

In spite of their numbers and training, the German spies in Britain had only served to deceive their masters about Allied intentions. Even in Latin America, where spies operated much longer and more freely, no ship was sunk and no military unit was weakened because of a spy report.[60] In the end, Germany only wasted its money and manpower in Britain and the Americas.

Funkspiele, Resistance, and the Normandy Landing

If German spies were unsuccessful in Allied territory, it was less through lack of skill than because the odds were so heavily against them. Radio, instead of liberating secret agents from the old constraints of physical communication, made them even more vulnerable. In their unequal struggle against counterespionage organizations, such agents could only hope to survive if they were numerous, well organized, and hidden by a friendly population. In the underground as in the visible war, the Allies suffered a long string of reverses before the tide of battle turned in their favor.

At the start of the war, British Secret Intelligence had sunk to a historic low point. Its agents were well known, for they earned their living as Passport Control Officers, a transparent cover. SIS had no agents in Germany, its agents in Switzerland had a radio receiver but no transmitter and had to send messages home via the Swiss post office, and its two key agents in the Netherlands were kidnapped by the Germans. After June 1940, the European continent seemed as free of British spies as it was of British soldiers.

Yet, like the Abwehr, British Intelligence built up an elaborate radio network. Its Section VIII, headed by Richard Gambier-Perry, erected a transmitter at Hanslope Park in Buckinghamshire and began manufacturing suitcase-sized transceivers at nearby Whaddon Chase.[61] The Special Operations Executive, Britain's sabotage organization, trained agents and parachuted them into the Netherlands to contact local resistance groups and set up espionage and sabotage rings. The first to arrive were located by German direction-finding vans and captured. In a mirror image of the double-cross system, Major Hermann Giskes of the Abwehr invented a Funkspiel or radio game called NORDPOL. The Abwehr made its captured agents radio false information to England and thus lure other agents into a trap. For twenty months, from January 1942 to November 1943, the Abwehr controlled the entire Dutch underground; it captured fifty-four agents and ninety-five parachute drops containing seventy-five transmitters, thousands of weapons, and large amounts of money. Although the agents had been instructed to omit certain security checks, such as deliberate errors, from their messages if they were captured, their handlers in Britain evidently ignored the lack of security checks; one even signaled back "Watch it, old boy, your mind must be wandering: you left out your security check."[62] It is odd, considering the sophistication of their double-cross system, that the British did not expect to be double-crossed in turn. But radio is a smooth deceiver, and secret organizations would evidently rather believe an ongoing hoax than admit a mistake.

The Germans were less fortunate in France than in the Netherlands. Things began badly for the French Resistance and its British allies. The first clandestine ring, set up in December 1940, was denounced to the Gestapo by its own radio operator. The next ring, code-named INTERALLIE, lasted longer. It was run by Captain Roman Garby-Czerniawski, a Polish refugee who transmitted from a flat in Paris the information he obtained from a network of associates. This network was also denounced by one of its members.[63] Others fell victim to denunciations by collaborators or to the Abwehr's increasingly sophisticated direction-finding vans. During the Occupation, clandestine radio operators or *pianistes* had the most dangerous job in France, with a life expectancy of three months. Of those recruited in 1941, 72 percent lost their lives; in 1942 and early 1943, the death rate was over 80 percent.

Yet, dangerous as it was, radio was the most important work in the Resistance, for it transmitted the information the British and the Free French wanted in exchange for the weapons, money, and agents the Resistance fighters desperately needed. Beginning in July 1943, Resistance networks proliferated more rapidly than the Germans could capture them. The death rate of their radio operators fell to 15 percent, and the number of messages sent rose from 226 a month in early 1943 to 3,472 in July 1944. The biggest network of all, ELECTRE, even ran a radio-operators' school in France.[64]

Communications between England and the French Resistance sometimes went over the BBC in the form of "personal messages" with hidden meanings. The best known were the lines from a poem by Paul Verlaine, "Les sanglots longs des violons de l'automne," broadcast on June 1, 1944, to alert the Resistance that a landing could be expected within fifteen days. Although the Germans had decoded this message, they disregarded the sequel broadcast on June 5—"blessent mon coeur d'une langueur monotone"—which announced the start of the invasion.[65]

That message also signaled the beginning of Plan Violet. In the years of German occupation, the Reichspostamt had extended the German telephone and teleprinter cable network to most of occupied Europe, and organized a European Postal and Telecommunications Union under German domination.[66] Knowing that the German armed forces used this cable network as much as possible to avoid radio interception, the Allies deliberately planned to disrupt it during the invasion. Starting at midnight on June 6, Resistance agents, many of them employees of the French Posts and Telegraphs, cut telephone lines, dug up cables, exploded repeater stations. Meanwhile Allied pilots, well briefed by the Resistance, bombed telecommunications buildings. One day after D-Day, thirty-two major long-distance cables were cut, and soon there were two thousand breaks in the French landline network.[67] On June 8, the German naval communications officer in France signalled to Captain U-boats, West: "All lines to Berlin, Kiel, Wilhelmshaven, Paris, Brest, Aix, La Rochelle down as a result of enemy action. One teleprinter line to Paris limitedly effective."[68]

Thus, at a most crucial time in the war, the Germans were forced to use the radio. And what they said on the radio, thanks to Ultra, was an open book to the Allies. Even Magic, the decryption of Japanese diplomatic messages, was helpful, for Hitler was quite open with the Japanese ambassador to Berlin, Baron Oshima. On January 10, 1943, Oshima visited the Atlantic Wall, Germany's defense against an invasion from the west, and sent a detailed report to Tokyo about its command structure and the location and strength of the German forces. Again, just before D-Day, the Japanese military attaché toured the German defenses in Normandy, and Oshima transmitted his report to Tokyo and also, inadvertently, to Washington and London.[69] After D-Day, the allies obtained precise information about German forces and intentions, from the highest strategic plans to small-scale tactical moves. For instance, on August 3, 1944, they decrypted Hitler's order in which he took personal command of the battle from General von Kluge and launched a massive armored attack on the Avranches Gap. Well forewarned, General Omar Bradley, commander of the American Twelfth Army Group, set a trap and destroyed nineteen German armored divisions.[70] It had been Hitler's last opportunity to destroy the Allied beachhead.

Late, very late in the war, the Germans seem to have begun having doubts about their communications security. As they retreated, they increasingly used landlines instead of the radio. For their high-level strategic messages they used the Geheimschreiber, the most complex cipher machine, not knowing that the British were reading that as well. In his final act of bravura, the Ardennes Offensive of December 1944, Hitler imposed absolute radio silence and the strictest security measures, and it worked, for it caught the allies by surprise and briefly sent them reeling.[71]

The Soviet Rings

In contrast to the flood of information about British and American intelligence, very little is known about Soviet activities during the war. The whole area of Soviet communications intelligence and cryptanalysis, for instance, is still shrouded in mystery. What we know the most are the spies caught by the Axis powers. The stories of their adventures and their methods of obtaining secret information are the stuff of spy thrillers, both historical and fictional. Our interest, however, is more specific: How did they get their reports out through the fine mesh of Axis counterespionage?

The first case is that of Richard Sorge, a German national who moved to Japan in 1933.[72] By posing as a Nazi journalist, he succeeded in ingratiating himself with Japanese politicians of the more moderate sort and with officials of the German embassy, and from them obtained high-level military and political information. To communicate with the GRU or Russian military intelligence, he first used couriers to Shanghai, but later employed a radio operator named Bruno Wendt, who was nervous and technically incompetent. In 1935 Wendt was replaced by a more competent radio operator named Max Clausen, who built a clumsy but functional suitcase transceiver out of spare parts and established a regular contact with the Russians once a week. Sorge and Clausen encrypted their messages by using a simple alphabetical substitution enciphered by random numbers chosen from the 1935 Statistical Yearbook of the German Reich. Not until 1938 did the Japanese government realize that clandestine radio transmissions were issuing from the Tokyo area. Their attempts to decrypt the messages or to locate the transmitter were fruitless, however.[73] In 1939 and 1940 Clausen stepped up the rate of transmission from once to twice or even three times a week.

While Sorge's communications slipped by the Japanese, he was not so lucky with Clausen. The latter had opened a business as a cover for his espionage activities, an experience that affected his political views, and he began spontaneously to cut Sorge's messages by one-half to two-thirds. In May 1942 Sorge discovered that Hitler was planning to attack Russia on June 20, and ordered Clausen to send the information to Moscow. Clausen sent an abridged version, deleting the best, such as the sentence "German troops had already started to gather near the Russian border in preparation for the attack on Russia." Clausen later commented: "I thought it was a very important subject, but since I had a favorable attitude already at the time toward Hitler's policies, I did not send out this information."[74] A few months later, Sorge, Clausen, and their contacts were arrested, ending one of the most successful, yet least consequential, spy rings in history.

Soviet spies also penetrated the German Reich. One ring, which began operating in June 1941 soon after the German invasion of Russia, was known as the Red Orchestra. Its leaders were Leopold Trepper, who operated an extensive network of agents in Brussels and Paris, and Harro Schultze-Boysen, a well-placed Luftwaffe officer who worked in the Ministry of the Air Force in Berlin. Members of the ring used Soviet-made radios said to be "superior to German transmitters and even to those used by British agents."[75]

To detect secret transmitters, the Abwehr and the Forschungsamt used vans equipped with direction-finding sets and even suitcases that could be carried by a pedestrian. With these devices, the Abwehr was said to be able to locate a transmitter in a large city like Paris within forty minutes on the average. Evidently the Russians were not aware of the German advances in direction-finding, for they insisted that the Red Orchestra agents transmit for hours at a time. The Berlin spy ring was compromised by a radio message from Moscow in October 1942, giving names and addresses. Schultze-Boysen was arrested the following August. In Brussels a first transmitter was located and captured in December 1941 and a second one in June 1941, as was the one near Paris. By the summer of 1943, almost all the transmitters in Paris had been captured. With the codes and ciphers they found, Abwehr agents discovered to their amazement that "there was not a sector in the political, economic and military life that was not known to the Russians in every detail."[76] That was only the beginning.

The most effective and at the same time most mysterious spy network of World War II was known as the Lucy Ring, which operated out of Lausanne and Geneva, Switzerland. Information from secret sources in Germany was channelled through a German refugee, Rudolf Rössler ("Lucy"), to Alexander Radolfi ("Radó"), the resident agent of the Soviet Ministry of State Security or MGB. The messages were then transmitted to Moscow by several radio operators: Margareta Bolli, Edmond and Olga Hamel, and the Englishman Alexander Foote. Communications with Moscow began in January 1941 and by 1942 were averaging eight messages a day.[77] And what information! Alexander Foote writes:

> I remember that in 1941 he supplied information regarding the manufacture of flying bombs and plans for the construction of ten-ton rockets. In effect, as far as the Kremlin

was concerned, the possession of Lucy as a source meant that they had the equivalent of well-placed agents in the three service intelligence staffs plus the Imperial General Staff plus the War Cabinet Offices. . . . Lucy provided Moscow with an up-to-date and day-to-day order of battle of the German forces in the East. This information could come only from the Oberkommando der Wehrmacht itself. In no other offices in the whole of Germany was there available the information that Lucy provided daily. . . . One would normally think that a source producing information of this quality would take time to obtain it. No such delay occurred in the receipt of Lucy's information. On most occasions it was received within twenty-four hours of its being known at the appropriate headquarters in Berlin. In fact, barely enough time to encipher and decipher the messages concerned. There was no question of any courier or safe hand route.[78]

At first the Soviets were suspicious of information that seemed too good to be true, especially since they did not know its source. Yet the information proved to be not only accurate, but extremely detailed. In July 1943, when the Wehrmacht launched its great tank offensive at Kursk, the Red Army knew the strength and position of the German forces, and defeated it. After that, however, the information became poorer.[79]

Some time in 1941, the Sicherheitsdienst, the Nazi party's security department, began intercepting the transmissions between Foote and Moscow. In April and May 1942 they located Foote's transmitter somewhere on the shores of Lake Geneva. Later, using several direction-finding stations, they pinpointed the transmitters at Geneva and Lausanne. In early 1943, they began breaking the code used by Foote and his associates. They also put pressure on the Swiss to crack down on the spy ring. Between October and December 1943 the Swiss police located the ring's transmitters and arrested Hamel, Bolli, and Foote, putting an end to the communications with Moscow. By that time the Soviets had lost interest in the ring and stopped sending them money.[80]

The Lucy Ring's methods of operation are clear, as was the importance of the information they transmitted. Only one mystery remains: Where did that information come from? Here, the sources disagree. Rössler himself, although pressured by the Soviets and the Swiss, would only say that his sources were inside the OKW, army, and Luftwaffe headquarters, but he refused to reveal their names.[81] Jozef Garlinski says the information came from Ultra decrypts that the British conveyed to Moscow via their embassy in Berne and the Swiss police because Stalin distrusted Britain too much.[82] Anthony Read and David Fisher maintain that it came from Bletchley Park via Alexander Foote, who was a double agent for both Britain and Russia.[83]

Accoce and Quet give a plausible, if unproven, explanation. According to them, it was none other than Generals Fellgiebel and "Fritz T" (obviously Thiele), who alone had access to Germany's most secret military information and also to the OKW's communications center with its hundred transmitters. Having supplied Rössler with a shortwave set, they were able to contact him with impunity, for the SD would hardly have located one illicit transmitter among the dozens all spewing out coded messages at once. It would be the perfect cover.[84]

Unfortunately this explanation clashes with the one proposed by Walter Laqueur, who maintains that Rössler had no shortwave radio at his disposal, and concludes:

The only plausible explanation is that he received some of the material from the Swiss and the rest by means of the occasional German courier. The Swiss . . . had excellent German sources at their disposal, above all the so-called "Viking Line" with Generals Oster, Thomas, and Olbricht as the chief informants. For obvious reasons, they have been reluctant to discuss to this day their sources of information during World War II.[85]

Until the Swiss open their archives and reveal the truth, those who like to speculate about such matters can choose which traitors to Hitler they prefer.

Conclusion

The great military theoretician Karl von Clausewitz (1780–1831) once described the unpredictable elements of battle as "the fog of war." The metaphor was appropriate in his day when generals chose to fight in daylight on open battlefields. In World War II battlefields were far too big for anyone's field of vision, and the advantage of fighting on a clear day was replaced by the knowledge provided by good intelligence. But unlike the sun, intelligence does not shine impartially on both sides. Thanks to communications intelligence, one side can be fighting in the sunshine while the other is lost in the fog. Starting in 1940, and increasingly as time went on, the light of knowledge shone on the Allies.

Notes

1. "Government Code and Cypher School: Institution under Admiralty Control" (December 17, 1919), in Public Record Office [hereafter PRO], ADM 1/8577/349; "Control of Interception" (1924), in PRO, WO 32/4897; Christopher Andrew, *Secret Service: The Making of the British Intelligence Community* (London, 1985), 259; Nigel West, *GCHQ: The Secret Wireless War 1900–86* (London, 1986), 71–72.
2. "Government Code and Cypher School"; "Official Secrets Act, 1920," in Cable and Wireless archives (London), B2/553; "Foreign Office Interception, 1938–1946," in ibid., B1/120.
3. "Report of Inter-Service Directorate Committee (9th April, 1923)" and "Reply by Lord Curzon (FO) (July 7, 1923)," in PRO, WO 32/4897; this document is mainly concerned with complaints by the armed forces that the Foreign Office, which controlled GC&CS, was ignoring their needs.
4. "Indo-China, Radio Installations (March 1920–June 1936)," in PRO, WO 106/5451; Andrew, 260–61 and 353.
5. "Report," in PRO, WO 32/4897.
6. Andrew, Chaps. 9 and 10; West, 76–79.
7. Heinz Bonatz, *Die deutsche Marine-Funkaufklärung 1914–1945* (Darmstadt, 1970), 73–74.
8. David Kahn, *Hitler's Spies: German Military Intelligence in World War II* (New York, 1978), 47–56 and 178–85; Erich Hüttenhain, "Erfolge und Miserfolge der deutschen Chiffrierdienste im Zweiten Weltkrieg," in Jürgen Rohwer and Eberhard Jäckel, eds., *Die Funkaufklärung und ihre Rolle im Zweiten Weltkrieg: Bericht über eine Tagung in Bad Godesberg und Stuttgart vom 15. bis 18. November 1978* (Stuttgart, 1978), 100–9; Bonatz, 89.

9. Kahn, *Hitler's Spies*, 96; Bonatz, 78–79, 90–91, and 113.

10. Bonatz, 93–95 and 115–16; David Kahn, *The Codebreakers: The Story of Secret Writing* (New York, 1967), 436–50.

11. Kahn, *Codebreakers*, 394–422.

12. More precisely, 3-rotor Enigmas had 3×10^{18} possible permutations; 4-rotor Enigmas had 4×10^{20}. Ronald Lewin, *Ultra Goes to War* (New York, 1978), 26 and 33; Kahn, *Codebreakers*, 422; West, 96–99.

13. Bonatz, 87. In a subsequent book, *Seekrieg im Äther: Die Leistungen der Marine-Funkaufklärung 1939–1945* (Herford, 1981), Bonatz rewrote the history of naval communications intelligence in the light of the Ultra revelations.

14. United States Army Security Agency, Historical Section, *Origin and Development of the Army Security Agency, 1917–1947* (Laguna Hills, Cal., 1978), 25; Lewin, *The American Magic: Codes, Ciphers, and Defeat of Japan* (New York, 1982), 33–35, and *Ultra*, 28; Arthur R. Hezlet, *The Electron and Sea Power* (London, 1975), 176; Kahn, *Codebreakers*, 426–27.

15. Patrick Beesly, *Very Special Intelligence: The Story of the Admiralty's Operational Intelligence Centre, 1939–1945* (Garden City, N.Y., 1978), 34; Hezlet, 164 and 175–76; West, 96.

16. Committee of Imperial Defence, Imperial Communications Committee, Memoranda (March 1937–August 1939), in PRO, Cab 35/35; "Emergency Office, Gibraltar, 1932–39," in Cable and Wireless, B2/812; "Code and Cipher School," memorandum of August 1939, in PRO, FO 366/1059; Andrew, 400.

17. "Code and Cipher School"; Hezlet, 302, No. 18; West, 95.

18. Beesly, 10–21; Hezlet, 177.

19. "Foreign Office Scrutiny Scheme, 1937–1938," in Cable and Wireless, B1/94; "Foreign Office Interception, 1938–1946," in ibid., B1/120; "War Office: U.K. Censorship, 1939–1945," in ibid., B1/86; letter from J. A. Calder, Colonial Office, to chairman, Cable and Wireless, December 1, 1938, in "Colonial Office Dealings, 1938–1943," in ibid., B1/104.

20. George A. Codding, *The International Telecommunications Union: An Experiment in International Cooperation* (Leiden, 1952), 181.

21. Kenneth C. Baglehole, *A Century of Service: A Brief History of Cable and Wireless Ltd. 1868–1968* (London, 1969), 23–24; Gerald R. M. Garratt, *One Hundred Years of Submarine Cables* (London, 1950), 44; Charles Graves, *The Thin Red Lines* (London, 1946), 181.

22. Kahn, *Codebreakers*, 611.

23. Committee of Imperial Defence, Standing Interdepartmental Committee on Censorship, Censorship Organisation Sub-Committee, Minutes, Memoranda & Report, 1934, in PRO, Cab 49/8; War Cabinet, Interdepartmental Committee on Censorship, Minutes of Meetings, 1939–40, in Cab 76/9; War Cabinet, Standing Inter-departmental Committee on Censorship, 1941, in Cab 76/10; "War Office: U.K. Censorship, 1939–1945," in Cable and Wireless, B1/86; "U.K. Censorship–Accounting, 1939–1941," in ibid., B1/119; Hugh Barty-King, *Girdle Round the Earth: The Story of Cable and Wireless and its Predecessors to Mark the Group's Jubilee, 1929–1979* (London, 1979), 269; Kahn, *Codebreakers*, 516; Graves, 15.

24. "Foreign Office Scrutiny Scheme, 1937–1938," in Cable and Wireless, B1/94; "Foreign Office Scrutiny Scheme no. 2, 1940–43," in ibid., B1/87.

25. G. E. C. Wedlake, *SOS: The Story of Radio Communication* (Newton Abbot, 1973), 133.

26. Lewin, *Ultra*, 68–71; Peter Calvocoressi, *Top Secret Ultra* (London and New York, 1980), 118; Bonatz, *Marine-Funkaufklärung*, 123–25; Hüttenhain, 106.

27. West, *GCHQ*, 119, 126, 162; and *MI6: British Secret Intelligence Service Operations, 1906–45* (London and New York, 1983), 187.

28. "Foreign Office Interception, 1938–1946," in Cable and Wireless, B1/120; Calvocoressi, 44–48; Lewin, *Ultra*, 61 and 115–16.

29. Hezlet, 178; Kahn, *Codebreakers*, 8–9; Calvocoressi, 46–47.

30. The book that revealed the secret was Frederick W. Winterbotham, *The Ultra Secret* (London and New York, 1974). Historical accounts based on archival sources include Patrick Beesly's *Very Special Intelligence* and Ronald Lewin's *Ultra Goes to War*, both published in 1978.

31. David Kahn, "Fernmeldewesen, Chiffriertechniken und Nachrichtenaufklärung in den Kriegen des 20. Jahrhunderts," in Rohwer and Jäckel, 17–47; Waldemar Werther, "Die Entwicklung der deutschen Funkschlüsselmaschinen: die 'Enigma,' " in ibid., 51–65; Lewin, *Ultra*, passim; Winterbotham, 64–75.

32. Tadeusz Lisicki, "Die Leistung der polnischen Entzifferundgsdientes bei der Lösung des Verfahrens der deutschen "Enigma"-Funkschlüsselmachine," in Rohwer and Jäckel, 66–81; Winterbotham, 26–28; Lewin, *Ultra*, 30–72; Beesley, 64.

33. Bonatz, *Marine-Funkaufklärung*, 87.

34. "Code and Cypher School. Erection of Wireless Intercept Stations and Staffing" (1939), in PRO, FO 366/1059; West, *GCHQ*, 187 and 220; Kahn, "Fernmeldewesen," 43–44.

35. Lewin, *Ultra*, 131; Beesly, 131–32; Kahn, "Fernmeldewesen," 37; West, *GCHQ*, 190–93 and 211.

36. Anthony Cave Brown, *Bodyguard of Lies* (New York, 1975), 165 and 200–201; Lewin, *Ultra*, 130 ad 214; Kahn, *Hitler's Spies*, 198–99.

37. Calvocoressi, 67–73; Lewin, *Ultra*, 63–65, 124–25, 140, and 278–81; Winterbotham, 42.

38. Memorandum of September 4, 1942, in PRO, ADM 116/5439: "Radio-telephone, 1942–5."

39. Kahn, *Hitler's Spies*, 162–76, 413, 451, and 460–61; and *Codebreakers*, 452–501, 554–56, and 649; Hüttenhain, 102–4; Cave Brown, 537; West, *GCHQ*, 144.

40. Lewin, *Ultra*, 75–87 and 185–95; Calvocoressi, 81; Winterbotham, 51–52.

41. Codding, 182.

42. Janusz Piekalkiewicz, *Rommel und die Geheimdienste in Nordakfrika 1941–1943* (Munich and Berlin, 1984), passim; Cave Brown, 102; West, *GCHQ*, 197; Lewin, *Ultra*, 139 and 165.

43. Raymond Daniell, "British Ire is High Over Tobruk Loss," *New York Times*, June 23, 1942.

44. Lewin, *Ultra*, 196–99; Winterbotham, 101–2.

45. Lewin, *Ultra*, 155–56.

46. Kahn, *Codebreakers*, 472–74; *Hitler's Spies*, 193–95; and "Fernmeldewesen," 25–26; Piekalkiewicz, 78–79; Cave Brown, 101.

47. Kahn, *Hitler's Spies*, 195, says the Americans had "somehow gotten wind of the Axis reading of the Fellers messages." Calvocoressi, 118–19, is more specific: "The British deciphered an Italian appreciation of the situation which stated that Rommel's successes had been in good measure due to his reading of the American military attaché cypher."

48. Piekalkiewicz, 150–58; Cave Brown, 101–2.

49. Piekalkiewicz, 158.

50. Winterbotham, 111–21; Lewin, *Ultra*, 172 and 267–68.

51. Piekalkiewicz, 158.

52. J. C. Masterman, *The Double-Cross System in the War of 1939 to 1945* (New

Haven, 1972); Lewin, *Ultra*, 300–308; Kahn, *Hitler's Spies*, 292 and 367–70; West, *GCHQ*, 118–19.

53. Cave Brown, 521, 550, and 604.

54. Kahn, *Hitler's Spies*, 491–92 and 510.

55. Lewin, *Ultra*, 304–5 and 317. See also Cave Brown, 673 and 685.

56. Robert Sobel, *ITT: The Management of Opportunity* (New York, 1982), 109.

57. "Resume of Reports of General Robert Davis, Comdr. George Shecklen and Mr. Philip Siling Regarding Efforts to Eliminate Axis Communications from South America" (August 28, 1942), in National Archives, Record Group 259, Box 13, file "Reports—Transradio Consortium"; "Spec Plan Comm on Intl. B.C.," in ibid., Box 33, file "Transradio Consortium Argentine"; Kahn, *Codebreakers*, 321–22 and 528–30.

58. "Debardeleben, John F.—Argentina" and "Chile—John Debardeleben," in National Archives, Record Group 173: FCC Radio Intelligence Division, Box 11: "On monitoring Axis in L. America" and Box 14: "On monitoring Axis in Chile" and "Weekly reports to the Chairman FCC, 1944–1946."

59. Kahn, *Hitler's Spies*, 320; and *Codebreakers*, 530; "Apfel, Pedro and Bach," *Time* (November 16, 1942), 44.

60. Kahn, *Hitler's Spies*, 327 and 369–70.

61. West, *MI6*, 147, 162–63, 269, and 338.

62. Kahn, *Codebreakers*, 531–38; Gilles Perrault, *The Red Orchestra* (New York, 1969), 499.

63. Roman Garby-Czerniawski, *The Big Network* (London 1961), 105–15; Jean Fleury, "La radio clandestine dans la Résistance (réseau Electre)," in Comité d'Histoire de la Poste et des Telécommunications, Institut d'Histoire du Temps Présent, *L'oeil et l'oreille de la Résistance: Action et rôle des agents des P.T.T. dans la clandestinité au cours du second conflict mondial. Actes du colloque tenu à Paris les 21, 22, 23 Novembre 1984* (Toulouse, 1986), 121–26.

64. Henri Michel, *Histoire de la Résistance en France* (Paris, 1980); Fleury, 121–26.

65. Kahn, *Hitler's Spies*, 511–13.

66. Frank Thomas, "Korporative Akteure und die Entwicklung des Telefonsystems in Deutschland 1877 bis 1945," *Technikgeschichte* 56, No 1 (1989), 59.

67. Michel de Cheveigné, "Les techniques, la guerre et la liberté, 1939–1947," in *Histoire des télécommunications en France*, ed. Catherine Bertho (Toulouse, 1984), 146–65; Jeanne Grall, "Sabotages de câbles dans le Calvados (1940–1944)," in *L'oeil et l'oreille de la Résistance*, 146–51; Lucien Simon, in ibid., 152–54.

68. Lewin, *Ultra*, 326.

69. Lewin, *American Magic*, 237; and *Ultra*, 134 and 353; Calvocoressi, 118.

70. Lewin, *Ultra*, 323–43.

71. Lewin, *Ultra*, 356.

72. Gordon Prange, *Target Tokyo: The Story of the Sorge Spy Ring* (New York, 1984).

73. Prange, 272–73; Kahn, *Codebreakers*, 656.

74. Prange, 371–72.

75. Perrault, 127.

76. Perrault, 133.

77. Jozef Garlinski, *The Swiss Corridor: Espionage Networks in Switzerland during World War II* (London, 1981), 68–69; Pierre Accoce and Pierre Quet, *The Lucy Ring* (London, 1967), 98–108; David J. Dallin, *Soviet Espionage* (New Haven, 1955), 190–201.

78. Alexander Foote, *Handbook for Spies* (Garden City, N.Y., 1949), 92–95.

79. Garlinski, 71–72 and 138–39; Accoce and Quet, 118–30; Dallin, 195–96.

80. Garlinski, 140–61; Dallin, 215–26; Accoce and Quet, 132–45, 159–61, and 192–210.

81. Garlinski, 72–73.

82. Garlinski, 79–83.

83. Anthony Read and David Fisher, *Operation Lucy: Most Secret Spy Ring of the Second World War* (London, 1980), 146–47.

84. Accoce and Quet, 71–73.

85. Walter Laqueur, *A World of Secrets: The Uses and Limits of Intelligence* (New York, 1985), 381, No. 21.

13

The War at Sea

When he launched his offensive in September 1939, Hitler, like Philip II, Napoleon, and the German General Staff before him, was playing out an age-old scenario: an ambitious ruler tries to conquer Europe but finds himself confronted by a small island nation that commands the sea and cannot be defeated by the largest armies. For the fourth time in as many centuries, Great Britain held out long enough to witness and assist the crumbling of yet another would-be European Empire. Yet Britain could not have done it alone, for each challenge to its mastery of the sea was more dangerous than the last, and in World War II as in World War I, Britain needed the help of its daughter-nation the United States. In the process, the United States inherited Britain's role at sea and in the world.

Another nation, meanwhile, coveted Britain's role as mistress of the seas and resented the American obstacle to its ambitions. Japan, an island just off the shores of Eurasia, was geographically a mirror image of Britain. But politically, their roles were opposite. Britain had learned centuries before to forsake territorial ambitions in Europe and divert its imperialism to other parts of the world. Japan, coming out of its long isolation at the height of European colonialism, directed its ambitions at nearby Korea, Manchuria, and China. Here the Japanese soon found their advance hampered by Britain and the United States. Thus in 1941 when Japan decided to become a world power, its ambition inevitably led to a naval war on the grandest scale.

The Cable War

In 1938 Cable and Wireless prepared a list of German and Italian cables to be cut in the event of war. When war broke out, British cable ships went out into the Channel as they had done twenty-five years before and cut the German cables to Spain, Portugal, and the Azores.[1] Ten months later, when Italy entered the war, British cable ships severed the Italian cables in the Mediterranean and the Atlantic. This time it mattered little, since Germany and Italy could easily communicate by radio with the rest of the world.

From February to April 1940, replaying World War I, the French and British governments discussed what to do with the severed German cables.[2] In July, with Italy at war and the French Atlantic coast in German hands, Edward Wilshaw, managing director of Cable and Wireless, wrote to the Imperial Communications Committee:

> The position in this war is that Germany, Italy and France have extensive submarine cable systems, and it is a matter for consideration whether and how these systems can best be adapted and employed to the advantage of the British Empire in the prosecution of the war.
>
> These suggestions are put forward not as a commercial proposition but in the interests of the prosecution of the war, the successful termination of which may well be dependent on rapid and secret communication.

He proposed to divert the German, Italian, and French Atlantic cables to form new links between England and Gibraltar, the Azores, West Africa, and the United States.[3] The Italian cable to Belgium was relaid to link England with Gibraltar, and the Malaga–Canaries cable became Gibraltar–Casablanca.[4] Cable and Wireless also planned to divert the French West African cable to Lagos, thereby cutting off French Equatorial Africa from the pro-Vichy colonies of French West Africa.[5] What Wilshaw hoped to gain from the war, in effect, was all the world's cables except the Americans'.

The Axis powers also tried to disrupt their enemies' communications. The Italians cut all the cables between Malta and Gibraltar and two of the five Malta-Alexandria cables. Due to the proximity of Axis airbases in Sicily, the British could not send a cable ship to repair the damage until January 1943. Although the cutting slowed down British cable communications, it did not break them off entirely, for cablegrams between Britain and Malta or Egypt could still go around Africa or even, for a time, via Canada and Australia.[6]

Elsewhere, the Germans and Italians were less successful. Italian bombers attacked the Aden cable station in June 1940, but caused no real damage. In August German bombers severed the land lines between London and Porthcurno, and for a time telegrams had to be transported by car. The Porthcurno station, the most vulnerable point in Britain's communications, was put underground.[7] Outside the Mediterranean, cable ships still operated, albeit with a destroyer escort, and somehow managed to keep cable network operating.[8] The British insistence on duplicate cables and "all-red" routes proved to have been a wise policy.

Yet in the heady days of July and August 1940, the Germans expected Great Britain to capitulate at any moment. This hope inspired those interested in global communications to make plans for the victorious peace Germany was about to enjoy. Major-General Thiele, head of communications in Western Europe, spared the French cable station near Brest because he expected an imminent peace followed by a quick reopening of transatlantic communications.[9] In July Herr Feuerhahn, a high official of the German Post Office, wrote a memorandum on "the shaping of Germany's position in world communications after the peace treaty." A month later, Herr K. Sonntag of the Deutsch-Atlantische Telegraphengesellschaft sent a memorandum on "the formation of a new cable network" to Postal Minister Ohnesorge. Both argued that after the war Germany would replace Britain as the political and economic center of Europe and recover the colonies it lost after World War I, and would therefore require an independent world cable network. Therefore Germany should demand the return of its old cables, along with reparations and raw materials sufficient to manufacture and lay a new network of loaded cables to North and South America. To ensure a lasting dominance in world communications, Germany should also demand Britain's landing rights abroad and acquire British shares in the Great Northern Company. What they advocated, in effect, was the fulfillment of Germany's pre-World War I cable projects.[10] Needless to say, had the Germans conquered Britain, Hitler's demands would have quite put to shame the modest wish list of the bureaucrats Feuerhahn and Sonntag. Even compared with Wilshaw of Cable and Wireless, they were inexperienced imperialists.

Cables in the Far East were much more vulnerable than in the Atlantic and Indian Oceans, for there the Royal Navy no longer ruled the waves. In June 1940, after Denmark was occupied by the German army, Japan abrogated the concession of the Danish Great Northern Company.[11] In the days after Pearl Harbor the Japanese cut the British cables to China, Indochina, the Dutch East Indies, and Singapore. They captured 29,300 kilometers of cable routes and eleven stations, but showed no interest in operating them.[12]

Two cables in the region really mattered to the British, namely the ones linking Australia to Canada and to South Africa. The Japanese never came close to the Pacific cable, but, like the Germans in World War I, they did attack the cable station at Cocos between Australia and South Africa. On March 3, 1942, a Japanese ship shelled the island, damaging the cable station and other buildings, but the cables survived. The next day, Cocos wired London: THINK POLICY SHOULD BE LET ENEMY THINK COCOS OUT OF ACTION. On the 5th, London radioed to Batavia (Java) in clear language: AS COCOS DESTROYED COMMUNICATION WITH YOU NO LONGER POSSIBLE SEE NO NEED YOU REMAIN BATAVIA . . . GOOD LUCK DO NOT REPLY TO THIS. Periodically thereafter the Japanese sent reconnaissance planes over the island, but seeing the cable station in ruins, assumed the cables were out of action. In fact Cocos continued to handle the cable traffic between Britain and Australia, in the greatest secrecy, for the remainder of the war. In November 1943 J. Denison-Pender, chairman of Cable and Wireless, wrote to F. W. Phillips of the Postal and Telegraph Censorship Department:

> It is possible that this scheme, which we agreed with the Admiralty at the time, may have worked even better than we dared hope, and that the Japanese may be under the impression that their attack did in fact destroy the station. It seems, however, too much to believe that they can really have been taken in so easily.[13]

Since World War I there had been speculation that cables might be cut by submarines or somehow intercepted. In 1924 the British Admiralty reported that "a modern submarine is capable of cutting cables up to a depth of 40 fathoms or less and under favourable circumstances if fitted with suitable gear up to 100 fathoms."[14] Herbert Yardley claimed in 1931 that "by stretching other wires alongside [a cable] for a distance of several hundred feet telegraph operators stationed in the submarines can copy the passing messages by induction."[15] In 1942 the U.S. Navy carried out experiments in intercepting cable communications by induction, not from a submarine but from a surface ship. What it found was that interception was possible, but with great difficulty and only relatively close to the sending cable station.[16] A representative of All-America Cables commented on these experiments:

> The fact that it is necessary to carry on such operations close to shore makes it almost impossible to accomplish in war time, because shore, ship and air patrol would detect any ship stationed over a cable for such purpose. Submarines, if used, would be spotted when they came to the surface and antisubmarine detective devices would also help to locate them. . . . [A]ny ship which has been able to receive such messages inductively from the cables must, of necessity, transmit the matter by radio to its headquarters, if it is to be of any use. In doing so they will run the immediate risk of detection by direction finders.[17]

There is no evidence from Allied intercepts or captured documents that the Germans or Japanese ever tapped Allied cables, or even tried.

Communications and Naval Warfare in the Atlantic

While armies have may ways to communicate, fleets rely almost totally on the radio. Hence in naval warfare, communications and communications intelligence have an importance found nowhere else.

At the beginning of the war, the Royal Navy had its own communications network with a high-powered longwave station at Rugby and shortwave transmitters scattered around the world; by the end of the war it had five times that number. Ships' radio equipment also multiplied: In 1939 battleships carried nine transmitters and receivers; by the end, they had sixteen transmitters and twenty-three receivers.[18] Merchant ships were first forced to suspend all radio communications in order to avoid detection by enemy direction-finders. Within a few months, however, they were grouped into convoys directed by radio from the Operational Intelligence Centre, the Headquarters Western Approaches, and the Coastal Command. Since ships in convoy also needed to communicate with one another in order to maneuver quickly, they were equipped with low-powered voice transmitters that made them vulnerable to detection by submarines. Toward the end of the war, convoys were equipped with very-high-frequency FM transmitters that could not be received beyond the horizon.[19]

Submarines had special communications problems. In World War I, German U-boats outside the North Sea had had difficulty communicating with their headquarters. By World War II, however, two effective means of communication were at their disposal. Submarines submerged to periscope depth or below could receive longwaves thousands of kilometers away. It was for this reason that the British maintained the Rugby station and that the Germans built the Goliath station at Frankfurt-an-der-Oder.[20] To transmit, however, submarines used shortwave because they could not carry longwave transmitters. Unlike the U-boats of World War I, which were essentially on their own like corsairs in the age of sail, those of World War II stayed in contact with the commander of the U-boats, Admiral Karl Dönitz, and thus under his control.

Dönitz had developed an answer to the convoy tactics that had defeated the U-boats in World War I: the wolf-pack. It required the U-boats to patrol a line that convoys were likely to cross. The one that spotted a convoy was then to keep it in sight and radio its position, direction, and speed every hour or two until other U-boats could converge and attack it together. U-boats were also required to report sinkings, minefields, the weather, and their own needs. U-boat movements were at first directed by a commanding U-boat until it was realized that emergency submersions cut off communications. After 1940, operations were directed from Dönitz's submarine tracking stations in Berlin or in Lorient (France).[21]

The wolf-pack tactic meant sacrificing radio silence. As Dönitz wrote in 1940: "Radio silence must not be an end in itself. One must not expect diminished results from the use of radio. If it is well used it increases our chances."[22] His goal was "for all units a shortwave program that should cover all distances in the Atlantic and allow every boat safe communication with the homeland several times a day."[23]

Of course Dönitz was well aware that the use of radio exposed his submarines to enemy direction-finding, but he thought the risk worth taking; in 1940 he wrote: "The English shortwave direction-finding service must from previous experience be considered efficient. . . . Seldom appearing short signals of at most three to four code groups sent if possible on irregular frequencies may above all be considered safe from enemy direction finding."[24]

Thus the battle between submarines and surface ships hinged largely on communications intelligence. The Germans needed direction-finding and cryptanalysis to track the convoys and the warships of the Royal and U.S. navies. The British and Americans needed the same to locate the German U-boats. In the Atlantic the two sides were more evenly matched than anywhere else in that war.

It did not start out that way. At first, the German B-Dienst was far ahead of British naval intelligence. By mid-1940 it had placed intercept and direction-finding stations across Europe from northern Norway to southern Spain, all linked to headquarters by teleprinter lines.[25] In the course of the war, it employed five to six thousand men, most of them military men, but also some businessmen and teachers with foreign language skills. Unlike the British, the B-Dienst thought "pure mathematicians were not always suitable, for they often lost themselves in theoretical investigations."[26] For a time, it was very successful in decrypting British messages. Although the Royal Navy used one-time pads for its high-grade traffic, for all other traffic it used old-fashioned codebooks and hand ciphers, which B-Dienst first began reading in 1936. The new codes and ciphers introduced by the Royal Navy just before the war broke out were soon broken as well, in part because the Germans had retrieved the codebooks from three British submarines sunk in the shallow waters of Heligoland Bight in January 1940 and from a destroyer run aground on the Norwegian coast in April.[27] The Royal Navy's own cipher was secure after 1940, but Germans penetrated the coastal shipping and convoy codes until August 1940, from July to November 1941, and again in 1941.[28] B-Dienst cooperated closely with the U-boat command; as Dönitz told the head of the B-Dienst, Heinz Bonatz, "Never forget that communications intelligence is the only intelligence than I can rely upon."[29]

The British vere a long time catching up. The German navy used Enigma machines of a more complex design than those of the Luftwaffe, and their procedures were tighter. As a result, the British were only able to decrypt German naval communications partially after June 1940, and sporadically thereafter.

To compensate, the British and Americans perfected their direction-finding beyond anything Dönitz could imagine. With long- and middle-wave transmitters direction-finding was fairly simple; shortwave, however, posed special problems because it did not go straight but bounced off the ionosphere. During the 1930s German engineers became convinced it could not be done, but engineers in Britain and the United States found ways to pinpoint the location of shortwave transmitters using pairs of sensitive receivers with special antennas.[30] This was known as HF/DF (high-frequency direction-finding), or "huff-duff."

The British thereupon built a network of direction-finding stations. By the end of 1941 they had sixteen in the North Atlantic, three in the West Indies, three in the South Atlantic, and five in the Mediterranean; by 1945 there were sixty-nine of them.[31] Stations as far apart as Gibraltar, Jamaica, and Ascension Island coordinated their fixes by cable or radio within a few seconds, and could locate a shortwave transmitter within eighty miles and often less.[32]

This was close enough for the Admiralty's Submarine Tracking Room to warn convoys away from an area known to contain U-boats, but not nearly good enough for destroyers to find and attack them. The Admiralty therefore experimented with mobile HF/DF sets, and in late 1941 began installing them on destroyers escorting convoys. In 1942 the U.S. Navy was producing its own HF/DF, and by 1943 every Atlantic convoy had two or three destroyers equipped with the sets. These sets could intercept even the shortest U-boat signals and pinpoint their transmitters within a mile or two.[33] At that point, radar took over, guiding destroyers and aircraft to a target as small as a periscope even in darkness and fog. By 1943, the mid-Atlantic was fast becoming dangerous for U-boats.

Yet it was also increasingly dangerous for convoys, as ever more U-boats joined the hunt and perfected their wolf-pack tactics. The Battle of the Atlantic hinged on many weapons systems working together: on the German side, submarines and cryptanalysis; on the Anglo-American side, convoys, destroyers, HF/DF, radar, and cryptanalysis as well. If the British had foolishly used vulnerable codes and ciphers for several years, at least they did not trust them and were willing to change. The Germans, however, started the war with a far more secure system, and refused to believe it could be penetrated (or feared to admit it). In September 1941 a naval staff report stated: "The decoded signal from the British Admiralty of September 6, a survey of the probable positions of German U-Boats, is completely true and can only have been gained by reported sightings and radio reports. An insight into our own cipher does not come into consideration." In March 1943 Dönitz wrote in his war diary that a thorough investigation "has, to some extent, allayed strong suspicions that the enemy has succeeded in breaking our ciphers."[34]

The Battle of the Atlantic, 1939–1944

At sea as in North Africa, the battle favored the best informed. When U-boats first struck a convoy in September 1939, when mines damaged the warships *Belfast* and *Nelson* in November, when the *Graf Spee,* the *Deutschland,* the *Scharnhorst,* and the *Gneisenau* made their sorties into the Atlantic that winter, the British were taken by surprise.[35]

In the spring of 1940, B-Dienst decrypted 30 to 50 percent of intercepted British naval messages and helped the Germans sink several British submarines. That summer and fall, 27 U-boats sank 274 merchant ships.[36] Yet the British were catching up. In February, the recovery of three Enigma rotors from the sinking *U-33* helped the naval cryptanalysts with the first breaks into the German naval Enigma cipher, known as Hydra. Though the cipher changed in December 1940, the Submarine Tracking Room was becoming skilled at locating U-boats by their radio signals and diverting convoys away from them.[37]

In 1941 Hitler, having abandoned his plan to invade Britain, attempted to starve it into submission by a submarine blockade, and to that end the navy launched dozens of new long-range U-boats. Despite the bombes at Bletchley Park, the British cryptanalysts needed an Enigma with its current keys in order to decrypt the German U-boat messages. In early 1941 the Royal Navy made several attempts to capture one. They seized three German trawlers off Iceland and got their rotors but no machine. During the famous chase after the *Bismarck* in May, the British had no decrypts on time, and finally located the battleship by direction-finding when Admiral Lütjens transmitted a thirty-minute signal announcing his arrival. Yet that same month, the Royal Navy achieved a victory that was more important in the long run than the sinking of the *Bismarck* when sailors snatched an Enigma with its rotors, keys, and charts from the damaged *U-110* before it sank. With this booty, the cryptanalysts not only read the Hydra traffic for several weeks (the duration of the keys the *U-110* had on board), but were able to break into Hydra and several other German naval codes until the end of the year.[38]

In 1942 the Battle of the Atlantic intensified yet more. Although American destroyers had been escorting convoys and attacking U-boats before Germany declared war on the United States on December 11, 1941, the Royal Navy and the U.S. Navy now coordinated their submarine tracking efforts and vastly expanded their HF/DF networks, their radar, and their aircraft cover for convoys. On the other side, B-Dienst was regularly decrypting the Allied convoy, aircraft, coastal, and minesweeper codes. On February 1, the U-boats began using a new Enigma with four instead of three rotors; the resulting cipher, called Triton, left the British cryptanalysts blind until December. Thus, while the Allies were building up their strength in equipment, the Germans had a substantial advantage in intelligence throughout the year, using it to good effect; in November, the worst month of the year, the U-boats sank 190 Allied ships.[39]

The Battle of the Atlantic reached its peak between March and May 1943. At the beginning of the year, B-Dienst was at maximum efficiency, with two hundred people working each shift on the convoy messages. Knowing exactly where the convoys were, Dönitz was able to direct his U-boats with uncanny precision; they did not even have to return to Germany to refuel, for they were being resupplied in mid-Atlantic by "milch-cow" submarines. In March his wolf-packs attacked two large convoys, SC122 and HX229, and sank 108 ships, fourteen of them on the night of March 16–17. Allied ships were going under far more rapidly than they could be replaced, and Britain faced imminent starvation.[40] The U.S. Navy, responsible for the western Atlantic, had no Operational Intelligence Centre and no Submarine Tracking Room, and only created one in April under British prodding.[41]

Then the tide of battle shifted. The British, finally realizing that the Germans were reading their signals, introduced a new convoy code in May and June, which left Dönitz suddenly blind. Meanwhile the British cryptanalysts were beginning to read German U-boat signals in the Triton cipher. This reversal in the balance of knowledge, along with better radar and long-range escort aircraft, helped the British and Americans locate the "milch-cow" U-boats at their rendezvous with the attack U-boats, and sink most of them. Until April the rate of U-boat losses—twelve a month—had been acceptable to Dönitz, but in April and May he lost fifty-six U-boats, faster than the German navy could train new crews, and he was forced to withdraw his U-boats from the Atlantic.[42]

Though they returned in June, their rate of loss—twenty a month—was twice as high as before, and the Allies were now building cargo ships faster than the U-boats could sink them. Not only were the Allied convoys better protected, they were also better guided, thanks to the penetration of the Triton cipher. The Germans suffered another setback in November 1943, when a bombing raid on Berlin damaged the building of the Naval High Command and destroyed much valuable cryptological material. Though B-Dienst moved to the country, it never recovered from the loss. The Allied convoys that ferried soldiers and materiel across the Atlantic in late 1943 and early 1944 in preparation for the invasion of Normandy suffered almost no losses. After an American destroyer captured the *U-505* with its Enigma, keys, charts, and codebooks in June 1944, wolf-pack attacks became suicidal. Dönitz still sent his U-boats out to sea, but they could no longer signal freely; they got their order before leaving and hunted alone, as in World War I. Even when they were vulnerable: Of the 679 U-boats lost in battle in World War II, almost half were sunk in the last eleven months of the war.[43] One statistic sheds light on the role of cryptanalysis in their defeat: The Public Record Office has 324,000 decrypted German naval signals dating from June 15, 1941, through January 5, 1945, an average of eleven decrypts per hour.[44]

The Battle of the Atlantic lasted throughout practically the entire war. In that time, weapons and tactics changed a great deal, but no part of warfare changed as much as electronics. All three aspects of electronic warfare—radar, direction-finding, and cryptology—became more powerful and sophisticated. And all three favored the Allies: radar and direction-finding from 1940–41 on, and the secret war of codes and ciphers after 1943. It is astonishing that Germany held its own so long against such unfavorable odds.

American Communications Intelligence before Pearl Harbor

In the United States, communications intelligence followed a different path than in Britain. If we can believe the self-glorifying account of its director, Herbert O.

Yardley, what successes there had been during the World War I were the work of the Army's cryptanalytic service MI-8, with the Navy contributing nothing at all.[45] At the end of the war, Yardley and General Churchill, head of Military Intelligence, were determined that America should continue to have a cipher bureau. Yardley and his staff moved to New York in 1919, where they operated the "American Black Chamber" under the cover of a commercial code company. Until 1928 they were funded by the Army and the State Department.

Yardley's biggest success was breaking the Japanese diplomatic code. Before and during the Washington Naval Arms Limitation Conference of 1921, the Black Chamber decrypted five thousand Japanese telegrams, intelligence that helped the State Department limit the ratio of Japanese to American warships.[46] Though Yardley tells all about the Black Chamber, he is secretive about his sources. American law, unlike the British, protected the secrecy of telegrams even from inquisitive government officials. To overcome this legal obstacle, Yardley began "a series of well-planned and secret inquiries at the Cable Companies as to whether it was possible for the United States to obtain copies of their code telegrams after they had been filed for dispatch." Evidently he succeeded, but as to "How? I shall not answer this question directly." By 1928, the world had drifted into an era of peace, as a result of which "It became increasingly difficult to obtain copies of the code telegrams of foreign governments, and we were forced to adopt rather subtle methods. Our superiors did not always assist us in the measures necessary to maintain the flow of telegrams into the Black Chamber."[47] Then came the final blow. In 1929 a new Secretary of State, Henry Stimson, ended the State Department's funding of the Black Chamber on the grounds that "gentlemen do not read one another's mail." The Chamber was closed, and its employees were dismissed without a pension.[48] Two years later, Yardley got his revenge by revealing all in *The American Black Chamber,* an instant best-seller, especially in Japanese translation.

While the State Department got out of the code-breaking business, the armed forces did not. The Army transferred the files of the Black Chamber to the Signal Corps and created the Signal Intelligence Service (SIS), under the civilian cryptanalyst William Friedman, which concentrated on Japanese diplomatic traffic. Since the cable companies were uncooperative, the SIS obtained what telegrams it could from two radio intercept stations in Virginia and New Jersey. Meanwhile, the Navy, worried about the Japanese navy, created a Code and Signal Section within the Office of Naval Intelligence in 1924, and sent a few officers to Japan to learn the language. Like the Army, it got its intercepts from radio listening posts from Maine to Florida and from California to the Philippines. A small intercept and cryptanalytic office at the U.S. consulate in Shanghai watched the Japanese naval traffic. From these beginnings was to grow the enormous American communications intelligence system of World War II and after, all under military jurisdiction.[49]

The imbalance between U.S. and Japanese communications intelligence was even greater than that between Germany and its enemies. Unlike Germany, which started with considerable advantages in communications intelligence, Japan was at a disadvantage from the beginning, and the gap only grew wider. While American cryptanalysts were reading some of the most sensitive Japanese secret messages, the Japanese never broke any high-grade American ciphers.[50]

When Yardley's *American Black Chamber* was published in Japan, the Japanese realized the weakness of their codes and ciphers, and made substantial improvements. After purchasing an Enigma, the Japanese navy introduced its own ciphering machine, Type No. 91, a version of which, the Type No. 91-A or "Red" machine, was used by the Japanese Foreign Ministry. A few years later, in 1937, it introduced a more sophisticated machine, the Alphabetical Typewriter Type 97, known to Americans as "Purple." To these machines they entrusted their most sensitive diplomatic traffic.[51]

In the late 1930s, a time of dangerous diplomatic tensions and impending war, the first task assigned to American cryptanalysts was to penetrate the Japanese secrets. The U.S. Army concentrated on diplomatic signals. Its Signal Intelligence Service grew from seven employees in 1929 to 331 in December 1941, and they were kept busy the whole time. Under the direction of William Friedman, SIS began reading the Japanese "Red" messages in 1937. The far more complex "Purple" messages resisted for two years; it began to give in to Friedman's efforts in August 1940 and only revealed the complete text of a message on September 25 of that year.[52] Friedman and his team had done so by constructing, from theory, a Purple machine of their own. Like the Germans, the Japanese placed great confidence in their machines; even after Ambassador Nomura in Washington obtained some evidence that the Americans had penetrated the Purple cipher, the Foreign Ministry in Tokyo continued to trust it.[53]

SIS built two replicas of the Purple machine for the Navy and two for the British. In the spring of 1941, the British began to collaborate with the Americans on communications intelligence. Two army and two navy cryptanalysts were invited to Bletchley Park. They brought with them a Purple machine and information about Japanese encryption systems, and in exchange they learned about Enigma. The British communications intelligence bureau at Singapore also began cooperating with the Americans at Corregidor on Japanese naval traffic. It was the beginning of an alliance that has persisted to this day.[54]

The U.S. Navy, meanwhile, worked on Japanese naval traffic. By 1941 its Mid-Pacific Strategic Direction-Finding Net stretched from Alaska to Samoa and from Hawaii to the Philippines. Decrypting signals was more difficult, for the Japanese used a codebook with superenciperment, known as JN25, among the most difficult in the world. The U.S. Navy had three communications intelligence units working on this traffic: in Washington, Op-20-G (formerly the Code and Cipher Section) under Lieutenant Lawrence Safford; at Pearl Harbor, "Hypo" (later renamed Fleet Radio Unit, Pacific, or FRUPac) under Lieutenant Commander Joseph Rochefort; and "Cast" under Lieutenant Rudolph Fabian in the Philippines (later evacuated to Australia). By 1941 these units had begun penetrating the Japanese naval traffic.[55] Their decrypts were called "Ultra," either to distinguish them from the diplomatic or "Magic" decrypts, or to confuse them with the British Enigma decrypts, also called "Ultra."

One source of information was for a long time off limits to military intelligence. By the Communications Act of 1934, American communications companies were forbidden to divulge the content of the messages they handled, even to agents of the government. (This explains why Americans could be so horrified at what the British—and every other government on earth—did quite naturally.) Thus the reports on the fleet in Pearl Harbor that the Japanese consul at Honolulu regularly sent home were safe from prying eyes, at least until November 1941 when David Sarnoff ordered the RCA office in Honolulu to let a naval intelligence officer see copies of them.[56]

From Pearl Harbor to Midway

By then events were moving quickly. Japanese attempts to draw a veil of secrecy over their actions were almost matched by American attempts to penetrate it; almost, but not quite. On November 1 the Japanese navy changed all its radio call signs, but they were broken by mid-month. On the 25th, the Japanese aircraft carriers, assembling for the attack on Pearl Harbor, left their radio operators behind to continue transmitting routine messages, as if the ships were still in harbor. Because many other Japanese warships were heading south toward Indochina, American naval intelligence assumed that the carriers had been left home as a reserve. In fact, they were on their way across the northern Pacific, in complete radio silence.

On December 2 a Japanese agent in Honolulu reported on the American fleet in Pearl Harbor. His telegram was duly intercepted and decrypted, as was the message from Tokyo to the ambassador in Washington to prepare to break diplomatic relations. On December 4, the Japanese navy introduced a new cipher, JN25b, a sure sign that something was afoot.

In the early hours of December 7, a naval radio station near Seattle intercepted a message from Tokyo to the ambassador in Washington with instructions to break relations at 1 p.m. By 11 a.m. Op-20-G and SIS had decrypted the message and understood its meaning. Not until an hour later did Chief of Staff General Marshall send a message warning General Short and Admiral Kimmel in Honolulu. For security reasons, the message was not sent by radio but by landline to San Francisco, then by cable to Hawaii. By the time it arrived, Japanese planes had already bombed Pearl Harbor.[57]

The combination of good information and total surprise has led to endless recriminations and exercises in hindsight analysis. Whatever else it did, Pearl Harbor proved that intelligence is not enough. It needs to be put to use, as military historian Ronald Lewin explains:

> The Americans before December 1941 had organized no effective system of evaluation and distribution. A misconceived and misapplied sense of security—stemming from the Chief of Staff himself, General Marshall—meant that those on the Magic list sometimes received information too late and sometimes not at all, while others who should have been on the list never had a chance of being informed.[58]

Seven moths later the U.S. Navy got its revenge for Pearl Harbor. On May 5, 1942, the Japanese Imperial Headquarters ordered Admiral Yamamoto to seize the island of Midway and the Western Aleutians a month hence. Since the fleet was at sea, all of Yamamoto's orders in preparation for this campaign had to be communicated by radio in the naval code J25b. For security reasons, the Japanese navy decided to change its codebooks and enciphering tables. This proved to be a staggering task, as Japanese units were scattered over millions of square miles of ocean, and the change-over, originally planned for April 1, was postponed to May 1 and then to June 1. This delay gave American cryptanalysts a precious breathing space in which to penetrate the new code and piece together the Japanese plan. They discovered that Yamamoto was assembling a task force of carriers and troop ships for an imminent attack on a place the Japanese called "AF." But where was AF? In Hawaii Combat Intelligence and Admiral Nimitz, commander-in-chief in the Pacific, were convinced it was Midway, but Op-20-G in Washington feared it might be Hawaii itself, or Alaska, or California.[59]

To find out, three intelligence officers—Rochefort, Jasper Holmes, and Joseph Finnegan—thought up a trick. They suggested that Midway be instructed by cable to send a message in plain language on the radio saying their water distilling plant had broken down and they were about to run out of fresh water. As Holmes relates the incident, "The Japanese took the bait like hungry barracuda. The next day, Wake radio intelligence reported that AF was short of fresh water because of a distilling-plant breakdown. . . . That ended the uncertainty about the identification of AF."[60] Having thus discovered the Japanese plans, the navy concocted another scheme to deceive the Japanese. By fake radio traffic, Admiral Halsey's carrier task force appeared to be near the Solomon Islands in the southwestern Pacific, instead of near Hawaii.[61] By June 1, the Americans knew where the Japanese fleet was, while the Japanese thought the American warships were too far from Midway to offer any resistance. In fact, as Lewin points out,

> Nimitz, on the eve of his next great battle, had a more intimate knowledge of his enemy's strength and intentions than any other admiral in the whole previous history of sea warfare. . . . The night before the action . . . Admiral Fletcher with his carriers was at exactly the right point on the surface of the Pacific—his presence unknown to the enemy.[62]

Taken by surprise, the Japanese navy lost four of its aircraft carriers—the *Akagi, Kaga, Soryu,* and *Hiryu*—to the loss of one American carrier, the *Yorktown.* From that moment on, Japan was on the defensive. At Midway more than anywhere else, victory and defeat hinged on communications intelligence.

After Midway

After Midway, American communications intelligence grew stronger and stronger, while the Japanese never realized to what extent their signals were being read. The task of decrypting signals, which was immense, had to be subdivided. The highest-level Japanese naval ciphers were so complex they could only be tackled with a series of tabulating machines, and were sent to Op-20-G in Washington to be decrypted. Less intricate ciphers were decrypted by FRUPac in Hawaii and in outlying stations.[63] Like everything else in that war, communications intelligence required an enormous increase in manpower, from 331 to 10,000 in the case of the army, and from 700 to 6,000 in the navy.[64]

Both the United States and Great Britain benefitted greatly from the cooperation they had begun in 1941. In April 1943 Friedman and two other American intelligence officers spent two months at Bletchley Park, learning British security procedures and cryptological advances. After complex negotiations, the British and American signed the secret BRUSA Pact by which the two nations agreed to share their communications intelligence methods and decrypts and to coordinate their handling of secret information. Bletchley Park and the U.S. Army's Signal Security Agency (formerly Signal Intelligence Service) divided up the German U-boat traffic between them.[65]

The Americans had learned, from the British and from the experience of Pearl Harbor, the importance of getting the right information to the people who needed it at the right moment. The American military never reached the level of perfection in the art of secrecy that the British achieved with their SLU system, and the press occasionally ran stories about code breaking. Nonetheless, they developed a sophisticated communications system. "Ultra advisors" were attached to command headquarters to convey Ultra intelligence and watch over communications security. Communications were sometimes achieved in a roundabout way. Coastwatchers in the Solomons sent messages via New Guinea, Australia, and Hawaii to the fleet operating among the nearby islands. When the navy refused to trust the army with decrypts of Japanese naval signals, they were routed to the British in Ceylon, and from them to General Claire Chennault in China. Ultra, Magic, and other high-level signals were encrypted on the Sigaba cipher machine. For combat communications in the Pacific, the Marine Corps recruited Navajos who spoke over the radio in a jargon code in their own language.[66]

None of these systems was ever broken by the Japanese. In fact, the Japanese seem to have had very little cyptanalytical success. They managed to break the codes used by guerrillas in the Philippines, a few low-level tactical military and diplomatic codes, but none of the codes and ciphers that might have mattered.[67] Even the Germans were aware of Japan's weakness. Conveying their experiences with a Japanese naval commission in Germany in the summer of 1941, the B-Dienst reported: "We got the impression that on the subject of communications intelligence the Japanese navy was either completely unapproachable or insufficiently prepared." They tried to persuade the Japanese of the importance of communications intelligence: "We offered to introduce Japanese officers without hesitation to the art of cryptanalysis, so that upon their return to Japan they would be able to set up, if necessary, a special service."[68] Evidently this plan did not work out, for there is no sign that Japanese cryptanalysis improved in the course of the war. Instead, they relied on traffic analysis and direction-finding.

In addition to Midway, American communications intelligence in the Pacific achieved two other victories. The first of these was the attack on Admiral Yamamoto, commander-in-chief of the southeastern air fleet and Japan's most talented and respected strategist. In January 1943 FRUPac obtained a large quantity of codebooks, charts, call signs, and other documents from the Japanese submarine *I-1*, which had run around off Guadalcanal. While the latest codebook was not among them, enough was lost to ease FRUPac's task and to cause confusion among the Japanese, who were forced to use compromised codes until they could replace them, a process that took months.[69] In April, FRUPac decrypted a message about Yamamoto's visit to bases in the Rabaul area. Thus warned, American fighter planes shot down his plane over Bougainville. Although the Japanese must have suspected that their signals had been read, they did not change their codes.[70]

Worse yet for Japan was the American submarine campaign. Japan, like Britain, was an island nation that needed a constant flow of fuel and raw materials from abroad, and this flow was vulnerable to submarine attacks. In contrast to the Battle of the Atlantic, in the Pacific the advantage of communications intelligence was all on the American side. Until 1942 Japanese cargo ships or *marus* had sailed singly and in radio silence. Their vulnerability to submarines and aircraft, however, forced them to sail in convoys. This meant they had to communicate by radio, in a code that FRUPac broke in early 1943. Close collaboration with Combat Intelligence allowed ComSubPac (the submarine command in Hawaii) to send wolf packs to attack the convoys, which the Japanese navy could not protect for lack of destroyers and escort planes. In 1943 Japan lost 308 merchant ships. Between January and April 1944 American submarines sank 179 ships and another 219 between May and August. Towards the end of the year, the rate of sinking tapered off as Japan ran out of ships and also out of the oil it needed to pursue the war. Vice-Admiral Lockwood, commander of U.S. submarines in the Pacific, later wrote: "The curve of enemy contacts and consequent sinkings almost exactly paralleled the curve of volume of Communication Intelligence available. . . . [T]hanks to Communication Intelligence, the submarines were always available at the same place as Japanese ships."[71]

As intelligence experts have often pointed out, nations on the defensive have a greater need for intelligence than have those on the offensive, in order to prepare for an enemy attack. Yet in modern wars of enormous complexity, intelligence is a major industry, one that takes a long time to develop. Both Germany and Japan, certain of a quick victory, paid insufficient attention to intelligence. Britain and the United States had a longer tradition of maritime trade and global communications, and, being on the defensive, were more sensitive to the need for intelligence.

Notes

1. Artur Kunert, *Geschichte der deutschen Fernmeldekabel. II. Telegraphen-Seekabel* (Cologne–Mülheim, 1962), 370–71; Charles Graves, *The Thin Red Lines* (London, 1946), 9.

2. "Use of Imperial and ex-enemy world wide cable networks, 1940–44," in Public Record Office (Kew) [hereafter PRO], ADM 116/5137; "War Operations, 1940," in Cable and Wireless archives (London), B2/889.

3. Memorandum on foreign cables, July 1940, in "French Communications and diversion of enemy cables (June 1940–February 1946)," in Cable and Wireless, B2/550; War Operations, 1940, in ibid., B2/889.

4. Kunert, 371; Graves, 23 and 85; Hugh Barty-King, *Girdle Round the Earth: The Story of Cable and Wireless and its Predecessors to Mark the Group's Jubilee, 1929–1979* (London, 1979), 270–71.

5. Memoranda of June 14 to December 10, 1940, in Cable and Wireless, B2/550; Graves 21.

6. Letters from Wilshaw to Colonial Secretary Lord Lloyd, November 6 and December 11, 1940, in Cable and Wireless, B1/112; Graves, 23, 105, 110, and 127; Kenneth C. Baglehole, *A Century of Service: A Brief History of Cable and Wireless Ltd. 1868–1968* (London, 1969), 23.

7. Barty-King, 268–80; Graves, 24–25 and 52.

8. On cableships and cable repairs in the war, see "Cable laying and charter of cable ships, 1939–45," in PRO, ADM 116/5433; "Cable communications and cable ships, 1941–45," in ibid., 5443; and Graves, passim.

9. Georges Bourgoin, "La Résistance dans le service des câbles sous-marins," in Comité d'Histoire de la Poste et des Télécommunications, Institut d'Histoire du Temps Présent (C.N.R.S.), *L'oeil et l'oreille de la Résistance. Action et rôle des agents des P.T.T. dans la clandestinité au cours du second conflit mondial. Actes du colloque tenu à Paris les 21, 22, 23 Novembre 1984* (Toulouse, 1986), 132–34.

10. Ministerial Feuerhahn (Deutsche Reichspost), "Denkschrift über die Ausgestaltung der Stellung Deutschlands im Weltnachrichtendienst nach dem Friedensschluß" (July 13, 1940); K. Sonntag (Deutsch-Atlantische Telegraphengesellschaft), "Gedanken über die Gestaltung eines neuen Seekabelnetzes" (August 29, 1940), with letter of acknowledgment from Reichspostminister Ohnesorge (February 10, 1941); both in the archives of Deutsche Fernkabel-Gesellschaft (Rastatt), kindly sent to me by Frank Thomas of the Max-Planck-Institut für Gesellschaftsforschung (Cologne).

11. "Great Northern Telegraph Company, 1938–1944," in Cable and Wireless, B1/644.

12. Graves, 68; Baglehole, 24; Barty-King, 280–85.

13. The letters, cables, and memoranda are in Cable and Wireless, B2/547; see also J. F. Stray, "Account of events in Cocos Islands, 1942–46," in ibid., 1551/43.

14. C.I.D., Imperial Communications Committee, 1924, Subcommittee to Consider the Strategical Importance of "Beam" Stations, Report (September 30, 1924), Appendix B, in PRO, Cab 35/14.

15. Herbert O. Yardley, *The American Black Chamber* (Indianapolis, 1931, reprinted 1981), 16.

16. "Report on experiment in intercepting cable transmissions," from Commander Eastern Sea Frontier to Vice Opnav (DNC) (October 12, 1942), in National Archives (Washington), Record Group 249, Box 4 "Cable Com." This document was exempt from automatic declassification by the National Security Agency in 1977 and declassified in 1988.

17. Letter from F. L. Henderson, All-America Cables and Radio, Inc., to E. K. Jett, chairman, Coordinating Committee, Board of War Communications, December 29, 1942, in National Archives, Record Group 259, Box 4.

18. Arthur R. Hezlet, *The Electron and Sea Power* (London, 1975), 248.

19. Jürgen Rohwer, "La radiotélégraphie: auxiliaire du commandement dans la guerre sous-marine," in *Revue d'Histoire de la Deuxième Guerre Mondiale* 18 (January 1968), 41–66; Hezlet, 209–10 and 247.

20. "Langwellenverkehr mit getauchten U-Booten," Memorandum from Nachrichten-mittelversuchsanstalt der Marine (Kiel) to Nachrichten-Inspektion (Kiel), November 21, 1938, in German Naval Records of the Second World War Captured by the British 1945, Reel 678, Frames 706–22, in Naval Historical Branch, Ministry of Defence (London); Hans Meckel, "Die Funkführung der deutschen U-Boote und die Rolle des xB-Dienstes (Deutscher Marine-Funkentzifferungsdienst)," in Jürgen Rohwer and Eberhard Jäckel, eds., *Die Funkaufklärung und ihre Rolle im Zweiten Weltkrieg: Bericht über eine Tagung in Bad Godesberg und Stuttgart vom. 15. bis 18. November 1978* (Stuttgart, 1978), 123; Helmuth Giessler, *Der Marine-Nachrichten- und -Ortungsdienst. Technische Entwicklung und Kriegserfahrungen* (Munich, 1971), 19; Hezlet, 160 and 210; Rohwer, "Radiotélégraphie," 43.

21. Patrick Beesly, *Very Special Intelligence: The Story of the Admiralty's Operational Intelligence Centre, 1939–1945* (Garden City, N.Y. 1978), 55–56; Hezlet, 198–99; Rohwer, "Radiotélégraphie," 56; Meckel, 122–23.

22. Rohwer, "Radiotélégraphie," 49.

23. PG/17332: Oberkommando der Kriegsmarine. Kriegstagebuch 2/Skl. (15.3.1940–30.6.1940), in German Naval Records, Reel 319, Frames 708ff, in Naval Historical Branch, Ministry of Defence (London).

24. Ibid.

25. See the map in Heinz Bonatz, *Seekrieg im Äther: Die Leistungen der Marine-Funkaufklärung 1939–1945* (Herford, 1981) 371.

26. Bonatz, *Seekrieg,* 103–5.

27. Nigel West, *GCHQ: The Secret Wireless War 1900–86* (London, 1986), 155–56.

28. Ronald Lewin, *Ultra Goes to War* (London, 1978), 125 and 195–96; David Kahn, *The Codebreakers: The Story of Secret Writing* (New York, 1967), 465–68; Beesly, 40–43; Hezlet, 176; Rohwer, "Radiotélégraphie," 59; Heinz Bonatz, *Die deutsche Marine-Funkaufklärung 1914–1945* (Darmstadt, 1970), 111–26, 139, and 155–56.

29. Bonatz, *Marine-Funkaufklärung,* 161.

30. Robert Sobel, *ITT: The Management of Opportunity* (New York, 1982), 106; Hezlet, 161, 177, and 188–89.

31. Hezlet, 202 and 248; see also Bonatz, *Seekrieg,* 214.

32. Beesly, 56; Graves, 96–107.

33. Hezlet, 229–30; Beesly, 82–83 and 210; Bonatz, *Seekrieg,* 214; Rohwer, "Radiotélégraphie," 58.

34. Quoted in Lewin, *Ultra,* 212–13. After the war, the same trust in the Enigma ciphers prevailed until 1974; see Karl Dönitz, *Memoirs* (London, 1959), passim; Bonatz, *Marine-Funkaufklärung,* 139; and Rohwer, "Radiotélégraphie," 57. See also Meckel, 128–30.

35. Beesly, 32; Bonatz, *Marine-Funkaufklärung,* 136–37; Hezlet, 191; Lewin, *Ultra,* 195; Rohwer, "Radiotélégraphie," 45.

36. Bonatz, *Marine-Funkaufklärung,* 136, and *Seekrieg,* 204–21; Hezlet, 192–98.

37. Lewin, *Ultra,* 195–210; Hezlet, 199.

38. Lewin, *Ultra,* 201–6; Beesly, 98; Hezlet, 209.

39. Beesly, 115 and 175; Bonatz, *Seekrieg,* 235–39, and *Marine-Funkaufklärung,* 111 and 140–41; Hezlet, 227–29; Lewin, *Ultra,* 209–13.

40. Beesly, 166; Bonatz, *Seekrieg,* 239–53, and *Marine-Funkaufklärung,* 136–41; Hezlet, 231–32; Lewin, *Ultra,* 216–17.

41. Lewin, *Ultra,* 243.

42. Beesly, 179–91; Bonatz, *Seekreig,* 243–56, and *Marine-Funkaufklärung,* 143–51; Hezlet, 232–36; Lewin, *Ultra,* 196 and 213–18.

43. Beesly, 167 and 256; Bonatz, *Seekrieg,* 274–75, and *Marine-Funkaufklärung,* 110 and 152; Kahn, *Codebreakers,* 506–7.

44. Peter Calvocoressi, "Aufbau und Arbeitsweise des britischen Entzifferungssdienstes in Bletchley Park," in Rohwer and Jäckel, 96.

45. Yardley, 4–150.

46. Yardley, 163–211; Kahn, *Codebreakers,* 355–58; Ronald Lewin, *The American Magic: Codes, Ciphers, and the Defeat of Japan* (New York, 1982), 21–22.

47. Yardley, 156–57, 184, and 246.

48. Lewin, *American Magic,* 31–32.

49. United States Army, Security Agency, Historical Section, *Origin and Development of the Army Security Agency, 1917–1947* (Laguna Hills, Calif., 1978), 6–9; Lawrence F. Safford, "A Brief History of Communications Intelligence in the United States," in *Listening*

to the Enemy: Key Documents on the Role of Communications Intelligence in the War with Japan* (Washington, 1988), 3–12; Kahn, *Codebreakers,* 5 and 12; Lewin, *American Magic,* 24–29.

50. Richard Deacon, *A History of the Japanese Secret Service: Kempei Tai* (New York, 1983), 129.

51. Lewin, *American Magic,* 35–43.

52. Kahn, *Codebreakers,* 389; Lewin, *American Magic,* 38–44; U.S. Army Security Agency, 23–24.

53. W. J. Holmes, *Double-Edged Secrets: U.S. Naval Intelligence Operations in the Pacific during World War II* (Annapolis, Md., 1979), 46; West, *GCHQ,* 172–76.

54. Lewin, *American Magic,* 46–47; *Ultra,* 134.

55. Holmes, 14–20 and 45–47; Kahn, *Codebreakers,* 8 and 562; Lewin, *American Magic,* 27, 45, and 83–87.

56. Kahn, *Codebreakers,* 13–14; Holmes, 13, 38, and 43.

57. Holmes, 6, 19, 27–28, and 52–53; Hezlet, 215; Lewin, *American Magic,* 85; Kahn, *Codebreakers,* 1, 32, and 40.

58. Lewin, *Ultra,* 234.

59. Lewin, *American Magic,* 88–89 and 99; Holmes, 117; Kahn, *Codebreakers,* 568 and 586.

60. Holmes, 89–91; Lewin, *American Magic,* 105–6.

61. Holmes, 96–97; Lewin, *American Magic,* 109.

62. Lewin, *American Magic,* 96 and 103.

63. Lewin, *American Magic,* 122 and 198; Holmes, 47.

64. Lewin, *American Magic,* 27 and 38.

65. On the complex negotiations between the two countries, see James Bamford, *The Puzzle Palace: A Report on America's Most Secret Agency* (New York, 1983), 392–99. See also Christopher Andrew, *Secret Service: The Making of the British Intelligence Community* (London, 1945), 491; Lewin, *American Magic,* 143–44; and *Ultra,* 254–56.

66. Doris A. Paul, *The Navajo Code-Talkers* (Bryn Mawr, Penn., 1973); Lewin, *American Magic,* 122, 140, and 165, and *Ultra,* 245–46 and 256.

67. Lewin, *American Magic,* 90, 153, and 303; Kahn, *Codebreakers,* 495 and 582–85; Holmes, 12–13 and 80.

68. "Oberkommando der Kreigsmarine. I Skl. Nachrichtendienst. B-Dienst" (January 1–December 31, 1942), PG/17329, in Ministry of Defence (London), Naval Historical Branch, Admiralty Project, Reel 320.

69. Holmes, 123–24.

70. Holmes, 134–35; Lewin, *American Magic,* 187.

71. C. A. Lockwood, "Contribution of Communication Intelligence to the Success of Submarine Operations against the Japanese in World War II" (June 17, 1947), in Ronald H. Spector, ed., *Listening to the Enemy: Key Documents on the Role of Communications Intelligence in the War with Japan* (Wilmington, Del., 1988), 134. See also Holmes, 125 and 190; Lewin, *American Magic,* 222–29; and Hezlet, 234–35 and 252–54.

14

The Changing of the Guard

Behind the scenes and overshadowed by the clash of warfare, the struggle for control of global communications continued between the United States and Great Britain. This was nothing new, for it had been going on for a quarter-century. American communications experts had long felt that America's means of communication were not proportional to the size, wealth, and importance of the nation, and that Britain was an obstacle to their "natural" growth. British experts, meanwhile, believed their country's network was necessary to defend its global responsibilities. By revealing Britain's weakness and America's strength, the war reopened this age-old question.

In July 1940, when Britain was fighting for its survival, Sir Edward Wilshaw, chairman of Cable and Wireless, saw the crisis not just as an Anglo-German war, but as an opportunity for Britain to seize the German, French, and Italian cables and thereby regain her old hegemony eroded by the United States:

> Up to the end of the last war British Overseas telegraphs practically dominated the world. England was the hub of a great system of world communications. Vast amounts of foreign traffic passed through London and were available for censorship.
>
> After the war American interests determined to change this state of affairs and they embarked on a world-wide system of communications development intended so far as possible to render them independent of London.[1]

At the same time in America, the Federal Communications Commission, headed by James Lawrence Fly, reported to the Senate Interstate Commerce Committee on the international telegraph industry.[2] This report bemoaned the sad fate of American cable companies squeezed by international telephone, radiotelegraph, and airmail and, worse yet, at the mercy of foreign administrations and companies, especially Cable and Wireless, which could play them off against one another. It advocated—

not for the first time—the unification of America's international cable and radiotelegraph companies in the interests of national defense: "It thus becomes important to have a single unified telegraph carrier in the international field on a secure basis, capable of maintaining the alternative methods and channels of communication in such a manner as to best serve the national needs."[3] The conflict of interest between the two countries had not changed that much in twenty years.

The approach of war hastened matters. By early 1941 the United States was deeply involved with Britain through the Lend–Lease program and joint protection of Atlantic shipping. Long before Pearl Harbor, America's communications were not merely a commercial matter but a question of defense. The Defense Communications Board, America's equivalent to the Imperial Communications Committee, was set up to deal with these urgent issues. Its members included representatives of the FCC, the Army, the Navy, and the State and Treasury Departments; under it was an Industry Advisory Committee with representatives of the major cable and radio companies. In April, recalling the bottlenecks and backlogs of World War I, the DCB investigated the "degree of coordination necessary to insure rapid handling of all international cable traffic" and concluded that "the cable cos. possess ample facilities."[4] A few months later, Sir Campbell Stuart, chairman of the Imperial Communications Advisory Committee, wrote to Fly, now also chairman of the DCB, about "the problem of wireless communication with North America in the event of the simultaneous interruption of all the trans-Atlantic cables."[5] Stuart believed that "sufficient radio transmitting facilities [are] available to handle all the outgoing traffic from this country."

The American Expansion

In October 1941 the DCB put together a "plan for communication between the United States and England in the event that cables should be interrupted." For Chairman Fly the German menace to Great Britain provided an opportunity to fulfill a long-standing American desire. In presenting the plan to the FCC, he wrote, "Final approval . . . should be withheld until I have the opportunity to discuss this matter with Sir Campbell Stuart and also discuss with him the desirability of permitting direct communication from the United States to South Africa and India."[6] This was a most sensitive issue, the very heart of British policy, for it is by channeling imperial communications through London that Britain had protected both its network and its empire for a century. In a letter to Secretary of State Cordell Hull, Fly gave several reasons for the American request. Some were purely practical: to expedite traffic by avoiding retransmission in the British Isles, to save time and improve security, to avoid lines that were vulnerable to war damage, and so on. But he gave another reason: "The Board believes that there is involved here a basic and permanent policy for the free development of international communications." By "free" he meant that American communications with the Commonwealth should be free from British control.

The question was how to pressure Britain into abandoning one of its most cherished policies. Fly came up with the solution in a letter to President Roosevelt on November 18, 1941, explaining the DCB's attitude towards British communications. He reminded the President that under existing conditions communications with the Commonwealth (e.g., San Francisco to Melbourne) all went through London. As a result, "commercial intelligence is unnecessarily controlled and leaked . . . the overall tendency is to make the United States commercial communications subservient to the British." He pointed out that under Lend-Lease Britain had requested four shortwave transmitters to be used in case cable communications with the United States were cut. Therefore, he wrote: "It is the unanimous view of the Defense Communications Board that the requisition for the four radio transmitters should be coupled with authoritative assurance from the British Government that the principle of direct communication with the British Empire is recognized."[7]

If the approach of war had called attention to this issue, the Japanese attack on Pearl Harbor precipitated events. Suddenly the United States was Britain's ally and the bulwark of the British Empire and there could be no question of refusing American requests.[8] On December 26, less than three weeks after Pearl Harbor, the Australian government authorized a direct radio link between Sydney and San Francisco.[9] It was a great victory for Fly. On January 19, 1942, he wrote to the FCC commissioners: "The British Government is prepared to acquiesce in the opening of direct radiotelegraph circuits between this country and countries in the British Empire for the duration of the war." Having won half a loaf, he proposed "carrying on the negotiations with the thought that, if the circuits are once established for the period of the war, they should be continued on a permanent basis."[10]

Under normal circumstances, policy precedes or at least influences events. In wartime, however, reality moves rapidly, and policy seems to be constantly running after the *fait accompli* and never catching up. After Pearl Harbor, America's worldwide interests exploded, spreading shipping, business enterprises, troop concentrations, military liaison units, and myriad other aspects of the American presence around the world. With the American presence came new or greatly expanded radio circuits. By May 1943 the United States was directly connected to many parts of the Commonwealth, including the Gold Coast, South Africa, Egypt, India, Australia, New Zealand, Jamaica, and other Caribbean colonies. In addition, new circuits had been opened to other parts of the world such as New Caledonia, Iran, French Equatorial Africa, the Belgian Congo, Algeria, Afghanistan, China, and the USSR. In effect, the whole world outside the Axis-occupied territories now communicated directly with the United States without going through British lines.[11]

The British had long feared the merger of America's international telecommunications companies, while in America Behn of ITT, Sarnoff of RCA, and Fly of the FCC had suggested it at one time or another, but never together or strongly enough to convince Congress and the President. Fly, in particular, continued to lobby for it throughout 1941 and 1942.[12] In July 1943, Roosevelt referred it to the State Department, where it got bogged down in committees.[13] Ironically, just two months later Western Union acquired the Postal Telegraph and Cable Company from ITT; instead of creating an irresistible giant, however, this merger only postponed the demise of the telegraph, increasingly beset by more modern means of communication.

Strategic Cables to North Africa and Europe

The sudden penetration of American interests into different parts of the world during 1942 and 1943 left several major issues to be resolved in a hurry. One of these was the Allies' need to communicate with their armed forces as they advanced into North Africa, then Italy, and finally France.

For strategic reasons, Great Britain had long maintained its cable network, as opposed to radio. In January 1942 an Admiralty memorandum criticized the Americans for their reliance on radio:

> American contention that W/T [wireless telegraph] installations are satisfactory alternative to cables is not in accordance with British policy. Risk of interception means use of high grade cypher essential on W/T and this entails extra delay and labour. In addition there are frequent occasions when unusual amount of traffic must be sent by cable for security reasons in order that hint of impending operations shall not be disclosed by increased volume of high priority traffic passing by W/T.[14]

Yet Americans—the military in particular—were well aware of the security advantages of cables. This became clear when British and American forces landed in North Africa in November 1942. Following the fleet that carried the American First Army to Algiers was the cableship *Mirror,* which diverted two of the Gibraltar–Malta cables to that city. In January it laid a cable from Gibraltar to Casablanca. Later that year, as the Allies advanced, cables were laid to Malta, Sicily, Naples, and Rome.[15] Now the British and American governments could communicate securely with their forces in North Africa. Or so it seemed to the British.

The Americans, however, were not happy to see their most secret military messages pass through British cable stations in Britain and Gibraltar. They wanted their own cables. On January 14, 1943, the American military communications staff suggested to the British that the former Italian cable, now linking Horta (Azores) and Gibraltar, and the former French Horta–New York cable, cut fifteen miles east of New York, be connected to form an American-controlled cable from New York to Casablanca; and furthermore that the severed German cable from Horta to Emden be used to link America with England.[16] To this the British Wireless Telegraphy Board (which, despite its name, was concerned with all military communications) responded: "These proposals are an attempt on the part of U.S. commercial interests to encroach on British interests on this side of the Atlantic, with a view to reaping post-war advantages."[17] At a meeting of the British Joint Communications Board on February 10, Brigadier General Rumbough, Chief Signal Officer of the U.S. Army, backed down from the demand for an exclusive cable and instead asked for a direct cable channel from Washington to Casablanca to be controlled by American personnel.[18] H. F. Layman, chairman of the Wireless Telegraphy Board, continued to protest against what he termed "commercial infiltration" and maintained that "the present set up of the British cable system should be disturbed as little as possible."[19] The American side, represented by the Board of War Communications (successor to the Defense Communications Board), remained adamant.[20] Finally on July 14 the two sides reached an agreement: Cable and Wireless was to lease one channel duplex (i.e., half the capacity of the cable) between Casablanca and Horta to the U.S. Army Signal Corps, to connect with Western Union's Horta–New York cable. This channel was to be operated with "automatic repeating equipment without retransmission or interception."[21] This stipulation was designed to alleviate American fears that the British might scrutinize their telegrams. These fears, perhaps justified in World War I, were now baseless, and disputes over security were very rare.[22] Yet the British resented this lack of trust. Long after the agreement, the British Joint Communications Board continued to protest:

> These groundless suspicions are creating worst possible impression here as large amount of detailed work entailed in refuting them is definite hindrance to war effort. British communications system is being operated as efficiently as possible in the equal interests of all the United Nations in spirit of the Atlantic Charter.[23]

The debate over dedicated channels went deeper than the particular military needs of the moment, deeper even than the mutual suspicions of the two allies. They revealed a different attitude towards communications. The Americans thought in terms of channels or leased lines linking pairs of correspondents, while the British saw the entire network as open to all customers, with priority to government messages. As the Imperial Communications Committee explained:

> In the course of seventy-odd years a world-wide British cable system has been built up and the experience gained over this period has shown how capacious and flexible such a system can be when treated as a whole. . . . United States cable experience has been limited broadly speaking, to the trans-Atlantic and North and South American routes. . . . The net result is lack of appreciation of cable potentialities when used in the proper way. The United States authorities tend to adopt a policy of securing exclusive cable circuits for the use of and even operation by a particular service or other Government department.[24]

But since the Americans held the purse strings, the British, however reluctantly, had to give in. In late 1943 U.S.-controlled transatlantic channels—to Algiers, to Italy, to England—proliferated. Electrical engineers had provided an elegant solution in the form of a system called *varioplex*. On the high-speed transatlantic cables, this technique allowed three channels at sixty words per minute in each direction, or more channels at slower speeds. In effect, channels could be switched on and off at will, giving the customers the advantage of a dedicated channel while the network retained the flexibility of individual messages. While most channels rented by pairs of government agencies on both sides of the Atlantic were of long duration, some were ephemeral. A small sample might include the War Department in Washington and the U.S. military attaché in London; U.S. Navy Anti-Submarine Warfare in Washington, and the Commander Western Approaches in Liverpool; the British Admiralty Delegation in Washington and the Admiralty and Air Ministry in London; and the Roosevelt–Churchill conference in Quebec (August 11–24, 1943) and the Foreign Office.[25]

By 1944 the Allies' mutual suspicions had abated somewhat as their efforts turned to the flood of words expected during and after the planned invasion of France. General Eisenhower appointed David Sarnoff, who had always liked to play soldier, as his special assistant for communications. In addition to the transatlantic cable space increasingly reserved for secret government traffic, Sarnoff obtained shortwave channels from the Signal Corps, the British Post Office, and Cable and Wireless, altogether enough for over half a million words a day.[26] On D-Day, the communications facilities were overprepared. Even though the traffic totaled well over a million words a day, the Board of War Communications could comment: "The anticipated enormous increase in traffic did not materialize and therefore the facilities of the American companies were ample to meet the demand."[27] As the Allies advanced, cables were laid across the Channel, landlines repaired, and radio transmitters erected. By September, the great French station at Sainte-Assise was restored and talking to New York. At no time did the Allies ever lack for communications facilities.

The Retreat of Britain

However impressive the new telecommunications links created during the war, they did not please everyone. The British, in particular, had to adjust rather suddenly to the American intrusion into their domain. On February 4, 1942, Sir Campbell Stuart had informed Sir Edward Wilshaw: "H.M. Government in the United Kingdom have informed the Government of the U.S.A. that they agree in principle to direct wireless circuits between the U.S.A. and any British Colony being opened in the interest of defence for the duration of the war, it being understood that such circuits be confined to terminal traffic between the two countries concerned."[28] This was exactly what Wilshaw had feared, and he reacted angrily. The American request, he wrote Stuart, was commercially motivated:

> The declared policy of American telegraph interests has been for many years, particularly since the last war, to break into British communication, and it would appear that foreign commercial interests have taken advantage of the present difficult times to endeavour to achieve this object.

The government's acquiescence to these demands violated the 1928 agreement to defend Imperial communications against any "attempt on the part of foreign interests to secure an increased share in the control and operation of world communications."

> It is therefore with profound misgivings that the Company is now forced to look upon a future where foreign interests have been permitted to make inroads on the communications of the British Empire, with possible disastrous results upon Empire communications as a whole and upon this Company in particular.

Knowing that the company's commercial prospects might not impress the government, he brought up a national security reason:

> It might be thought undesirable, from a security point of view, that messages which up to date have transitted London should no longer continue to do so, but should go direct between the countries concerned without the same facilities for the interception and scrutiny of such messages by those charged with the preservation of security.[29]

The company's counsel pointed out that they had no legal case against the government, and that "the only way in which my clients are likely to achieve any remedy is by pressure on the Government of a non-legal kind."[30] At a meeting of the company's directors, "the possibility of a direct approach to the Prime Minister was examined," but evidently it did not seem politic to protest Winston Churchill's policy of friendship with the United States. The interests of Cable and Wireless no longer coincided with those of Great Britain. Not only was the British government in no position to refuse reasonable American demands, it could no longer even dominate events within the Commonwealth. Wilshaw, who represented the past, found himself overruled by events.

With that, Britain's century-old monopoly of Empire communications began to crumble. In its place there appeared a new policy of "partnership," with the United States as a benevolent patron. Sir Campbell Stuart later recalled: "With the entry of America into the war it was found to be neither practicable nor desirable to maintain the pre-war policy of regarding the British empire as if protected by an unscalable wall with its main gateway to the world through London."[31] The United States was not alone in wanting direct communications. The dominions themselves, particularly Australia and New Zealand, which had long chafed at their dependence on Cable and Wireless, felt the same need, especially in that desperate year 1942 when the United States alone stood between them and a Japanese invasion.

A major conference on imperial communications was held in the fall of 1942, not in London but in Canberra at the invitation of the prime minister of Australia, John Curtin. Wilshaw was invited but refused to attend, thereby losing the opportunity to present his case. His views in any case would not have overcome the consensus of the conference, which Stuart described as "a striking demonstration of the new quality of Empire partnership which has at long last triumphed over the hard-dying bogy of London control, and from this point of view alone it was a significant landmark in Empire history."[32] (It is also significant that Stuart, the man with the greatest influence over British telecommunications policy, was a Canadian.)

Once Great Britain had accepted direct communications between the dominions and the United States, it was only a matter of time before the dominions raised the issue of communications within the Commonwealth. In April 1943 the Imperial Communications Advisory Committee was renamed the Commonwealth Communications Council to reflect the increasing power of the dominions. Under Stuart's chairmanship, it endorsed a scheme proposed by Australia and New Zealand to nationalize Commonwealth communications, on the grounds that "Australia and New Zealand are not prepared to subscribe to any measures limiting, in the interests of a London-based Corporation, the fullest possible development of cheap communications for their peoples."[33]

Thus, in addition to the conflict between British and American interests, the long-simmering dispute between Cable and Wireless and the dominions had reappeared. The British government was caught in the middle. The Committee on Empire Telecommunications Services of the War Cabinet sided with Wilshaw, while Stuart supported the Australia–New Zealand or "Canberra" scheme.[34] Hoping to patch up the differences, the government sent Lord Reith on a mission around the Commonwealth. On his return Reith endorsed the Canberra plan, but the British government balked and called a Commonwealth Telecommunications Conference.[35] That conference, which met in London in July and August 1945, basically endorsed the Canberra scheme: Each Commonwealth nation, including the United Kingdom, was to nationalize the local assets of Cable and Wireless, leaving the "ocean" and foreign assets in British hands. In November of that year, at a conference with the United States, the British government accepted the recommendations of the London Conference and acquiesced to the nationalization of Cable and Wireless by the Commonwealth countries and to direct communications between countries.[36] The old communications system centered on London, which had served Great Britain well for seventy years, was disintegrating along with the empire it had served.

The Organization of Postwar Communications

Seen from the perspective of the Allies in 1945, future global communications had two characteristics. On the one hand, each country, including members of the Commonwealth, would control its own telecommunications and communicate directly with every other country. On the other hand, the United States was certain to dominate world communications because it alone had an economy expanding rapidly enough to require new circuits for business and the press, and the resources to satisfy that demand. No matter what policies the British government might have adopted, the new realities of power and wealth meant that, in Wilshaw's phrase, "New York would inevitably tend to usurp London's present position as the hub of the communications world."[37]

This left one other issue to be resolved, namely communications in the defeated Axis countries. At the end of World War I, it will be recalled, the Allies confiscated Germany's ocean cables but did not interfere with its other telecommunications facilities. In World War II the Allies were determined to go much further. Yet in this, as in many other matters, the American attitude differed from that of the British.

The American attitude was contained in a "Report of the Special Interdepartmental Committee on Communications regarding Peace Terms," which Secretary of State Cordell Hull sent to President Roosevelt in September 1943. Roosevelt showed it to Winston Churchill, who sent it to the British Joint Staff Mission in Washington and to Foreign Secretary Anthony Eden.[38] That report assumed that after the war there would be a United Nations and an international telecommunications organization. It proposed therefore to transfer all enemy telecommunications facilities outside their boundaries to the United Nations, and to establish some form of supervision of domestic facilities in order to eliminate "objectionable material" from broadcasts. The report as a whole was vague and idealistic. It also left open the touchy issue of whether Italy was an "enemy" or not.

British ideas about enemy telecommunications were much more precise and less idealistic. In March 1943 the Cable and Wireless Company presented a plan to the government entitled "Post-war Control of Axis Telecommunications."[39] It maintained that "rigid control of the aggressor nations' Telecommunications Services, at least for a period, will be vitally necessary following the present War." "Rigid control" was specified in detail: all telegraph, telephone, and telex traffic in the Axis countries would be tapped and scrutinized by outsiders; all overseas traffic would be funneled through London, Malta, Guam, or Shanghai, where it would be scrutinized; all radio transmissions would be controlled by U.N. officials; and no codes and ciphers would be allowed.

In August 1945, after the war had ended, E. S. Herbert, director of postal and telegraph censorship in Britain, put forth a similar proposal:

> Complete control over Germany's external communications for, say, the next 20 years would help to provide against any revival of German war-like aggression under the cloak of peaceful business or peaceful scientific endeavour such as occurred between 1919 and 1939. . . .
>
> Censorship control should be exercised now in such a way that it will be clear to those Germans who are anxious to help the Allies that they have nothing to fear from Allied Censorship control of communications. Censorship control should, therefore, not interfere with the free expression of democratic ideas.[40]

Herbert's memorandum focused on Germany, for the British government was by then consciously turning its back on the Far East. In March 1945 the Foreign Office sent a memorandum on the "future of the Japanese islands in the Pacific" to the Imperial Communications Committee. In that memorandum it acquiesced to the American acquisition of all the Japanese Pacific islands and saw "no reason why this should be contrary to the interests of the United Kingdom or to those of Australia, New Zealand and Canada." Furthermore it stated: "As regards telecommunications it does not appear *prima facie* that we have any special interest." Another memorandum, from the Post Office to the Imperial Communications Committee, confirmed this: "There is no special imperial interest in the area from a telecommunications point of view."[41]

By 1945 the main concern of Britain's telecommunications experts was to prevent the resurgence of Germany. The Pacific was graciously handed over to the Americans, as Great Britain increasingly turned toward Europe.

Conclusion

Communications had a greater impact on the course of World War II than on any previous event in history. The very nature of that war—massive and motorized—demanded continuous, instant, and secure communications. Victory did not smile upon the boldest nations, as the Axis leaders believed, but upon the best informed.

The Allied advantage had an element of luck, but it was largely the result of a seventy-five-year-long British experience with global telecommunications. During those years, Britain had learned better than other nations how to safeguard its own secrets and how to penetrate those of its enemies. From the late 1920s on, when shortwave radio threatened to bankrupt the cable companies, the British government chose to make it subsidize the cable network. On a broader scale, this meant protecting the security of Britain's overseas communications at the expense of its commercial competitiveness.

Even with secure communications and the help of its Commonwealth partners, however, Britain might not have survived the German onslaught. With the coming of war, it formed three concentric alliances: on the outside, an ephemeral anti-German alliance that only lasted as long as its common enemy; within it, a league of North Atlantic nations that endures to this day; and at the core, the long friendship (some would call it a conspiracy) between Britain and the United States. To avoid defeat, Great Britain had bequeathed its position in the world—including its mastery of the global information flow—to the United States.

Notes

1. Secret and confidential memorandum on foreign cables from Edward Wilshaw to the Imperial Communications Committee, July 1940, in Cable and Wireless archives, B2/550.

2. U.S. Federal Communications Commission, "Report of the Federal Communications Commission on the International Telegraph Industry submitted to the Senate Interstate Commerce Committee investigating telegraphs," United States Senate, Appendix to Hearing before Subcommittee of the Committee on Interstate Commerce (77th Congress, 1st Session, part 2), 450–81, reprinted in *The Development of Submarine Cable Communications*, ed. Bernard S. Finn (New York, 1980).

3. Ibid., 473.

4. "Topic No. 3: Degree of coordination necessary to insure rapid handling of all international cable traffic," April 28, 1941, in National Archives, Record Group 259, Box 48, File "Com. III D.C.B."

5. Letter from Sir Campbell Stuart to J. L. Fly, August 31, 1941, in National Archives, RG 259, Box 1, File "DCB—Direct Com w Br Emp."

6. Memorandum from J. L. Fly to FCC, October 14, 1941, re "Plan for Communication," ibid.

7. Letter from J. L. Fly, chairman, DCB, to President Franklin D. Roosevelt, November 14, 1941, in National Archives, Record Group 259, Box 1, File "DCB—Direct Com w Br Emp."

8. On U.S.–British relations and the colonial question in World War II, see William Roger Louis, *Imperialism at Bay, 1941–1945: The United States and the Decolonization of the British Empire* (Oxford, 1977); unfortunately it does not mention telecommunications.

9. Hugh Barty-King, *Girdle Round the Earth: The Story of Cable and Wireless and its Predecessors to Mark the Group's Jubilee, 1929–1979* (London, 1979), 288–89.

10. Memorandum from J. L. Fly, chairman, to FCC, January 19, 1942, in National Archives, RG 259, Box 1, File "DCB—Direct Com w Br Emp."

11. "DCB—International Circuits—General," May 17, 1943, and "DCB Direct Circuits," July 14, 1943, in National Archives, RG 259, Box 2; FCC Engineering Department, International Division, "Maps of Radiotelegraph and Radiotelephone Circuits in Active Operation between the United States and Territorial Possessions and Foreign Countries," July 1, 1943, ibid., Box 61; "BWC Office of War Information, Report on United States Communications in the War," September 29, 1943, ibid., Box 62.

12. See e.g., letter from J. L. Fly, chairman FCC, to Joseph F. Chamberlain, Columbia University, August 14, 1942, in National Archives, RG 173, Box 596: "FCC, Office of the Executive Director."

13. Letter from President Roosevelt to J. L. Fly, chairman of the Board of War Commu-

nications, June 1, 1943, in National Archives, RG 259, Box 3, File "BWC. Unification of International Facilities of American Carriers."

14. Admiralty memorandum to British Admiralty Delegation, Washington, January 30, 1942, in Public Record Office, ADM 116/5443; "Cable Communications and Cable Ships, 1941–45."

15. Charles Graves, *The Thin Red Lines* (London, 1946), 85, 91–93, and 123; Barty-King, 292.

16. Memorandum "Naval Cypher XD plug by Cable," from Commonwealth Joint Communications Committee to British Joint Communications Board, January 14, 1943, in Cable and Wireless archives B2/550.

17. Memorandum from Wireless Telegraphy Board re "U.S. proposals concerning transatlantic submarine cable communications," January 26, 1943, in PRO, ADM 116/5137.

18. Memorandum from Brigadier General W. S. Rumbough to British Joint Communications Board, February 10, 1943, in PRO, ADM 116/5137: "Use of Imperial and ex-enemy world-wide cable network, 1940–44."

19. Memorandum from H. F. Layman, chairman of the Wireless Telegraphy Board, to the Imperial Communications Committee, February 26, 1943, re "U.S. proposals concerning trans-Atlantic submarine cable communication," ibid.

20. Memorandum from BWC Committee III (cables) to BWC re "American Cable Communications Plan," April 6, 1943, in National Archives, RG 259, Box 47: "Board of War Communications (1941–45)," File "Com III."

21. Agreement of July 14, 1943, in Cable and Wireless archives B2/550; memorandum from British Chiefs of Staff, July 21, 1943, in PRO, ADM 116/5137.

22. George Kennan, U.S. chargé d'affaires in Lisbon, complained that the Cable and Wireless employees leaked American diplomatic and commercial telegrams to both the British and the Axis; the company denied the allegation. See Kennan's letters to Secretary of State Hull, October 21 and November 20, 1943, re "Eastern Cable Company and Marconi Wireless Company of Lisbon," in National Archives, RG 259, Box 34, File "Cables & Wireless, Ltd."

23. Memorandum from British Joint Communications Board to Commonwealth Joint Communications Committee, August 25, 1943, in PRO, ADM 116/5137.

24. Memorandum from the IC to the Chiefs of Staff, October 20, 1943, in PRO, ADM 116/5137.

25. Letter from Ivan Coggeshall (formerly of Western Union) to Donard de Cogan, May 19, 1985, cited with permission.

26. Kenneth Bilby, *The General: David Sarnoff and the Rise of the Communications Industry* (New York, 1986), 143–47.

27. Memorandum from E. K. Jett, chairman, Coordinating Committee to Board of War Communications, June 10, 1944, in National Archives, RG 259, Box 61, File "BWC International Communications, efficient handling of trans-Atlantic."

28. Letter from Campbell Stuart to Edward Wilshaw, February 4, 1942, in Cable and Wireless archives, B1/93: "Direct Services USA, 1942–1943."

29. Letter from Wilshaw to Stuart, February 13, 1942, ibid.

30. Letter from D. N. Plitt, April 3, 1942, ibid.

31. Sir Campbell Stuart, *Opportunity Knocks Once* (London, 1952), 228–29.

32. Ibid, 229. See also Barty-King, 289–90.

33. Commonwealth Communications Council, "Interim Report to the Governments," May 10, 1944, in PRO, Cab 76/7. See also Stuart, 125–26.

34. First Report of the Official Committee on Empire Telecommunication Services, James Rae, chairman, October 27, 1944, in PRO, Cab 76/7.

35. "Commonwealth Telecommunications. Report by Lord Reith on his Mission to the Dominions, India and Southern Rhodesia," March 30, 1945, in PRO, Cab 76/7; "Reorganization Commonwealth Telecommunications. Lord Reith's Report, 1945," in PRO, ADM 116/5444; J. C. W. Reith, *Into the Wind* (London, 1949), 497–506.

36. Reith, 506–17; Barty-King, 313–20.

37. Barty-King, 294.

38. Secret File, British Embassy, Washington, No. G.285/1: "Special Committee on Communications: Peace Terms," in PRO, FO 115/3571.

39. Report by Cable and Wireless to Government "Post-war control of Axis telecommunications," March 12, 1943, in Cable and Wireless archives, B2/552.

40. Memorandum by E. S. Herbert, chairman, Committee on Censorship and Director General, Postal and Telegraph Censorship, re: "Germany—Policy Concerning the Control of Communications by the Allies," August 30, 1945, in PRO, Cab 76/11: Minutes of Interdepartmental Committee on Censorship, 1942–45.

41. Memoranda from the Foreign Office, March 16, 1945, and the Post Office, March 21, to the Imperial Communications Committee of the War Cabinet in PRO, ADM 116/5438: "Japanese islands in the Pacific. British telecommunications interests and future policy."

15

Telecommunications, Information, and Security

The history of telecommunications is first of all the story of one of mankind's most admirable achievements: a technology that informs, entertains, and reassures millions of individuals, an indispensable tool of modern business and government. On a global level, the trade and prosperity of the world depend on a constant flow of information that only modern telecommunications can provide. Among nations, it has mainly been the object of cooperation. In the past 150 years, electrical communications have become rapid, reliable, and cheap, and have spread throughout the developed world and into many parts of the poorer countries as well. As a result, people no longer complain that they do not know enough, but that they are flooded with too much information. And all this has taken place without polluting the environment or depleting natural resources. While so many technologies of the same era, such as railroads, automobiles, and mass production, seem to have reached a plateau after spectacular beginnings, telecommunications have never ceased improving and the future promises miracles as astonishing as those our forefathers marveled at. It is only natural that most books about the telegraph, the telephone, the radio, and other communication media should celebrate the blessings these inventions have brought to mankind.

Here we have looked at the question from a special perspective, that of international relations. Alas, in the period we have studied, the relations between nations have as often been a curse as a blessing for mankind. In the century from the 1850s to the 1940s, two macro-events transformed the world: the expansion of the great powers into weaker parts of the globe, followed by two world wars among those some great powers. If the nineteenth century showed how technology increases the power of humans over nature, the twentieth has proved how easily that power over nature can be transformed into the power of some people over others. In an era of conflicts, telecommunications has been both a weapon and a cause of national rivalries. Its history reflects the nature of its time.

While many nations played a part in the development of the telegraph and of radio, none contributed as much as Britain. For that reason, the history of global telecommunications is closely tied to the growth and decline of the British Empire. In the 1860s, when submarine cables became reliable, only Britain had sufficient industry and finance to create a world network and sufficient trade to warrant the investment. From the 1870s on, the British Empire was increasingly bound together by strands of copper. Thanks to its cable network, Great Britain possessed the power to control the global flow of information at a time when information was becoming increasingly vital to great-power status and to economic prosperity. The history of Britain illustrates this interdependence: If it remained a great power for several decades after its industries had been surpassed by those of other nations, it is thanks to its empire, its navy, and its global trade, all of which required secure and efficient communications.

Other European nations involved in imperialist expansion and world trade benefitted from the British network. The era of cooperation only lasted as long as there were enough non-European territories to satisfy the great powers' expansionist drives. Although the British had built and operated their network as a commercial medium available to all customers, it soon became clear that Britain's power could be used against other nations. By the turn of the century, growing international tensions and the realization that Britain would not hesitate to use its power over global communications whenever its interests were threatened stimulated France and Germany to create rival networks. These politically motivated networks were not profitable enough to undermine the British hegemony, however. Only in the North Atlantic did British cable companies lose ground to American firms that did not threaten British access to information.

The first half of the twentieth century was an age of wars and preparation for wars. War adds a special dimension to telecommunications, for information is a weapon and so is secrecy. Experience showed that submarine cables, controlled at both ends by one nation and its allies and protected by a powerful navy, provided the most secure communications; but only Britain and the United States had this option. While World War I put an end to German ambitions in cables, it stimulated the development of a newer technology, the radio, which seemed to undermine Britain's advantages in information, but in fact enhanced it.

In wartime, security requires much more than secret communications: It also requires access to the enemy's secrets, the ability to deceive the enemy by feeding him misleading information, and sufficient military forces to take advantage of the resulting information gap. Although radio messages were never entirely secure, Britain enjoyed a substantial lead in communications intelligence over Germany. In both world wars, Great Britain possessed the advantage in information, even if it had to wait for America to enter the war before it could parlay that advantage into victory.

It was not Germany's military might but the economic power of the United States that threatened Britain's preponderance in international communications. In

World War II the United States inherited Britain's role as the world's leading industrial and naval power, and in so doing it also became the center of international trade and information. In the process, Americans developed both a global communications network and an obsession with security and communications intelligence.

This book ends with the year 1945. Needless to say, the story does not end there, only the historian's access to reliable sources. Since 1945 the technology has continued to improve at an accelerating pace, partly because of technological momentum and partly to meet an ever-expanding demand. The year 1956 saw the first transatlantic cable to be laid in thirty years, a telephone cable that made the old telegraph cables obsolete overnight. Shortly thereafter, in the 1960s, the era of telecommunications satellites began, only to be followed, twenty years later, by fiber-optic cables that are making the older telephone cables and even some satellites obsolete in turn.

While technology progresses apace, the human response lags far behind. In the field of international communications, the habits of suspicion born in the age of world wars have carried over into the postwar era and turned communications intelligence into a major industry. The United States, an apprentice in the art before 1941, joined Britain as a master in the game of communications intelligence and created the largest cryptological service ever known, the National Security Agency. Yet neither past successes nor huge budgets guarantee secrecy, for time and again, spies have sold both nations' most jealously guarded secrets to the Soviet Union.

It is dangerous to confuse communications security with national security. In peacetime, far from ensuring security, secrecy only breeds suspicion and resentment, whereas more knowledge, whether freely given or surreptitiously obtained, can allay these suspicions. In the age of information, less secrecy may well mean less fear of sudden surprises, and therefore more security. Perhaps it is not too late to hope, as Ferdinand de Lesseps did a century ago, that "men, by knowing one another, will finally cease fighting."

Bibliographical Essay

The published literature on telecommunications is very uneven. Apart from the technical literature, which is enormous but of limited value for an economic and political study, there are essentially two categories of published works. One is the large literature on submarine telegraph cables dating back to the mid-nineteenth century and reaching a peak around the time of World War I. In comparison, the literature on radio is relatively scant. Instead, the late twentieth century has produced an outpouring of books on communications intelligence, cryptology, and espionage, understandably so after World War II. This flood of books shows no sign of abating, and the archives are constantly declassifying documents from the war. The present study can therefore make no claim to be definitive or complete. Readers should consider it a starting point for their own investigations and discoveries.

Books on Submarine Telegraph Cables

A few books deal with the origins and early impact of submarine telegraph cables. Two of the earliest are Willoughby Smith, *The Rise and Extension of Submarine Telegraphy* (London, 1891) and Charles Bright, *Submarine Telegraphs, Their History, Construction and Working* (London, 1898) For a lucid introduction to the technology of cables, see Gerald R. M. Garratt, *One Hundred Years of Submarine Cables* (London, 1950). Kenneth R. Haigh, *Cableships and Submarine Cables* (London and Washington, 1968) is a good reference work. A recent attempt to describe the role of cables in shaping the modern world is Vary T. Coates and Bernard Finn, *A Retrospective Technology Assessment. Submarine Telegraphy. The Transatlantic Cable of 1866* (San Francisco, 1979).

Many books deal with specific aspects of cables. Maxime de Margerie, *Le réseau anglais de câbles sous-marins* (Paris, 1909), considers the British network from a political and economic point of view. The relations between the cable companies and the British government in the age of imperialism are the subject of Robert J. Cain's excellent but unfortunately unpublished "Telegraph Cables in the British Empire, 1850–1900" (Ph.D. dissertation, Duke University, 1971). The strategic implications of cables before World I have been described in P. M. Kennedy, "Imperial Cable Communications and Strategy, 1879–1914," *English Historical Review* 86 (1971), 728–52.

Three books deal with the German cable network, two of them written at the time of its creation. For a German point of view, see Hugo Thurn, *Die Seekabel mit besonderer Berücksichtigung der deutschen Seekabeltelegraphie. In technicher, handelswirtschaftlicher and strategicher Beziehung dargestellt* (Leipzig, 1909). The Frenchman Charles Lesage wrote an anti-German but well-documented study *La rivalité franco-britannique. Les câbles sous-marins allemands* (Paris, 1915). A thorough, if pedantic, study of the German cables is Artur Kunert's *Geschichte der deutschen Fernmeldekabel. II. Telegraphen-Seekabel* (Cologne–Mülheim, 1962), written in the 1930s and privately printed in 1962. Alas, no similar studies exist on the French and American cable networks.

Two studies have focused on telegraphy in Asia. The origins of British communications with India are best described in Halford L. Hoskins, *British Routes to India* (London, 1928). Jorma Ahvenainen has written an excellent monograph, *The Far Eastern Telegraphs: The History of Telegraphic Communications between the Far East, Europe and America before the First World War* (Helsinki, 1981). On the origins of telegraphy in China, see Saundra P. Sturdevant, "A Question of Sovereignty: Railways and Telegraphs in China 1861–1878" (unpublished Ph.D. dissertation, University of Chicago, 1975).

Books on Radio and Telecommunications

The literature on radio contains a few excellent works, especially Hugh Aitken's *Syntony and Spark: The Origins of Radio* (New York, 1976) and *The Continuous Wave: Technology and American Radio, 1900–1932* (Princeton, 1985). The military origins of radio have intrigued several historians; see Susan J. Douglas, *Inventing American Broadcasting, 1899–1922* (Baltimore, 1987) and Rowland F. Pocock, *The Early British Radio Industry* (Manchester, 1988). For a more general work on military electronics, see Arthur R. Hezlet, *The Electron and Sea Power* (London, 1975). The legal aspects of radio are best described in John D. Tomlinson, *The International Control of Radiocommunications* (Geneva, 1938).

Since the advent of radio and the telephone, telegraphy has become telecommunications, a broader subject that has attracted considerable attention. The late 1920s, a time of massive reorganization in the telecommunications business, saw the appearance of several interesting books: George A. Schreiner, *Cables and Wireless and Their Role in the Foreign Relations of the United States* (Boston, 1924); Frank J. Brown, *The Cable and Wireless Communications of the World: A*

Survey of Present Day Means of International Communication by Cable and Wireless, Containing Chapters on Cable and Wireless Finance (London, 1927); and Leslie B. Tribolet, *The International Aspects of Electrical Communications in the Pacific Area* (Baltimore, 1929). More recent surveys include Hugh Barty-King, *Girdle Round the Earth: The Story of Cable and Wireless and its Predecessors to Mark the Groups' Jubilee, 1929–1979* (London, 1979), a company history with an emphasis on British cables; and, for French telecommunications, Catherine Bertho, *Télégraphes et téléphones de Valmy au microprocesseur* (Paris, 1981). See also George A. Codding, *The International Telecommunication Union: An Experiment in International Cooperation* (Leiden, 1952).

Communications Intelligence

The dramatic role of espionage and intelligence in two world wars has given rise to a torrent of books. The best general history of cryptology remains David Kahn, *The Codebreakers: The Story of Secret Writing* (New York, 1967). For British undercover activities, see Christopher Andrew, *Secret Service: The Making of the British Intelligence Community* (London, 1985). On World War I, three books are especially valuable: Barbara Tuchman, *The Zimmermann Telegram* (New York, 1958); Patrick Beesly, *Room 40: British Naval Intelligence, 1914–18* (London, 1982); and Alberto Santoni, *Il primo Ultra Secret: L'influenza delle decrittazioni britanniche sulle operazioni navali della guerra 1914–1918* (Milan, 1985). Herbert O. Yardley's memoir, *The American Black Chamber* (Indianapolis, 1931), though self-serving, nonetheless makes fascinating reading.

For literature on the history of World War II, the year 1974 marks an important turning point with the publication of Frederick W. Winterbotham's *The Ultra Secret* (New York, 1974), which revealed the extent of British penetration into Germany's secret communications. For that reason, books written after that date are much to be preferred to those written before. In particular, Ronald Lewin, *Ultra Goes to War* (London and New York, 1978) and Anthony Cave Brown, *Bodyguard of Lies* (New York, 1975) cover most of the war. Janusz Piekalkiewicz, *Rommel und die Geheimdienste in Nordafrika 1941–1943* (Munich and Berlin, 1984) deals with the North African campaign, while Patrick Beesly's *Very Special Intelligence: The Story of the Admiralty's Operational Intelligence Centre, 1939–1945* (Garden City, N.Y., 1978) is still the best book on British naval intelligence in that war. On German espionage, see David Kahn, *Hitler's Spies: German Military Intelligence in World War II* (New York, 1978). Communications intelligence in the Pacific is the subject of two important studies: W. J. Holmes, *Double-Edged Secrets: U.S. Naval Intelligence Operations in the Pacific during World War II* (Annapolis, Md., 1979) and Ronald Lewin, *The American Magic: Codes, Ciphers, and Defeat of Japan* (New York, 1978).

Those interested in communications intelligence after the war, a subject not covered in this book, should begin with James Bamford, *The Puzzle Palace: A Report on America's Most Secret Agency* (Boston, 1982).

Primary Sources

In addition to the books listed above and in the references, the author consulted documents from a number of archives. The role of Great Britain in the history of international telecommunications is reflected in the importance of its archival collections, in particular those of the Cable and Wireless Company in London, heir to the Eastern and Marconi companies. The author is deeply grateful for the friendly welcome he received at Cable and Wireless during his stay in London. Equally important are the papers found in the Public Record Office in Kew, in particular the collections prefaced ADM, CAB, FO, and CO. The collection of the Ministry of Defence also proved useful.

In France the author consulted the Archives Nationales Section Outre-Mer in Paris (since transferred to Aix-en-Provence) and the archives of the Ministry of Posts and Telecommunications.

In the United States the National Archives in Washington contain important collections of papers of the Board of War Communications (1940–1947), the Foreign Broadcast Intelligence Service (1940–1947), and the Federal Communications Commission.

Index

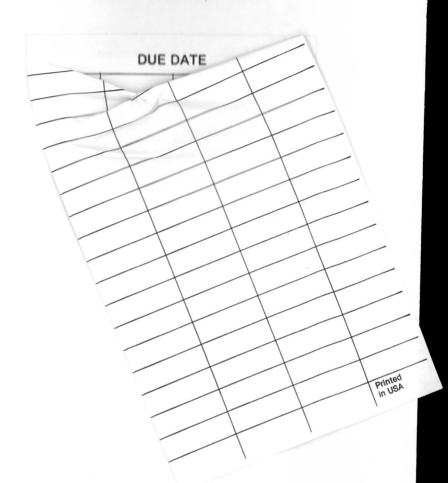

DUE DATE

Printed
in USA